THE FEDERAL CABINET
of PAKISTAN

FORMATION AND WORKING
1947–1977

THE FEDERAL CABINET
of PAKISTAN

FORMATION AND WORKING
1947–1977

Naumana Kiran Imran

OXFORD
UNIVERSITY PRESS

OXFORD
UNIVERSITY PRESS

Oxford University Press is a department of the University of Oxford.
It furthers the University's objective of excellence in research, scholarship,
and education by publishing worldwide. Oxford is a registered trade mark of
Oxford University Press in the UK and in certain other countries

Published in Pakistan by
Ameena Saiyid, Oxford University Press
No.38, Sector 15, Korangi Industrial Area,
PO Box 8214, Karachi-74900, Pakistan

First Edition published in 2016

ISBN 978-0-19-940337-0

Typeset in Adobe Garamond Pro
Printed on 80gsm Local Offset paper

Printed by Ilma Printers, Karachi

I dedicate my book to
*Holy Prophet Muhammed (*PBUH*) who has given a clear*
thought of learning and peace to humanity.

May Allah accept my efforts and help
all researchers, scholars, and readers of this book!

Contents

List of Tables and Graph

Acknowledgements

During the course of my research study, I have incurred the debt of many individuals and institutions. I am grateful to Prof. Dr Massarrat Abid for her guidance, cooperation, and support. It proved to be indispensable at every stage.

I acknowledge the advice and encouragement I received from Prof. Dr Mohammad Iqbal Chawla and Dr Fraz Anjum, my teachers and colleagues. They read some of the chapters, proposed ways and means for improvement, and were a source of guidance for me throughout. I thank them for their unfailing support, comments, and cautions.

I owe a personal debt to a number of scholars. Among those whose guidance was most helpful in understanding the complexities of the research study in the initial stages include Dr Mohammad Waseem, Dr Rafique Afzal, Dr Hassan Askari Rizvi, Prof. David Gilmartin, Prof. Robert Nichols, and Dr Aslam Syed. In the later stages of the research study those whose advice and suggestions helped include Dr Bettina Robotka, Prof. Mathew Nelson, and Dr Pippa Virdee. I am grateful for their valuable suggestions and scholarly feedback.

I also take this opportunity to offer my heartfelt gratitude to the library staff of the Department of History, Pakistan Study Centre, Department of Political Science, and Central Library of the University of the Punjab, Punjab Public Library,

Quaid-i-Azam Library, Lahore, Museum Library, Lahore, Punjab Assembly Library, National Documentation Centre, Islamabad, and the National Archives, Islamabad.

Finally, my family has been a great source of strength for me. The encouragement, support, and prayers of my parents have always remained with me. I also express my gratitude to my father-in-law who helped and supported me throughout the period of my research. My husband, Imran Sharif Sadberg, has always stood by me and has encouraged me in my endeavours. I admire his patience and endurance. My children, Qamar, Amna, and Taha, tolerated my busy schedule and cooperated with me as much as was possible for them.

Naumana Kiran
2016

Introduction

This study explores the role of the federal cabinet of Pakistan in the decision-making process and policy formulation from 1947 to 1977. It challenges the common perception that only the military and civil bureaucracies played pivotal roles in the decision-making process. It argues that the federal cabinet was not a voiceless institution. It does not refute the concept of the effectiveness of the civil and military bureaucracies, but adds to the existing knowledge that, along with these two institutions, the cabinet was also an effective body, especially when dealing with political and economic matters. As far as foreign policy is concerned, all three institutions, the civil bureaucracy, military bureaucracy, and the cabinet, were effective, along with a few prominent individuals.

The main aims of this study are to investigate the different appointment criteria under different systems of government, the socio-economic backgrounds of the ministers; the role of the cabinet in policymaking, especially in the realm of the political issues which emerged at the provincial level, in economic policy formulation and planning, and in foreign policy matters. It also looks into the rifts which emerged between the members of various cabinets and the effects of these on the working of the institution. It further examines the relationships that developed between the chairman and the members of the cabinet.

The hypothesis of the study is that the cabinet played an important role in the decision-making process with variations, i.e. greater or lesser in different eras and under different regimes. The representation of one or other social group, i.e. urban professionals, civil or military bureaucrats, businessmen, or rural-based ministers in the cabinet had an impact on the formulation of policies to a great extent. Moreover, the ideological, regional, and sometimes personal rifts within the cabinet had an impact on the performance of this institution.

The term 'cabinet' is derived from the Italian word '*cabinetto*' meaning 'a small private room; a good place to discuss important business without being interrupted'.[1] The concept of cabinet originated with the first monarch in the world, with different names, powers, and ideologies. Heads of states or monarchs needed a group of advisors who were like their ministers. During a monarchical period, certain members of the nobility worked as principal advisors to the monarch and functioned as heads of different administrative departments. Their powers were limited, but they were available at the monarch's discretion to discuss, and sometimes to decide issues.

However, despite having some commonalities, the ancient and medieval councils of advisors were fundamentally different from modern cabinets. The former was an informal political structure, deriving all its authority from the will of the monarch. The modern cabinet is a formal body, having constitutional authority and responsibility to the legislature. The concept of the modern cabinet or cabinet government originated more or less in 1660, after the restoration of the monarchy in Britain. 'The cabinet emerged as, by the standards of the age, a small, businesslike committee of that truly ancient institution the Privy Council ... the prototype cabinet was known variously in the 1660s and 1670s as the Foreign Committee or the Intelligence Committee of the Privy Council'.[2] Before the Glorious Revolution of 1688, the term 'cabinet' was used for an elite group of advisors who circled around the monarch. After the revolution, this small group of elites played the role of a bridge between the Parliament and the British monarch. The Glorious Revolution was a turning point in minimizing the powers of the monarch, and the legislative process of the nineteenth century gradually diminished the monarch's powers. The Parliament, especially the House of Commons, gained more powers. The majority of the cabinet members were taken from the House of Commons instead of from the House of Lords.[3] After 1717, the cabinet ceased to hold meetings in the presence of the king or queen. With the emergence of political parties in the 1860s and 1870s, the cabinet system in Britain gained more strength than ever before.[4]

The traditional and constitutional role of the cabinet in the British political system is dual: it proposes legislation, and then supervises the administration of that legislation. In the hierarchy of the government or institutions of the government, the British cabinet sits at the apex.[5] The major functions of the cabinet are to determine the main directions of domestic and foreign policy; to control the agenda in the Parliament, to coordinate the policies of the government; to allocate the government's expenditure; long-term strategic planning; and to deal with any unforeseen difficulties and problems.[6] Problems of a political or economic nature are dealt with and legislation is recommended by the cabinet. Foreign policy is also discussed by it. No change in policy can be introduced without prior sanction by the cabinet.[7]

By the 1690s, an inner group within the cabinet had also emerged that was very close to the monarch. When an inner cabinet is formed, the whole cabinet is weakened. The ministers in an inner cabinet are markedly and regularly consulted by the prime minister (PM). These influential ministers persuade the cabinet if a policy is questioned in cabinet meetings.[8] The inner cabinet necessarily consists of political figures, which is not essential for a 'kitchen cabinet', which may also include some non-political figures. This is an informal support network for the PM. It may include bureaucrats, technocrats, businessmen, journalists, and private secretaries. In the opinion of some critics, the presence of the inner or kitchen cabinet is harmful for a healthy, effective, and efficient government.[9]

To Americans, 'cabinet' means 'an enclosed place with shelves for storing dishes, clothes, and supplies of some kind'.[10] In the political context, it means the top officials who work for the president. James Madison, the fourth president of the USA, under the influence of British customs, used the word 'cabinet' for the first time for the top officials in the president's executive branch of government.[11] George Washington, the first president of the USA, appointed only four members to a council of ministers in 1790, to aid and advise him. This grew and reached eighteen members. as under President Barack Obama in 2013. Apart from these, seven other officials have the status of cabinet-rank, including the White House Chief of Staff, the Chairman of the Council of Economic Advisors, and others. However, the increase in number resulted in a reduction of the influence and power of the cabinet.[12] The role of a cabinet under the presidential system is different and limited. The cabinet is answerable to the president, unlike under the parliamentary system where it is answerable to the legislature and 'stands at the pinnacle of government'.[13]

CABINET IN THE SUBCONTINENT UNDER BRITISH COLONIAL RULE

The origin of Pakistan's cabinet system lies in the colonial rule of the East India Company. Its business was run by a council whose senior-most member was called the 'governor' or the 'president'.[14] The council enjoyed decision-making powers which was based on a majority vote. The powers of the governor general in the council increased with the expansion of territory under the East India Company. In 1786, the governor general was given authority to take decisions at his discretion if the situation required it. Normally, he was bound by the advice of the council. This power of the governor general in India continued till the transfer of power to the governments of India and Pakistan in 1947.[15] The basis of dual government was retained in India: one for normal circumstances, and the other for emergency situations. The emergency powers were used so frequently that it became a normal phenomenon for the governor general to use his emergency powers.

The British Crown assumed direct control over India after the uprising of 1857 under the Government of India Act of 1858. The Crown appointed the governor general and the members of the council of the governor general. The council included only British members until 1909; no Indian was included. The governor general had the power to override the majority decision of his council, which included both bureaucrats and non-bureaucrats.[16] Elected members were included for the first time in 1909, though in small numbers, but their representation increased gradually. They were permitted to raise questions, to discuss the budget, and to present resolutions on administrative questions.[17] In the colonial period power proceeded downwards from the 'king to the people'.[18] In colonial India, the cabinet or council of ministers could not become a strong institution.

The cabinet system was introduced into India by Lord Canning in 1861. On his suggestion, departments were distributed among members of the Viceroy's Executive Council, except for a few which were kept under the direct control of the viceroy himself. Besides a minister, each department was assigned a secretary who was as powerful as the minister and had direct regular access to the governor general.[19] Since 1909 the commander-in-chief (C-in-C) of the armed forces had been an ex-officio member of the Viceroy's Council. Since he had the defence portfolio under his control, he was thus regarded as the second-most powerful member after the viceroy. This practice continued even under the 1935 Act. Had the C-in-C been removed from the cabinet of the British governor general, the political power of the military would have been reduced. The same convention was inherited by Pakistan.[20] However, it is important to mention that Sardar Baldev Singh was appointed as the last Minister of Defence of British India in 1946.

The other tradition inherited from colonial rule was the powerful bureaucracy. The bureaucrats were in the habit of overruling the ministers on issues of importance. The general secretary at the centre, and the chief secretaries in the provinces were extremely powerful. The civil servants had always enjoyed the power to advise their ministers, and during the days of the British, some important departmental issues were even decided by them without bringing them to the notice of the ministers.[21]

Under Section 9 of the Government of India Act, 1935, the governor general was the most powerful executive. He was assisted by the council of ministers but was not bound by the advice of the council, especially in matters of special responsibilities, including the peace and tranquility of India, the financial stability of the federal government, the safeguarding of the legitimate interests of the minorities, the protection of the Indian states' rights, and many others. Ministers were to be chosen by the governor general from among the members of the legislature, and must not exceed ten in number. The governor general could preside over meetings of the council of ministers at his discretion.[22] Under the terms of the 1935 Act, ministers had limited powers.

They had no right to tender advice on matters which came under the discretionary powers of the governor general, on which the governor general could exercise his individual judgment, and which came under the jurisdiction of his special duties.[23]

THE CABINET IN PAKISTAN

The cabinet system introduced in Pakistan in August 1947 was highly influenced by the colonial traditions in which the governor general was exceedingly influential. In Pakistan, this institution worked efficiently, even in the presence of strong governors general during the first decade of independence. Prime Ministers like Liaquat Ali Khan took important policy decisions in the fields of economy, politics, and foreign policy. The cabinet remained influential in decision-making from 1947 to 1954, but afterwards the effectiveness of the office was minimized during the period of coalition ministries due to the frequent fall of governments. The significance and working capability of the cabinet increased during the Ayub Khan era (1958–1969), as most issues were decided in cabinet meetings. Again, the institution lost its influence during Yahya Khan's regime (1969–1971), which witnessed the hegemony of the military high command. It regained its value and status during the early years of Zulfikar Ali Bhutto's rule (1971–1974), when it was empowered to decide almost all issues except matters of foreign policy. The situation was reversed during the post-1974 era as the cabinet gradually lost its influence. Overall, this institution remained significant in the areas of policy formulation and decision-making.

This study is an attempt to understand the role of the cabinet during the period under discussion in the light of documents which have not been consulted by previous researchers. The study has accumulated sufficient evidence to show that the cabinet in Pakistan has performed an important role in decision-making, though its influence and power varied during different eras and under different systems.

The study challenges the general perception that it was mostly the feudal lords who attained cabinet seats. Sociopolitical analysis in this regard has revealed that professionals, rather than feudal lords, generally remained in the majority and other groups, including civil and military bureaucracies, industrialists, and businessmen, were also appointed to important portfolios. It looks into the role and status of inner or kitchen cabinets, the cabinet's role in dealing with the political problems that arose in the provinces, its role in the formation of economic institutions, economic planning, and policymaking in the fields of agriculture, business, and industry. The study also brings to light the effects of the personal understanding and attitude of the heads of the state or government on the involvement of the cabinet in foreign policy issues. Finally, it highlights the rifts that existed among cabinet colleagues and the impact of these rifts on the decision-making process. The nature of the relationship between the prime minister and the president with his cabinet is another area of exploration. It focuses on the nature of the debates and struggles which took place once an issue came to the cabinet's attention, and how these affected the direction of policy.

The study explores the prevailing belief that the most important decision-making authority in the country from 1947 to 1977 was the civil and military bureaucracy. The truth lies in the fact that the three institutions, the cabinet as well as the civil and military bureaucracies, played their parts in the formulation of foreign policy, but in deciding economic and political issues, the cabinet was more involved than the other two institutions. It challenges the perception that the first martial law that was imposed in the country in 1953 was done with the involvement of the president, defence secretary, and military high command, while bypassing the cabinet. However, it is pointed out here that the order imposing martial law was issued by the cabinet on 6 March 1953. Furthermore, all economic policies of development, investment, import and export, and others were devised and approved by the cabinet. The presence of a large number of professionals in the cabinet resulted in the implementation of pro-urban plans of development in most eras. This is evidence that the cabinet was playing an important role in decision-making and in introducing policies.

To study the formation and working of the institution of the cabinet in Pakistan the period researched has been divided into three phases. The first phase is from 1947 to 1958 with a parliamentary form of government; seven prime ministers took control, one after the other, with eight cabinets during this period. These eight cabinets are divided into three types, i.e. single party cabinets (1947–1954), the Cabinet of All

Talents (1954–1955), and coalition cabinets (1955–1958). The second phase witnessed the rule of two military heads from 1958 to 1971, and has been further divided into three parts to examine the performance of the institution of the cabinet: the martial law period (1958–62); the presidential period (1962–1969); and the period consisting of the cabinets of the second martial law regime of Yahya Khan (1969–1971). The third phase is the second parliamentary period from 1971 to 1977. During this period four cabinets were formed: two before the introduction of the 1973 Constitution, the first of which worked under the martial law system from December 1971 to April 1972, whereas, the second cabinet worked under the Interim Constitution, from April 1972 to August 1973. The last two cabinets of this era functioned under the parliamentary form of government established by the Constitution of 1973. However, to study the rifts and inner dynamics of the institution of the cabinet, the division of the phases is different: it is on the basis of the type of cabinet, i.e. single-party cabinets, the Cabinet of All Talents, coalition cabinets, military cabinets, and presidential cabinets, etc.

No significant study has so far been undertaken to evaluate the institution of the cabinet alone, and there is a striking gap in the literature available. The absence of any full-length discussion on how the cabinets of Pakistan performed in the realm of policymaking and dealt with issues has made research on this theme essential. An equally striking omission is the absence of any work on the fertile area of rifts and groupings in the cabinets. It is this gap which this study seeks to fill. This work is produced on the basis of primary source materials, declassified cabinet files, and cabinet papers which have not been consulted by political scientists and the historians of Pakistan to evaluate the working, role, and limitations of the cabinet. These cabinet papers provide a detailed insight into the workings of this important institution. The use of cabinet files on various issues has enhanced the importance of this research work and sheds new light on various issues. It also reveals the true value of the institution of the cabinet in policymaking and decision-taking.

The declassified record of the cabinet files includes not only the minutes and decisions of the cabinet meetings, but also the summaries presented to the cabinets on various important issues. It includes the political problems prevailing in the provinces, the economic condition of the country, the formation and performance of economic institutions, land reforms, industrialization, Pakistan's relations with other countries, and many others. These cabinet files are important in providing first-hand knowledge of the government's stand on various matters. The record includes ministers' discussions on various issues, specifically from 1947 to 1958. Except for a few files, the cabinet files for the whole period of study have been declassified. Furthermore, the declassified files of the Ministry of Interior, Ministry of Finance and Economic Affairs, and the Ministry of Foreign Affairs were also consulted and were found to be most helpful in analysing the working of the cabinet. Files related to governors' conferences were another important source material, especially with reference to provincial political matters.

Keeping in mind the basic prerequisites of the research, the primary sources related to cabinet have been given the highest priority. In addition to cabinet records, the prime ministers' papers from 1947 to 1953, the National Assembly of Pakistan's debates, British High Commissioners' reports, and other materials available in London Archives have also been used. Interviews of a few relevant personalities and ministers who served in the cabinets during the period of the study were also conducted, and their memories have been used as an important source material. Interviews were also conducted with living members of Ayub Khan and Z. A. Bhutto's cabinets, including S. M. Zafar, Mubashir Hasan, Abdul Hafiz Pirzada, etc., the available close relatives of deceased ministers, and a few journalists and bureaucrats. Their first-hand knowledge has enhanced the significance of this study. Newspapers were also consulted to analyse the ongoing events on a broad level. Various books on Pakistan's politics, institutions, political personalities, economy, foreign policy, speeches and memoirs of political leaders, biographies and autobiographies of politicians, etc. were studied to obtain the views presented by historians, economists, political scientists, and politicians regarding cabinet's role in the governance and decision-making process in Pakistan. Articles in various research journals of international repute were also assessed. One major problem with the whole range of secondary sources available was that the cabinet was not discussed directly, hence, a detailed or in-depth study of the complete data had to be conducted.

The general format of the research was to review all related source material, including primary and secondary sources. Moreover, the authenticity of the primary sources has been carefully validated. Analytical, descriptive, and comparative methods have been applied to assess the findings of the research.

Quantitative research techniques have also been applied to present collected data in a precise form. The most important contribution in terms of quantitative research are the tables and graph prepared to assess the socio-economic profile of the various ministers who served in the cabinets under different regimes. For this, data has been collected from cabinet records, NDC, London Archives, newspapers, encyclopedias, research journals, and books. The available data regarding the socio-economic backgrounds of the ministers were counter-checked against different sources. Short biographies of almost all ministers of the given period have also been provided in the appendices.

The book contains five chapters along with an introduction and conclusion. Chapter One deals with the formation of cabinets in Pakistan under working constitutions, criteria of appointment, social backgrounds of ministers from the perspective of its impact on decision-making, and inner or kitchen cabinets. Chapter Two examines the cabinets' roles in the formation of economic institutions, planning, and the introduction of industrial, agricultural, trade, and business policies. Chapter Three explores the cabinets' performances in dealing with the political problems which arose in the provinces. Chapter Four examines the cabinets' role in dealing with foreign policy issues and the formulation of foreign policy. It further explores whether the cabinet was taken into confidence or bypassed during the signing of important agreements with India, China, the USA, and Afghanistan. Chapter Five seeks to explore the reasons for the rifts that existed between cabinet members, and the regional and ideological groupings. It also explores the impact of rifts and groupings on decision-making.

Notes and References

1. Sam Wellman, *Your Government: How it Works? The Cabinet,* (Philadelphia: Chelsea House Publishers, 2001), 12; and Robert Longday, About.com Guide US Government Info Google 15.07.2011.

2. Peter Hennessy, *Cabinet* (New York: Basil Blackwell Ltd., 1986), 8. Privy Council was originally a committee of the monarch's closest advisors to give confidential advice on affairs of state. It was a powerful institution but most of its power was transferred to its committee, called 'Cabinet' after the revolution.

3. Stephen Buckley, *The Prime Minister and Cabinet* (Edinburgh: The University Press, 2006), 26–7.

4. Hennessy, *Cabinet,* 10 and Buckley, *The Prime Minister,* 29 and 32.

5. Michael Laver and Kenneth A. Shepsle, *Making and Breaking Governments: Cabinets and Legislature in Parliamentary Democracies* (Cambridge: Cambridge University Press, 1996), 29.

6. Ivor Jennings, *Cabinet Government* (Cambridge: Cambridge University Press, 1961), 232–42.

7. Ibid. 151.

8. Laver and Shepsle, *Making and Breaking Governments: Cabinets and Legislature,* 4.

9. Ibid. 39.

10. Wellman, *Your Government: How it Works? The Cabinet,* 12.

11. Ibid.

12. Ibid. 57.
13. Christopher Hill, *Cabinet Decisions on Foreign Policy: The British Experience October 1938–June 1941* (Cambridge: Cambridge University Press, 1991), xvii.
14. A. B. Rudra, *The Viceroy and Governor General,* (London: np, 1940), 22.
15. K. J. Newman, 'The Diarchic Pattern of Government and Pakistan's Problems', *Political Science Quarterly*, 75 (March 1960), 94.
16. Masud Ahmad, *Pakistan: A Study of its Constitutional History 1857–1975* (Lahore: Research Society of Pakistan, 1978), 1.
17. Newman, *The Diarchic Pattern of Government and Pakistan's Problems,* 95.
18. M. Rashiduzzaman, *Pakistan: A Study of Government and Politics* (Dacca, The University Press, 1967), 108.
19. Newman, *The Diarchic Pattern of Government and Pakistan's Problems,* 97.
20. Ibid. 99.
21. Ibid. 105.
22. Govt. of India Act, 1935, Section 9 cited in C. L. Anand, *The Government of India Act 1935* (Karachi: Law Publishers, 1939), 127.
23. Masud Ahmad, *Pakistan: A Study of its Constitutional History,* 10.

CHAPTER 1

Formation of Cabinets

This chapter examines the formation of the cabinets and the different appointment criteria followed by the various heads of state or government of Pakistan under different systems of government. It looks into the constitutional status of the various cabinets under different constitutions, i.e. the Provisional Constitution of 1947, which was an amended form of the Government of India Act, 1935, the 1956 Constitution, the 1962 Constitution, the Interim Constitution of 1972, and the 1973 Constitution. It further examines the social backgrounds of the ministers and the groups they represented. Another aspect discussed is the existence of inner or kitchen cabinets within the cabinets.

The appointment criteria for cabinet members are different under the parliamentary and the presidential systems of government. A limited number of members of parliament are available to be selected as ministers in a parliamentary system, whilst under the presidential system there is no restriction for the selection of ministers from among the members of the parliament. Under the British parliamentary system, three major principles are followed when appointing ministers: representation in relation to political factions and tendencies as well as social origin, loyalty to the PM, and ministerial competence.[1] Full cabinet ministers are selected from those with experience. If they have successfully worked as cabinet secretaries and junior ministers or ministers of state, they have better chances of selection.[2] Though Pakistan followed the British parliamentary and cabinet system, the inherent weaknesses and the colonial traditions[3] did not enable a cabinet system to flourish in Pakistan on a strong footing.

The chapter has been divided into three parts to study the question of the formation of the cabinets in the first parliamentary period (1947–1958), under martial law and the presidential regime (1958–1971), and during the second parliamentary era (1971–1977).

1.1. THE FIRST PARLIAMENTARY PERIOD, 1947–1958

1.1.1. STRUCTURE AND CONSTITUTIONAL STATUS OF THE CABINETS

(i). *Single Party Cabinets 1947–1954*

From 1947 to 1954, three cabinets worked under the amended 1935 Act which was adopted as the Interim Constitution of Pakistan in 1947. The cabinet was made collectively responsible to the Constituent Assembly of Pakistan (CAP). No individual discretion was given to the governor general; he was bound to act on the advice of the cabinet. In some cases he was given the power to issue ordinances subject to the approval of the cabinet and CAP.[4] Section 17 of the Interim Constitution gave the power to appoint ministers to the governor general in place of the PM. Section 10(A) of the Interim Constitution stated that 'The governor general's ministers shall be chosen and summoned by him, shall be sworn in as members of the council, and shall hold office during his pleasure'.[5] He could also allocate any department for himself. Under this section of the constitution a new Ministry of States and Frontier Regions was created in July 1948 which was headed by Governor General Muhammad Ali Jinnah himself. That the governor general could have a ministry under his own control created a unique precedent.[6] In theory, the cabinet was more powerful than the governor general, who was bound to exercise his powers on the advice of the cabinet.[7] Since there were no organized political parties, and the PM had less political backing with a stable majority, the governor general could exercise more power than the cabinet.[8]

The first cabinet appointed by Governor General Muhammad Ali Jinnah on 15 August 1947 was the cabinet of Liaquat Ali Khan, the first PM of Pakistan. This cabinet 'was designed to give a balance of sectional interests and under strong leadership, it was capable of working as a team'.[9] It included Fazlur Rehman, Minister of Education who later headed the Commerce ministry, Ibrahim Ismail Chundrigarh, Minister of Industries and Commerce until May 1948, and Jogandar Nath Mandal, Minister of Law. They were all from Bengal. Then there was Ghazanfar Ali Khan, Minister of Food, Agriculture, and Health, Malik Ghulam Mohammad, Minister of Finance and Economic Affairs, Mohammad Zafrullah Khan, Minister of Foreign Affairs and Commonwealth Relations from Punjab; Abdus Sattar Pirzada, Minister of Health and later Law and Labour from Sindh; and Sardar Abdur Rab Nishtar,

Communications Minister from the North-West Frontier Province (NWFP, presently called Khyber Pakhtunkhawa).[10] Later, some internal changes took place and some additions were made so that it included Khawaja Shahabuddin as Minister of Interior, Information and Refugees and Rehabilitation, and Dr A. M. Malik as Minister of Minority Affairs, from East Bengal; and Mushtaq Ahmad Gurmani as Minister Without Portfolio and later Kashmir Affairs, and Chaudhry Nazir Ahmad as Minister of Industries after Chundrigarh, from Punjab, and Sardar Bahadur Khan Minister of Health and later Communications from the NWFP.[11]

The first Cabinet of Pakistan set a convention which was a requirement of the time but which established a negative precedent. Under the working constitution, the Governor General was only a constitutional figurehead. But due to the special circumstances, PM Liaquat and the cabinet decided that none of them wanted the Father of the Nation, Quaid-i-Azam, to be only a constitutional head because they needed his guidance in the true sense of the word.[12] To this end, cabinet signed a convention on 30 December 1947 under which the Quaid-i-Azam's authority and superiority was accepted over the cabinet:

> The Cabinet agreed that the Quaid-i-Azam's presence was the greatest factor making for the stability and progress of the state ... no question of policy or principle should be determined and decided except at a meeting of the Cabinet to be presided over by the Quaid-i-Azam ... in the event of any difference of opinion between the Cabinet and the Quaid-i-Azam, latter's decision should be final.[13]

It was further approved that if any minister disagreed with the Quaid-i-Azam, he would resign. Although the cabinet approved the convention, Malik Ghulam Mohammad, Finance Minister, and Mohammad Zafrullah Khan, Foreign Minister, argued that no extra burden should be placed on the Quaid because of his ill health, and that the convention should not damage the ideal of an independent democratic country. The finance minister said, 'Since our ideal was a democratic state the convention should be worked in such a manner as to steer a course between democracy on the British model on the one hand and one-man rule on the other'.[14] The most important decision of the cabinet regarding the convention of the Quaid-i-Azam was that 'the convention be confined to the person of the Quaid-i-Azam until the final constitution of Pakistan came into force'.[15]

Unfortunately this convention could not remain limited to the person of the Quaid-i-Azam. Succeeding Governors General Malik Ghulam Muhammad and Iskandar Mirza misused their powers and either dismissed or conspired to dissolve cabinets. They did not consider themselves bound by the advice of the cabinet. In 1954, an effort was made to change the convention by the first CAP, but Governor General Malik Ghulam Mohammad dismissed the CAP.[16]

Almost the same cabinet of Liaquat Ali Khan continued to hold office under Khawaja Nazimuddin (1951–1953), who was appointed PM by the cabinet[17] in October 1951 after the assassination of Liaquat Ali Khan.[18] He acknowledged that the cabinet had put the 'onerous responsibility of being Pakistan's Prime Minister'[19] on him. It changed the real spirit of the working constitution under which the Governor General had the authority to appoint all members of the cabinet including the PM, and the cabinet was supposed to work under the supervision of the PM. Baxter has mentioned that Nazimuddin himself assumed the office of PM in consultation with the ministers present in the capital.[20] Discussing the same point, Ziring added that ministers including Shahabuddin, Nazimuddin's brother, manoeuvered to appoint Nazimuddin as PM. The former finance minister, Malik Ghulam Mohammad, was promoted to the seat of Governor General, and Choudhury Muhammad Ali was appointed finance minister by the Governor General. Dr Ishtiaq Hussain Qureshi and Dr Mahmud Husain were inducted into the cabinet as Minister of Kashmir Affairs and Refugees, and Rehabilitation respectively on 26 November 1951.[21] Each of them had already served as a minister of state in Liaquat's cabinet.

Nazimuddin's cabinet was dismissed by the Governor General in April 1953.[22] In Nazimuddin's words, on the demand for resignation from the Governor General Ghulam Mohammad, 'I told the Governor General that constitutionally and legally he had no right to make such a demand because he was purely a constitutional Governor General'.[23] Furthermore, the budget had recently been passed by the Legislative Assembly with an overwhelming majority, so he refused to resign.[24] On Nazimuddin's refusal to resign, he and his cabinet were dismissed. Constitutionally, the Governor General was bound to gain approval for his decisions from the cabinet, but he did not care for the constitution.

The weakness of the institution of the cabinet became evident for the first time in 1953 when six out of thirteen members of Nazimuddin's cabinet expressed their readiness to work in the new cabinet. They were more concerned about self-gain than democracy.[25] The third cabinet of this period was formed under Muhammad Ali Bogra in April 1953. The ministers were nominated by Governor General Ghulam Mohammad. Bogra was then the ambassador of Pakistan to the USA. The six ministers of Nazimuddin's cabinet who continued in Bogra's cabinet were Mohammad Zafrullah Khan, Minister of Foreign Affairs, Choudhury Muhammad Ali, Minister of Finance, Nawab Mushtaq Ahmad Khan Gurmani, Minister of Interior, States and Frontier Regions, Sardar Bahadur Khan, Minister of Communications, Ishtiaq Hussain Qureshi, Minister of Education, and Dr A. M. Malik, Minister of Labour, Health and Works. The new inductions were A. K. Brohi, Minister of Law and Parliamentary Affairs from Sindh, Khan Abdul Qayyum Khan, Minister of Food and Agriculture from the NWFP, Shoaib Qureshi, Minister of Information, Refugees and Kashmir Affairs from Punjab, and Tafazzal Ali, Minister of Commerce from East Bengal.[26]

Through a legislative act, the CAP repealed the Public and Representative Offices (Disqualification) Act (PRODA) on 21 September 1954, and made the Governor General bound to the advice of the cabinet. It further amended Article 10-A of the constitution, and the right to dismiss the PM was taken away from the Governor General, which resulted in the dissolution of the CAP on 24 October 1954 by the Governor General, who took it as a personal insult.[27]

(ii). *Cabinet of All Talents 1954–1955*

The fourth cabinet of the first parliamentary era was nominated by Governor General Ghulam Mohammad under Bogra's premiership and included almost all new faces. They were Habib Ibrahim Rahimtoola, Minister of Commerce, Col. Syed Abid Hussain, Minister of Food and Education, and Sardar Mumtaz Ali Khan, Minister of Information and Kashmir Affairs from Punjab; M. A. Ispahani, Minister of Industries and Commerce, and Ghulam Ali Talpur, Minister of Information, Broadcasting, and Education from Sindh; Maj. Gen. Iskandar Mirza, Minister of Interior, States, and Kashmir Affairs, Ayub Khan, Commander-in-Chief of the Forces, Minister of Defence, Dr Khan Sahib, Minister of Communications from NWFP; Huseyn Shaheed Suhrawardy, Minister of Law, and Abu Hussain Sarkar, Minister of Health from East Bengal. Ghayasuddin Pathan, Choudhury Muhammad Ali, and Dr A. M. Malik continued from the previous cabinet.[28]

It was called the 'Cabinet of All Talents'[29] by Muhammad Ali Bogra as he claimed that it included all experts and people qualified in their respective fields. In Ziring's opinion it was a 'non-Muslim League civil-military complex',[30] but practically it was a civil-military-cum-Muslim League (ML) and opposition partnership as it also included some Muslim Leaguers like Sardar Mumtaz, Rahimtoola, and Abid Hussain. It was called the government of 'national unity' by Callard.[31] In Wheeler's view it was like an 'official government'[32] as had worked in the colonial period, or like the viceroy's council before Partition. It was like a military dictatorship in disguise.[33] It is further claimed that it was an 'Emergency Government'.[34] It was practically a national government in which all elements of society were included.

The so-called Cabinet of All Talents was not answerable to any legislature. It was not a normal, responsible government.[35] PM Bogra stressed on 31 October 1954 that since the cabinet was directly responsible to the people, it was therefore a democratic body.[36] A draft constitution was prepared by Sir Ivor Jennings, a British expert on constitutional law and an advisor to the government of Pakistan. Under the draft constitution, the cabinet was made responsible to the president of Pakistan, not to the legislature, as has been the pattern of the American Constitution. The cabinet approved the draft in February 1955. Governor General Ghulam Mohammad had planned to promulgate the constitution, but the Federal Court of Pakistan halted the constitution-making process by the Governor General alone through an exclusive decree, declaring that only the CAP could design the constitution.[37]

(iii). *Coalition Cabinets 1955–1958*

As a result of indirect elections in August 1955, the second CAP came into being. The composition and party position was totally different in this CAP. The sweeping majority so far enjoyed by the ML was lost and other parties such as the Awami League (AL), United Front (UF), etc. also won seats. The ML won twenty-five, AL twelve, UF sixteen, Congress four, Scheduled Caste Federation three,[38] and other smaller parties and independents won ten. This new party position in the second CAP left no chance for the establishment of a single party government.[39]

Meanwhile, Choudhury Muhammad Ali, the new PM who took charge on 11 August 1955, convinced the ailing Governor General Malik Ghulam Mohammad to take two months' leave. The application for leave was presented in the cabinet meeting, and was approved.[40] On the proposal of Choudhury Muhammad Ali, the cabinet decided to send a formal recommendation to Her Majesty Queen Elizabeth II to the effect that the acting Governor General, Iskandar Mirza, should be appointed Governor General in place of Ghulam Mohammad from 6 October.[41] Suhrawardy has recorded that Iskandar Mirza's nomination was accepted by a cabinet vote. The result of the vote[42] was a tie and the deciding vote in favour of Iskandar Mirza was cast by Ayub Khan.[43]

During 1955–58, four coalition governments were formed. The first was formed by a coalition of the ML and UF under Choudhury Muhammad Ali, the leader of the ML parliamentary party. This cabinet included five ministers from the ML and four from the UF. Each party in the UF nominated one minister: A. K. Fazlul Haq, Minister of Interior, Kamini Kumar Dutta, Minister of Health, Hamidul Haq Chowdhry, Minister of Foreign Affairs and Commonwealth Relations, Nurul Haq Chaudhry, Minister of Labour, Works and Minority Affairs, Abdul Latif Biswas, Minister of Food and Agriculture, and I. I. Chundrigarh, Minister of Law. All of them were from East Pakistan. The West Pakistani ministers were Dr Khan Sahib, Minister of Communications (remained for only two months), Habib Ibrahim Rahimtoola, Minister of Commerce and Industries, Syed Abid Hussain, Minister of Kashmir Affairs, Pir Ali Mohammad Rashdi, Minister of Information and Broadcasting, Syed Amjad Ali, Minister of Finance and Economic Affairs, M. R. Kayani, Minister of Communications, and Abdus Sattar, Minister of Interior and Education. Abdus Sattar replaced A. K. Fazlul Haq.[44] The inclusion of two non-Muslim ministers in the cabinet gave it a non-sectarian look. Democracy seems to have been working successfully at that moment.[45] The absence of the leading Punjabi politicians in the cabinet was due to their priority to get cabinet seats in the newly-created unified West Pakistan Province, the One Unit.

The first permanent constitution prepared by the second CAP was introduced in Pakistan on 23 March 1956. It established a federal and parliamentary system of government. It provided for a cabinet of ministers, with the PM as its head, to aid and advise the president in the exercise of his functions. Under Article 37 of the constitution the president was required 'to act in accordance with the advice of the Cabinet except in those matters in which he was empowered by the Constitution to act in his discretion'.[46] The most important discretionary power given to the president was in regard to the appointment of the PM from among the members of the National Assembly. The other ministers were to be appointed by the PM with the consent of the president.[47] The cabinet was made responsible to the National Assembly, and decisions taken by the cabinet on any issue were to be conveyed to the president by the PM under Article 42.[48]

Ambiguity evidently existed in the distribution of powers between the legislature, the cabinet, and the president. On the one hand, the president was bound to follow the advice of the cabinet in the exercise of his duties and functions. On the other hand, there was no solution provided in the constitution should the problem arise of the president refusing to follow the advice. The cabinet, under Article 52 of the constitution, was collectively responsible to the National Assembly,[49] but if the cabinet were to lose the confidence of the legislature, there was no provision for its resignation or dismissal. The PM was to hold office during the pleasure of the president,[50] but at the same time, the president could not exercise his powers unless he was satisfied that the PM had lost the confidence of the majority in the National Assembly.

Choudhury Muhammad Ali resigned from the premiership on 8 September 1956 after the creation of the Republican Party from within the ML.[51] The next coalition government of the AL and the Republicans was formed under the premiership of Suhrawardy on 12 September 1956. It included four AL ministers, including Suhrawardy himself, Abul Mansur Ahmad, Minister of Commerce and Industries, Abdul Khaleque, Minister of Labour and Works, and Dildar Ahmed, Minister of Food and Agriculture, from East Pakistan. The five Republican ministers were Malik Firoz Khan Noon, Minister of Foreign Affairs and Commonwealth Relations, Syed Amjad Ali, Minister of Finance, Mir Ghulam Ali Talpur, Minister of Interior, and Sardar Amir Azam Khan, Minister of Information, Broadcasting, Parliamentary Affairs, and Law, from West Pakistan.[52] Suhrawardy claimed that it was the first time in Pakistan that a government had been formed in direct response to parliamentary forces, and that the government had demonstrated political maturity and shown improved performance.[53] This government came to an end in October 1957 due to a dispute within the cabinet on the issue of One Unit and the intrigues of Iskandar Mirza.[54]

The next coalition government was formed by four political parties led by the ML under the premiership of Ibrahim Ismail Chundrigarh on 18 October 1957. Huge differences of opinion among coalition partners brought the fate of this cabinet to an end on 11 December 1957. It was dissolved within two months because of severe disagreement on the issue of electorates.[55] The twelve ministers of this cabinet were taken from the ML, Republican Party, Krishak Sramik Party (KSP), and Nizam-i-Islam Party (NIP). Ministers from West Pakistan included Amjad Ali, Minister of Finance, Malik Firoz Khan Noon, Minister of Foreign Affairs and Commonwealth Relations, Mozaffar Ali Qizilbash, Minister of Industries, Ghulam Ali Talpur, Minister of Interior, and Mian Jaffar Shah, Minister of States and Frontier Regions, from the Republican Party. The ML ministers from West Pakistan were Mian Mumtaz Mohammad Khan Daultana, Minister of Defence, Yousuf Haroon, Minister of Kashmir and Parliamentary Affairs, and Fazlur Rehman, Minister of Commerce and Law from East Pakistan. KSP's ministers were Abdul Latif Biswas, Minister of Food and Agriculture, Lutfur Rehman, Minister of Health and Education, and Misbahuddin, Minister of Communications, from East Pakistan. NIP ministers included later in the cabinet were

Nurul Haq and Farid Ahmed.[56] One minister of state was from the Scheduled Caste Federation. It had a total of sixteen ministers and ministers of state in the last days.[57] This cabinet had to resign due to the disunity and differences of opinion among the coalition partners, specifically on the issue of electorates.

The next government was formed by the Republican Party in coalition with the National Awami Party (NAP), KSP (Hamid ul Haq Chowdhry group), the Pakistan National Congress, and the Scheduled Caste Federation, under the premiership of Malik Firoz Khan Noon in December 1957. All the smaller parties had their origins in East Pakistan. This government was also supported by the AL. The basis of this partnership was the continuation of joint electorates.[58] The only powerful party in this coalition was the Republican Party, so all the important portfolios were given to members of that party, and the decision-making authority was, in practice, in the hands of a single party.[59] The ministers in this cabinet from West Pakistan included Syed Amjad Ali, Minister of Finance, Mozaffar Ali Khan Qizilbash, Minister of Industries and Commerce, Ghulam Ali Talpur, Minister of Interior, Mian Jaffar Shah, Minister of Food and Agriculture, and Haji Moula Bukhsh Soomro, Minister of Rehabilitation. The East Pakistani ministers were Abdul Aleem, Minister of Labour, Works, Minority Affairs, and Information, Ramizuddin Ahmad, Minister of Communications, Kamini Kumar Dutta, Minister of Health, Education and Law, and Mahfuzul Haq, Minister of Social Welfare and Development Division.[60]

There was a reshuffle of some portfolios in March 1958 due to the addition of some new ministers. These were Basenta Kumar Das, Minister of Education, and Hamidul Haq Chowdhry, Minister of Finance from East Pakistan, who were appointed only on 16 September 1958. Sardar Abdur Rashid, Minister of Commerce and Industries, Sardar Amir Azam Khan, Minister of Economic and Parliamentary Affairs, and M. A. Khuhro, Minister of Defence, were from West Pakistan, which was given less representation than East Pakistan. Sahiruddin, A. H. Dildar Ahmad, and Nur ur Rahman had been included in the cabinet only five days before its dismissal with the imposition of martial law on 8 October 1958. The AL supported this government but was not part of the cabinet as it could not agree with the Republican Party on the distribution of portfolios.[61] Ziring argues that all the cabinet partners were opportunists and working to gain personal benefits.[62] The total number of ministers at the time of inauguration was nine, but changes were made time and again. Eighteen people held portfolios in different months. The more consistent ministers were Syed Amjad Ali, Qizalbash, Talpur, Jaffer Shah, Abdul Aleem, Ramizuddin Ahmad, and K. K. Dutta.

1.1.2. Appointment Criteria to the Cabinet

The appointment criteria were different in all three types of government. When appointing the first cabinet, which functioned until 1953 with only one major and some minor changes, Quaid-i-Azam Muhammad Ali Jinnah's only condition was qualification. He appointed the best available brains to different positions. Secondly, he tried to give representation to the different regions of Pakistan. He appointed three ministers from East Bengal, and one each from Punjab, NWFP, and Sindh.[63] He also gave representation to the minorities and Jogandar Nath Mandal was appointed.

While selecting his cabinet, the third Governor General, Ghulam Muhammad, gave consideration to his personal contacts and picked individuals loyal to him. He also made some appointments on the basis of need. He suspected that Abdul Qayyum Khan, Chief Minister of NWFP, would oppose the dismissal of Nazimuddin, so he was invited to be part of the cabinet. He accepted the offer and remained Minister of Food and Agriculture during Bogra's first premiership (1953–1954).[64] The Governor General also took into account the individuals' qualifications and experience in his specific field. The characteristic feature of that cabinet was the presence of military as well as bureaucratic elites. Along with these, a new social group was added, that of the industrialists represented by M. A. Ispahani and Rahimtoola. Strong Muslim Leaguers were unable to gain positions in the cabinet because Ghulam Mohammad did not trust them, and most of them had been tested during the previous regimes. Some appointments were made to reach a compromise, for example, Suhrawardy, who accepted a cabinet portfolio to secure his provincial government in East Pakistan.

During the third period of the first parliamentary phase, i.e. the coalition cabinets' period (1955–1958), the appointment criteria were quite different due to the 1956 Constitution and different party position in parliament. After the introduction of the 1956 Constitution, the nomination authority was the prime minister, not the president, who only gave his approval. All four cabinets formed during this period were coalitions, and the coalition partners were always given due shares. The nominees proposed by the coalition partners were accepted into the cabinet. If the coalition was led by AL, the AL prime minister had to accept all those names which were forwarded by the Republican Party, or by NIP, or by any other coalition partner. The PM had little or no choice in this regard and depended on his coalition partners for the nomination of cabinet members. As the One Unit had been introduced in West Pakistan, parity was maintained between the East and West Wings when appointing ministers. Equal numbers of ministers were appointed from each wing during this period and qualification was not always based on the best criteria, unlike in early cabinets.

1.1.3. SOCIAL BACKGROUNDS OF THE MINISTERS

The social backgrounds of the ministers influenced the policies devised by the cabinet. Urban professionals and the intelligentsia had dominated the cabinets up until 1955. They introduced economic reforms in favour of urban areas; industry flourished, but agriculture was neglected due to the absence or small representation of landlords. The cabinet had direct access to the problems, weaknesses, and areas in need of improvement in the urban vicinity, but were ignorant of the problems that needed to be addressed in the rural areas. It was because of this weakness that no large-scale reform package was introduced for the development and well-being of the millions of poor who were living in the villages. The social backgrounds of the ministers who served in the cabinet from 1947 to 1958 are given below:

Table: 1-A

Social Group	1947–1954 Single Party Cabinets	1954–1955 Cabinet of All Talents	1955–1958 Coalition Cabinets	1947–1958 Total
Professionals	17	6	21	44
Landowners	4	2	6	12
Civil Bureaucrats	2	1	2	5
Industrialists and Businessmen	0	2	3	5
Military Bureaucrats	0	3	1	4
Professions Unknown	0	0	4	4
Total Ministers	23	14	37	74

Source: The above table was prepared by the researcher on the basis of information collected through different sources including reports from the British High Commissioner to the Commonwealth Relations Office in London, cabinet files, newspapers, and various books including autobiographies, biographies, and others.

The table illustrates that most of the ministers belonged to five major social groups of the upper- and upper-middle classes including landowners, businessmen, bureaucrats, military personnel, and professionals (mostly lawyers). The other professionals included judges, educationists, and journalists.[65] Some of the professionals had a feudal background, but their profession is considered the decisive factor in assessing their social status. Of the seventeen professionals who served during 1947–1954, ten were practising lawyers, three were educationists, one was a retired justice, one was a journalist, and two belonged to other professions. In the period of the first parliamentary phase, of the four landlords, two were big feudal lords and the rest owned small landholdings and belonged to the middle class of landlords. There were only two civil bureaucrats in the cabinet before 1954.

The Cabinet of All Talents included six professionals—three were lawyers, one was a doctor, and the other two belonged to other professions. The two landlords belonged to the class of big feudal lords. The two new social groups that emerged were military bureaucrats and industrialists-cum-businessmen. There were three military bureaucrats and two industrialists and businessmen.

The total number of ministers rose to thirty-seven during the coalition cabinet era. Professionals formed the largest group here as under previous regimes. Again lawyers were in the majority among professionals, numbering thirteen out of twenty-one members. The cabinets of that period included two journalists and educationists, one retired justice and a doctor. The remaining members were from other professions. Of the six landlords, five belonged to the upper strata of landlords and only one was a middle-class landlord. Industrialists and businessmen maintained their positions but the ratio of civil and military bureaucrats decreased: there were two civil bureaucrats and only one military bureaucrat.

From the above data it can be concluded that most of the cabinet ministers were highly educated and qualified, no matter which social group they belonged to. Secondly, none, or very few ministers came from the lower-middle class and not even a single minister had his roots in the lower class. In fact, the lower class had no direct access to politics at the national level.

1.1.4. THE INNER CABINET

Professionals, especially lawyers, were dominant in the cabinets in all regimes from 1947 to 1958, but their large presence did not mean that they were the most influential members of the cabinet. During 1947–1954, the most influential cabinet ministers were Malik Ghulam Mohammad, Choudhury Muhammad Ali (both were bureaucrats), Sir Mohammad Zafrullah Khan (lawyer), and Dr Fazlur Rehman, who to some extent, particularly in Liaquat's premiership, enjoyed special status. Liaquat was a towering personality,[66] a man of opinion and a good decision-maker. However, he gave weight to the opinions of his ministers. It was after Liaquat's assassination that the two bureaucrats, Malik Ghulam Mohammad and Choudhury Muhammad Ali, were the most influential in the decision-making.[67] Hamza Alavi's opinion is that the most influential among all members of the inner cabinet was Malik Ghulam Mohammad.[68] This is true, since he had the bureaucracy under his control and the army stood behind him. He also enjoyed the US' blessings. The place of the inner cabinet was taken over by the kitchen cabinet during Nazimuddin's premiership. It was established by Governor General Ghulam Mohammad rather than the PM, and included some civil and military bureaucrats, Iskandar Mirza and Ayub Khan, as well as Finance Minister Choudhury Muhammad Ali.[69] Almost the same kitchen cabinet existed during Mohammad Ali Bogra's period.

During the coalition cabinet period, the changes in governments were so abrupt and frequent that no permanent inner cabinet could be formed. The PM depended on the members of the cabinet belonging to his political party. In other words, decisions of the political leadership of that specific party were normally approved. The ML under the leadership of Choudhury Muhammad Ali was influential in the decision-making during this period. Malik Firoz Khan Noon and Amjad Ali both had political and administrative experience and were significant in decision-making during Suhrawardy's premiership although they belonged to the Republican Party. He himself possessed great self-confidence and decision-making powers.[70] The prominent figures during Chundrigarh's premiership were Malik Firoz Khan Noon and Mian Mumtaz Mohammad Khan Daultana, the Defence Minister.[71] The prominent minister in Noon's cabinet was Mozaffar Ali Qizilbash.

1.2. MILITARY PERIOD, 1958–1971

On 8 October 1958, martial law was imposed in Pakistan and the first parliamentary phase then came to an end. All hopes of the political parties for elections vanished. The parliamentary system had not worked satisfactorily due to frequent changes of government. Even the CAP was unable to play its role in strengthening the democratic processes, so much so that the deputy speaker of the East Pakistan Assembly was injured during the proceedings and later died due to severe injuries.[72] Cabinets had hardly any time to introduce reforms or to formulate policies during 1956–1958.

1.2.1. STRUCTURE AND CONSTITUTIONAL STATUS OF THE CABINETS

(i). *Martial Law Era 1958–1962*

The imposition of martial law brought an end to the life of the 1956 Constitution and the country remained without any constitution until June 1962. The status and powers of the cabinet remained undefined during this period. It consisted of technocrats and non-political figures. Besides the cabinet, Ayub Khan appointed a number of commissions to propose recommendations for socio-economic reforms in the country. Some of these commissions included cabinet ministers and needed approval for their policies from the cabinet.[73]

The first cabinet of Ayub Khan, formed on 28 October 1958 following the exile of Iskandar Mirza, included four generals, i.e. Ayub Khan, the president, Lt Gen. Azam Khan, Minister of Rehabilitation, Lt Gen. W. A. Burki, Minister of Health and Social Welfare, and Lt Gen. K. M. Sheikh, Minister of Interior. The latter three were excellent administrators and highly trusted by Ayub Khan. This cabinet also included four ministers from West Pakistan and four from East Pakistan. From West Pakistan Manzur Qadir, Minister of Foreign Affairs and Commonwealth Relations, Mohammad Shoaib, Minister of Finance, F. M. Khan, Minister of Railways and Communications, and Zulfikar Ali Bhutto,

Minister of Commerce were included. From East Pakistan, Habib ur Rehman, Minister of Education, Information, and Minority Affairs, Hafiz ur Rehman, Minister of Food and Agriculture, Mohammad Ibrahim, Minister of Law, and Abul Kasem Khan, Minister of Industries, Works, and Irrigation were made members of the cabinet.[74] None of the ministers were politicians and generally speaking none had a good reputation.[75] Moreover, this cabinet was not military-oriented since the majority of the ministers were civilians. Aziz Ahmed, a civil bureaucrat, was appointed as Deputy Chief Martial Law Administrator (DCMLA) and Secretary General. His position as Secretary General was not inferior to that of the First Secretary General of Pakistan Choudhury Muhammad Ali.[76]

The second cabinet of Ayub was formed under the Presidential Order of 1960 on 17 February 1960. It retained all the military generals and all seven civilian ministers, who continued with their positions in the cabinet with minor changes of portfolio. The new additions were Akhtar Hussain, Minister of National Reconstruction and Information from West Pakistan, and Zakir Hussain, Minister of Interior from East Pakistan. General K. M. Sheikh was given the Ministry of Home Affairs.[77]

(ii). *Cabinets under the 1962 Constitution, 1962–1969: The Presidential Cabinets*

The Constitution Commission was appointed by Ayub Khan under the chairmanship of Justice Mohammad Shahabuddin and was asked to prepare a draft of the constitution.

Its report, presented to the president in May 1961, was thoroughly examined by him and his cabinet. It was also discussed at the Governors' Conference, held from 24 to 31 October 1961. It appointed a drafting committee under Manzur Qadir, Minister of Foreign Affairs, to draft the final constitution. It took four months to complete its work and Ayub Khan announced the constitution to the nation on 1 March 1962.[78] Later, while addressing the National Assembly on 8 June 1962, Ayub Khan said, 'The Constitution … represents my political philosophy in its application to the existing condition of Pakistan and it deserves a fair trial'.[79]

The presidential form of government was introduced under the 1962 Constitution. In theory the cabinet is not as significant and effective under the presidential system as in the parliamentary system. The president has the right to appoint his council of ministers.[80] The significance of the cabinet in decision-making varies depending on the president, and what status he gives to the cabinet. Under the American presidential system, the cabinet does not play a central role in any administration as a collective body,[81] but in Pakistan it did under Ayub Khan's 1962 Constitution. The exact nature of the relationship between the president and his cabinet was not defined in the constitution. Unlike the parliamentary system, the president's personal desire was the key variable in determining the role for any particular cabinet.[82]

Under Article 33 of the 1962 Constitution, the president had absolute freedom to appoint his ministers from among persons qualified to be elected as members of the National Assembly.[83] 'He could both set the tone and temper of policy and select the men to carry it out'.[84] The ministers had no claim to public standing or, for that matter, to competence in all areas. They were a team in the sense that all owed loyalty to the president, at whose pleasure they held office. Under Article 118 of the constitution the president was authorized to dismiss any minister from office without giving any reason.[85] In addition, the president was authorized to disqualify any minister from holding any office for five years on charges of delinquency in relation to his duties.

The cabinet ministers were not members of the National Assembly under the 1962 Constitution. If any member of the National Assembly was appointed to the cabinet, he would lose his seat in the assembly. This provision was later amended by the president.[86] The amendment altered the real character of the cabinet or council of ministers. Ministers could participate in discussions on the floor of the assembly; they could address the house and could be members of committees, but they did not have the right to vote under Article 25 of the 1962 Constitution.[87] This was introduced to keep the powers of the executive and the legislature independent. Furthermore, the ministers were not answerable to the legislature.

The third cabinet of Ayub Khan was the natural outcome of the 1962 Constitution. It excluded all military personnel.[88] Mohammad Shoaib, Finance Minister, and Zulfikar Ali Bhutto, Minister of Industries and Natural Resources, had retained their positions in the cabinet since 1958. In addition, it included only two ministers from the second cabinet: they were Abdul Qadir, temporarily appointed as

Minister of Finance, from West Pakistan, and Muhammad Munir, Minister of Law and Parliamentary Affairs, from East Pakistan. Both ministers resigned from the cabinet in December 1962 and two new ministers were inducted, Mohammad Ali Bogra, Minister of Foreign Affairs. Abdul Monem Khan, Minister of Health, was later appointed as Governor of East Pakistan. Wahiduzzaman, Minister of Commerce and Health, was appointed after Monem Khan; Abdus Sabur Khan, Minister of Communications, and K. M. Fazlul Qadir Chowdhary, Minister of Food and Agriculture, were from East Pakistan. The cabinet included Habibullah Khan, Minister of Home and Kashmir Affairs, and Shaikh Khursheed Ahmad, Minister of Law and Parliamentary Affairs, after the exit of Muhammad Munir and Rana Abdul Hamid, Minister of Labour, Rehabilitation, Food and Agriculture, from West Pakistan.[89] This cabinet started work with four former and six new ministers. In the later years, new ministers were added to the cabinet due to the death or resignation of working ministers. Abdul Waheed Khan from West Pakistan, Abu Talib Mohammad Mustafa, Abdullah-al-Mahmood, and Al Haj Abd-Allah Zaheer ud Deen from East Pakistan were appointed to ministerial positions in the later years.[90]

The fourth cabinet of Ayub Khan, formed after the presidential elections of 1965, consisted of all new faces except for Mohammad Shoaib and Z. A. Bhutto from West Pakistan who continued in office. The other ministers included Khawaja Shahabuddin, Minister of Information and Broadcasting, Abdus Sabur Khan, Minister of Communications, Altaf Hussain, Minister of Industries and Natural Resources, Qazi Anwarul Haq, Minister of Education, Health and Labour, and Shams ud Doha, Minister of Food and Agriculture, from East Pakistan. West Pakistani ministers were Ghulam Faruque, Minister of Commerce, Syed Mohammad Zafar, Minister of Law and Parliamentary Affairs, and Chaudhry Ali Akbar Khan, Minister of Home and Kashmir Affairs. The whole cabinet consisted of five ministers from East Pakistan and five from West Pakistan.[91] The later additions were Sharifuddin Pirzada, Minister of Foreign Affairs, Nabi Bakhsh Mohammad Sadique Uquaili, Minister of Finance, Vice Admiral A. R. Khan, Minister of Defence, and Nawabzada Abdul Ghafur Khan Hoti, Minister of Commerce, after the exit of Ghulam Faruque, and Mohammad Arshad Hussain, Minister of Foreign Affairs from West Pakistan, and Ajmal Ali Choudhry, Minister of Industries and Natural Resources from East Pakistan.[92] It seems, especially after the exit of Mohammad Shoaib and Bhutto, that Ayub wanted a cabinet in the Gaulist mould. No minister had a strong, popular following.[93]

Ayub Khan was forced to resign on 25 March 1969 because of huge demonstrations and agitation against him. In a cabinet meeting explaining the reasons for his resignation he said that politicians were 'disrupting the country' and the economic life of Pakistan had come to a halt. No discipline was observed by workers or even by government officials. With the resignation of the president, all ministers, and governors stood as dismissed.[94]

(iii). *Cabinets under General Yahya Khan, 1969–1971*

Yahya Khan imposed martial law in the country on 25 March 1969 and took charge. He introduced a Provisional Constitutional Order in April 1969[95] in which basic principles for running the government were set out, but the status of the council of ministers or cabinet was not defined. During this period, the institution of the cabinet was the most neglected. According to Fazal Muqeem Khan, the cabinet was among those institutions which were totally destroyed during Yahya Khan's period. Its power was limited in his early years and later the institution was vanquished.[96] The government was run purely by the military-oriented council of ministers from March to August 1969. One civilian cabinet was appointed in August 1969 which worked till February 1971. Its status remained undefined and it was just a ceremonial body.[97]

Yahya Khan established his Advisory Council in March 1969 which consisted of the Vice Admiral A. R. Khan, Mian Arshad Hussain and Fida Hassan, all from West Pakistan. He further appointed three Deputy Chief Martial Law Administrators (DCMLAs). They were Lt Gen. Abdul Hamid Khan, Army Chief of Staff, Vice Admiral S. M. Ahsan, Commander-in-Chief of the Navy and Air Marshal Nur Khan, Commander-in-Chief of the Air Force, all from West Pakistan. Six portfolios were held by Yahya in his own hands and the rest of the departments were given to the three-member Cabinet of Generals. Besides these, General Pirzada, Yahya's Principal Staff Officer (PSO), looked after all the affairs of government, but he was not a formal member of the military cabinet.[98] The other prominent figures in the ruling junta were Lt Gen. Gul Hassan (NWFP) Armour Specialist, Maj. Gen. Ghulam Omar (Punjab), Chairman of the Pakistan National Council, Chief of the General Staff, and Maj. Gen. Mohammad Akbar, Head of Intelligence (Punjab).[99] Thus three DCMLAs also performed the functions of the military cabinet. It was popularly known as the Council of Administration.[100]

This set-up worked until a civilian cabinet was sworn in on 4 August 1969. This civilian cabinet included five ministers each from East and West Pakistan. The East Pakistani ministers were Dr Abdul Motaleb Malik, Minister of Health, Labour and Communications, Abdul Khair Muhammad Hafizuddin, Minister of Industries and Natural Resources, Muhammad Shams ul Huq, Minister of Education and Scientific Research, Ahsan ul-Huq, Minister of Commerce, and Golam Waheed Choudhry, Minister of Communications. The West Pakistani ministers were Sardar Abdul Rashid, Minister of Home and Kashmir Affairs, Nawab Mozaffar Ali Qizilbash, Minister of Finance, Nawabzada Mohammad Sher Ali Khan, Minister of Information and Broadcasting, Mahmood A. Haroon, Minister of Agriculture and Works, and A. R. Cornelius, Minister of Law.[101] This civilian cabinet included Nawabzada Mohammad Sher Ali Khan, a retired major general. Two parallel institutions were working in this period: one was the civilian cabinet and the other was the military cabinet.[102]

The civilian cabinet was dismissed on 22 February 1971 after the elections of 1970. From February 1971 to December 1971 the country was run without any formal cabinet. Yahya was surrounded by some advisors. They were M. M. Ahmed,

A. R. Cornelius, M. H. Sufi, and Ghiasuddin Ahmad. All were bureaucrats except Cornelius, who was a former Judge of the Supreme Court. During this period Yahya again relied heavily on his kitchen cabinet consisting of members of the junta or military.[103] He introduced a 'laboriously contrived system of administration'.[104] All issues had to be brought to General Pirzada (PSO); if he approved, only then were they presented to the president. In the provinces, civil issues needed the approval of the martial law authorities. The whole system of administration was militarized[105] because Yahya lacked sufficient political acumen.[106]

1.2.2. Appointment Criteria to the Cabinet

The appointment criteria to the cabinet were different during the two military regimes. According to Rashiduzzaman, Ayub Khan took account of two major factors when appointing his cabinet members. First, to include financial and legal experts like Mohammad Shoaib and Manzur Qadir,[107] who were experts in their respective fields, and second to include experienced politicians like Mohammad Ali Bogra, especially after the introduction of the 1962 Constitution.[108] From 1958 to 1962 Ayub Khan's cabinet had not included any political personalities.[109] In Rushbrook William's opinion, Ayub used to include in the cabinet all such men who were faithful to the country, expert in their fields, and loyal to the president.[110] However, Robert Laporte has presented a different view saying that family or personal connections were always important criteria for inclusion in the cabinet. Additionally, administrative skills were also given considerable weight by

Ayub.[111] However, the best criterion for appointment, in Ayub's opinion, was experience. Only experts were appointed to control foreign affairs, finance, railways, education, commerce, local administration, law, and industries. He always appointed the best available brains. Manzur Qadir, Mohammad Ali Bogra, Zulfikar Ali Bhutto, Syed Sharifuddin Pirzada, and Arshad Hussain were all experienced experts.[112] Pirzada owed his position as Foreign Minister mainly to the impression he made on Ayub in efficiently conducting his business as Attorney General, especially in relation to the Rann of Kutch dispute.[113] Next he gave equal representation to both East and West Pakistan after the introduction of the 1962 Constitution. If one West Pakistani minister died or resigned from the cabinet, the new minister was taken from West Pakistan. The same rule was followed for East Pakistan. The number of ministers never exceeded twelve, including the president himself.

During the pre-1962 era, military personnel were given important portfolios in the cabinet; however, this trend was not followed in the post-1962 constitutional period, with only the one exception of Vice Admiral A. R. Khan, who was appointed as Minister of Defence and Kashmir Affairs due to his wide experience as Commander-in-Chief of the Navy and his understanding of the subject. It is further noted that important or key portfolios were given to West Pakistani ministers, except for Mohammad Ali Bogra who was appointed as Minister of Foreign Affairs in 1962. He served as ambassador to the United States of America twice so he could play the role of a transmission belt and followed the instructions of the president always.[114] Ayub was of the opinion that East Pakistan had a dearth of intelligent people and that most of the East Pakistanis thought in terms of being Bengalis, not in terms of being Pakistanis.[115] East Pakistani ministers always felt neglected.[116]

The appointment criteria underwent a change in the later period, 1966–69. Now loyalty was considered by Ayub to be the indispensable requirement for ministers. Secondly, he appointed men who would unquestioningly carry out his policies without danger of forming an independent political basis and who had, apparently, little political future. Thirdly, they should be men of technical and administrative competence. When appointing Arshad Hussain as Foreign Minister, Ayub told him that he was appointed for his 'professional efficiency' as Pakistan's foreign policy was a complicated and difficult task to tackle.[117] He also looked for political balance[118] and started trusting those politicians who agreed or accepted his system of Basic Democracies. Some of them were included in the cabinet also. These were Abdus Sabur Khan, Bogra, Fazlul Qadir Chowdhary, and Wahiduzzaman.[119] The whole team of ministers in the last cabinet were loyal servants of the state and did not question the authority of the president. His cabinet 'quickly developed considerable corporate responsibility',[120] a sense of common purpose, and strong ties of loyalty to the president.

Yahya had not designed any proper standard of appointment to the cabinet, yet he visited East Pakistan for the selection of his cabinet ministers. He held informal interviews with the prospective candidates and made inquires through different sources including collecting information from intelligence reports. Lastly, the top of the military hierarchy was consulted regarding the suggested list and only then were the names of the ministers finalized.[121] It is believed that Yahya's civilian cabinet was only mediocre in wisdom, skills, and in work.[122] Practically, if they were given appropriate time and suitable power, they could have demonstrated better skills and performance. Yahya never trusted them, and most of the business was done by his military advisors or members of the kitchen cabinet who were not even part of the cabinet but belonged to the military high command. The cabinet was given less-important political, social, defence, and foreign policy issues to consider.[123]

Another negative aspect of Yahya's cabinet was the absence of any minister of foreign affairs. General Pirzada and Maj. Gen. Omar considered themselves experts in foreign affairs, but they were both inexperienced and incompetent in this regard. Issues related to foreign policy were never discussed in the meetings of the civilian cabinet.[124] It happened for the first time in Pakistan's history that cabinet worked without a foreign minister. Yahya simply fulfilled the requirement of appointing a civilian cabinet; in reality the government was run by his military and some civilian bureaucrats.[125] General Yahya Khan had designed a government set-up in which the politicians were given no representation in the cabinet.[126]

1.2.3. THE SOCIAL BACKGROUNDS OF THE MINISTERS

The cabinets of this period included both urban elites and professionals in large numbers whose presence had an impact on the policies of the government. The urban professionals, including civil and military bureaucrats and others, initiated policies of industrial development and international trade. Simultaneously, General Ayub Khan and Z. A. Bhutto had an understanding of rural society and had sought help from urban professionals. This ushered in agricultural development, the Green Revolution, and an increase in agricultural output. The social backgrounds of the cabinet members of this period are given below:

Table: 1-B

Social Group	1958–1962 Martial Law Era	1962–1969 The Presidential Cabinets	1969–1971 Yahya's Period	Total
Professionals	4	15	6	25
Landowners	1	2	0	3
Civil Bureaucrats	6	8	7	21
Military Bureaucrats	4	2	6	12
Industrialists and Businessmen	1	01	1	3
Total Ministers	16	28	20	64

Source: The above table was prepared by the researcher on the basis of information collected through different sources including reports from the British High Commissioner to the Commonwealth Relations Office London, cabinet files, newspapers, and various books including autobiographies, biographies, and others.

In the first period of this phase, the largest group was of bureaucrats who were highly qualified and experienced. They were given charge of only those departments in which they had worked as secretaries or in other higher positions. Two groups, military bureaucrats and professionals, occupied equal numbers of seats in cabinet. This time the professionals included only two lawyers and two retired judges. Two remaining social groups, landowners and industrialists and businessmen were very insignificant and held only one seat each.

In the cabinets of the constitutional period (1962–1969), the professionals recovered their position as the largest group. This time there were fifteen, of whom seven were lawyers, three retired judges, one educationist, one journalist, and three from other professions. Civil bureaucrats emerged as the second-most influential group, occupying eight seats in the cabinet. Of the two landlords, one, Z. A. Bhutto, was a big feudal lord, and the other, Mohammad Ali Bogra, belonged to the middle class of landlords. Of the two military bureaucrats, one was Ayub Khan and the other was retired Commander-in-Chief of the Navy, Vice Admiral A. R. Khan. There was only one minister, Nawabzada Abdul Ghafur Khan Hoti, who belonged to the social group of the industrialists and businessmen.

The composition of Yahya Khan's ministry was very different from the all the previous cabinets except during the pre-1962 constitutional period of Ayub's military regime. This time the most prominent group was the civil and military bureaucrats, including seven civilian and six military bureaucrats out of the total of twenty. The second most important group was that of the professionals. The composition of this group was varied: it included two educationists, one medical doctor, a retired judge, a lawyer, and an ex-ambassador. It was the first occasion that lawyers were least represented. The social group of industrialists and businessmen maintained their position with only one representative.

According to Hasan Askari Rizvi, the cabinets of both military rulers were similar in one way or another. Ayub's cabinets consisted mainly of ex-civil and military officials, which seem to be one reason for his fall. The same mistake was repeated by Yahya, and it also became the reason for his failure.[127] However, this study emphasizes that Yahya Khan trusted and relied on the military junta more than on civil bureaucrats. The decisions of the military junta were accepted and implemented. On the other hand, Ayub left the governance of the country to the civilians, including bureaucrats, professionals, and others. This is also supported by the fact that Aziz Ahmed, a senior ICS officer, was appointed as DCMLA.[128]

1.2.4. THE INNER CABINET AND THE KITCHEN CABINET[129]

Ayub Khan's era witnessed the existence of an inner cabinet in the early years, which was later transformed into a kitchen cabinet. At times Ayub had prior discussion with his close associates in the cabinet and the cabinet would take decisions accordingly. In some cases only West Pakistani ministers were called to special meetings of the cabinet to discuss specific issues. The most influential cabinet ministers during the martial law period (1958–1962) were Z. A. Bhutto, Manzur Qadir, and Muhammad Shoaib.[130] Shoaib had great personal influence on Ayub Khan and played an effective role in deciding economic issues.[131] Unlike Bhutto, the other two were non-political figures. The members of the cabinet from East Pakistan were the main sufferers in this regard.[132] Their opinions were not given considerable importance during the formulation and approval of various policies by Ayub Khan, though he employed teamwork in day-to-day matters.[133]

The Constitution Commission had prepared and agreed a report which was totally changed by Ayub Khan in consultation with Manzur Qadir.[134] The consent of Z. A. Bhutto, who agreed with the president, was also sought. There were three military generals in Ayub's cabinets during this period, but they were less influential than the three ministers named above, and more influential than the East Pakistani ministers at the same time, though General Azam Khan was relatively stronger than his other military colleagues in the cabinet.[135] During the 1962 Constitution period, Z. A. Bhutto and Muhammad Shoaib continued to be the most influential ministers.

They both left Ayub Khan's cabinet in 1966, after which the places of these influential ministers were taken over by Ghulam Faruque, Commerce Minister, A. K. Sabur, Minister of Communications, and Khawaja Shahabuddin, Information Minister. They were technocrats not politicians, with little apparent political future. At the same time, no one had power like Bhutto and Shoaib to influence Ayub.[136] However, Ghulam Faruque and Shahabuddin were in a position to talk frankly to the president on occasions.[137] A. K. Sabur was relatively more influential among East Pakistani ministers and brought political issues relating to East Pakistan into cabinet meetings for discussion.[138] The last cabinet of Ayub Khan, especially after the exit of Ghulam Faruque in 1967, could not achieve the status of an advisory body as it then contained less powerful personalities like Altaf Hussain, Qazi Anwarul Haq, Shams ud Doha, Sharifuddin Pirzada, and Chaudhry Ali Akbar Khan. The later additions also lacked political background and influence.

Ayub gave more places in his kitchen cabinet to the civil and military bureaucrats in later years by including Mr Yusuf, Secretary of the Ministry of Foreign Affairs, Altaf Gauhar,[139] Secretary of the Ministry of Information and Broadcasting, Qudruttullah Shahab,[140] Secretary of Education, and Yahya Khan, Commander-in-Chief of the Forces. These performed the role of kitchen cabinet after 1966.[141] In the last year of Ayub's regime, the military high command enjoyed tremendous influence due to Ayub's prolonged sickness and anti-Ayub agitation. The influential ministers of Ayub Khan in both regimes were, apart from Bhutto, non-political figures. East Pakistanis were the main sufferers in this whole scenario as they had felt ignored.[142]

Ayub fell seriously ill at the beginning of 1968. Yahya responded to the crisis by staging an unofficial coup. Ayub's contacts with politicians and civilian associates were terminated.[143] In reality, the government was controlled by the military generals, including Yahya Khan, the C-in-C of the armed forces, General Mohammad Musa, Governor of West Pakistan, A. R. Khan, Defence Minister and ex-Commander of the Pakistan Navy, Air Marshal Nur Khan, Commander of the Pakistan Air Force, and Khawaja Shahabuddin.[144]

During the Yahya Khan period, a kitchen cabinet of five military generals emerged which tried to improve the image of Yahya and the military.[145] It included General Pirzada, PSO, and the de facto PM, Brigadier Rahim, Chief Military Officer, and Brigadier Karim, Chief of Civilian Affairs. Rahim and Karim were also super secretaries; all files had to pass through them. This kitchen cabinet also included General Abdul Hamid Khan, Chief of Staff Army, and Maj. Gen. Ghulam Umar, Chief of National Security.[146] It functioned independently of the formal cabinet as a whole and 'took all major decisions, providing a kind of collective leadership'.[147] The real powers remained with the kitchen cabinet of the military high command.

1.3. SECOND PARLIAMENTARY PHASE, 1971–1977

The fall of Dacca on 16 December 1971 caused political change in Pakistan, and on 20 December the Yahya regime was forced to step down in favour of a civilian set-up. Following the separation of East Pakistan, people came out onto the streets demanding the trial of General Yahya and his advisors, who were declared traitors.[148] Yahya Khan was left with no option but to resign. Bhutto, who was out of the country, and was the leader of the largest political party in West Pakistan, now the new Pakistan, decided to come back to his country. He returned on 20 December 1971 and met Gul Hasan, Rahim Khan, and then Yahya Khan. They handed over power to Bhutto, whose Pakistan Peoples Party (PPP) had won the majority of the West Pakistan seats in the 1970 elections. He took the oath as president and civilian chief martial law administrator because Pakistan was being governed without any constitution.

1.3.1. Structure and Constitutional Status of the Cabinet, 1971–1977

(i). *Presidential Cabinets, 1971–1973*

Bhutto's period witnessed four cabinets. The first was formed on 24 December 1971 and continued till April 1972. During this period, the country remained under martial law with a civilian martial law administrator, Z. A. Bhutto. The first cabinet consisted of fourteen ministers. Bhutto was the president and the vice president was Nurul Amin, a prominent ML politician from former East Pakistan. Raja Tridiv Roy, Minister of Minorities Affairs, was also from former East Pakistan. Six ministers from Punjab were Mian Mahmud Ali Kasuri, Minister of Law and Parliamentary Affairs, Mubashir Hasan, Minister of Finance, Shaikh Muhammad Rashid, Minister of Social Welfare, Health and Family Planning, Malik Miraj Khalid, Minister of Food and Agriculture, Rana Mohammad Hanif, Minister of Labour, Works and Local Bodies, and Maulana Kausar Niazi, Minister of Information and Broadcasting. J. A. Rahim, Minister of Presidential Affairs and Town Planning, Ghulam Mustafa Jatoi, Minister of Political Affairs, Communications and Natural Resources, and Abdul Hafiz Pirzada, Minister of Education, Information and Provincial Coordination, were from Sindh. Justice Faizullah Kundi, Minister of Establishment, and Khan Abdul Qayyum Khan, Minister of Home Affairs, States, and Frontier Regions, were from NWFP.[149] This cabinet decided to resign on 20 April 1972.[150]

In this cabinet, Balochistan was not represented directly; Yahya Bakhtiar from Balochistan, the Attorney General of Pakistan, was given the status of cabinet minister.[151]

An interim constitution was introduced in April 1972. Bhutto took the oath of office as president under the Interim Constitution of the Islamic Republic of Pakistan.[152] The Interim Constitution was a mixture of the presidential and parliamentary forms of government in terms of the status of the cabinet. The president was the head of state and the government. He, under Article 62 of the constitution, worked with the aid and advice of a council of ministers.[153] It was imperative for the ministers to be members of the National Assembly, a feature of the parliamentary form of constitution. Nurul Amin was given the status of vice president and took precedence over other members of the council of ministers.[154] The ministers were answerable to the president, who was responsible to the legislature.[155]

His cabinet also took oath under the Interim Constitution on 1 May 1972.[156] It continued with all the ministers of the previous cabinet except Justice Kundi and Malik Miraj Khalid. It included three new ministers, Hayat Mohammad Khan Sherpao, Minister of Fuel, Power and Natural Resources from NWFP, Khursheed Hasan Meer, Minister without Portfolio from Punjab, and Sardar Ghaus Bakhsh Raisani, Minister of Food and Agriculture from Balochistan; with this Balochistan was directly represented in the cabinet. Sherpao and Raisani were opposition leaders in NWFP and Balochistan respectively during that time. According to Wali Khan this was a strange situation.[157]

(ii). *Cabinets under the 1973 Constitution, 1973–1977*

This cabinet came to an end with the introduction of the permanent constitution on 14 August 1973. On the same day, the third cabinet took its oath of office as the PM's cabinet in place of the president's council of ministers. The PM and federal ministers were collectively made responsible to the National Assembly under Article 90 of the 1973 Constitution.[158] They were to be taken from the parliament and were appointed by the PM. It is a convention of the parliamentary system that cabinet ministers are appointed by the president on the advice of the PM, but in the 1973 Constitution the president was not given any power in this regard; only the PM had the authority to appoint his cabinet. Another feature of the parliamentary system is that usually 'the executive authority of the federation is vested in the President and is to be exercised by him in accordance with the Constitution'.[159] This was also altered in the 1973 Constitution. Under Article 90 of the 1973 Constitution, the executive authority of the federation was to be exercised in the name of the president by the federal government consisting of the PM and the cabinet.[160]

Not more than one quarter of such federal ministers and ministers of state were to be taken from the upper house, the Senate.[161] The president was bound by the advice of the PM. Under Article 46 of the constitution, the PM was made responsible for informing the president about matters of internal and foreign policy that the federal government intended to bring before parliament.[162] No discretionary powers were delegated to the president.

The third cabinet (August 1973–October 1974) included all ministers of the previous cabinet with no additions. They were Dr Mubashir Hasan, Shaikh Muhammad Rashid, Raja Tridiv Roy, Ghulam Mustafa Khan Jatoi, Abdul Hafiz Pirzada, Muhammad Hanif, Maulana Kausar Niazi, Abdul Qayyum Khan, J. A. Rahim, Hayat Muhammad Khan Sherpao, Khursheed Hasan Meer, and Sardar Ghaus Bakhsh Raisani. Members had to take the oath of office again because of the introduction of the 1973 Constitution. Only its status was changed from a presidential council of ministers to a parliamentary cabinet.[163] Rafi Raza joined the cabinet later.[164]

In October 1974 Bhutto's fourth cabinet took the oath of office and functioned till March 1977.[165] The composition of this cabinet was quite different from the previous three. Seven ministers of the previous cabinet were asked to continue. They were Shaikh Muhammad Rashid, Minister of Food and Agriculture, Abdul Hafiz Pirzada, Minister of Education and Provincial Coordination, Rana Mohammad Haneef Khan, Minister of Finance, Planning, and Economic Affairs, Maulana Kausar Niazi, Minister of Religious Affairs, Khan Abdul Qayyum Khan, Minister of Interior, Khursheed Hasan Meer, Minister of Labour, Health, and Social Welfare, and Rafi Raza, Minister of Industries and Production. It included eleven new ministers, mostly added in different months of 1975 and 1976. They were Malik Miraj Khalid, Minister of Law and Parliamentary Affairs, Hafizullah Cheema, Minister of Labour, Health, and Social Welfare, appointed after the resignation of Khursheed Hasan Meer, Malik Mohammad Akhtar, who held different portfolios including Law and

Parliamentary Affairs and Fuel, Power, and Natural Resources, Nasir Ali Rizvi, Minister of Housing and Works, and Mian Mohammad Ataullah, Minister of Industries from Punjab. Mumtaz Ali Bhutto, Minister of Communications, and Syed Qaim Ali Shah Jilani, Minister of Kashmir and Northern Affairs, were from Sindh. Muhammad Yusuf Khattak, Minister of Fuel, Power, and Natural Resources, Mir Afzal Khan, Minister of Commerce, and Muhammad Hanif Khan, Minister of Information and Broadcasting, were from NWFP, and Mir Taj Muhammad Khan Jamali, Minister of Labour, Health, and Population Planning was from Balochistan.[166] Almost the same group of ministers continued in the first three cabinets. The most prominent among them were Mubashir Hasan, J. A. Rahim, Shaikh Muhammad Rashid, and Khursheed Hasan Meer.

1.3.2. APPOINTMENT CRITERIA

Different appointment criteria were applied by Bhutto. It appears that most appointments were made on the basis of Bhutto's family or personal connections. Besides personal friendships, political acumen and skills were also given some importance.[167] Under this consideration the appointments of Abdul Hafiz Pirzada, Mustafa Jatoi, Mubashar Hasan, J. A. Rahim, and Shaikh Mohammad Rasheed were made.[168]

At times the opposition was also given a place in the cabinet by Bhutto for political reasons. Khan Abdul Qayyum Khan, and later Muhammad Yusuf Khattak, from the Muslim League, were included in the cabinet. Qayyum Khan was given the important portfolio of Home Affairs. It was claimed by Wali Khan that Qayyum was given this portfolio so he could provide valuable secret information about NAP to Bhutto.[169] This view is supported by Hamid Khan with the addition that Bhutto wanted to use Khan against the NAP-Jamiat-i-Ulema-i-Islam (JUI) government in NWFP.[170] He worked for the same purpose in later years. Another opinion is that Qayyum was included in the cabinet to minimize the role of the opposition in national politics. Both Bhutto and Qayyum Khan had distinct approaches towards politics. Their only point of consensus was a strong centre and hostility towards India.[171] The induction of Qayyum Khan provided representation for the smaller province of NWFP where PPP had lost the elections.[172] Hayat Mohammad Khan Sherpao, leader of the opposition party in NWFP, was included in the federal cabinet to help Qayyum Khan topple the NAP-JUI government in the two smaller provinces.[173]

Another important consideration when appointing ministers was to give all provinces representation in the cabinet. To this end Ghaus Bakhsh Raisani, the most trustworthy and important Baloch leader for Bhutto, was assigned the portfolio of Food and Agriculture in May 1972. He had already served as governor of Balochistan before Bizenjo. He kept Bhutto informed about political activity in Balochistan including reports about Bugti and his companions.[174]

The fourth and most important criterion of appointment in the early years was the belief in and strong support of the ideology of the PPP on the basis of which many leftists were given a place in the cabinet. However, in later years the position of socialist or leftist ministers such as Mubashir

Hasan, J. A. Rahim, and Khursheed Hasan Meer, was taken over by a new support group, the feudal lords.[175] In the last years of his rule, Bhutto depended more on the civil bureaucracy, especially during his election campaign with Rafi Raza in charge. It appears that Bhutto's level of trust in his cabinet colleagues gradually decreased.[176] Also, unlike the practice under the British parliamentary system,[177] hardliners were sometimes appointed to the cabinet, like Khursheed Hasan Meer and Meraj Khalid who were hard-line socialist in their ideologies.

The prominent feature of the cabinets of Bhutto was their socialist ideology, especially before 1974. But the socialist agenda gradually faded away after 1974 as the socialist ministers were replaced by the feudal lords. Secondly, smaller provinces, especially Balochistan, were the least represented. The main reason seems to be the absence of PPP representatives in the Balochistan Assembly and the limited support enjoyed by the party in NWFP. Most of the cabinet portfolios were given to Punjab and then to Sindh, followed by NWFP. In the first period (1971–1973) almost half of the cabinet ministers were from Punjab. In the second period (1974–1977), almost the same trend was followed. The number of ministers in the first three cabinets did not exceed fourteen but it rose to twenty in the last cabinet. One prominent feature of Bhutto's cabinets was the absence of a minister of foreign affairs as this ministry was kept under the direct supervision of the PM who took a great interest in foreign affairs. Since huge differences of opinion could emerge between him and his minister of foreign affairs, he avoided making this appointment.

1.3.3. SOCIAL BACKGROUNDS OF THE MINISTERS

The social backgrounds of Bhutto's cabinet members, especially in the pre-1974 era, was different from the previous regimes as some groups were totally excluded and others had a significant position which had an impact on policy. The following table will make this point clear:

Table: 1-C

Social Group	1971–1973 Presidential Cabinets	1973–1977 Parliamentary Cabinets	1971–1977 Total
Professionals	11	9	20
Landlords	5	11	16
Industrialists and Businessmen	0	3	3
Civil Bureaucrats	1	1	2
Religious Elites	1	1	2
Military Bureaucrats	0	0	0
Total Ministers	18	25	43

Source: The above table was prepared by the researcher on the basis of information collected through different sources including reports from the British High Commissioner to the Commonwealth Relations Office London, cabinet files, newspapers, and various books including autobiographies, biographies, and others.

In the pre-constitutional period, middle-class professionals were the largest group.[178] They constituted eleven out of eighteen; there were seven lawyers, one retired justice, one civil engineer, a poet, and one was Attorney General of the federal government of Pakistan. Of the five landlords, four, Z. A. Bhutto, Ghulam Mustafa Khan Jatoi, Hayat Mohammad Khan Sherpao, and Sardar Ghaus Bakhsh Raisani, were big feudal lords and only one, Raja Tridiv Roy, belonged to the middle-class of landlords. His cabinet also included one former civil bureaucrat, J. A. Rahim, who had retired from the Foreign Service and was the main brain behind preparing the PPP manifesto.[179] Besides J. A. Rahim, no other military or civil bureaucrat was given a place in the cabinet. For the first time in the history of Pakistan, civil and military bureaucrats were not welcomed in this high level, decision-making institution.[180] Bhutto wanted to establish a purely political and democratic government where public institutions would remain within their limits.

The group of industrialists and businessmen, who had always had one or two seats in the cabinet, were also denied a portfolio in the first two cabinets. The PPP's socialist manifesto[181] did not permit the induction of industrialists and businessmen: according to the slogans produced by the leadership, it was a party of labourers and the poor.

While denying a place to three of the major social groups, the PPP government did give representation to the religious elite; Maulana Kausar Niazi was the symbol of religious representation.

The composition of the cabinets of the second period (1973–1977) and especially of the fourth cabinet (1974–1977), was dramatically different from that of the previous cabinets.

This time the big feudal landlords were in the majority, constituting eleven out of twenty-five members. Of the nine professionals, seven continued from the previous cabinet and only two were new entries, Rafi Raza and Hafizullah Cheema. Six professionals were lawyers, one was a civil engineer, one a poet, and one was the Attorney General.

The group of businessmen and industrialists regained their position in the cabinet when Muhammad Yusuf Khattak, Malik Mohammad Akhtar, and Mian Mohammad Ataullah were appointed. The religious elite maintained its position in the cabinet, but the civil and military bureaucrats were again given no place. However, some of them were given portfolios as ministers of state, but this is beyond the scope of this study since a minister of state is not formally a member of the cabinet.[182]

In both periods there were similarities and differences between Bhutto's cabinets. The presence of a large number of professionals and the absence of civil and military bureaucrats from the cabinets show consistency in his policy of appointment. But at the same time, the number of landlords was raised from five to eleven, and of the businessmen from zero to three. Bhutto's cabinet was conservative in 1976. 'Scientific Socialists'[183] who represented the middle-class were mostly out, and their places were taken by the feudal lords. Here, PPP's leadership deviated from its manifesto and instead of welcoming the representatives of labourers and the downtrodden it appointed big landlords and businessmen. The ideology and approach of the cabinet was changed and the leftist element was quite insignificant in the last cabinet. Only Sheikh Rashid remained and he found himself unable to voice leftist ideas as there was no one to support him within the cabinet. The changed composition of the cabinet had an impact on policy.[184]

1.3.4. THE INNER CABINET

In the first period, the leftist ministers Hasan, Sheikh Rashid, and Meer[185] were the most influential and their plans and policies, including the nationalization of industries, banking, and insurance, were approved by the PM. They were part of Bhutto's inner cabinet[186] and all decision-making and important portfolios including finance, production, industries and labour, were controlled by them. All were urban-based professionals from the middle class. Although their ideology had an impact on that of Bhutto, decision-making power, regarding foreign policy matters resided with Bhutto alone.[187] The status of the inner cabinet of influential ministers was taken over by rightists like Maulana Niazi and by some of Bhutto's personal friends like Abdul Hafiz Pirzada in the later period. Niazi's influence increased because of his 'obsequiousness and personal relations to Bhutto'.[188] The status of Pirzada was similar to that of Bhutto in the early years of Ayub Khan. He was obedient to Bhutto.[189] Thus the whole nature and composition of the cabinet changed from leftist to right.[190]

In Laporte's opinion, from 1947 to 1977, political elites who were members of the cabinet belonged to three groups: military, civil bureaucracy, and large land-owning representatives. He believed that more or less all cabinet members were selected from these three groups. But the situation was different to a large extent in the early years of Bhutto's rule and none of the elite groups was given a prominent position in the cabinet; these were in the hands of the urban and rural middle-class professionals. Most of them were highly qualified and belonged to the professions of law, medicine, education, and engineering. This phase was not permanent, as in Bhutto's later years the cabinet again adopted the same composition as in the pre-Bhutto regime when, in Laporte's opinion, the middle-class was voiceless in the decision-making process.[191] The findings of this study, as shown in the table and bar graph below, are quite different from the established theory.

Table: 1-D

Social Group	1947–1958		1958–1971		1971–1977	
	Ministers	Per-centage	Ministers	Per-centage	Ministers	Per-centage
Professionals	44	59.45	25	37.87	20	46.51
Landowners	12	16.21	3	4.54	16	37.2
Civil Bureaucrats	5	6.75	21	31.81	2	4.65
Military Bureaucrats	4	5.40	12	18.18	0	0
Industrialists and Businessmen	5	6.75	3	4.54	3	6.97
Religious Elite	0	0	0	0	2	4.65
Unknown Professions	4		2			
Total	74		66		43	

Graph: 1-A

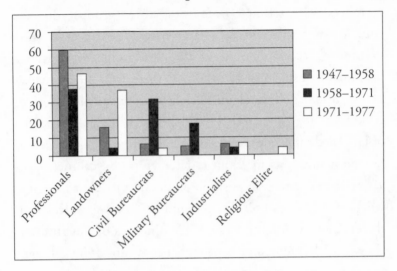

The most prominent change is that the cabinet ministers were not taken from three social groups but represented five social groups till 1971 and the sixth group added to Bhutto's cabinet, the religious group, was represented by one seat. The other five groups represented in the cabinet were professionals, landowners, civil and military bureaucrats, and industrialists and businessmen. The composition of these groups remained different in the three phases. In the first phase professionals were the most prominent with forty-four seats in the cabinet out of the seventy-four. Landowners were the second-most important social group with twelve seats. The number of civil and military bureaucrats was only one-fifth that of the professionals, with nine cabinet portfolios. The least represented group was businessmen and industrialists, with only five portfolios.

In the second phase, the most prominent social group represented in the cabinet was the civil and military bureaucracy. Their total representation was thirty-three out of sixty-six ministers. Professionals were second in number with twenty-five seats. The least represented groups were the landowners with three seats, and businessmen and industrialist with only two seats.

Some dramatic changes occurred in the third phase: the civil and military bureaucracy was totally unrepresented in the cabinet. Only J. A. Rahim, who had retired from the Foreign Service, was included. He was one of the founding fathers of the PPP and struggled against the control of affairs by civil servants. There were three reasons behind the primacy of politicians over bureaucracy. Firstly, the ministers were the product of electoral politics, unlike the ministers of previous regimes. Secondly, some ministers held the view that the bureaucracy must be subordinate to the political leadership, and thirdly, some of them were striving to implement the socialist objectives of the PPP. All of them were active politicians. The most prominent social group was of the professionals with twenty seats in the cabinet out of forty-three. Although the landowners also had comparatively more seats in the cabinet than under the previous regimes, when they occupied only sixteen seats, they controlled less-significant portfolios. It was the group of industrialists and businessmen which maintained its ratio in all periods, with three seats. During this period a new group, the religious elite, also emerged in the cabinet, represented by just one seat. Thus Laporte's assertion of the presence of three social groups in the cabinet is shown to be incorrect since this study has identified the presence of six different social groups in the cabinet.

To conclude, it may be pointed out that the appointment criteria in different periods followed diverse patterns. The first phase included qualifications, party affiliation, representation of different regions, and sometimes personal contacts of the Governor General and PM. However, Ayub Khan's appointment criteria included experience in the related field, loyalty to the president, equal representation for East and West Pakistan, etc. Some politicians were also included after the introduction of the 1962 Constitution. Most of the administrative affairs in Yahya Khan's era were run by military personnel, so he did not take a keen interest in the business of his civilian cabinet. During the third phase, Z. A. Bhutto's appointment criteria included personal connections, political acumen, support for the ideology of the PPP, and representation of all the provinces. Ministers were mostly selected from five social groups, i.e. professionals, landlords, the civil and military bureaucracy, and industrialists and businessmen. The difference in the ratio of representation of various social groups in the cabinet resulted in the introduction of different policies in all three phases. An inner, or kitchen cabinet existed in all regimes, but its presence rarely impacted the normal working of the cabinet. It was only during General Yahya's era that the military-oriented kitchen cabinet was the only decision-making authority, and it failed badly to solve the issues. Otherwise, the full cabinet duly performed its role in the other eras.

Notes and References

1. Richard Rose, 'The Making of Cabinet Ministers', *British Journal of Political Science* 1 (October 1971), 397.
2. Buckley, *The Prime Minister and Cabinet*, 41.
3. One council of the Governor General was established which theoretically enjoyed the decision-making powers on the basis of majority votes. Practically, the power of the Governor General increased with the expansion of territory. In 1786, the Governor General was given authority to take decisions on his own responsibility if the situation required. Normally, he was bound by the advice of the council. The power of the Governor General continued under British rule till the transfer of power to Indians in 1947. This colonial tradition was widely accepted in the newly-created state of Pakistan.
4. *Government of India Act 1935* (as Adapted, Modified and Amended); *The West Pakistan Constitutional Manual Vol. 1* (Lahore: Government Printing Press, 1958), 6; *The Pakistan (Provisional Constitutional) Order 1947*; The Gazette of Pakistan Extraordinary (hereafter called GPE), Notification No. 25/PSC/47, 1 September 1947, Government of Pakistan (hereafter called GOP), Cabinet Secretariat, Karachi; and Richard Symonds, 'State-making in Pakistan' *Far Eastern Survey* 19 (March 1973), 47.
5. Ibid.
6. Khalid Bin Sayeed, *Pakistan: The Formative Phase 1857–1948* (Karachi: Oxford University Press, 969), 239.
7. Ibid. 238, and G. W. Choudhury, *Constitutional Development in Pakistan* (Lahore: The Ideal Book House, 1969), 29.
8. Choudhury, *Constitutional Development in Pakistan*, 30.
9. Keith Callard, 'The Political Stability of Pakistan', *Pacific Affairs* 29 (March 1956), 9.
10. The GPE, Notification, No. 1-C/CF/47, 15 August 1947, GOP, Cabinet Secretariat, Karachi. Ministries of the Federal Government, Official Record prepared by Cabinet Wing, National Documentation Centre (hereafter called NDC), Islamabad.

11. Ministries of the Federal Government, Official Record prepared by Cabinet Wing, NDC, Islamabad. For the detailed treatment of the internal changes in the cabinet, please see Farooq Ahmad Dar, *Jinnah's Pakistan: Formation and Challenges of the State* (Karachi: Oxford University Press, 2014), 35–8.

12. Cabinet mtg, 30 December 1947, 21/CF/48, NDC, Islamabad.

13. Ibid.

14. Ibid.

15. Ibid.

16. K. K. Nayyar, *Pakistan at the Crossroads* (Delhi: RUPA Co, 2003), 102.

17. Normally cabinet is appointed by the PM but due to special circumstances created after the assassination of Pakistan's PM Liaquat Ali Khan, cabinet assumed the responsibility with the approval of Governor General Khawaja Nazimuddin and decided for the future of the country.

18. GPE, NO. 4(1)-Cord/51-1 and 4(1)-Cord/51-11, GOP, Cabinet Secretariat Karachi; Keith Callard, *Pakistan: The Political Study* (London: George Allen and Unwin Ltd., 1957), 57, and M. A. Chaudhuri, *Government and Politics in Pakistan* (Dhaka: Puthighar Ltd, n.d.), 165.

19. Address of Khawaja Nazimuddin to the Nation from Radio Pakistan, Karachi on 17 October 1951 cited in Ziauddin Ahmad, ed., *Quaid-i-Millat Liaquat Ali Khan* (Karachi: The Oriental Academy, 1970), 61.

20. Craig Baxter ed., *From Martial Law to Martial Law: Politics in the Punjab 1919–1958* (Lahore: Vanguard, 1985), 313.

21. Ministers of the Federal Government, Official Record prepared by Cabinet Wing, NDC, Islamabad and *Dawn,* 27 November 1951.

22. GPE, No. 4 (1)/53-Cord-1, GOP, Cabinet Secretariat, Karachi. The details of the reasons for dismissal have been given in Chapter 5.

23. *Dawn,* 19 April 1953.

24. From United Kingdom High Commissioner (hereafter called UKHC) Karachi to Commonwealth Relations Office (hereafter called CRO) London, 17 April 1953, DO 35/5106, The National Archives (hereafter called NA), London.

25. Rafique Afzal, *Pakistan, History and Politics 1947–71* (Karachi: Oxford University Press, 2001), 117.
26. GPE, No. 4(1)/53-Cord-11, GOP, Cabinet Secretariat, Karachi.
27. From UKHC Karachi to CRO London, 21 September 1954, DO 35/5111, NA, London; Almost identical details are given in another file DO 35/5043 and Noor Ahmed, *From Martial Law to Martial Law*, 343. In addition, the formation of the One Unit was a point of grave disagreement between the Governor General and PM Bogra, so his cabinet was also dismissed.
28. Ibid. and Hamid Yousuf, *Pakistan: A Study of Political Developments 1947–97* (Lahore: Sang-e-Meel Publications, 1999), 61.
29. Callard, *Pakistan: A Political Study,* 67, and *Dawn,* 31 October 1954.
30. Lawrence Ziring, *Pakistan in the Twentieth Century: A Political History* (Karachi: Oxford University Press, 1997), 169.
31. Callard, *Pakistan: A Political Study*, 142.
32. Richard S. Wheeler, 'Governor General's Rule in Pakistan', *Far Eastern Survey* 24 (Jan. 1955), 4.
33. Rashiduzzaman, *Pakistan: A Study of Government and Politics* (Dhaka: The University Press, 1967), 98.
34. From UKHC Rawalpindi to Secretary of the State for CRO London, 16 February 1960, PREM II-3902.
35. Callard, *Pakistan: A Political Study*, 142.
36. *Dawn*, 31 October 1954, and *Nawa-i-Waqt*, 31 October 1954.
37. Afzal, *Pakistan, History and Politics,* 146. For further details please see G. W. Choudhury, *Constitutional Development in Pakistan*, 84–102.
38. Choudhury, *Constitutional Development*, 93.
39. Kausar Parveen, *The Politics of Pakistan: Role of the Opposition, 1947–1958* (Karachi: Oxford University Press, 2013), 197.
40. Cabinet mtg., 4 August 1955, 230/CF/55, NDC, Islamabad.
41. Cabinet mtg., 18 September 1955, 236/CF/55, NDC, and Baxter, *From Martial Law to Martial Law,* 351.
42. Voting was not a normal phenomenon and it was not a secret ballot. The individual opinion of ministers was sought whenever required.
43. Mohammad H. R. Talukdar, *Memoirs of Huseyn Shaheed Suhrawardy* (Dhaka: The University Press Ltd., 1987), 90.

44. GPE, No. 4(10)55- Cord-1, GOP, Cabinet Secretariat, Karachi, and *Pakistan Times,* 12 August 1955.

45. Stanley Maron, 'A New Phase in Pakistan Politics', *Far Eastern Survey* 24 (1955), 162.

46. *The Constitution of the Islamic Republic of Pakistan 1956,* Article 37 (Karachi: Government of Pakistan, 1956), 12, Library of the Punjab Assembly, Lahore.

47. Ibid. 13.

48. Ibid. Article 42.

49. *Constitution of the Islamic Republic of Pakistan, 1956*; Article 52, and Hamid Khan, *Constitutional and Political History of Pakistan,* (Karachi: Oxford University Press), 102.

50. Newman, 'The Dyarchic Pattern of Government,' 103–4, and Choudhury, *Constitutional Development,* 120–2.

51. The details of his resignation are given in Chapter 5.

52. *Pakistan Times,* 13 September 1956.

53. Huseyn Shaheed Suhrawardy, 'Political Stability and Democracy in Pakistan', *Foreign Affairs* 35 (April 1957), 425, and Rashiduzzaman, *Pakistan: A Study of Government and Politics,* 121.

54. The details are given in Chapter 5.

55. Ibid.

56. The Gazette of Pakistan Notification, No Cord (1)-4/1/57, 18 October 1957, GOP, Cabinet Secretariat, Karachi; *Nawa-i-Waqt,* 19 October 1957; *Pakistan Times,* 18 October 1957. Details of some ministers are taken from the Record of Ministers, prepared by Cabinet Wing, NDC, Islamabad.

57. Afzal, *Pakistan: History and Politics,* 199 and *Pakistan Times,* 16 December 1957.

58. Ibid. 201, and From BHC Karachi to CRO London, 11 December 1957, PREM 11/2027.

59. Mushtaq Ahmed, *Government and Politics in Pakistan,* (New York: Frederick A. Praeger Publishers, 1963 revised), 69.

60. The Gazette of Pakistan Notification, No Cord (1)-4/2/57, 16 December 1957, Government of Pakistan, Cabinet Secretariat Notification, Karachi.

61. 'Political Situation in Pakistan', Note by the Secretary of State for CRO, 28 July 1956, DO 35/8936, NA, London, and Talukdar, *Memoirs of Huseyn Shaheed Suhrawardy,* 125. Ministers of Federal Cabinet, Cabinet Wing, NDC, Islamabad.

62. Lawrence Ziring, *Pakistan: At the Crosscurrent of History* (Lahore: Vanguard, 2004), 78.

63. Richard Symonds, 'State-Making in Pakistan', *Far Eastern Survey 19 (March 1950),* 46.

64. Baxter, *From Martial Law to Martial Law,* 322.

65. For further details please see Appendix II, 'Short Biographies of the Ministers'.

66. Mushtaq Ahmad, *Jinnah and After: A Profile of Leadership* (Karachi: Royal Book Company, 1994), 70.

67. Firoz Khan Noon, *From Memory* (Lahore: Ferozsons, 1966), 84.

68. Hamza Alavi, 'Pakistan-US Military Alliances', *Economic and Political Weekly 33* (June 1998), 1554.

69. Noor Ahmad, *From Martial Law to Martial Law,* 317–18.

70. From UKHC Karachi to CRO London, 25 October 1956, DO 35/5407, NA, London.

71. Rashiduzzaman, *Pakistan: A Study of Government,* 121. This portfolio remained with PM except during the Cabinet of All Talents.

72. Preliminary Report on Pakistan Section, A, Internal Affairs 'The Revolution' by P. J. Griffiths, 25 October 1958. DO 35/8345, NA, London.

73. Altaf Gauhar, *Ayub Khan: Pakistan's First Military Ruler* (Lahore: Sang-e-Meel Publications, 1998), 159.

74. The Gazette of Pakistan Notification, No Cord (1)-4/2/58-11, 28 October 1958, GOP, Cabinet Secretariat, Rawalpindi; Record of the Cabinet prepared by Cabinet Wing, NDC, Islamabad; Khalid bin Sayeed, 'Martial Law Administration in Pakistan', *Far Eastern Survey* 28 (May 1959) 75, Gauhar, *Ayub Khan,* 53, Herbert Feldman, *Revolution in Pakistan; A Study of the Martial Law Administration* (London: Oxford University Press 1967), 13, and Draft Brief for Prime Minister prepared by Fouller High Commissioner Karachi, 27 October 1958, DO 35/8944, NA, London.

75. From UKHC Karachi to CRO, London, 25 October 1958, DO 35/8945, NA, London.

76. Ibid. 27 October 1958, DO 35/8944, NA, London.

77. The Gazette of Pakistan Notification, No Cord (1)-103 (2)/60 and No. Cord (1)-105 (22) 60-1, 14 June 1960, GOP, Cabinet Secretariat, Rawalpindi, and *Dawn,* 2 June 1960.

78. Choudhury, *Constitutional Development in Pakistan*, 178.

79. *National Assembly of Pakistan Debates,* Official Report, 8 June 1962, Vol. 1, No. 1.

80. Muhammad Munir, *Constitution of the Islamic Republic of Pakistan* (Lahore: All Pakistan Legal Decision, 1965), 249.

81. *'Cabinet' Dictionary of American History,* 2003. Encyclopedia.com, 5 July 2010 at http://www.encyclopedia.com

82. Choudhury, *Constitutional Development,* 197.

83. *The Constitution of the Republic of Pakistan 1962,* Article 33, 1 March 1962, The All-Pakistan Legal Decisions (hereafter called PLD), Central Statutes, 1962, Vol. XIV, 164.

84. Afzal, *Government and Politics in Pakistan,* 222.

85. *The Constitution of the Republic of Pakistan 1962,* Article 118.

86. Removal of Difficulties (Appointment of Ministers) Order, 1962. President's Order No. 34 of 1962. PLD. 1962, Central Statutes, 647.

87. Muhammad Munir, *Constitution of the Islamic Republic of Pakistan: A Commentary on the Constitution of Pakistan, 1962* (Lahore: The Punjab Educational Press, 1965), 234.

88. *Nawa-i-Waqt,* 8 June 1962.

89. The Gazette of Pakistan Notification, No. 102(13)/62-Min, 13 June 1960, GOP, Cabinet Secretariat, Rawalpindi.

90. Record Prepared by the Cabinet Wing, NDC, Islamabad.

91. GPE, No. 101/5/65-Min, 29 March 1965, GOP, Cabinet Secretariat Notification, Rawalpindi; *Pakistan Observer,* 30 March 1965; *Nawa-i-Waqt,* 30 March 1965 and Record prepared by Cabinet Wing. NDC, Islamabad.

92. The details of changes in the cabinet are given in Chapter 5.

93. From BHC Rawalpindi to CRO London, 1 August 1966, DO 35/316, NA, London.

94. Cabinet Mtg., 26 March 1969 cited in Craig Baxter, *Diaries of Field Marshal Muhammad Ayub Khan 1966–1972* (Karachi: Oxford University Press, 2007), 309.

95. Provisional Constitutional Order, PLD, Vol. XXI, Central Statutes, 1969, 41–2.

96. Fazal Muqeem Khan, Pakistan's Crisis in Leadership (Islamabad: National Book Foundation, 1973), 29.

97. G. W. Choudhury, *The Last Days of United Pakistan* (Karachi: Oxford University Press, 1998), 56.

98. Lawrence Ziring, *Pakistan in the Twentieth Century: A Political History,* 320, Hasan Askari Rizvi, *The Military and Politics in Pakistan 1947–1986* (Lahore: Progressive Publishers, 1986), 182, Muqeem Khan, *Pakistan's Crisis in Leadership*, 20.

99. The Gazette of Pakistan, Proclamation of Martial Law, No. S.1033/L-7646, 25 March 1969, GOP, Cabinet Secretariat, Rawalpindi and Lawrence Ziring, 'Militarism in Pakistan: The Yahya Khan Interregnum', *Asian Affairs* 1 (July-August 1974), 402–4.

100. G. W. Choudhury, *The Last Days of United Pakistan* (Karachi: Oxford University Press, 1974, paperback 1993), 51, and *Imroze,* 26 March 1969.

101. The Gazette of Pakistan Notification, No. 102/18/69-Min-11, 4 August 1969, GOP, Cabinet Secretariat, Rawalpindi, *Pakistan Times,* 5 August 1969, and Record prepared by Cabinet Wing, NDC, Islamabad.

102. Interview of Nawabzada Sher Ali Khan (minister in Yahya's civilian cabinet) to *Imroz,* 21 April 1972, and Ziring, *Pakistan in the Twentieth Century,* 321.

103. Ziring, *Pakistan in the Twentieth Century,* 346; Choudhry, *The Last Days of United Pakistan,* 75.

104. Gul Hassan Khan, *Memoirs* (Karachi: Oxford University Press, 1993), 252.

105. Ibid. Burhanuddin Hasan, *Breaking Point* (Karachi: Royal Book Company, 2009), 69.

106. Ziring, 'Militarism in Pakistan', 410.

107. Mohammad Shoaib was a financial expert and Manzur Qadir was a legal expert.

108. Rashiduzzaman, *Pakistan: A Study of Government and Politics*, 171.

109. Ronuaq Jahan, *Pakistan: Failure in National Integration* (New York: Columbia University Press, 1972), 56.

110. Rushbrook Williams, *The State of Pakistan* (London: Faber and Faber, 1962), 185.

111. Robert Laporte Jr, *Power and Privilege, Influence and Decision-Making in Pakistan* (Berkeley: University of California Press, 1975), 7.

112. Mushtaq Ahmed, *Government and Politics in Pakistan*, 223.

113. From UKHC Rawalpindi to CRO London, 1 August 1966, DO 196/316, NA, London.

114. Ziring, *The Ayub Khan Era*, 49.

115. Baxter, *Diaries of Field Marshal*, 238.

116. W. M. Dobell, 'Ayub Khan as President of Pakistan', *Pacific Affairs* 42 (Autumn 1969), 299.

117. Ibid. 219.

118. From UKHC Rawalpindi to CRO London, 20 March 1967, DO 134/33 a similar report was sent by BHC to the Secretary of State for CRO London, 14 September 1966, DO 196/316, NA, London.

119. Salman Taseer, *Zulfiqar Ali Bhutto: Bachpun Sei Jawani Tuk* (Urdu) *(Lahore: Iman Printing, 1988)*, 40–1.

120. William, *The State of Pakistan*, 185.

121. Choudhury, *The Last Days of United Pakistan*, 55.

122. Talbot, *Pakistan: A Modern History* (Lahore: Vanguard Books, 1999), 191.

123. Hasan Askari Rizvi, *Military State and Society in Pakistan* (Lahore: Sang-e-Meel Publications, 2003), 122, Talbot *Pakistan: A Modern History*, 191, Muqeem Khan, *Pakistan's Crisis in Leadership*, 20, and Afzal, *Pakistan, History and Politics 1947–1971*, 359.

124. Choudhury, *The Last Days of United Pakistan*, 67.

125. Rizvi, *The Military and Politics*, 183; Talbot, *Pakistan: A Modern History*, 191, Ziring, 'Militarism in Pakistan', 410, and Morris Janowitz, *The Military in the Political Developments of New Nations* (Chicago: The University Press, 1964), 44.

126. Shahid Javed Burki, *Pakistan: The Continuing Search for Nationhood* (Boulder: West View Press, 1986), 56.

127. Rizvi, *The Military and Politics,* 183.

128. Mohammad Ayoob, 'Pakistan's Political Development 1947 to 1970: Bird's Eye View', *Economic and Political Weekly* 16 (January 1971), 200.

129. Inner Cabinet necessarily consists of the cabinet ministers and generally exists in the parliamentary system, whereas a kitchen cabinet may include the cabinet ministers, civil and military bureaucrats, journalists and other experts. It normally operates in the presidential system.

130. Public Record Office. Ref. DO 35/8946 cited in Roedad Khan, *The British Papers, Secret and Confidential India Pakistan Bangladesh Documents 1958–1969* (Karachi: Oxford University Press, 2002), 115.

131. Interview with S. M. Zafar, 104, 4th Floor, Siddique Trade Centre, Lahore, 9 December 2012.

132. B. M. Bhatia, *Pakistan's Economic Development 1947–1990* (Lahore: Vanguard, 1990), 18.

133. From UKHC Karachi to CRO London, 16 February 1960, DO 35/8950, NA, London, and Taseer, *Zulfiqar Ali Bhutto*, 40.

134. Shahab ud Din Muhammad, *Recollections and Reflections* (Lahore: P.L.D. Publications, n.d.), 121.

135. Public Record Office, DO 35/8946 cited in Khan, *The British Papers*, 115.

136. From BHC Karachi to CRO London 14 September 1966, DO 196/316 and DO 196/318, NA, London.

137. Ibid., 30 June 1967, FCO 37/178, NA, London.

138. Interview with S. M. Zafar.

139. As well as being a civil bureaucrat he was chief editor of *Dawn* (Karachi) and *Muslim* (Karachi), ex-Secretary General Third World Foundation, ex-Chief Controller Imports and Exports and writer of many books including *Ayub Khan: Pakistan's First Military Ruler.*

140. He started his career as Secretary General of the Government of Azad Kashmir in April 1948, served as Deputy Commissioner Jhang, Director Industries Punjab, Private Secretary of Governor

General Ghulam Mohammad, President Iskandar Mirza and Ayub Khan till 1962, worked as ambassador in Holland, and worked as Secretary of Information and Education also. He was founder of Writers' Guild and was author of many books including *Shahab Nama*.

141. Khalid Bin Sayeed, 'Pakistan: New Challenges to the Political System', *Asian Survey* 8 (February 1968), 98, and From BHC Rawalpindi to CRO London, 20 March 1967, DO 134/33, and FCO 37/79, NA, London.

142. B. M. Bhatia, *Pakistan's Economic Development 1947–1990*, 18.

143. Altaf Gauhar, 'Pakistan: Ayub Khan's Abdication', *Third World Quarterly 7* (January 1985), 17.

144. Ibid. and from BHC Rawalpindi to CRO London, 9 July 1968, FCO 37/181. NA, London.

145. M. S. Korejo, *Soldiers of Misfortune: Pakistan under Ayub, Yahya, Bhutto and Zia* (Karachi: Ferozsons, 2004), 60.

146. Ibid.

147. Stanley Kochanek, *Interest Groups and Developments, Business and Politics in Pakistan* (Karachi: Oxford University Press 1983), 54.

148. Talbot, *Pakistan: A Modern History*, 213.

149. GPE, Notification No 102/33/71, 25 December 1971, 424/CF/71, NDC, Islamabad.

150. Cabinet mtg, 18 April 1972, 187/CF/72, NDC and *Dawn*, 19 April 1972.

151. Office memorandum, 9 March 1972, 113/CF/74, NDC, Islamabad.

152. Proclamation, 21 April 1972, 424/CF/71, NDC, Islamabad.

153. *The Interim Constitution of the Islamic Republic of Pakistan 1972*, Article 62 (Islamabad: Printing Corporation of Pakistan, 1972), 14.

154. Ibid.

155. Z. A. Bhutto, *A New Beginning: Reforms Introduced by the People's Government in Pakistan, December 20, 1971-April 20* (Karachi: Ministry of Information and Broadcasting Department of Films and Publication Government of Pakistan, 1972), 50.

156. GPE, No. 102/21/72-Min, 3 May 1972, GOP, Cabinet Division, Islamabad.

157. Khan Abdul Wali Khan, *Aasal Haqaiq Yai Hain* (Urdu) (Karachi: Shabul Publications, 1988), 30.

158. *The Constitution of the Islamic Republic of Pakistan 1973,* Article 90, PLD, 1973, Vol. XXV, Central Statutes, 335.

159. G. W. Choudhury, *Pakistan, Transition from Military to Civilian Rule* (Essex: Scorpion Publishing Ltd., 1988), 169.

160. *Constitution of the Islamic Republic of Pakistan, 1973*, Article 90, and Muhammad Munir, *Constitution of the Islamic Republic of Pakistan* (Lahore: Law Publishing Company, 1975), 264.

161. Ibid. Article 92.

162. Ibid. Article 62.

163. GPE, No. 102/39/73-Min, 16 August 1973, Cabinet Secretariat, Islamabad.

164. *Dawn,* 4 July 1974, and *Pakistan Times,* 4 July 1974.

165. Elections were held in the country in March after which the situation reached a point of no compromise between the government and the opposition. So martial law was imposed in the country on 4 July 1977.

166. *Nawa-i-Waqt,* 23 October 1974, and *Pakistan Times,* 23 October 1974.

167. Laporte, *Power and Privilege; Influence and Decision-Making,* 7.

168. Stanley Wolpert, *Zulfi Bhutto of Pakistan: His Life and Times* (Karachi: Oxford University Press, 1993), 171–3.

169. Khan Abdul Wali Khan, *Aasal Haqaiq Yai Hain,* 84; Wolpert, *Zulfi Bhutto of Pakistan,* 203.

170. Hamid Khan, *Constitutional and Political Development,* 259.

171. Satish Kumar, *The New Pakistan* (New Delhi: Vikas Publishing House Pvt. Ltd., 1978), 14–15.

172. Kausar Niazi, *Jhinain Mai Nai Dhekha* (Urdu) (Lahore: Jang Publishers, 1989), 165.

173. Hamid Khan, *Constitutional and Political Development,* 260.

174. Wolpert, *Zulfi,* 225–6.

175. Eric Gustafson, 'Economic Problems of Pakistan under Bhutto', *Asian Survey* 16 (April 1976), 369.

176. Kausar Niazi, *Zulfikar Ali Bhutto of Pakistan: The Last Days* (New Delhi: Vikas Publishing House, 1992), 43.

177. Richard Rose, 'The Making of Cabinet Ministers', *British Journal of Political Science* 1 (October 1977), 401.

178. Laporte, *Power and Privilege,* 125.

179. Wolpert, *Zulfi,* 103; Department of State, Secret, From American Embassy Islamabad to Secretary of State Washington, December 1971 cited in Roedad Khan, ed., *The American Papers Secret and Confidential: India-Pakistan-Bangladesh Documents 1965–73* (Karachi: Oxford University Press, 1999), 775.

180. Burki, *State and Society,* 155.

181. The manifesto of the PPP prioritized the nationalization of industry and the socialization of the economy, where industrialists were denied prominent positions. Hasan Askari Rizvi, *Pakistan Peoples Party, The First Phase 1967–71* (Lahore: Progressive Publishers, 1973), 17.

182. They only look after departmental affairs and are allowed to attend cabinet meetings in the case of the absence of cabinet ministers from the country.

183. Anwar H. Syed, 'Pakistan in 1976: Business as Usual', *Asian Survey, 17* (February 1977), 185.

184. Ibid. 108–09; Gustafson, *Economic Problems of Pakistan under Bhutto,* 367.

185. Wolpert, *Zulfi,* 239.

186. Mubashir Hasan, *The Mirage of Power, An Inquiry into the Bhutto Years 1971–1977* (Karachi: Oxford University Press, 2000), 10–1; Burki, *State and Society,* 112 and Laporte, *Power and Privilege,* 124–5.

187. Niloufer Mahdi, *Pakistan's Foreign Policy 1971–1981: The Search for Security* (Lahore: Ferozsons Pvt LTD, 1999), 31.

188. Salman Taseer, *Bhutto: A Political Biography* (London: Ithaca Press, 1979), 194.

189. Lawrence Ziring, 'Pakistan: A Political Perspective', *Asian Survey* 15 (1975), 635.

190. Surendra Nath Kaushik, *Pakistan under Bhutto's Leadership* (New Delhi: Uppal, 1985), 129.

191. Laporte, *Power and Privilege,* 1–8.

CHAPTER 2

Economic Policy and Planning:
The Role of the Cabinet

The focus of this chapter is on the federal cabinet's contribution to the formulation of Pakistan's economic policy and planning which was crucial in the early phase specifically, and in later years generally. It looks into the cabinet's role in the formation of a large number of economic institutions, and long-term and short-term economic planning and policy in the fields of agriculture, industry, trade, and business, which is not generally brought to light in academic works on the politics and economy of Pakistan. Cabinets also looked into the details of the periodic reports of the development schemes.[1] The view that the prime ministers of Pakistan in the early period did not have a full understanding of economic planning[2] seems to be unrealistic. They not only understood economic affairs, but also involved their cabinets in formulating economic policies. The role of the cabinet remained important in economic decision-making during the military period as well, except during Yahya Khan's regime. Its role was far greater during Bhutto's era, especially until 1974 when economic ministries including finance, economic affairs, industries, commerce, and trade were dominated by leftist ministers and they were designing economic policies.

The minister for finance and economic affairs enjoyed a high status in all the cabinets, as did the minister of foreign affairs. Policy and planning in the fields of the formation of economic institutions, industry, agriculture, and business and trade will be analysed generally in three phases i.e. the first parliamentary period (1947–1958), the regimes of the two military leaders (1958–1971), and the second parliamentary period (1971–1972).

In 1947, Pakistan inherited a weak economic structure which consisted of predominantly rural areas with a small number of towns. It was essentially an agricultural country with no industrial base; there was no banking network and only a small amount of business activity was controlled by the Muslims. The bulk of its population lived and worked in villages. Pakistan's main raw materials were cotton, produced in the western wing of Pakistan, and jute, produced in the eastern part of Pakistan, but at the time of independence Pakistan inherited only 14 out of 394 cotton mills and not a single jute mill. The two ports of Pakistan, Karachi and Chittagong, were poorly equipped and dealt with very little cargo. Although the economy depended on agriculture, agricultural methods were outdated and rudimentary.[3] Along with all these physical problems, Pakistan faced a shortage of trained staff for banks and other economic institutions; arrangements were made for training,[4] but the transitional phase was difficult.

2.1. THE FORMATION OF ECONOMIC INSTITUTIONS AND PLANNING

The first cabinet of Pakistan attempted to play its appropriate role to bring the country through the crises. The vision of the state with regard to the economy was well defined in the first statement of policy, approved by the cabinet. The aims were to improve the standard of living, to generate employment opportunities, to initiate industry based on agriculture, and to develop agricultural facilities.[5] All institutions related to economic affairs, including planning, industry, business, etc. received approval from cabinet for their formulation and were bound to submit their monthly reports to it.[6] The Economic Committee of the Cabinet (ECC) consisting of the PM, minister of finance and economic affairs, minister of commerce and industries, minister of food and agriculture, and the cabinet secretary was responsible for designing general policy regarding development.

The federal cabinet established various institutions including the Development Board, formed in early 1948 under the chairmanship of Minister for Finance, Ghulam Mohammad,[7] the Planning Advisory Board,[8] the Planning Commission set up in 1950, which was replaced by the Planning Board in 1953[9] with Zahid Hussain as its chairman,[10] the Pakistan Industrial Development Corporation[11] (PIDC) established in 1952 with Ghulam Faruque[12] as chairman, and finally the National Economic Committee (NEC), established by Choudhury Muhammad Ali's government in 1956. It included four federal ministers and three ministers of provincial cabinets with the president, Iskandar Mirza, as its head. The responsibilities of the NEC were to look after the economic development of the country, to present its recommendations to the provincial governments on trade goods and economic planning, and to keep the level of development equal across the whole state.[13]

Ayub Khan's cabinet followed these traditions with some innovations. The government's economic institutions played an active, influential, and constructive role in the establishment of private sector capital in Pakistan during Ayub Khan's regime (1958–69). The cabinet reformulated the objectives and status of all inherited institutions including the Planning Board, PIDC, ECC, etc. The Planning Board was renamed the Planning Commission (PC) after its reorganization. It was made part of the president's secretariat and was chaired by the president. His deputy at the PC was Minister of Finance and Economic Affairs, Mohammad Shoaib. This commission enjoyed influence in decision-making[14] and introduced an 'effective mechanism of policy'.[15] Besides preparing a Five-Year Plan and development schemes, it was also given the new responsibility of preparing schemes to install heavy industries in consultation with private entrepreneurs.[16] Provincial authorities were bound to bring their suggestions to the Planning Commission regarding industrial development and the working of the Second Five-Year Plan every six months, or once a year.[17]

The status and functions of the PIDC, which had played an important role in industrial development during the previous regime, were redefined by the cabinet.[18] Cabinet advised the PIDC to submit its plans regarding the disposal of projects to the cabinet.[19] Two parallel steps were taken: on one hand the status of the Planning Commission was upgraded, and on the other hand, the status of the PIDC was minimized.

The Economic Committee of the Cabinet, in accordance with the decision of the cabinet, functioned as the supreme economic body in this phase, unlike during the previous one.[20] Its members were President Ayub Khan, Minister for Finance Mohammad Shoaib, Minister for Food and Agriculture Lt Gen. Azam Khan (later others), Minister of Industries Abul Kasem Khan, Minister of Commerce Z. A. Bhutto, and some officials. Its functions included the approval and oversight of the implementation of the Five-Year Plan and the Annual Development Programme. It could sanction development schemes of all types and would report to the cabinet periodically regarding the implementation of the plans. Furthermore, an Economic Coordination Committee of the Cabinet consisting of the ministers of finance, commerce, industries, and natural resources, and foreign affairs was also working. Its charter included the preparation of papers on vital economic issues.[21]

The National Economic Council was a new institution[22] which comprised of the federal ministers of finance, agriculture, education, information, communication, defence, and commerce, provincial governors, provincial finance ministers, and some officials. It prepared all provincial development schemes, national-level development projects, and annual plans.[23] The responsibility for the implementation of policies and programmes rested with the Executive Committee of the National Economic Council (ECNEC), chaired by the federal minister of finance and included federal ministers in charge of development ministries, provincial governors or their nominees, and provincial ministers in charge of planning and development departments.[24] The presence of provincial governors and finance ministers was very significant in this federal institution. The points of view and problems of the provincial governments concerning economic matters could formally and directly reach the federal government through this institution.

Other institutions included the Agricultural Development Corporation,[25] the National Finance Commission[26] established in March 1964, and the Economic Coordination Committee of the Cabinet formed in 1966.[27]

The imposition of the second martial law changed many aspects of economic policy and planning. No formal cabinet existed for most of the time, except from August 1969 to March 1970, so there was no question of cabinet having a share in policymaking. Most issues were not brought before the civilian cabinet meetings. It was the only time of the period under research when cabinet's role in decision-making was insignificant or non-existent. The only decision-making authority was the military high command.

No new economic institution was set up, but the status and working style of some of the institutions was changed. The NEC now included only military personnel i.e. CMLA-cum-President Yahya Khan, members of the military cabinet including Nur Khan, CMLA of the Air Force, Navy, and Army, martial law administrators of Zones A and B (East and

West Pakistan), Personal Staff Officer S. G. M. Pirzada, and some civilian bureaucrats including the cabinet secretary and the deputy secretary to the cabinet.[28]

The Planning Commission was also dominated by military personnel. The ECCC, working on a bureaucratic level,[29] was responsible for the formulation of reports on policy issues and then the presentation of them to the higher policymaking institution. In July 1969 it prepared a report on the formulation of export policy and on reasons for the decline in exports.[30]

Cabinet-oriented institutions were revived immediately after the establishment of Z. A. Bhutto's government. These institutions included the Economic Coordination Committee of the Cabinet (ECCC), the Executive Committee of the National Economic Council (ECNEC), and the NEC itself.[31] The ECCC was chaired by Mubashir Hasan and included the ministers of industry, commerce, agriculture, communication, production, and planning.[32] All economic matters except taxation, the budget, and pricing of agricultural produce came under its jurisdiction. It met once a week and decided most issues. Final approval was sought from the cabinet, which sometimes did not approve the plans.[33] The NEC was chaired by President Bhutto, seconded by Mubashir Hasan.[34] Periodical reports on the implementation of major decisions of the NEC, cabinet and governors' conference were submitted to it. The intention was to keep the cabinet informed of such decisions.[35]

The Council of Common Interests was a new economic institution established under Article 153 of the 1973 Constitution. Its purpose was to safeguard the economic interests of all the provinces and to regulate economic policies. It comprised of Bhutto as chairman, federal cabinet ministers, and provincial chief ministers. As provincial chief ministers were from the PPP, federal cabinet ministers were also from the PPP and Bhutto was leading this council, so there was always one-way political-cum-economic communication, from the centre to the provinces.[36]

The Planning Commission was the least effective institution during the Bhutto regime. Its powers were curbed due to the influence of the leftist ministers in the cabinet and the restructuring of the civil bureaucracy. Its chairman, Qamar ul Islam, was dismissed and it became only a division of the Ministry of Finance.[37] This commission was totally overlooked when policies were introduced in the later period. The long gestation projects, including nuclear plants, steel mills, etc. were approved by the cabinet without any formal feasibility studies by the Planning Commission.[38] The only major task assigned to it was the preparation of the Fifth Five-Year Plan in later years, and this was not implemented.[39]

The cabinet's planning for economic development during the first phase was based on the choice between capitalism and socialism rather than on practical needs,[40] and the plans were prepared to obtain maximum aid from capitalist countries. The cabinets approved two major economic plans including the Six-Year Plan (1951–1957)[41] and the First Five-Year Plan (1955–1960). The Six-Year Plan was only a general statement about 'goals and a list of specific projects'.[42] Work started on the formulation of the First Five-Year Plan in 1953 but the Planning Board could not acquire the support of the cabinet, and there was little coordination between the two institutions. The First Five-Year Plan received final approval only in 1958, after many revisions.[43] It was a comprehensive and detailed document.[44] The Harvard Advisory Group and the Ford Foundation provided support to the Planning Board[45] for preparing the plans. Top priority was given to agriculture, transport and communication, industry and mining, fuel and power, and schemes of social uplift, but the plan could not be implemented.

Pakistan's economic condition at the advent of martial law on 8 October 1958 was deteriorating due to political instability and the neglect of economic development in the previous couple of years. The First Five-Year Plan, whose period was due to lapse in 1960, still awaited implementation. The martial law government of Ayub Khan was deeply concerned with economic development and demonstrated its consciousness by planning in the economic field.[46] The planning process was institutionalized, through opening planning departments in the provinces and planning cells in the ministries besides establishing decision-making committees of the PC. The finance minister was a member of all such committees and of the NEC.[47] The cabinet approved and introduced two Five-Year Plans during the military period: the Second Five-Year Plan (1960–1965) and the Third Five-Year Plan (1965–1970) were prepared and introduced with proper homework and planning.[48] All the economic institutions, the cabinet, ministers, and their ministries played their parts in the whole process. The Planning Commission was mainly responsible for preparing the plan but the ECC, NEC, and finally the cabinet provided support to the Planning Commission. At the request of the ECC, the ministries had expedited the finalization of schemes and programmes for the Planning Commission to enable it to achieve the targets set for the Second Five-Year Plan.[49]

The objectives of the Second Five-Year Plan, as approved by the cabinet, were agricultural and industrial development in particular, and development in other areas in general. The Planning Commission sent the outline plan to the cabinet for comments. The cabinet sent it to the central ministries and the provincial governments and advised them to send their comments as early as possible.[50] After receiving these comments, the finance minister summarized the major problems and presented them to the meeting of the ECC. The committee suggested solutions to the problems.[51] The total outlay for the planning, which also included rural development schemes, was Rs. 2,300 crore.[52]

The Third Five-Year Plan was also prepared with the same efficiency and hard work of the cabinet and other economic institutions, but there was a difference in the levels of success of the plans. The Second Five-Year Plan was more successful than expected. It witnessed a 30 per cent increase in national income rather than the 24 per cent which had been set by the planners.[53] The increase in GDP was 6.7 per cent per annum compared to 5.6 per cent.[54] The reasons for lesser success during the Third Plan period included increased military expenditure due to the 1965 Pakistan-India war, political uncertainty, less foreign aid, and political troubles during the last years of the period. The targets were revised on the recommendation of the finance minister and suggestions of the ministries.[55] In addition, Yahya Khan's government abandoned the Third Five-Year Plan in March 1969 and work on the Fourth Five-Year Plan was stopped.[56] The Fourth Five-Year Plan could not be implemented as it was drawn up for both the East and the West Wings of the country.[57]

No major economic plan apart from the Annual Economic Plan for 1969–1970 was prepared during Yahya's period. It was

Table: 2-A, Targets and Achievements of the First Three Five-Year Plans

Per cent increase over plan period	First Plan (1955–1960)		Second Plan (1960–1965)		Third Plan (1965–1970)	
	Target	Achievement	Target	Achievement	Target	Achievement
GNP	15	12	24	32	37	28
Agricultural output	14	7	14	18	28	24
Manufacturing output	42	32	51	61	61	45
Exports	33	11	15	30	57	38
per capita GNP	7	0	10	16	22	12

Sources: Pakistan Planning Commission: The First, Second, and Third Five-Year Plans; *Final Evaluation of Second Five-Year Plan* (Karachi, 1966) and Pakistan, C. S. O., *25 Years of Pakistan in Statistics 1947–1972* (Karachi, 1972) cited in Dharma Kumar, *The Cambridge Economic History of India* (New Delhi: Cambridge University Press [expanded edition], 2005).

presented to the NEC for final endorsement but due to a gap between resources and projects, it was not approved. The responsibility for covering the gap was given to the federal and provincial finance secretaries,[58] but no formal action was taken on it.

Bhutto's cabinet stopped the introduction of the Fourth Five-Year Plan, whose 'draft documents were already in circulation'.[59] In place of the Fifth Five-Year Plan, a two-year crash plan was introduced to explore new West Asian markets. A second type of plan introduced during this period was the Annual Development Programme.[60] One plan was introduced for Balochistan in 1974. It was of an overall value of Rs. 18 crore added to which was an additional grant of Rs. 1.4 crore. It included development projects in the fields of water, agriculture, physical planning, housing, industry, education, health, communications, transport, manpower studies, and research.[61]

A large number of economic institutions were established during the period 1947–1977 under the supervision of the federal cabinet which had mostly worked to achieve their set target while gaining approval for the plans from the cabinet. Sometimes differences of opinion occurred which affected the speed of work during the first phase. Generally, cordial relations had developed during Ayub Khan's period between economic institutions and the cabinet, whereas the economic institutions worked as subordinate institutions to the federal cabinet during the Bhutto era. The First Five-Year Plan could not be introduced in the country due to the rapid change of the governments and late approval of the plan by the cabinet. However, Ayub Khan's period witnessed the successful implementation of the Second Five-Year Plan and partial success of the Third Five-Year Plan. Nevertheless, due to the shift of priorities during Yahya Khan's period and change in the planning process during the Bhutto era, the work on Five-Year Plans was stopped.

2.2. INDUSTRIAL POLICY

During the first phase, the government's economic policy was biased in favour of urban industrial development through 'exchange rate, trade, investment, and pricing policies'.[62] Only 6 per cent and 7 per cent of total public sector investment went towards agriculture between 1950–55 and 1955–60 respectively. Industrial investment was 36 per cent between 1950–55, and 31 per cent between 1955–60.[63] The absence of industry in Pakistan, and the control of the economic ministries by urban professionals like Malik Ghulam Mohammad, Minister of Finance (1947–1951), Choudhury Muhammad Ali, Minister of Finance (1951–1955), Syed Amjad Ali, Minister of Finance (1955–1958), Chaudhry Nazir Ahmad, Minister of Industries, Fazlur Rehman, Minister of Commerce, and others, prioritized investing maximum energy and resources in building an industrial base. Liaquat Ali Khan, conscious of industrial development, said: 'Government must take an active part in planning, encouraging, and developing industry and helping those who are desirous of taking an active share in the development of their country.'[64] The first industrial policy was approved by the cabinet on 12 December 1947. Its emphasis was on planned industrial development and the building of agriculture-related industry.[65]

Although development of industries was a provincial subject under the Interim Constitution, yet on the recommendation of the Pakistan Industries Conference, planning related to twenty-seven industries was brought under the federal government's jurisdiction.[66] On a proposal from the Ministry for Industries, the cabinet sent a bill to CAP to make a law that would give the centre authority for industrial planning.[67]

The absence of a planning institution resulted in the growth of only the manufacturing industrial sector before 1950.[68] Minister of Industries, Fazlur Rehman, continuously urged the formation of an autonomous corporation 'to promote and develop certain specified industries'.[69] The Planning Board was a positive development in this regard, but the conflict between the board and the cabinet did not enable the Planning Board to get approval or to implement its policies properly and on time.

Conflict originated between consolidators and expansionists[70] within the cabinet and bureaucracy too. The chairman of the PIDC, Ghulam Faruque, was an expansionist who wanted to encourage investment in heavy industry, but Finance Minister Choudhury Muhammad Ali and Zahid Hussain, chairman of the Planning Board, were consolidators who believed that self-sufficiency in food was essential before investment in heavy industry. It was due to the consolidators' influence that the manufacturing industries of fertilizers, medicine, petroleum products, chemicals, light and medium engineering products, and essential defence requirements, along with consumer goods and agricultural-based items, flourished.[71] As consolidators like Choudhury Muhammad

Ali were present within the cabinet, the idea of heavy industry was not entertained in the 1950s[72] except for one heavy industrial venture of the ordinance factories at Wah. These were maintained as independent entities under the direct control of the government.[73]

The cabinet managed industrial policy strictly through control on foreign exchange earnings, the licensing system, and tariff structure, and through incentives including tax concessions,[74] export promotion schemes, export credit guarantees, and infrastructure aids including training, water, and power[75] encouraged the manufacturing and consumer goods industries to flourish. The government permitted the import of industrial machinery at subsidized prices, but only for medium- and small-scale industries.[76] The import of all consumer items which were produced in Pakistan was banned.[77] The government also had strict control on credit through the Pakistan Industrial Credit and Investment Corporation[78] (PICIC) and the Pakistan Industrial Finance Corporation (PIFCO). Minister of Industries, Nishtar Hussain, directed PIFCO to extend its support to private companies and individual industrialists.[79] These firms provided funds and loans to manufacturing industries and to 'larger more established firms which had adequate security and a high profit rate'.[80] Half of PICIC's loans were given to a tiny group of West Pakistani industrialists.[81] Besides providing incentives to indigenous industrialists, the government, with the approval of the cabinet, permitted foreign investment in Pakistan. Teams of US investors who wanted to visit and study the new opportunities for investment and to start new projects were welcomed.[82] Cabinets looked into utilizing handsome amounts of foreign aid in industrial development. Cabinet's industrial policy was largely pro West Pakistan because of the political strength of West Pakistani ministers. Whatever its results, the main point is that cabinet was very prominent in taking decisions regarding industrial development.

The martial law regime announced a new industrial policy in early 1959 which aimed at rational development based on indigenous raw materials and agriculture, and the development of cottage- and small-scale industry on a priority basis.[83] The cabinet kept direct and indirect control on private industrial development. It was responsible for industrial development and planning, fixing targets and priorities, the location of selected industries in specific areas, determination of the level of production, and prescription of standards and quotas for exports. The provincial governments were given responsibility for implementing the industrial policy.[84]

The cabinet issued industrial investment schedules which contained a list of projects on a province-wise basis. The granting of permission to install such industries listed in the schedule was smooth and less time-consuming. Investment permission procedure was more difficult in the Third Plan period as an investor would also need permission from the ECC.[85] In this way, cabinet's grip on policymaking was even greater than during the first phase of economic development, which was revised and relaxed in 1966.

Unlike in the first phase, there was no conflict between the cabinet and the economic institutions related to industrial development. Government and the private sector encouraged by the government invested in new and major industries with more complex technology, larger capital requirements, and longer payback periods. These industries included paper, cement, chemicals, and engineering industries. Intermediate and capital goods industries also flourished. One negative element of this development was its dependence on imported materials; here the government's policy was unsuccessful.[86]

Acting on cabinet's advice, PIDC sold all industrial units which were complete to the private sector.[87] This helped to remove inflationary pressures. Cabinet advised PIDC to survey what areas of industrialization needed investment at the provincial level,[88] so that neglected areas and major problems could be identified. It was assigned the task of investing in major projects and then privatizing those projects.[89] It completed fifty-five industrial projects by 1962 and another twenty-five by 1969; these were transferred to financial industrial groups.[90] This policy of the cabinet successfully created a group of private entrepreneurs under governmental patronage.[91]

Industry remained a federal concern till 1962, but with the introduction of the 1962 Constitution, it was transferred to the provinces; the role of the federal government was limited to national industrial planning and coordination.[92]

Cabinet planned to establish heavy industries in Pakistan both in the public and private sectors. Capital was invested in stabilizing ordinance factories to fulfill maximum possible military requirements, especially after the 1965 war.[93] Power generation capacity for heavy industries was also increased.[94] Under cabinet's direction, foreign investment in industry, trade, and banking was encouraged and economic ministers and senior officials visiting foreign countries were advised to convince investors about the favourable economic conditions in Pakistan.[95]

Under the ECC's decisions, secretaries of the ministries of finance, commerce, and industries were bound to meet periodically. They were to review and submit a report to the ECC on a quarterly basis regarding new foreign investment, problems faced and solved limiting such investment, and further incentives.[96] This facilitated foreign investment. The ECC took an important and beneficial step regarding the Pakistanization of foreign firms in Pakistan.[97] On Mohammad Shoaib's recommendation, the ECC asked the Investment Promotion Bureau to prepare a programme of *Pakistanization* for each group of firms and to enforce it vigorously within five years.[98] This helped to reduce unemployment in the country.

Industry flourished during this period, especially before the Pakistan-India War in 1965. Its contribution to GDP had increased from 9.2 per cent to 11.4 per cent by the end of the Second Five-Year Plan period.[99] The negative elements of the industrial policy designed by Ayub and his ministers were the increased reliance on foreign aid, repression of the rights of industrial workers, and the ban on trade unions.[100]

No other major industrial policy except nationalization was introduced during the second parliamentary regime. Industries of different categories were nationalized in three steps. The issue of nationalization was brought into the cabinet meeting only one day after its formation. Cabinet formed a committee of three ministers, Mubashir Hassan, J. A. Rahim, and Kasuri, to complete the preparation for nationalization.[101] The work was completed within a few days and thirty-four industrial units from ten categories were nationalized on 2 January 1972.[102] Serious debate continued among socialist and rightist ministers, Bhutto, and the bureaucracy on the question of the nationalization of the textile industry. The leftists ministers were in favour of nationalization. While rightist elements, including Abdul Hafiz Pirzada and Maulana Kausar Niazi, pressured Bhutto to take time in nationalizing the industry. Bhutto decided in favour of the latter group for the moment.[103]

Only management, not ownership, was nationalized. The Board of Industrial Management (BIM), created under the chairmanship of the federal minister of production, looked after the management.[104] This policy reduced the power of former economic elites and gave authority to the leftist ministers to introduce favourable policies for the benefit of the workers.[105] Burki claims that most of the new managers in all nationalized units were dishonest.[106] Anwar Syed opined that the poor performance was due to lack of experience and marketing sense, and overemployment.[107] Both opinions are partially true.

Bhutto promised that there would be no more nationalization, but a large number of medium-sized *ghee* industrial units were nationalized in August 1973. Mubashir Hasan blamed private industrialists and businessmen for creating 'a national crisis for personal advantage'.[108] He convinced Bhutto to nationalize the vegetable oil industry. This wave of nationalization hurt the PPP constituency as it affected medium-sized and small industrialists. Besides creating resentment, this group of industrialists pressurized Bhutto to reduce the influence of the left in economic decision-making.[109]

The greatest blow to industrial policy during this regime was witnessed in 1976 when the third round of nationalization was introduced. Rice husking, flour mills, and cotton-ginning units were nationalized; as a result, low-level investment stopped coming to Pakistan. Unfortunately, no prior approval was given by cabinet. Only some bureaucrats were taken into confidence including the secretary general of finance, food and agriculture, the cabinet secretary, and Feroze Qaisar, Special Assistant for Economic Affairs. Qaiser, who was later dismissed, opposed it. Cabinet, who were informed along with the public, endorsed it only formally and pointed out its negative impacts.[110] The businessmen and industrialists who were affected by this wave of nationalization played an important role in the anti-Bhutto movement.[111]

Landlord members of cabinet successfully introduced a pro-landlord policy for the management of the industries. They created close links with the managers of three-quarters of the nationalized units. It was the first time that, along with crop production, agro-based industry came under the control of the feudal lords.[112] This wave of nationalization was political in nature. Bhutto wanted the support of the landlords in the next election and that is why he benefited them by handing over control of the agro-based industries.[113]

Overall, the industrial policy of this regime was anti-investment. The tax holiday scheme for industry was abolished and no export subsidy was given for finished industrial goods. Import duty on finished goods was reduced, and price control was instituted. As a result, private investment decreased.[114] Existing investment shifted to small-scale industry only, but after the nationalization measures of 1976, small entrepreneurs were also discouraged.[115] Public sector investment increased to 70 per cent due to structural changes in the economic system.[116] The setting-up of basic industries was the jurisdiction of the federal government, and provincial governments could only invest in medium-sized and employment-generated industries.[117] Labour reforms were introduced but not implemented properly as no institution was made responsible for implementing medical, low-cost housing, and free education reforms.[118]

Foreign investment decreased due to the policies of the government.[119] Wali Khan claimed that Bhutto's federal cabinet was not ready to support the provincial governments in their efforts to establish industry. The provincial government of NWFP demanded tax-relaxation for small entrepreneurs, which was not approved by the federal cabinet.[120] Finance Minister Rana Mohammad Hanif presented a summary regarding the encouragement of private investment, but this was rejected by the cabinet on the basis that no proposal contrary to the party's manifesto should be entertained and that the cabinet would only encourage public sector investment.[121]

2.3. AGRICULTURAL POLICY

Agriculture was the 'sick man'[122] of economic development during the 1950s. The absence of landlords from the cabinet or their handling of less important portfolios in later years (except Malik Firoz Khan Noon (1957–1958)) was one of the major reasons for the neglect of agricultural issues. None of the economic institutions formed in this period included agriculture among their priority issues. The proposed formation of the Agricultural Commission was presented by Minister of Agriculture, A. H. Dildar Ahmad, and was approved by the cabinet in September 1957, but it did not materialize due to the change of government after only a month.[123] Later, PM Malik Firoz Khan Noon said in the cabinet meeting on 5 February 1958:

> ... there was no need to appoint an Agricultural Commission. In his view this Commission would serve no useful purpose. He already knew what the problems were and what the remedies were. The setting up of this Commission would be just a waste of time and money ... the previous Cabinet's decision should be reversed and no further action should be taken to appoint the Agricultural Commission.[124]

The fate of the idea of establishing an Agricultural Bank was no different from that of the Agricultural Commission, the summary for which was presented by the Ministry of Finance in September 1956;[125] it could not be implemented due to the quick change of government. The First Five-Year Plan, prepared by the Planning Board, emphasized reforms in the agricultural field and set high export targets based on agriculture, but successive governments criminally neglected the agriculture sector. Agricultural yield decreased during the period of the plan, which led to the revision of targets.[126]

No broad reforms were introduced to support agricultural production. From 1953 onwards, Pakistan continuously faced food shortages. The area which used to produce food for most of the Indian region in the colonial era had to import it from the USA, Britain, and the other countries.[127] During the period of the coalition government, landlords could occupy some positions in the federal cabinet and tried to discuss measures for enhanced agricultural yield in the meetings. Suhrawardy's cabinet decided that the Ministry of Food, in consultation with the Ministry of Finance, should examine the question of appointing a high-powered committee to supervise and sanction 'Grow More Food Schemes'.[128] Provincial governments were advised, following cabinet's decision, to make special arrangements for the distribution of fertilizers and to control smuggling.[129] The scheme could not be implemented, again due to the quick change of government.

The dominant urban professionals sitting in the cabinets initiated policies that led to the decline in food production.[130] The policies included lower prices for agricultural products,[131] since cabinet had always determined the prices of major agricultural items;[132] an overvalued exchange-rate policy, which made agricultural products very expensive; high export taxes, etc.

Neglecting land reforms was the second main problem for agricultural development. The First Five-Year Plan proposed land reforms, but the suggestion was totally ignored by successive governments.[133] In the absence of landlords from the early cabinets, it was easy to approve and implement land reform initiatives, but no serious effort was made in this regard. In July 1953 Minister of Finance Choudhury Muhammad Ali proposed in the cabinet meeting the redistribution of land in order to prevent a few landlords from reaping the benefits,[134] but no steps were taken. The effort was revived during his premiership and his finance minister, Syed Amjad Ali, said in his budget speech on 15 March 1956, 'The first phase of industrial development is over and it is now necessary to pay greater attention to agricultural development'.[135] He claimed that the devaluation of the currency in 1955 was carried out in the same light. The government wanted to introduce some other agricultural reforms including subsidized prices for fertilizer and seed, and control of waterlogging, salinity, etc. but no plan was introduced.[136]

Suhrawardy's government appointed a committee under the chairmanship of Bengali Minister of Food and Agriculture, A. H. Dildar Ahmad, to solve agricultural problems. The committee and the AL Agrarian Conference suggested 'a constitutional amendment legalizing the state's confiscation of land without compensation'.[137] West Pakistani landlords in the cabinet and outside of it voiced loud protests against this 'un-Islamic' proposal. They founded the Pakistan *Zarai*

(Agricultural) Federation to safeguard the rural structure and to protect the rights of landlords.[138] Land reforms could not be introduced in West Pakistan. Chundrigarh's cabinet reversed this policy too, and the next PM, Noon, continued with the status quo.

Ayub's cabinet consisted mostly of urban-based bureaucrats and professionals, but they did not neglect the agricultural sector for two major reasons: first they may have learnt from the mistakes of the past governments, and second was the rural background of Ayub Khan who belonged to a lower-middle class family from Abbotabad. He personally was interested in raising the status of poor farmers. He declared that his main purpose was to end social inequality in rural areas where many Pakistanis were working as serfs.[139] The Finance Minister declared that the government's economic policy would be balanced towards industry and agriculture. Greater attention was paid to agricultural development with the aim of achieving self-sufficiency in food supplies.

The first steps included the exclusion of landlords from his first cabinet, a direct blow to the landed aristocracy, and the second step was the introduction of land reforms.[140] Furthermore, he did not want to destroy agriculture as a profession so the land ceiling was reasonable.[141] The president informed the cabinet that there was no cause for unnecessary fear regarding land reforms as these were not based on emotional and ideological considerations, but on scientific and realistic lines. He further stated that the government was just towards all concerned.[142] Cabinet constituted the Land Reforms Commission on 31 October 1958, which presented its report in January 1959, and cabinet approved it within a few weeks. The land ceiling was fixed for the first time in Pakistan's history and a significant proportion of land was distributed to landless peasants. The reforms were not radical in scope, but originated with the middle-class of landlords who, through the Basic Democracies System played a significant role in the economic decision-making process at the local level, and in bringing in the Green Revolution.[143]

The federal economic institutions had strict control over agricultural development during the whole period. A National Agricultural conference was called once or twice a year by the federal minister of food and agriculture to which representatives of provincial governments and the chairman of the Agricultural Development Corporation (ADC) were invited to review the progress made and to suggest to the appropriate authorities ways and measures for overcoming difficulties and bottlenecks.[144]

A number of agricultural development projects were introduced for the provinces. Cabinet advised the provincial governments to guide the ADC to initiate special projects for selected areas, such as fruit cultivation in hilly areas, banana growth in former Sindh, and coconut plantations in East Pakistan, under the direction of export project directors, etc. They further advised that nurseries should be developed for the projects.[145] The ECC continuously monitored the activities of the corporations through the provincial governments and criticized them if dissatisfied. The NEC also introduced some development projects.[146] Cabinet introduced price incentives schemes and price support policies for agriculturists. An attempt was made to settle the water problem in West Pakistan through the Indus Water Treaty, ground water irrigation and treatment of the problems of waterlogging and salinity. All these steps increased the contribution of agricultural products to the GNP from 7 per cent to 13 per cent during the Second Plan period.[147]

Cabinet's Green Revolution policy gave first priority to attaining self-sufficiency in food production during the Third Plan period. It was decided that the food shortage should be tackled on a war-like footing. A detailed programme for achieving the targets was fixed by the Agricultural Policy Committees (APCs) under the advice of the NEC.[148] Additionally, the APCs of two provinces were given the responsibility to prescribe production targets for each district and division and to obtain periodical reports about the progress made in achieving the targets. Fertilizers were made available to farmers at subsidized prices and a price-freeze on fertilizers was also introduced.[149] High quality seed was provided to the farmers and modern agricultural machinery was imported from other countries[150] to improve harvest times.

In addition, in accordance with a decision of the governors' conference, subsidies were provided to industrialists for establishing domestic industries producing agricultural machinery, tube wells, and water pumps.[151] The major beneficiary in this whole process was West Pakistan.[152] The Third Plan period saw the fastest agriculture growth period since independence, but it was confined mainly to West Pakistan. The Green Revolution failed in East Pakistan due to the unfriendly climate, lack of adequate investment for the control and development of water resources, and non-installation of tube wells in absence of the big landholdings.[153] Unfortunately, self-sufficiency in food could not be achieved.

Table 2-B: Annual Growth Rate, 1958–1970, at 1959–1960 factor cost (% per annum)

Year	Agriculture	Manufacturing	
		large-scale	small-scale
1958/59	4.0	5.6	2.3
1959/60	0.3	2.7	2.3
1960/61	-0.2	20.3	2.9
1961/62	6.2	19.9	2.9
1962/63	5.2	15.7	2.9
1963/64	2.5	15.5	2.9
1964/65	5.2	13	2.9
1965/66	0.5	10.8	2.9
1966/67	5.5	6.7	2.9
1967/68	11.7	7.6	2.9
1968/69	4.5	10.6	2.9
1969/70	9.5	13.9	3.0
1958–1964 (ave)	3.0	13.3	2.7
1965–1970 (ave)	6.2	10.4	2.9

Source: Government of Pakistan, *Pakistan Economic Survey, 1984–85,* Islamabad, 1985 cited in S. Akbar Zaidi, *Issues in Pakistan's Economy.* (Karachi: Oxford University Press, 2009).

During the second parliamentary phase, most of Bhutto's ministers came from the urban areas and were therefore more interested in urban development. His cabinet was divided on the issue of land reforms. The leftist ministers wanted pure socialist land reforms, but the rightist and landlord ministers wanted a soft land reforms package.[154] Both elements were partially successful in introducing their desired reforms. The package was better than Ayub's land reforms,[155] but was not radical. Under the reforms, the individual land ceiling was 150 acres of irrigated and 300 acres of unirrigated land. Interior Minister Khan Qayyum stated that the land reforms were like a 'Charter of emancipation'[156] for peasants. Mohammad Hanif, Minister of Labour, said that the entire economic structure of the country would be revolutionized.[157]

A mixed reaction of ministers on the issue of the implementation of reforms was noticed. Agricultural Minister Sheikh Rashid and some other leftists were happy at the introduction of the reform package, but some other political figures including Mustafa Jatoi, Minister of Political Affairs, and Sadiq Hussain Qureshi, ignored implementing the reforms.[158] Cabinet was informed that a small surrendered area would be available in Punjab for distribution. The situation in Sindh was satisfactory; however Balochistan and NWFP were thought to be the trouble spots in the implementation of reforms, as the sardars and *khans* were not ready to surrender their lands without compensation.[159] Police and local levies were deployed to enforce the implementation.

Bhutto warned the cabinet on 14 December 1973, that '… if the provincial governments did not act more vigorously, he might call for a new general election'.[160] The cabinet was blamed that the commission, formed under the chairmanship of the federal minister, for the distribution of the resumed land, distributed it on the basis of favouritism and nepotism.[161] Khalid Bin Sayeed holds the view that Bhutto, himself a landlord, did not wish to eradicate the system from Pakistan abruptly, and at the same time wanted to give some benefits to the peasants, so this type of reform package was introduced.[162] Provincial assemblies passed amendment acts and provided a number of concessions to the landlords, so the average land ceiling remained very high.[163]

Cabinet had started work on the abolition of the *sardari* (feudalism) system in Balochistan as early as 1972, but work progressed slowly.[164] The first step in this connection was taken in April 1976, when the *Sardari* Abolition Ordinance was issued. According to the ordinance, the *sardars* (feudal) were not allowed to keep private jails and were debarred from forcing anyone to provide free labour and payment of tributes. Unfortunately, the ordinance could not be implemented successfully.[165]

Bhutto's fourth cabinet, consisting mainly of the rightist politicians and landlords, initiated some positive measures to increase agricultural yield as a rural bias had entered into the decision-making process.[166] Land revenue tax was abolished for all those peasants who held less than twenty-five acres of land, and simultaneously the ratio of tax for landlords who owned more than fifty acres was increased. According to Gustafson, it was meaningless as the land revenue rate was only Rs. 12 per acre for first grade land and Rs. 2.43 for rain-fed land.[167] A scheme of credit and loans was introduced and small farmers were given preference in receiving agricultural credit.[168] Choudhury Mohammad Haneef Khan, Minister of

Finance, told the members of the National Assembly on 6 February 1975, '... agricultural credit has necessarily to be provided to the farmers where it is most needed ... Tractors, seeds, fertilizers etc., have necessarily to be linked with the credit.'[169] Prices of agricultural machinery were lowered in 1974–75. The Agricultural Development Bank was under the control of the government, which also controlled agricultural loans. Additionally, fuel for agricultural machinery was made available at subsidized prices.[170] The prices of all types of fertilizers were reduced in November 1974 for at least the next six months.[171]

None of the efforts of the pro-rural decision-makers was successful due to floods, inflation, and the high increase in petroleum prices. Pakistan's economy went continuously downwards.[172] Estimates of the yields of many crops proved wrong due to 'unforeseen circumstances'.[173] On the initiative of the big landlords in the cabinet, landlords kept control of the introduction of price policies and subsidies, the ownership of agro-industries, and the restructuring of local institutions. Owing to these policies, the middle-sized farmers turned against Bhutto.[174]

Some economic schemes including the Rural Works Programme and the People's Works Programme were introduced. But these were unsuccessful because of the poor and inefficient rural administrative structure.[175] The landlord-oriented cabinet had taken the strange step of introducing land reforms. Two powerful feudals, Malik Khuda Bakhsh Bucha, and later, Malik Hayat Muhammad Khan of Tamman were advisors to Bhutto.

The cabinets of the first phase totally neglected the agricultural sector, whereas Ayub Khan's and Zulfikar Ali Bhutto's cabinets spent valuable time designing policy for the development of this area of the economy.

2.4. BUSINESS AND TRADE POLICY

Cabinets in the first phase designed policy to have strict control on business and trade. Import controls were relaxed during the Korean War boom (1950–53) due to the availability of capital, but were imposed again after the end of war. The balance of trade due to import controls, especially on consumer goods, remained in favour of industry.[176] Export policy was also decided by the cabinet.[177] Import and export licenses were given with the approval of the government through specified economic institutions which were bound to follow the policy formulated by the cabinet.[178] Most of the import and export licenses were given to West Pakistani, mostly Karachi-based, businessmen.[179] 60 to 80 per cent of foreign exchange was earned through the export of jute, but most of it was reinvested in West Pakistan.

Severe import restrictions and an overvalued exchange rate penalized exports of agricultural goods.[180] The Minister for Industries, M. A. Ispahani, was against the Export Incentive Scheme as it had resulted in artificial growth, but the Minister of Commerce, Ibrahim Rahimtoola, insisted on continuing it. The latter's idea was endorsed by the cabinet in March 1955.[181] Cabinet often looked into the trends related to import and export.[182]

The control of the ministries of finance and commerce and industry by West Pakistani ministers, after the exit of Commerce Minister Fazal ul Haq, resulted in a pro-West Pakistan approach, where most of the development projects had been initiated. Manufacturing output was greater in West Pakistan, i.e. 34 per cent from 1950 to 1955, whereas it was only 21 per cent in East Pakistan during the same period.[183] East Pakistani politicians and businessmen were against the disparity that existed between the two parts of the country. They demanded parity in import-export licenses. PM Suhrawardy, who came from East Pakistan, brought this issue before the cabinet and with cabinet's approval parity was awarded in issuing import and export licenses and in the distribution of foreign exchange earnings. Minister for Commerce Abul Mansur Ahmad's role was significant in introducing this policy.[184] After gaining approval from the National Economic Council (NEC), it was implemented in February 1957. A separate Directorate of Supply and Development, and an office of the Controller of Import and Export were opened in East Pakistan. Cabinet allocated foreign exchange to East and West Pakistan on the ratio of 42 per cent and 16 per cent respectively and advised the Planning Board to revise the Five-Year Plan in order to give an equal share to East Pakistan.[185]

The West Pakistani businessmen and industrialists created trouble on this issue in 1957 and pressurized the cabinet of Suhrawardy to either accept their decisions or resign. Many chambers and associations, including the Chamber of Commerce and Industries (CCI) were established.[186] They approached President Mirza and invited him to a meeting of the CCI. The president of the CCI attacked Suhrawardy's government and said that politicians had created a mess not only in the political sphere, but also in the economic sphere. He was against parity in the economic sphere.[187]

Suhrawardy defended his government's policy later, saying that one part of the country must not be developed at the expense of the other. He also criticized the fact that only one-third of all development projects were allocated for East Pakistan.[188] The situation was worsened when Suhrawardy's cabinet decided to distribute $10 million of foreign aid in favour of East Pakistan in September–October 1957 and to establish the Public Shipping Corporation for Coastal Trade between East and West Pakistan. The West Pakistani businessmen approached the West Pakistan based president to redress the situation, and the president forced Suhrawardy and his cabinet to resign.[189]

Chundrigarh's predominantly West Pakistan based cabinet washed away the efforts to eliminate economic disparity between the two parts of Pakistan by reversing all the policies and decisions of Suhrawardy's cabinet. His commerce minister, Fazlur Rehman, while upholding cabinet's policy, assured West Pakistan's Chambers of Commerce that his government would keep politics away from economic affairs.[190] West Pakistani traders and businessmen were further assisted by Malik Firoz Khan Noon's government. The landlord ministers of his cabinet, including himself, were against giving more incentives to businessmen, but at the insistence of Finance Minister Syed Amjad Ali, some compensation was granted to businessmen on 20 February 1958, which included the lifting of price control on many commodities, excluding foodstuffs, cement, iron, steel, newsprint, and mechanically-propelled vehicles.[191] The control of cabinet by either West Pakistan or East Pakistan based prime ministers resulted in a dramatically different approach towards economic affairs. If cabinet was not an influential decision-making institution, different approaches could have not been introduced.

Trade activities were tightly controlled and closed in the early years of martial law. The stock market was a playground for a handful of people, supported by the economic institutions and the policymakers.[192] The cabinet's presence was as active in making trade policy as in other fields of the economy. All trade delegations travelling abroad needed clearance from the Ministry of Foreign Affairs.[193] Trading bodies for the import and export of all major items were established after receiving the approval of the cabinet. Ayub Khan had mentioned that this was his idea, but Commerce Minister Ghulam Faruque (March 1965–July 1967) took a long time to be convinced, so the idea was only approved by cabinet after a lengthy discussion.[194] The general perception that the military cabinet was only a 'rubber stamp' is not true: Ayub Khan consulted his ministers on important issues.

Cabinet provided incentives for exports through indirect subsidies, and industrialists were given permits to establish export industries.[195] The philosophy of the finance minister, who believed in encouraging exports, building up foreign exchange, and improving the balance of payment position, was reflected in the design of trade policy. An Export Bonus

Scheme also promoted exports, especially of manufactured goods.[196] Also, imports were liberalized except for that of luxury goods and of domestically-produced goods.[197] A free list of importable items was issued in 1964 which further relaxed the government's control and reduced the prices of many commodities.[198] The manufacturing industries, which depended on imported goods, flourished greatly in this period due to import liberalization. Foreign aid was a major factor in the increase of imports.[199]

Minister of Commerce Zulfikar Ali Bhutto, with the approval of the cabinet, took many initiatives to increase Pakistan's exports. These steps included regulations for government quality control on exports, the creation of export promotion centres and the introduction of Bonus Voucher Schemes.[200] The later Minister of Commerce Ghulam Faruque continued the trend of introducing new initiatives with the approval of the cabinet, including a study programme in Hong Kong to see 'how it developed its exports potentials'.[201] The cabinet reduced or eliminated export taxes on agricultural products after the introduction of the Third Five-Year Plan. Construction of some major roads was crucial in enhancing smooth internal and external trade. The Executive Committee of the NEC approved the scheme for the construction of the Karakorum Highway through the Indus Valley from Besham to Gilgit via Chilas at an estimated cost of Rs. 332 lakhs.[202] It was mainly constructed to facilitate trade between Pakistan and China. Exports were boosted because of the effective trade and business policies of the government. Its contribution to the GNP increased by 6 and 7 per cent in the Second and Third Plan periods respectively. It should be noted that there was no growth in the First Plan period.[203] Ministers' share, who were in control of economic ministries, was significant in this regard. They were always eager to work and introduce new policies.

The cabinet of Zulfikar Ali Bhutto introduced some drastic changes in import and export policy due to the loss of East Pakistan and structural changes in the economic system. The export bonus scheme and multiple exchange rate systems were abolished in May 1972 and the currency was devalued.[204] Mubashir Hasan abolished the licensing system.[205] Federal cabinet held frequent meetings over a few days in May 1972 to settle this single issue. Consensus could not be established as different opinions emerged, including Rs. 9.50 per dollar and Rs. 10 per dollar. Finally, the cabinet approved the devaluation of the Pakistani rupee to the exchange rate of Rs. 11 per dollar on 11 May.[206]

The leftists ministers wanted to bring trade in some major goods under government control. Cabinet, in its meeting held on 18 April 1972, decided that the import and export of pharmaceutical raw materials would be made only through the Pakistan Trading Corporation.[207] Contrary to the policies of Ayub Khan, import duties were raised. This put a constraint on industry-oriented imports. Incentives were provided to maximize exports, which was favourable for agriculturists who could export raw materials for better prices due to the devaluation of the currency in May 1972. After devaluation, Pakistan entered into a standby arrangement with the IMF for a loan of $100 million and imposed export duties.[208] Leftist cabinet ministers also gained approval for the nationalization of some aspects of trade in the second wave, including the nationalization of the purchase of cotton from the growers, the rice export trade, and, after some months, the cotton export trade was also nationalized.[209] Exports of manufactured goods showed poor performance, especially after 1974, largely due to exchange, trade, and industrial policies.[210]

The Economic Coordination Committee of the cabinet was responsible for the design and review of the import policies and their effects on production and investment. It was also responsible for evaluating export performance from time to time in relation to specific policies and measures for the promotion of exports.[211] Cabinet adopted an on-off policy after the exit of the leftist ministers. Cabinet did not have any formal guidance due to its mistrust of bureaucracy. For example, in August 1973 the government had announced that there would be no ban on the export of onions. Later, the ban was imposed. However, the ban was lifted in May 1974, which caused inflation. When the onion crop was ready for export, the ban was imposed again, prices went down, and investors suffered losses. This shows the absence of well thought-out policy and planning. It increased economic uncertainty because the government did not have a proper understanding of the economy, especially market activity.[212]

The reform measures of 1976 also had an impact on trade. They diminished the power of the *arthis* (brokers) who were blamed for taking profit from both consumers and farmers. Many *arthis* were medium-sized farmers or operated medium-sized industries. In place of the *arthis*, 4,000 officials were appointed by the government to perform the functions of the *arthis*. Most of them were inexperienced, inefficient, and sometimes corrupt. They had close feudal connections. The breakdown of the grain trade badly damaged the image of the government with three segments of society: consumers, farmers, and middlemen. This reform measure was not successful because of the lack of economic foresight. It left both feudal landlords and consumers dissatisfied.[213]

Table 2-C: Trade Pattern in Millions of Rupees, 1970–1977

Year	Exports	Imports	Balance
1970/71	1,998	3,602	−1,604
1971/72	3,371	3,495	−124
1972/73	8,551	8,398	153
1973/74	10,161	13,479	−3,318
1974/75	10,286	20,952	−10,666
1975/76	11,253	20,465	−9,212
1976/77	11,294	23,012	−11,718

Source: Government of Pakistan, *Pakistan Economic Survey, 1995–96,* Islamabad, 1996, cited in S. Akbar Zaidi, *Issues in Pakistan's Economy* (Karachi: Oxford University Press, 2009).

2.5. PERFORMANCE OF THE CABINET

During the first phase (1947–1958) of Pakistan's independent existence, the direction to Pakistan's economic growth was given by the urban professionals who dominated the cabinet. Shahid Javed Burki's belief that landlords or rural elites started sharing decision-making with urban elites after Liaquat's assassination in 1951 is not true. According to him, a third element in this regard was the bureaucracy.[214] Practically, landlords or rural elites could not occupy decision-making portfolios in the economic sector before 1957, at least at the federal level. No economic portfolio was entrusted to a landlord in the federal cabinet during this period.

The nature of the control of the economy was direct as the government did not trust businessmen.[215] Syed Akbar Zaidi's claim that the bureaucracy tried to keep Pakistan on its feet economically in the first decade[216] is again only partially true. In reality, the cabinet, with the help of the bureaucracy, did this as some bureaucrats who were part of the cabinet were representing cabinet rather than the bureaucracy. Both elements helped in planning the economic development in the first decade. All economic decisions were taken by the cabinet and its economic institutions rather than by the bureaucracy.

Federal cabinet's economic policies widened the economic gulf between East and West Pakistan. Cabinet came to the conclusion, after long discussions, that devaluation of the currency would be beneficial for agriculturists and rural people, and non-devaluation would be beneficial for fixed-income urban dwellers[217] and, of course, industrialists. Ayesha Jalal stressed the fact that the federal cabinet decided to import military supplies at lower rates and allow imports for West Pakistani industrialists.[218] This policy had negative implications for the Eastern Wing. The jute trade, which was closely tied to India, was stopped, and a recession occurred that worsened relations between the two wings.[219] This was followed by the devaluation of the currency in 1955. Minister of Finance Choudhury Muhammad Ali, in consultation with

Minister of Commerce Habib Ibrahim Rahimtoola, prepared the plan for devaluation which was criticized by ex-Minister of Commerce, Fazlul Huq.[220] Cabinet, following this decision, wanted to transfer its priority to the export of agricultural raw materials;[221] however, it benefitted the export of manufactured goods.

Almost all the prime ministers had some understanding of the importance of planning and that was the reason behind the establishment of several institutions and the introduction of Year Plans. Dobell's opinion seems to be wrong in light of the above analysis. They made mistakes as they and their cabinets had no experience in financial matters, but most of them made sincere efforts to stabilize Pakistan's economy. It is true that the last two governments attached low priority to economic development plans and were unable and unwilling to adopt the necessary policies for general economic development. Landlords were in the cabinets by then in comparatively prominent positions, but they were disinterested, or perhaps did not have sufficient time to introduce agricultural reforms; although the idea of the establishment of the Agriculture Commission, the first institution in the agriculture sector, was approved by the cabinet, due to the change of government it could not be established. The neglect of the agricultural sector for different reasons was largely responsible for the failure of the First Five-Year Plan.[222] Overall, 'despite some negative consequences of the economic policies pursued in the first decade by the governments, it would be fair to say that the early cabinets initiated an era of industrial growth and development which laid the foundation for the decade of development between the years 1958–68'.[223]

Ayub Khan's period is significant in Pakistani history from the point of view of economic development. It was a period of successful economic management; all policies were well-debated, well-planned and well-followed, though some failed.[224] Burki believes that Ayub was the sole decision-making authority in the economic policymaking and all other groups, including civil and military bureaucracies, landed aristocrats, big industrialists, and merchants, added to later by middle-sized farmers and small industrial producers, were only decision-influencers, not makers.[225] In Mohammad Waseem's opinion, the bureaucracy controlled policymaking and commercial fields and the decision-making was the preserve of the Planning Commission and the other economic institutions.[226] Zaidi points out that the bureaucrats defined policy.[227] This study reveals the fact that the economic policies of Ayub's government were not the creation of Ayub's mind only. No doubt he dominated affairs, but his ministers, Mohammad Shoaib and Z. A. Bhutto specifically, and others including Gen. Azam Khan, Gen. K. N. Sheikh, and Ghulam Faruque, generally played their part in making and implementing economic policies. Finance Minister Mohammad Shoaib was pro-America and had a continuing relationship with the Harvard Advisory Group (HAG), which remained in Pakistan throughout Ayub's period and performed an important role in creating and guiding the planning and economic institutions in Pakistan.[228] The high-level growth of his period was possible due to sharing his authority and power with his ministers, who were also economic planners.[229]

The situation changed considerably in 1966 after the exit of Mohammad Shoaib and Bhutto, who were symbolic of a balanced economic policy, with Mohammad Shoaib trying to get maximum financial support from the USA and the West, and Bhutto, who succeeded in getting aid from the USSR and later, China. The exit of these two and other urban professionals left room for the traditional landlords with their traditional economic ideology i.e. the status quo. From 1966 onwards, a downward trend in the economy was observed; one reason was the new social group of policymakers who were sitting in the cabinet. Burki's point that Ayub was a sole decision-maker is not true. If he had been the sole decision-maker, the exit of urban professionals from the cabinet would not have had such an impact on policy.

Ayub's cabinet and his economic institutions were well-knit and did not cause any controversy. The Planning Commission and State Bank recommended the devaluation of the currency, but the finance minister and other ministers opposed it. The ministers of industries and foreign affairs opposed devaluation on the grounds that it would destroy Pakistan's image and would be harmful for industry. Following the stance of the majority, the cabinet decided not to devalue the currency.[230]

Ayub's cabinet and his government followed the theory that 'a poor country anxious to develop be well advised not to worry too much about distribution of income'.[231] Dr Mahbub-ul-Haq held a similar opinion. He said: 'the underdeveloped countries must consciously accept a philosophy of growth and shelve for the distant future all ideas of equitable distribution and welfare state ... these are luxuries which only developed countries can afford.'[232] This ideology was reflected in the economic policies of Ayub's cabinet. All economic reforms resulted in enhancing inequality and disparity on two levels: between the classes, and between the two provinces, though overall production increased.[233] Industry and trade flourished a lot but it brought real benefits to the entrepreneurial class.[234] The Green Revolution swelled the income of the landlords,[235] but did not benefit the small farmers. Nor did land reforms change the situation significantly.

The real problem was that 70 per cent of the budget was spent on a West Pakistan-based defence system and a large share was spent on redeveloping the West Pakistan based Indus Basin System. As a result, East Pakistan was neglected. The blame is put again on the policymakers, including the cabinet ministers who were West Pakistan based. In mid-1961, three Bengali federal cabinet ministers, Minister of Commerce Mohammad Hafizur Rehman, Minister of Industries Abul Kasem Khan, and Minister of Law Mohammad Ibrahim, demanded, in a letter to the president, a separate economy for East Pakistan. They were not happy with the unjust attitude of West Pakistani policymakers in the cabinet and outside it.[236] East Pakistan, while supplying two-thirds of the country's foreign exchange earnings, had been allocated about one-third of the foreign exchange for imports. East Pakistanis were also unhappy when the East Pakistan Planning Board was abolished.[237] It is, however, important to note that

Balochistan territory in West Pakistan also did not enjoy the results of the Green Revolution and other economic reforms.[238]

West Pakistani members of the cabinet, including the president, claimed that they had done a lot to overcome disparity between the wings. The president told the cabinet that 'he had already taken a large number of steps to saddle East Pakistanis with important responsibilities so that they would come to know where the bottlenecks lay and how difficult it was to get anything done in a hurry.'[239] He could not understand many causes of the friction between the two wings. Ayub said in his foreword to the Third Five-Year Plan: 'It will be our firm policy, therefore, to prevent excessive concentration of income and wealth in the hands of a few.'[240] Finance Minister Abdul Qadir told journalists that 'no government has done so much for the people in East Pakistan as this regime.'[241] The disparity was inherited by Yahya's regime, which was unable to address many economic problems. The issue between East and West Pakistan had reached such a point that it ultimately caused the civil war in which the Eastern Wing gained its independence.

Besides disparity, the other negative element of development was its dependence on foreign aid. Policymakers believed that dependence on foreign aid was compulsory in the early stage of development and that almost all developed countries of the day had, in their early stages of development, depended on aid.[242] When the flow of aid dwindled, the policymakers were troubled because it was the main source of Pakistan's economic development. The cabinet discussed the issue in detail and looked into different ways of overcoming the crisis in its special meeting held on 15 July 1965 and decided that the Pakistani administration must seek internal resources to overcome the problem, and a serious effort must be made to obtain aid from sources other than the USA.[243] Despite serious efforts, the shortage of foreign aid could not be overcome.[244] This problem was also encountered by the succeeding regime.

Economic disparity in the country, decreasing foreign aid, heavy defence expenditure, and the fall in investment after the 1965 Indo-Pakistan War had put the country in a difficult situation. This was exacerbated by the absence of brilliant economists and policymakers Z. A. Bhutto and Mohammad Shoaib. Less sharp and less experienced economists took over who could not introduce effective policies to take Pakistan out of this crisis. New Finance Minister N. M. Uquailli, in the words of Ayub, 'was not brilliant but has a lot of industrial and banking experience and had sound common sense and is down to earth'.[245] He was submissive and followed instructions, unlike Mohammad Shoaib and Bhutto who were men of opinion and possessed the qualities to convince Ayub Khan.

The last year of Ayub's regime was crisis-oriented on the economic and political fronts. The food shortage was one cause of the crisis. Commerce Minister Abdul Ghafur Hoti, a sugar mill owner, earned the title of *Cheeni Chor* (sugar thief). He was forced to resign as he was not ready to do so willingly.[246] Ayub's cabinet, while he was bedridden with pneumonia, decided to celebrate Ayub's regime as a decade of development. This specific meeting was presided over by

Khawaja Shahabuddin.[247] The celebration of this decade had a negative impact as people were dissatisfied by inequality on a large scale. Ayub had to hand over the government to Yahya, but the new government was without any economic plan or defined policy. No economic problem could be overcome during this regime; not even the problems of rising prices,[248] economic disparity, decreased investment and foreign aid, etc. could be addressed properly.

The economic situation of the country was bad during Yahya's period and investment in the private sector plummeted. Production and exports declined by 8 per cent, imports declined and prices were under pressure. Foreign exchange reserves were below a satisfactory level and smuggling increased.[249] The civilian cabinet decided that the commerce ministry must introduce measures to improve private sector investment and also decided to lift the state of emergency. The cabinet further decided that Minister of Commerce Ahsan-ul-Huq, Minister of Finance Mozaffar Ali Qizilbash, and Minister of Planning Abdul Motaleb Malik should prepare an agreed-upon proposal.[250] On different occasions the civilian cabinet decided that exports must be increased by seeking new markets for rice and other agricultural products,[251] and to introduce a liberalized import policy,[252] but no steps were taken to implement these decisions.

The scattered and unplanned decisions of the cabinet could not be implemented due to persistent political uncertainty, the East Pakistan crisis, severe economic conflict between East and West Pakistan, increasing defence expenditure, and the inexperience and low level of interest of the military junta, which was the only decision-making authority during this period. The civilian cabinet of Yahya was powerless. Its decisions could not be implemented as the military-oriented kitchen cabinet that took control of affairs was not properly aware of economic planning, so no economic policy could be introduced during this period.

The economy was facing acute problems at the time of the transfer of power to Bhutto due to the 1971 war, the separation of East Pakistan, and the bad governance during Yahya's regime. Industrial production had declined, while agricultural production remained static. Global inflation impacted badly on the economy of Pakistan, which had inherited foreign debt worth $600 million.[253] The new cabinet had designed a complete programme of reforms on the basis of socializing the economy, minimizing inequality in society, and curbing 'the concentration of wealth'[254] in a few hands. It included increased wages, job security, an agenda for the rural economy, and social service packages including education, health, and housing.[255]

Most of the political scientists, biographers of Bhutto, and historians of Pakistan, including Burki, Saeed Shafqat, and Salman Taseer, have agreed that the role of the Leftist ministers in the formulation of economic policy and planning was significant;[256] the civil and military bureaucracies had no place in the decision-making. Louis D. Hayes added the opinion that Bhutto was more interested in international ventures and left the economic decision-making to the leftist members of his cabinet who had introduced policies and plans of development.[257] Anwar Syed's point of view is quite the opposite of these historians. He emphasized that it was Bhutto, not the leftist ministers, who took many important economic decisions such as nationalization.[258] This study seeks the reality which lies in the middle. Both the prime minister and his leftists ministers introduced mutually decided and agreed economic policies and plans at least up until October 1974, when the cabinet included Dr Mubashar Hasan, J. A. Rahim, Sheikh Muhammad Rashid, and Khursheed Hasan Meer. They all were firm and rigid socialists and headed important economic ministries. Finance Minister Mubashar Hassan, was more influential than the others. They all tried in their fields and capacities to fulfill the PPP's electoral promise of socialism.[259] Mubashir's plan to nationalize all industry was not approved due to the rightist elements in the cabinet.[260]

After the reformulation of the cabinet in 1974, landlords were again seated in the cabinet. Almost all economic ministries were given to rightist ministers. Rana Mohammad Hanif was appointed as minister of finance[261] in place of Mubashar Hasan. Rafi Raza[262] was appointed as minister of production in place of J. A. Rahim. Another rightist, Yusuf Khattak, was appointed as minister of fuel, power, and natural resources. Feroze Qaisar[263] was put in charge of the Ministry of Industry and was made a special advisor to the PM. Only one economic ministry, less influential, was given to a leftist minister, Sheikh Mohammad Rashid who was minister of agriculture. Now ministers were without any defined economic ideology.[264] Bhutto was largely guiding his cabinet to introduce economic measures or was more prominent in economic decision-making than his cabinet during the later years. His personality was far stronger[265] than those of his ministers.

Instead of following his socialist agenda, some grand projects of a political rather than an economic nature, were introduced during this period,[266] which included establishing a steel mill in Karachi, construction of a highway on the right bank of the Indus River, a nuclear power plant, and a sports complex in Islamabad. Such projects were very costly and as a result, other fields of the economy were neglected.[267]

The first and second series of nationalization measures were strategic due to left-wing ministers, but the motives and effects of the third phase were ad hoc responses to various situations.[268] 'His moves became governed more by the need for survival and re-election than systematic application of his avowed principles.'[269] Some economists believe that plans of the hard leftist ministers, especially of Mubashir Hasan, were the single most important reason for the failure of Bhutto's economic policies. The cabinet of Bhutto had no comprehensive strategy for economic development and the socialist ideology was also not well-developed. However, one important success of this period was that the economic policies decreased the concentration of wealth in a few hands.[270]

The other negative element of Bhutto's economic policy was its reliance on foreign assistance. Pakistan's foreign debt was $3.1 billion in December 1971 and rose to $6.3 billion in June 1977.[271] The USA maintained its influence on Pakistan's economy, especially through the IMF and the

World Bank after the exit of the leftist ministers from the cabinet. They, especially Mubashir Hasan, always resisted the policies initiated by the IMF and the World Bank, including the elimination of subsidies and increased prices of certain basic commodities and utilities. He always promoted the policy of 'improved terms of trade rather than aid'.[272] Policy was changed after the exit of the leftist ministers; no more subsidies were given and prices of commodities were also increased.

In a nutshell, the comparison of economic policy and planning of all the three phases (1947–1977) of Pakistan's history makes it abundantly clear that cabinets' role and contribution varied in the field of economic policymaking. The general perception that the civil and military bureaucracies, and sometimes landlords, dominated the decision-making in the economic field has been challenged in this study. The cabinet always remained an effective institution in this regard. It was dominated by urban professionals for most of the first phase and consequently, economic policies initiated by these cabinets favoured industry, business, and trade. Development was highly controlled. Agriculture was neglected during this phase. The policy of Ayub Khan's cabinets was relatively balanced between both urban and rural areas, so the economy witnessed growth in both sectors, but at the same time was unbalanced concerning the development of East and West Pakistan, which resulted in an increase in economic disparity between the two wings. Yahya Khan's military cabinet was least efficient in the introduction of formal economic policy and planning. His civil cabinet was not powerful enough to implement such a policy. Bhutto's period can be divided into two parts vis-à-vis economic policy: first the left-oriented cabinet which mostly consisted of urban professionals, and second, the rightist ministers, who were big landlords themselves. The presence of leftist ministers in the cabinet and their exit from it had a significant impact on the economic policy and planning of this era. The leftist ministers generally introduced urban-based economic policies and neglected agricultural development. Agriculture developed mostly after 1974 but industry could not flourish due to the nationalization policy. The economy had started showing good results in 1972–1973, but due to some factors[273] which were out of the cabinet's control, the growth level decreased. The economy was under the control of the landlords in the post-1974 era. As well as agriculture, they also controlled manufacturing industry and its trade. The dominance of one or other group in the cabinet had an impact on economic policy to a large extent. If the cabinet had not been playing its part in the economic policymaking, changes of membership within the cabinet could not have had an impact on economic policies.

Notes and References

1. Aftab Ahmad Khan, 'Economic Development' in *Pakistan in Perspective 1947–97,* ed. Rafi Raza (Karachi: Oxford University Press, 1997), 179.

2. W. M. Dobel, 'Ayub Khan as President of Pakistan', *Pacific Affairs* 42 (Autumn 1969), 297.

3. Mohammad Uzair, *Economy of Pakistan: Perspective and Problems* (Karachi: Royal Book Company, 2004), 2; L. F. Rushbrook

Williams, *The State of Pakistan* (London: Faber and Faber, 1962), 155; and Talbot, *Pakistan: A Modern History*, 178.

4. Cabinet mtg, 19 August 1948, 36/CF/48, NDC, Islamabad.
5. Statement of the Industrial Policy, Approved by the Cabinet, 27 March 1948, 213/CF/47.
6. Ibid. 24 July 1953, 144/CF/53-1 NDC, Islamabad.
7. It was responsible for co-ordinating development plans between the centre and the provinces, to make recommendations regarding priorities among development plans, and to keep watch on the progress of development schemes. Cabinet mtg, 27 March 1948, 213/CF/47, NDC, Islamabad.
8. Ibid. 179–80. Its functions were to advise the government on issues of planning, to review progress, and to educate the public regarding various schemes of development. This board prepared various schemes of development for the provinces. The cost of the projects was met by the loans and grants given by federal government to the provinces.
9. This institution was responsible for preparing a comprehensive development plan covering all aspects of national life. Cabinet approved accepting the services of foreign experts for the proposed board. Cabinet decision, 22 May 1953, 144/CF/53-1, NDC, Islamabad.
10. Zahid Hussain was Governor of the State Bank of Pakistan.
11. It invested in those areas in which the private sector was not taking an interest or was slow to move. Such sectors were fertilisers, sugar, cement, coal, irrigation, hydel projects and exploration and distribution of gas. Shahid Javed Burki, 'Politics of Economic Decision-making during the Bhutto Period' *Asian Survey* 14 (Dec. 1974), 1131; and Massarrat Abid, 'Chaudhary Mohammad Ali Ki Wizarat-i-Uzma Pur Aik Nazar,' *Journal of the Research Society of Pakistan* (April 1988), 86.
12. He was an ex-bureaucrat and a strong-willed, powerful individual who gained so much significance that he started criticizing Finance Minister Amjad Ali on 30 July 1957. Cabinet reacted and Ghulam Faruque was warned following a decision of the cabinet. It was decided that in future no division, department, or statutory

autonomous organizations like the PIDC should contradict cabinet or any other institution of the government, 31 July 1957, 335/CF/57, NDC, Islamabad.

13. Abid, 'Chaudhary Mohammad Ali', 86.

14. Aftab Ahmad Khan, 'Economic Development', 185; Talbot, *Pakistan: A Modern History*; Stephen Lewis, *Economic Policy and Industrial Growth in Pakistan* (London: George Allen and Unwin Ltd., 1970), 12; and Dobel, 'Ayub Khan as President', 297.

15. John Adams and Sabiha Iqbal, *Exports, Politics and Economic Development in Pakistan* (Lahore: Vanguard, 1986), 79.

16. Decision of the Governors' Conference, 23 to 26 October 1962, 121/CF/62_IV, NDC, Islamabad.

17. Governors' Conference, 25 May 1962, 359/CF/62, NDC, Islamabad.

18. Cabinet issued to the PIDC prohibiting it to make any future commitment in regard to capital expenditure without the prior approval of the government.

19. Cabinet mtg, 15 November 1958, 512/CF/58, NDC, Islamabad. The secretary general gave a briefing to the cabinet regarding this particular directive.

20. Cabinet mtg, 19 March 1959, 454/CF/58, NDC, Islamabad.

21. Ibid. Mtg of the Economic Coordination Committee of the Cabinet, 1 February 1966, 48/CF/66.

22. It was set up following the pattern of the National Economic Committee, initiated by Choudhury Muhammad Ali's government in 1956.

23. The Annual Plan of 1968–69 was prepared and approved by this council. For further information see details of the mtg of NEC 4 May 1968, 189/CF/68, NDC, Islamabad.

24. Viqar Ahmad and Rashid Amjad, *The Management of Pakistan's Economy 1947–82* (Karachi: OUP, 1984), 59.

25. Cabinet mtg, 23 April 1962, 121/CF/62-IV, NDC, Islamabad.

26. It was responsible for making recommendations for the distribution of revenue between the central and provincial governments and for removing the disparity between the provinces and different areas of the provinces. It was chaired by Finance Minister Mohammad

Shoaib and included the law minister, finance ministers from the provinces, the secretary of the ministry of finance, the economic advisor to the PC, and Professor Nurul Islam from Dhaka University. *Dawn*, 21 March 1964 and 136/CF/64.

27. It was responsible for coordination of foreign policy and the economic and commercial policies of the country. It was chaired by the secretary of the department of foreign affairs and included the secretaries of the ministries of finance, commerce, information and broadcasting, economic affairs, and defence, and the personal secretary to the president. The committee met once in a fortnight and briefed the president and ECC on all economic and foreign policy matters. Cabinet mtg, 22 June 1966, 229/CF/66, NDC, Islamabad.

28. Members of NEC, 7 May 1969, 201/CF/69, NDC, Islamabad.

29. Members of Economic Coordination Committee, 22 July 1969, 102/CF/69, NDC, Islamabad.

30. Mtg of ECC, 22 July 1969, 201/CF/69, NDC, Islamabad.

31. Decision of the Governors' Conference, 2 January 1972, 20/CF/72, NDC, Islamabad.

32. Charter of Economic Coordination Committee of the Cabinet, 17/CF/74, NDC, Islamabad. The details of the charter are given in this file.

33. Hasan, *The Mirage of Power*, 45. It decided that as well as national insurance companies, international insurance companies must also be nationalized, but cabinet did not endorse this plan.

34. He was appointed as deputy chairman after the dismissal of Qamar ul Islam. Burki, *State and Society*, 113.

35. Cabinet mtg, 27 May 1972, 369/CF/71/II, NDC, Islamabad.

36. Husain, *Elite Politics*, 151.

37. Viqar Ahmad, *The Management of Pakistan's Economy*, 58; and Parvez Hasan, *Pakistan's Economy at the Crossroads; Past Politics and Present Imperatives* (Karachi: Oxford University Press, 1998), 218. The Planning Commission was assigned new responsibility to prepare a document which defined short-, medium-, and long-range goals to achieve and introduce a socialist economy in the country. Hayes, *The Struggle for Legitimacy*, 237.

38. Ibid. 146 and Parvez, *Pakistan, Economy*, 228.
39. W. Eric Gustafson, 'Economic Problems of Pakistan under Bhutto', *Asian Survey 16* (April 1976), 367.
40. William, *The State of Pakistan*, 156.
41. It was introduced under the Colombo Plan, inaugurated in 1951 for member countries of the Commonwealth of Nations belonging to South and East Asia. Its purpose was to save these countries from communism. The plan was prepared without proper and reliable knowledge regarding the population nor its economic and financial magnitudes. Raza, *Pakistan in Perspective*, 183.
42. Stephen R. Lewis, Jr., *Economic Policy and Industrial Growth in Pakistan* (London: George Allen and Unwin Ltd., 1970), 10, Viqar Ahmad and Amjad Rashid, *The Management of Pakistan's Economy 1947–82* (Karachi: Oxford University Press, 1984), 56.
43. Ahmed, *The Management of Pakistan's Economy*, 56; Parvez Hasan, *Pakistan's Economy*, 133; Jalal, *The State of Martial Rule*, 241 and Arshad Zaman, 'Economic Strategies and Policies in Pakistan, 1947–1997', in *Pakistan: The Contours of State and Society*, ed. Sofia Mumtaz, Jean Luc Reine and Imran Anwar Ali (Karachi: Oxford University Press, 2002), 160.
44. Its size was revised from Rs. 11,500 million to Rs. 10,800 million. Its main objectives were to increase national income and exports by 15 per cent each, food-grain production by 9 per cent and to generate 2 million new jobs. Khawaja Amjad Saeed, *The Economy of Pakistan* (Karachi: Oxford University Press, 2007), 199.
45. Speech of Choudhury Muhammad Ali in the CAP 1955 in Ali, *The Task Before Us*, 39.
46. Hassan Said, *Pakistan: The Story Behind its Economic Development* (New York: Vantage Press, 1971), vii.
47. Viqar Ahmad, *The Management of Pakistan's Economy*, 50.
48. Aftab Ahmad Khan, 'Economic Development', 185.
49. Mtg of the ECC, 24 July 1959, 448/CF/59, NDC, Islamabad.
50. Special mtg of the cabinet, 29–30 December 1959, 448/CF/59, NDC, Islamabad.
51. Special mtg of the cabinet, 8 February 1960, 448/CF/59. The problems included (a) imbalance between wage and price levels

during the Second Plan period, (b) inefficient production and production under monopoly conditions, (c) financing the plan. The ECC decided that (a) the economic affairs division of the Ministry of Finance should undertake a detailed study in respect to measures needed to stabilize the wage and price levels during the Second Five-Year Plan period, (b) The minister of industries should, in consultation with the Planning Commission, prepare a detailed paper on measures needed to deal with inefficient production and production under monopoly conditions.

52. Khan, 'Economic Development', 186.
53. Ibid. and Parvez Hasan, *Pakistan's Economy*, 145.
54. Gilbert T. Brown, 'Pakistan's Economic Development After 1971', in *Pakistan the Long View*, ed. Lawrence Ziring, 173.
55. Mtg of NEC, 26 May 1966, 176/CF/65, NDC, Islamabad.
56. Viqar Ahmad, *The Management of Pakistan's Economy*, 57.
57. Khan, 'Economic Development', 187.
58. Mtg of the National Economic Council, 7 May 1969, 93/CF/69, NDC, Islamabad.
59. Pandav Nayak, *Pakistan: Political Economy of a Developing State* (New Delhi: Patriot Publishers, 1988), 114.
60. Ibid.
61. Working paper on the implementation of the Annual Development Plan 1973–74 in Balochistan, 221/CF/74, NDC, Islamabad.
62. Hasan, *Pakistan's Economy at the Crossroads*, 132.
63. Swadesh R. Bose, 'The Pakistan Economy since Independence (1947–70)', *The Cambridge Economic History of India Vol. II 1757–2003*, ed. Dharma Kumar (New Delhi: Oriental Longman, 2005), 1010.
64. Address of Liaquat to the first meeting of the Planning Board on the need for a master plan on 2 February 1949 in Ziauddin Ahmad, *Liaquat Ali Khan: Builder of Pakistan* (Karachi: Royal Book Company, 1990), 248.
65. Cabinet mtg, 12 December 1947, 213/CF/47, NDC, Islamabad.
66. Cabinet decision, 27 March 1948, 213/CF/47 and Omar Noman, *Pakistan: Political and Economic History Since 1941* (London: Kegan Paul International, 1980), 25. The Pakistan Industries Conference

was held from 13 to 17 December 1947 in Karachi to attract new investors. Its final plan and programme were approved by the cabinet in its meeting held on 12 December 1947. The representatives of provincial governments also attended the conference.

67. Cabinet mtg, 24 February 1949, 358/CF/48, NDC, Islamabad.

68. Bose, 'The Pakistan Economy', 1015.

69. From Fazlur Rehman, Minister of Industries, Education, Commerce and Works to Prime Minister Liaquat Ali Khan, 29 August 1949, 3(6) PMS/48, GOP, NDC, Islamabad.

70. Jalal, *The State of Martial Rule*, 249.

71. A. R. Kemal, 'Pattern and Growth of Pakistan's Industrial Sector' in *50 Years of Pakistan's Economy: Traditional Topics and Contemporary Concerns*, ed. Shahrukh Rafi Khan (Karachi: Oxford University Press, 2006), 151; and Hasan, *Pakistan's Economy at the Crossroads*, 126–7.

72. Jalal, *The State of Martial Rule*, 249–50.

73. Mtg of the Defence Committee of the Cabinet, 25 June 1958, 189/CF/58, NDC, Islamabad.

74. Cabinet mtg., 17 November 1953, 7/CF/53-11, NDC, Islamabad.

75. Stanley Kochanek, *Interest Groups and Development: Business and Politics in Pakistan* (Karachi: Oxford University Press, 1983), 76; and S. Akbar Zaidi, *Issues in Pakistan's Economy* (Karachi: Oxford University Press, 2009), 95.

76. Wasim, *Politics and the State in Pakistan*, 192 and Jalal, *The State of Martial Rule*, 249.

77. Abid, 'Choudhry Muhammad Ali', 73; and Bose, The Pakistan Economy', 1012.

78. Summary for the cabinet, prepared by Ministry of Finance, 427/CF/57, NDC, Islamabad.

79. Syed Mujawar Hussain Shah, *Sardar Abdur Rab Nishtar: A Political Biography* (Lahore: Qadiria Books, 1985), 180.

80. Zaidi, *Issues in Pakistan*, 96.

81. Gustav Papanek F, *Pakistan's Development: Social Goals and Private Incentives* (Harvard: The University Press, 1967), 154.

82. Cabinet mtg, 15 September 1954, 781/CF/54, NDC, Islamabad.

83. Summary prepared by the Ministry of Industries, New Industrial Policy, 529/CF/60 and From UKHC Karachi to CRO London, 19 December 1958, DO 35/8946 in Roedad Khan, The British Papers, 112.

84. Ibid.

85. Rashid Amjad, *Private Industrial Investment in Pakistan 1960–70* (Cambridge: Oxford University Press, 1984), 35; Viqar Ahmad, *The Management of Pakistan's Economy*, 85 and Mahbub ul Haq, *The Strategy of Economic Planning* (Karachi: Oxford University press, 1963), 50–1.

86. Bose, 'The Pakistan Economy', 1018.

87. Cabinet mtg, 19 November 1958, 512/CF/58, NDC, Islamabad.

88. Cabinet mtg, 1 November 1958, 592/CF/58, NDC, Islamabad.

89. Husain, *Pakistan: The Economy of an Elitist State,* 16.

90. Ibid. and Husain, *Pakistan: The Economy of an Elitist State,* 16.

91. Economic Survey of Pakistan 1961–62, in Shafqat, *Contemporary Issues in Pakistan*, 103.

92. Statement of Industrial Policy, Summary for cabinet, prepared by Ministry of Industries, Natural Resources and Works, 261/CF/63, NDC, Islamabad.

93. Cabinet mtg, 20 December 1965, 422/CF/65, NDC, Islamabad.

94. Cabinet mtg, 2 November 1966, 335/CF/66-II, NDC, Islamabad.

95. Cabinet mtg, 20 May 1960, 98/CF/60, NDC, Islamabad.

96. Mtg of ECC, 5 January 1961, 98/CF/60, NDC, Islamabad.

97. Minister of Finance, Mohammad Shoaib, told the ECC that a large number of countries in the world did not permit foreign firms and companies to employ foreign nationals in order to employ their own population.

98. Mtg of ECC, 16 March 1962, 130/CF/62, NDC, Islamabad.

99. Jalal, *The State of Martial,* 305.

100. Ishrat Husain, *Pakistan; The Economy of an Elitist State* (Karachi: Oxford University Press, 2002), 18; Choudhury Muhammad Ali also criticized the fact that industrial development during the Ayub period was largely due to foreign aid, in the inaugural address at a Symposium on Foreign Aid and its Impacts on Pakistan in Karachi University, February 1963, Choudhury Muhammad Ali, *The Task*

Before Us; Selected Speeches and Writings (Lahore: Research Society of Pakistan, 1974), 161.

101. Hasan, *The Mirage of Power*, 37.

102. Its output was not more than 12.8 per cent of the gross domestic product. Syed, *The Discourse and Politics*, 121; Talbot, *Pakistan: A Modern History*, 233.

103. Shafqat, *Civil-Military Relations*, 140–1; and Burki, *State and Society*, 115.

104. Ibid. 132. Later 10 basic nationalized industries were regrouped and reorganized into 10 corporations.

105. Hayes, *The Struggle for Legitimacy*, 238

106. Burki, *State and Society*, 117.

107. Syed, *The Discourse and Politics*, 122.

108. Prices of edible oil increased due to increased international oil prices, heavy floods, crop failure and shortage of consumer goods. *Pakistan Times*, 17 August 1973.

109. Burki, *State and Society*, 117. An similar account is given by Shafqat, *Civil Military Relations*, 142 and Syed, *The Discourse and Politics*, 121.

110. Rafi Raza, *Zulfiqar Ali Bhutto and Pakistan*, 284.

111. Ibid. 285.

112. Burki, *State and Society*, 159–61.

113. Parvez Hasan, *Pakistan's Economy*, 211.

114. Kemal, 'Pattern and Growth', 154.

115. Adams and Sabiha, *Export, Politics*, 30 and Waseem, *Politics and the State*, 308.

116. Hasan, *Pakistan's Economy*, 208 and Husain, *Pakistan: The Economy*, 92–3.

117. Cabinet mtg, 13 February 1976, 73/PROG/76.

118. Waseem, *Politics and the State*, 299.

119. Bhutto's government gave the message to foreign and internal investors in later years that the Bhutto government was neither anti-foreign investment nor anti-capitalist. This message from Bhutto did not help a lot for new investment. Laporte, *Power and Privilege*, 110.

120. Wali Khan, *Aasal Haqaiq Yei Hain*, 38.

121. Cabinet mtg, 22 January 1976, 18/PROG/75, NDC, Islamabad.

122. Papanek, *Pakistan's Development*, 145.

123. Cabinet mtg, 20 September 1957, 322/CF/57, NDC, Islamabad.

124. Cabinet mtg, 5 February 1958, 437/CF/57-1, NDC, Islamabad.

125. Cabinet mtg, 19 September 1956, 395/CF/56, NDC, Islamabad.

126. Jalal, *The State of Martial Rule*, 251. A similar view is given by Mohammad Waseem, *Politics and the State in Pakistan*, 192.

127. Ibid.

128. Cabinet decision, 3 June 1956, 203/CF/56, NDC, Islamabad. Almost the same decision was taken on 9 January 1957 in Cabinet mtg, 203/CF/58, NDC, Islamabad.

129. Ibid.

130. Ishrat Husain, *Pakistan; The Economy of an Elitist State*, 65.

131. Papanek, *Pakistan's Development*, 146 and Akmal Hussain, *Strategic Issues in Pakistan's Economic Policy* (Lahore: Progressive Publishers, 1988), 65.

132. For details see the Cabinet file 247/CF/50, NDC, Islamabad.

133. Bose, 'The Pakistan Economy', 1015.

134. Cabinet mtg, 8 July 1953, 144/CF/53-1, NDC, Islamabad.

135. Viqar Ahmad, *The Management of Pakistan's Economy*, 68.

136. Ibid.

137. Jalal, *The State of Martial Rule*, 258.

138. Ibid.

139. Ayub Khan, *Friends Not Masters*, 111.

140. Shahid Javed Burki, 'West Pakistan's Rural Works Program: A Study in Political and Administrative Response', *Middle East Journal* 23 (1969), 331.

141. Ayub Khan, *Friends Not Masters*, 111.

142. Cabinet mtg, 7 November 1958, 630/CF/58, NDC, Islamabad.

143. Burki, 'Politics of Economic Decision Making', 1132.

144. Governors' Conference, 14 and 16 January 1964, 9/CF/64, NDC, Islamabad.

145. Cabinet mtg, 23 April 1962, 121/CF/62-IV, NDC, Islamabad.

146. It approved a power pump irrigation scheme in East Pakistan at a cost of Rs. 529.20 lakhs. It was decided that the East Pakistan government should prepare a scheme for bringing additional land

under cultivation and raising a larger winter crop through power pump irrigation and mechanised cultivation. Mtg of the Executive Committee of the National Economic Council, 2 December 1964, 490/CF/64, NDC, Islamabad.

147. Bose, 'The Pakistan Economic', 1019.

148. Mtg of the Executive Committee of the National Economic Council, 21 October 1966, 437/CF/66, NDC, Islamabad.

149. Mtg of National Economic Council, 14 December 1966, 475/CF/66, NDC, Islamabad; Khan, 'Economic Development' in Raza, *Pakistan in Perspective*, 185 and Bose, 'The Pakistan Economy', 1017.

150. Cabinet mtg, 27 June 1968, 205/CF/68, NDC, Islamabad.

151. Governors' Conference, 1 February 1962, 116/CF/62, NDC, Islamabad.

152. Parvez Hasan, *Pakistan's Economy*, 167–9.

153. Viqar Ahmad, *The Management of Pakistan's Economy*, 88; and Husain, *Pakistan: The Economy*, 19.

154. Talbot, *Pakistan: A Modern History*, 230.

155. The major difference was that landlords were not given any compensation unlike under Ayub and the resumed land was divided amongst the peasants without any payment.

156. Bruce J. Esposito, 'The Politics of Agrarian Reform in Pakistan', *Asian Survey* 14 (May 1974), 433.

157. Ibid.

158. Raza, *Zulfiqar Ali Bhutto*, 149.

159. Secret working paper on the Law and Order Situation in West Pakistan: Prepared for Governors' Conference dated 21 March 1972, 128/CF/72-V.

160. Anwar H. Syed, 'The Pakistan People's Party; Phase One and Two', in *Pakistan: The Long View*, 113.

161. Ronald J. Herring, 'Zulfikar Ali Bhutto and the Eradication of Feudalism in Pakistan', *Comparative Studies in Society and History* 21 (October 1979), 554. A similar opinion is given by Mohammad Asghar Khan, *Generals in Politics, Pakistan 1958–1982* (New Delhi: Vikas Publishing House Pvt Ltd, 1983), 55.

162. Khalid Bin Sayeed, *Politics in Pakistan: The Nature and Direction of Change* (New York: Praeger, 1980), 923.

163. Waseem, *Politics and the State*, 303.

164. Cabinet was informed that the file concerned had been sent to the law division for legal procedure. Cabinet mtg, 4 August 1972 and mtg in May 1974. 228/CF/74, NDC, Islamabad.

165. Shafqat, *Civil-Military Relations*, 154.

166. Burki, *State and Society*, 155.

167. Gustafson, 'Economic Problems', 369.

168. Cabinet mtg, 20 November 1974, 444/CF/74 and Zirnig, *Pakistan in the Twentieth Century*, 403.

169. *National Assembly of Pakistan Debates*, Vol. II, No. 12, 6 February 1975 (*Karachi: The Manager, Printing Corporation of Pakistan Press, 1972*), 101.

170. Burki, *State and Society*, 158.

171. Cabinet mtg, 20 November 1974, 444//CF/74, NDC, Islamabad.

172. Kaushik, *Pakistan under Bhutto*, 236–37 and Aftab Ahmad Khan, 'Economic Development', 202. The GNP decreased from the envisaged growth of 10 per cent to 44 per cent. The average growth of GDP was 4.2 per cent.

173. *National Assembly of Pakistan Debates, Vol. II, No. II*, Sheikh Mohammad Rashid, Minister of Agriculture, starred question and answer, 4 February 1975, *27*.

174. Burki, *State and Society*, 156.

175. Ibid. 141.

176. Viqar Ahmad, *The Management of Pakistan's Economy*, 66 and Lewis, *Economic Policy and Industrial Growth in Pakistan*, 76.

177. Cabinet suggested an export policy for Pakistan after reviewing the international cotton position. Summary prepared for cabinet by Ministry of Commerce and Works on 'Cotton Export Policy 1949–50', 234/CF/49 NDC, Islamabad.

178. Policy has already been discussed under which import and export licences were given to firms which had a sound economic record. The import of consumer goods was permitted and the export of consumer goods was carried out on a large scale. The import of such items as were produced in the country was banned and the export

of such agricultural items as were required for domestic industry was very costly.

179. Sayeed, *Politics in Pakistan*, 58 and Burki, 'Politics of Economics', 113.

180. Lewis, *Economic Policy and Industrial Growth in Pakistan*, 10; and Kemal, 'Pattern and Growth of Pakistan', 151.

181. Cabinet mtg, 30 March 1955, 59/CF/55 NDC, Islamabad.

182. It expressed its concern about the unsatisfactory movement of cotton and jute exports and instructed the minister of commerce to look into the issue. Cabinet mtg, 30 March 1955, 59/CF/55 NDC, Islamabad.

183. Although the government alone was not responsible for it, as most private investors came from West Pakistan and foreign investors also started projects in West Pakistan, the whole blame was placed on the government. Furthermore, East Pakistanis were not interested in investment in industry as they found themselves unable to compete with West Pakistani industrialists. S. J. Burki, 'The Management of Crises', *Foundation of Pakistan's Political Economy: Towards an Agenda for the 1990s*, ed. W. E. James and Subroto Roy (New Delhi: np, 1993), 38.

184. Talukdar Muniruzaman, 'Group Interests in Pakistan Politics, 1947–1958', *Pacific Affairs* 39 (Spring-Summer 1966), 90; and Husain, *Elite Politics*, 118.

185. Ibid. and Afzal, *Pakistan: History and Politics*, 189.

186. It represented West Pakistani business interests. About 96 per cent of Muslim private industrialists and businessmen in West Pakistan were members. Its management committee was the most powerful pressure group in Pakistan.

187. *Dawn*, 27 June 1957.

188. From BHC Karachi to CRO London, 28 March 1962, DO 189/217, NA, London.

189. Muniruzaman, 'Group Interests', 91.

190. Ibid. and Jalal, *The State of Martial Rule*, 262.

191. Ibid.

192. Zaidi, *Issues in Pakistan's Economy*, 6.

193. Mtg of Economic Coordination Committee of the Cabinet, 21 May 1966, 195/CF/66, NDC, Islamabad.
194. 'Diary of Ayub', 26 January 1967, in Baxter, *Diaries of Ayub*, 54.
195. Cabinet mtg, 2 November 1966, 335/CF/66-II, NDC, Islamabad.
196. John Adams and Sabiha Iqbal, *Exports, Politics and Economic Development in Pakistan* (Lahore: Vanguard, 1987), 11; Kemal, 'Pattern and Growth', 151; William, *The State of Pakistan*, 190. As finance minister he successfully introduced many policies like treasury centre, decimal currency, etc., Viqar Ahmad, *The Management of Pakistan's Economy*, 249 Lewis, *Economic Policy and Industrial Growth in Pakistan*, 10.
197. Omar Noman, *Pakistan: Political and Economic History since 1947* (London: Kegan Paul International, 1988), 39.
198. Papanek, *Pakistan's Development*, 131–32.
199. Bose, 'The Pakistan Economy', 1017–18.
200. Kaushik, *Pakistan under Bhutto*, 76.
201. Cabinet mtg, 2 November 1966, 335/CF/66-II, NDC, Islamabad.
202. Mtg of the National Economic Council, 8–9 April 1963, 223/CF/63, NDC, Islamabad.
203. Amjad, *Private Industrial Investment*, 19.
204. Viqar Ahmad, *The Management of Pakistan's Economy*, 251.
205. Waseem, *Politics and the State*, 308; Brown, 'Pakistan's Economic Development', 176.
206. Hasan, *The Mirage of Power*, 183.
207. *Dawn*, 19 April 1972.
208. Hasan, *The Mirage of Power*, 184.
209. Gustafson, 'Economic Problems of Pakistan', 365.
210. Parvez Hasan, *Pakistan's Economy*, 204.
211. Charter of the ECCC, 17/CF/74, NDC, Islamabad.
212. Gustafson, 'Economic Problems', 378.
213. Adams and Iqbal, *Export, Politics*, 86 and Shafqat, *Civil Military Relations*, 154–5.
214. Ibid.
215. Papanek, *Pakistan's Development*, 142.
216. Zaidi, *Issues in Pakistan's Economy*, 5.

217. Cabinet mtg, 18 September 1949, 53 (b), Lord/49–50–1, GOP, NDC, Islamabad; Lewis *Economic Policy*, 13.

218. Jalal, *The State of Martial Rule*, 243.

219. Husain, *Pakistan: The Economy*, 88; Zaidi, *Issues in Pakistan's Economy*, 96; and Burki, 'The Management of Crises', 137.

220. Cabinet mtg, 2 August 1955, 222/CF/55, NDC, Islamabad.

221. Viqar Ahmad, *The Management of Pakistan's Economy*, 70.

222. Bose, 'The Pakistan Economy', 1016.

223. Zaidi, *Issues in Pakistan's Economy*, 97 and an almost identical opinion is given by Parvez Hasan, *Pakistan's Economy*, 136.

224. Hasan, *Pakistan's Economy at the Crossroads*, 182.

225. Burki, 'Politics of Economic Decision-Making', 1133.

226. Waseem, *Politics and the State in Pakistan*, 185.

227. Zaidi, Issues *in Pakistan's Economy*, 6.

228. From BHC in Pakistan to CRO London, 2 April 1964, DO 196/316 and Shafqat, *Contemporary Issues in Pakistan*, 100–1.

229. Parvez Hasan, *Pakistan's Economy*, 180.

230. Viqar Ahmad, *The Management of Pakistan's Economy*, 81.

231. Harry Johnson, *Money, Trade and Growth* (London: Allen and Unwin, 1962), 153.

232. Haq, *The Strategy of Economic Planning*, 30.

233. Pandav Nayak, *Pakistan: Political Economy*, 79.

234. The media wrongly publicised Dr Mehbub ul Haq's statement that 80% share of the wealth was with 22 families. His figures stated that 80% of industrial shares were in the control of 22 families, not of the whole economy, and industry's share in the economy was only 18% of GNP. Income inequality existed, but it was not so intense.

235. Nayak, *Pakistan: Political Economy*, 96.

236. Ibid.

237. Talbot, *Pakistan: A Modern History*, 169. The income inequality which emerged at the provincial level was not due to the policy-makers of Ayub's regime only. Public sector investment increased a great deal in East Pakistan. It increased by 128 per cent from the First to the Second Five-Year Plan period in East Pakistan, whereas it increased by only 55 per cent during the same period in West Pakistan. It increased by 150 per cent during the Third Plan Period

for East Pakistan, whereas it was 90 per cent for West Pakistan. Private entrepreneurs were offered a lot of incentives to invest in East Pakistan, but private sector investment decreased in East Pakistan. Jahan, *Pakistan: Failure in National*, 75–6, and Nayak, *Pakistan Political Economy*, 96, and from INR—Roger Hilsmen to NCA. Mr Talbot, Research Memorandum, 28 March 1962, Intelligence and Research, Department of State, DO 189/217.

238. Interview with Dr Abdul Hai Baluch (member of National Assembly from 1971 to 1977 on NAP's seat), Superintendent House, Hostel No 4, Punjab University, Lahore, 6th June 2012.

239. Mtg of Cabinet, 15 February 1962, 137/CF/62, NDC, Islamabad.

240. Government of Pakistan, Planning Commission, Third Five-Year Plan, 1965–70), cited in Lawrence J. White, *Industrial Concentration and Economic Power in Pakistan* (New Jersey: Princeton University Press, 1974), 43.

241. From UKHC to CRO, 9 February 1962, DO 189/217.

242. Mtg of the Executive Committee of the National Economic Council, 21 October 1966, 437/CF/66.

243. Special mtg of the Cabinet, 15 July 1965, 309/CF/65, NDC, Islamabad.

244. In the later years of the Ayub regime, American aid declined gradually from $380 million in 1963 to $282 million in 1968. Shafqat, *Contemporary Issues in Pakistan*, 107. For details see the books by John Adams and Sabiha Iqbal, Export, *Politics and Economic Development*, 8 and Mohammad Waseem, *Politics and the State in Pakistan*, 197.

245. Baxter, *Diaries of Ayub Khan*, 4 March 1967, 69–70.

246. Gauhar, *Ayub Khan*, 435.

247. Ziring, *Pakistan in the Twentieth Century*, 311 and Ziring, *Pakistan at the Crosscurrent of History*.

248. Yahya's cabinet advised the Ministry of Industries to submit monthly reports to cabinet indicating the price-trends of essential commodities, a forecast of their likely behaviour, and the remedial measures being undertaken to deal with the rising prices. The step could not be proved effective. Mtg held on 12 November 1969.

249. Cabinet mtg, 19 November 1969, 297/CF/69, NDC, Islamabad.

250. Ibid.

251. Mtg of ECC, 22 July 1969, 201/CF/69, NDC, Islamabad.

252. Cabinet mtg, 19 November 1969, 247/CF/69, NDC, Islamabad.

253. Nayak, *Pakistan Political Economy*, 114.

254. Shafqat, *Civil Military Relations*, 125.

255. Brown, 'Pakistan's Economic Development', 187.

256. Shafqat, *Civil Military*, 125, Burki, 'Economic' In Ziring, *Pakistan: The Long View*, 188 and Taseer, *Bhuto: Political Biography*, 168.

257. Louis D. Hayes, *The Struggle for Legitimacy in Pakistan* (Lahore: Vanguard, 1986), 237.

258. Anwar Syed, *The Discourse and Politics*, 125.

259. Shafqat, *Civil Military Relations*, 116,

260. Burki, *State and Society*, 115.

261. He was a mild-natured lawyer from Sahiwal, a city of medium-sized industry and without a powerful group of urban intelligentsia. Here owners and operators of small industries, merchants, shopkeepers, and farmers formed the influential group. These classes were happy with his appointment. Eric Gustafson claims that he was low-profile. W. Eric Gustafson, 'Economic Problems of Pakistan', 366.

262. He was a lawyer, a rightist, member of senate, not a politician.

263. He was a certified accountant from Karachi and rightist.

264. Gustafson, 'Economic Problems', 366.

265. Ziring, *Pakistan in the Twentieth Century*, 399.

266. Burki, *State and Society*, 146–7.

267. Ibid.

268. Omar, *Pakistan: A Political and Economic History*, 75.

269. Adams and Iqbal, *Export, Politics*, 77 and Omar, *Pakistan: A Political and Economic*, 75.

270. Ibid. 84.

271. Nayak, *Pakistan: Political Economy*, 120.

272. Raza, *Zulfiaqr Ali Bhutto and Pakistan*, 290.

273. Floods of 1973 and price increase of oil by oil-producing countries damaged Pakistan's economy.

CHAPTER 3

Centre-Province Relations: Political Issues

This chapter discusses the role played by the cabinet in handling some of the political issues originating in the provinces, and argues that cabinet's role was decisive in solving political matters in the provinces. Political issues in the provinces were given priority in the cabinet. Sometimes cabinet directed actions on the basis of majority opinion, while at other times, presidents and prime ministers played a decisive role. The major provincial problems which were brought under consideration by the federal cabinets included the language issue, mass movements including the anti-Ahmadiyya movement, anti-One Unit movement, student agitation, and the anti-Ayub movement, and issues of provincial administration including Balochistan's administration, the Six Points of Mujibur Rehman, the Agartala Conspiracy Case, Yahya Khan's mishandling of East Pakistan, and dealing with the NAP-JUI coalition in NWFP and Balochistan.

From 1947 to 1955 West Pakistan consisted of three provinces, namely Punjab, Sindh, and NWFP, six states, the Federally-Administered Tribal Areas, Balochistan territory, and a capital area, while East Pakistan consisted of only one province, East Bengal. West Pakistan was merged into one province in 1955, and Pakistan became a federation of two provinces only—West Pakistan and East Pakistan. The One Unit system was abolished in 1970 and four provinces were established in West Pakistan: Punjab, Sindh, NWFP, and Balochistan, and again only one province in the East. With the separation of East Pakistan in 1971, Pakistan was left with only the four provinces of former West Pakistan.

3.1. THE LANGUAGE ISSUE

3.1.1. NATIONAL LANGUAGE (BENGALI OR URDU)

Bengali was the language of almost 90 per cent of the population of East Bengal who constituted 56.5 per cent of the total population of Pakistan, whereas Urdu was the language of only 7 per cent of the population of Pakistan. However, Urdu was understood in almost all urban areas of Pakistan. Furthermore, it was closely associated with the Indian Muslim heritage and the Pakistan Movement.[1]

The people of East Bengal wanted the Bengali language to be the national language of Pakistan. It became a great source of tension between the centre and the provinces, since the Quaid-i-Azam, while on a visit to East Bengal, announced on 28 March 1948, that Urdu would be the national language of Pakistan.[2] The issue emerged again in January–February 1952 when students started a campaign to give national stature to the Bengali language. Strong public reaction came to the forefront when several student demonstrators were killed in the province. This time the language movement was widely spread among the masses of East Bengal as well as the students. The use of force by the provincial government resulted in further support for the language movement throughout the whole of the province.[3] The question of a national language was taken up by the cabinet in 1952. Governor of East Bengal Malik Firoz Khan Noon requested the centre to discuss the issue in the legislature. He wrote to the PM on 28 February 1952:

> ... this Bengali language question must be settled once for all, and I do not think that you can get out of it without accepting Bengali as one of the state languages, but it must be Bengali written in the Arabic script. The sooner this resolution is passed the sooner this controversy be settled.[4]

A cabinet meeting was held on 12 March 1952 to discuss the language issue. Nazimuddin suggested that the cabinet should plan a course of action on the language question before it was raised in the CAP and the legislature. If the question was raised, 'Government side must try to postpone it till April 1952'[5] when the CM of East Bengal would be there and a better line of action could be followed then. If the language question was raised by the opposition, the government should say that the Basic Principles Committee had already dealt with the question as well as other committees, and that the issue would be addressed in the constitution. The view was put forward that the unity of the country could be endangered by the question of language,[6] so a final decision should be delayed.

Unfortunately, the cabinet opted for delaying tactics while dealing with the question of the Bengali language. On 15 November 1953 it was decided that the appropriate time had not yet come to decide the national language issue because provincial elections were going to take place soon in East Bengal. A precarious situation might be created if the issue was raised, so it was thought best to discuss it after elections.[7] After a year's delay, the cabinet of PM Bogra decided, in a party meeting held on 19 April 1954, to announce the appointment of a committee to examine the question of the adoption of Bengali as the state language. The committee was comprised of PM Bogra, Finance Minister Choudhury Muhammad Ali, Nurul Amin, ML's leader from East Bengal, and Sardar Abdur Rab Nishtar, ML's leader from West Pakistan.[8] The issue of language was finally settled in the 1956 Constitution when Bengali was declared a state language along with Urdu.

3.1.2. Tensions in Sindh on the Language Issue

The second language controversy came to the surface in Sindh in 1972 after the separation of East Pakistan. As a result of the post-Partition migration in 1947, the *muhajir* (refugees) population had increased in Karachi, Hyderabad, and other urban areas of Sindh. Most of the industry and commerce was dominated by them, and Sindhis felt deprived. The Muhajirs claimed themselves to be superior in learning. The Sindhis demanded the replacement of Urdu by the Sindhi language at the provincial level so they could qualify as competent. Zulfikar Ali Bhutto had attracted Sindhis into his party by dealing with the Sindhi-Muhajir question before coming into power. He had announced that he would overcome the Sindhi-Muhajir divide, and declared that Muhajirs were 'capitalists' and 'exploiters'.[9] He was successful in acquiring the support of Sindhis but violent clashes broke out between Sindhis and the Muhajirs in March 1972 on the issue of language[10] which assumed an alarmingly militant aspect.

Sindhis burned Urdu newspapers in Larkana, Dadu, and Shikarpur. They also tried to spread the movement to rural areas. President Bhutto, expressing his opinion in a cabinet meeting, accepted that 'the law and order situation especially in Sindh was fast getting out of hand',[11] and that Khan Abdul Qayyum Khan, Minister of Home Affairs, must issue suitable instructions to the provincial government on the subject of the poor law and order situation. Further, he must direct the provincial government to 'exercise' the utmost vigilance and to deal with the situation firmly.[12] At the insistence of the cabinet, Law Minister Mian Mahmud Ali Kasuri presented the 27th Amendment to the Interim Constitution under which the provinces were given the right to introduce their respective provincial languages as compulsory subjects in educational institutions in addition to Urdu. While presenting the resolution he said:

> It would be extremely unfortunate if even now we did not learn a lesson from the loss that we have suffered due to this language issue in the past, and allow the dismemberment of the country on this issue. We recognize the fact that the national language of this country is Urdu. We want to promote the Provincial languages.[13]

Bhutto declared that both Sindhis and Muhajirs were Pakistanis and both must have justice.[14] This attempt of the federal cabinet was not successful and violence continued. The provincial assembly of Sindh approved the Language Bill on 7 July 1972 in which Sindhi was upgraded to be an official language within the province. Amendments presented by the Muhajir members of the assembly were not accepted by the Speaker of the Assembly. The Urdu-speaking community reacted violently on the issue.[15] Bhutto instructed Governor Rasul Bakhsh Talpur to postpone the signing of the Bill due to the violent clashes between the Muhajirs, Sindhis, members of *Jiye Sindh*, and *Sindhu Desh*.

The federal cabinet decided to form a cabinet committee consisting of four members including Hayat Mohammad Khan Sherpao, Minister of Fuel, Power and Natural Resources from NWFP, Malik Miraj Khalid, Governor of Punjab, Miraj Mohammad Khan, Minister of State for Public Affairs, an Urdu speaker, and Abdul Hafiz Pirzada, Minister of Law and Parliamentary Affairs, a Sindhi, to settle the issue. It invited Muhajir and Sindhi delegates for dialogue. The Muhajir delegation included I. H. Qureshi, Hussain Imam, Professor A. B. Haleem, Prof. Ghafoor Ahmad, and G. A. Madni, while the Sindhi delegation consisted of Shaikh Ayaz, a famous Sindhi poet, Qazi Faiz Mohammad, Ali Bakhsh Talpur, Mohammad Khan Soomro, and two ministers of the Sindh cabinet, Law Minister Qaim Ali Shah, and Education Minister Dur Mohammad Usto.

The first meeting was held on 10 July at which both delegations presented their demands to the committee. In the meetings of 13 and 14 July, Pirzada recommended that the governor of Sindh should sign the Language Bill, but Malik Miraj Khalid warned them about the possible bitter reaction in the Punjab, as Punjabis were also in favour of Urdu. Students in the Punjab held a demonstration in favour of Urdu on 15 July. The stand of the Punjab on the issue was alarming for Bhutto since it was a power base for the PPP. Bhutto announced a compromise on the recommendation of the cabinet committee that Sindhi would be the official language and Urdu would be the national language[16] and that no person would be discriminated against for appointment or promotion for the next twelve years, 'on grounds of want of knowledge of Sindhi or Urdu'.[17]

The law and order situation was restored in Sindh after this decision. The cabinet of Z. A. Bhutto did not linger on the problem but settled it on a priority basis, unlike the earlier cabinets of Pakistan who had delayed reaching an acceptable decision on the Bengali-Urdu controversy.

3.2. MASS MOVEMENTS

Cabinets played a decisive role in dealing with the mass movements raised in different provinces of Pakistan during various regimes, except during the coalition cabinet's era (1956–1958) and during Yahya Khan's martial law regime (1969–1970). The cabinet of Khawaja Nazimuddin held several meetings to deal with the anti-Ahmadiyya movement raised in 1953. Ayub Khan's cabinets had to deal with many mass movements including student agitation, the anti-One Unit movement, and the anti-Ayub movement.

3.2.1. ANTI-AHMADIYYA MOVEMENT

The problem, which later became the Punjabi-Bengali tussle, was the 'anti-Ahmadiyya Movement' in the Punjab. The problem started due to the shortage of wheat in Pakistan. Daultana, the CM of Punjab, gave the federal cabinet a hard time by not following its decisions. The government was trying to obtain a loan from the USA to buy wheat. The cabinet was informed by Abdus Sattar Pirzada, Minister of Food and Agriculture, on 16 May 1953 that Daultana had been issuing statements to say that wheat was 'flooding'[18] Punjab markets, which had been creating trouble for the federal government. Nazimuddin and other ministers criticized these statements of Punjab's CM which, in their view, were weakening Pakistan's case for a wheat loan from the USA. Abdus Sattar Pirzada told the cabinet that instructions had been delivered to the secretary of the Ministry of Food to explain the whole situation to the CM of Punjab and to ask him to refrain from issuing such statements.[19]

Some historians have suggested that Nazimuddin's cabinet was in a state of indecision regarding the anti-Ahmadiyya Movement,[20] which seems incorrect. The cabinet of Nazimuddin was neither a silent spectator nor in a state of indecision. Many cabinet meetings were held exclusively to discuss the question of dealing with the anti-Ahmadiyya movement.[21] The *Khatam-e-Nabuwat* party[22] threatened to start direct action from 23 February 1953. The PM and Minister of Industries Sardar Abdur Rab Nishtar met the leadership of the *Khatam-e-Nabuwat* party on 20 February to settle the issue peacefully. Nazimuddin suggested seeking the *ijma* (consensus) of the ulama from the Muslim countries to decide whether *qadianis* were Muslims or non-Muslims.[23] It was a positive suggestion and if the ulama of Pakistan accepted it, the situation could be controlled at an early stage.

Cabinet agreed in its meeting held on 25 February that the question of declaring Ahmadis as non-Muslims should be decided by the CAP and not by the government, and that the issue should be presented in the CAP. It further decided that the governors and CMs of Punjab, Sindh, and NWFP, chief secretaries, and inspectors general of police must be invited to the special cabinet meeting to be held on 26 February 1953, at which the course of action to tackle the anti-Ahmadiyya movement was to be decided after further discussion.[24]

Cabinet decided to issue a press communiqué, and provincial governments were also informed officially about the central government's course of action. It stated that neither Ahmadis nor any other community could be declared as a minority against their will.[25] Secondly, Ahmadis could not be removed from key posts solely on the grounds that they were Ahmadis. Nor could the demand for the removal of Foreign Minister Mohammad Zafrullah Khan be entertained on the grounds that he was an Ahmadi. Cabinet decided:

> There was constitutional machinery provided for the removal of any Minister from office. So long as he continued to enjoy the confidence of his colleagues and the elective representatives of the people in the Central Legislature, he could not be removed from his office. No one could be removed on the basis of religion.[26]

The question of army action to deal with the issue was also decided by the cabinet. Ayesha Jalal says that after failing to get sanction from the federal government, on 6 March 1953 the area commander, General Azam Khan, had taken the decision to impose martial law in Lahore entirely on his own.[27] The study of the cabinet files has brought to light the fact that it was the cabinet, and not General Azam, who decided that direct action by the *Ahrars* must be dealt with firmly and the army could be used for the purpose. Further, that the leaders of the movement must be arrested.[28] The cabinet had directed Defence Secretary Iskandar Mirza on 6 March 1953 to issue instructions regarding the proclamation of martial law in Lahore. The following telegram was authorized to be issued at once to the C-in-C of the Pakistan Army:

> The Punjab Government has intimated their inability to control situation in Lahore. General Azam has been directed to take over in Lahore and declare Martial Law ... It is possible that Army may have to take over other towns and districts in the Punjab and you will prepare a complete plan to meet the situation.[29]

The minutes of the cabinet meeting are evidence of the fact that the decision was taken by the cabinet itself and not by General Azam.[30] In line with the decision of the cabinet, the people were informed through the media that the anti-Ahmadiyya movement was basically political and was supported by a few ulama only and the majority were against it. The following telegram was also issued to the district magistrates by the cabinet:

You must now use all your resources and use whatever force may be necessary to put down lawlessness wherever it takes place. Law and order must be fully restored and maintained. Where army help is required the fullest cooperation should be extended ...[31]

Cabinet also decided that authority in Punjab should be directed immediately to intercept the Punjab *jatha* (group of people) and prevent them from entering the NWFP, and instructions were issued to the frontier government to prevent the infiltration of the volunteers into the tribal areas.[32] Evidently the federal cabinet was not a silent spectator, but was busy sorting out the problems. The accusation of not taking timely action against the anti-Ahmadiyya movement is based on misinterpretation and therefore the conclusion that Nazimuddin's dismissal was on this ground is incorrect. It came to the surface later that the agitation was supported by the Punjab government who gave large subsidies to 'the Press from the Government's secret fund to promote the cause'.[33] The cabinet of Bogra decided later that the PM must tell the CAP in the upcoming budget session that it was purely a political movement and the actions taken by the central government had the approval and confidence of the provincial governments.[34]

Though the cabinet of Khawaja Nazimuddin worked vigorously to solve the poor law and order situation in Punjab, his cabinet did not want to take the decision of declaring Ahmadis as non-Muslims. Order was restored with the help of the military, at the invitation of the cabinet.

3.2.2. STUDENT AGITATION

The way of dealing with provincial political matters during Ayub Khan's period was different and more organized than during the early parliamentary phase. Besides cabinet, a new forum, the Governors' Conference, was introduced where governors of the provinces and some provincial ministers were invited to take part in discussions with the president and the cabinet ministers. In this way, the provinces remained in direct and continuous contact with the cabinet, and cabinet was in a position to play an active role in decision-making concerning provincial political matters. In the early years of Ayub's martial law, political calm was observed in both provinces of Pakistan. Akhtar Hussain, a retired civil servant, was appointed governor of West Pakistan who remained in office till 1960. The province enjoyed peace apart from some student disturbances and occasional rumbles of trouble in Balochistan and the Frontier areas. Law and order was maintained by the next governor of West Pakistan, the Nawab of Kalabagh Amir Mohammad Khan, who turned West Pakistan into a strong base for Ayub's regime.[35]

However, students were dissatisfied and reacted to the educational reforms introduced by the government. They demonstrated against them in both provinces. This later became a political issue due to the interference of AL and some other political parties of East Pakistan. Cabinet took action against the student agitation that took place in Karachi in 1961. President Ayub asked the governor of West Pakistan, Nawab Amir Mohammad Khan, to stay in Karachi for a few days to maintain law and order.[36] Ayub instructed

Amir Mohammad Khan to run the administration of Karachi University through the civil servants and to change the principals of the troubled colleges.[37] Besides this, he received much more advice through the forum of the Governors' Conference, including separation of part-time students and teachers from the regular ones, reorganization of the management committees, and the involvement of parents to reform the behaviour of their children. He was finally asked to seek help from the secretary of the Ministry of Education and Scientific Research to implement the plan given to him by the federal cabinet.[38] He did not encounter any problem in overcoming the trouble in Karachi.

The student agitation which erupted in East Pakistan in February 1962 was far more serious and deep-rooted than that seen in West Pakistan, and had the support of AL. Many student demonstrations were held in Dhaka, Barisal, Kushtia, Chittagong, Sylhet, Khulna, and Naokhali in February 1962. A special meeting of the cabinet was convened on 15 February 1962 to discuss the issue. Governor of East Pakistan, General Azam Khan was also invited to the meeting. Ayub Khan stated in his introductory remarks that the East Pakistan disturbances should be studied with two objectives in view: firstly restoring normalcy, and secondly, seeking ways for a permanent solution to the problem. General Azam Khan briefly informed the cabinet that the provincial government was in complete control of the situation and action against disruptive students had been taken under the Safety Acts. He further informed them that the provincial government was prosecuting individuals for specific offences.[39] Besides those strict measures, some attempts at conciliation had been made. The government had permitted students to construct 'Shaheed Minar' (Martyr's Tomb) in honour of those who were killed during the language movement of 1952. This had an impact on the politics of the province, the people, and the students.

After listening to this brief, the president asked the ministers to express their opinions on different points. Minister of Fuel and Natural Resources Bhutto was of the opinion that students liked spectacular things and the government should deal with them as the situation demanded. But firm action should be taken if any attempt was made to disrupt law and order.[40] Manzur Qadir said that although he 'had nothing to say against the decision of the Government regarding the construction of Shaheed Minar, he wanted the Government of East Pakistan to bear in mind the point that this action may imply confirmation and ratification of the method that was used during those disturbances'.[41] Lt Gen. K. M. Sheikh, Minister of Home Affairs agreed with Manzur Qadir and said that permission should not be given for the construction of Shaheed Minar. Abul Kasem Khan, minister of Industries, expressed the opinion that there was no immediate necessity for taking over AL's newspaper, Ittefaq.[42] Lt Gen. K. N. Sheikh and the director of the Intelligence Bureau disagreed with Abul Kasem and were of the view that the pro-Suhrawardy, AL newspaper Ittefaq must be banned. Z. A. Bhutto added that Suhrawardy must also be arrested on the grounds that he was organizing a united front all over Pakistan against the government, and that he was misleading the people, and any delay in taking action against him would bring about a far more serious situation after the promulgation of the constitution. Mohammad Shoaib, Minister of Finance, said that Suhrawardy's arrest would create disturbances, so it must be avoided at least till the promulgation of the constitution.

While keeping in view the majority's opinion, the president said, 'Suhrawardy's arrest was a realistic step as he was poisoning the relations between the two wings ... the great harm was being done at the present moment by politically-minded mullahs. The provincial governments should have the lists of such political mullahs, particularly those amongst Jamat-i-Islami for possible action.'[43] Cabinet's decisions included the immediate arrest of Suhrawardy, and action against political mullahs, and *Ittefaq*.[44]

The provincial government tried to implement the orders of the cabinet but it failed to control the students. In May, Governor of East Pakistan, Azam Khan, widely respected and appreciated by East Pakistanis, was replaced by Ghulam Faruque.[45] He remained governor of East Pakistan for only five months. During his tenure, students agitated against the three years' BA degree programme and the government had to surrender to the students' demands. The federal government was of the view that India and anti-Pakistan elements were behind the student agitation.[46] This point of view was adopted on the basis of intelligence reports. The government decided to take strong action against such elements. The president proposed to initiate a campaign against such elements to create awareness among the public, so they could distance themselves from the movement.[47] The introduction at university level of many healthy activities like sports, debates, etc. was proposed. The Governors' Conference decided to move university campuses out of the cities; it was also decided not to invite students to official functions, and all activity of the Arts Council and student-related organizations should be carefully watched. Furthermore, all government officials, politicians, and journalists who were trying to instigate student unrest must be strictly dealt with, powerful decision-makers must be appointed as heads of educational institutions, and students who were creating trouble must be removed from these institutions.[48]

Along with this, a conciliatory policy was adopted towards students while releasing and pardoning all arrested students one month before the introduction of the 1962 Constitution. The government appealed to the students to stay out of politics.[49] Abdul Monem Khan was appointed governor of East Pakistan in October 1962 and served till March 1969. During this whole period, 'he faithfully pursued the policies and interests of General Ayub'.[50] Federal cabinet's policy regarding students had been successful in resolving the crisis.

3.2.3. THE ANTI-ONE UNIT[51] MOVEMENT

Smaller provinces' leaders, especially Baloch leaders, were unhappy, even violent, on the introduction of One Unit in West Pakistan. Many organizations demanded the formation of a unified Balochistan. Widespread demonstrations were mobilized by the Khan of Kalat specifically, and by the other leaders generally, to dismember One Unit.[52] The Khan of Kalat was arrested on 6 October 1958, due to his anti-One Unit movement, in an army operation in Kalat.[53] The study of the declassified cabinet record has proved that coalition cabinets (1955–1958) had not discussed the anti-One Unit movement in Balochistan, and the other demands of the Balochis had also not been discussed, perhaps because of the rapid changes of governments and cabinets.

With the lifting of martial law in 1962, opposition forces in West Pakistan gradually emerged on the political scene. The centre of opposition was the issue of the formation of One Unit in West Pakistan.[54] Almost all previous provinces of West Pakistan raised opposition against One Unit. The opposition was stronger in Balochistan than in the other areas. The opposition leaders included Mir Bagi Baluch, Malik Ghulam Jilani, Hyder Bakhsh Jatoi, Ghaus Bakhsh Bizenjo, Ataullah Khan Mengal, and Abdus Samad Khan Achakzai. They suffered in pursuit of their objective.[55] The unrest in Balochistan was successfully concealed from the outside world. It was very difficult to get news as the troubled areas were inaccessible for a long time. The troubled areas were those of the Marris, Bugtis, and Mengals. Troops were often used in much the same way as they had been used under British rule.[56]

In Sindh, Karachi was most active in the anti-One Unit demonstrations. It was as late as 1967 that Ayub realized that the anti-One Unit movement had become too strong and something should be done about it as national unity was in danger. Sindhis, Balochs, and Pathans continuously opposed One Unit because West Pakistan was dominated by the Punjab. They blamed the Punjab for the socio-economic backwardness of their areas. They argued that the greater part of development funds went to the Punjab and that their own problems and needs received little sympathy.[57] Ayub's cabinet decided that the anti-One Unit movement must be resisted with force. In a few cases some concessions, such as a grant of land, were also given to stop resistance against the One Unit.[58] Cabinet decided at a later stage, in 1968, to include some well-written articles on the benefits of the One Unit scheme in the textbooks for schools and colleges to educate the younger generation, and to curb the tendency for regionalism.[59] The other feature related to the anti-One Unit movement was the political murders whose perpetrators had never been arrested. All this gradually led to unrest among the masses of West Pakistan.

The major issue in West Pakistan during Yahya's period was again the dissolution of the One Unit. His advisors prioritized the break-up of One Unit. According to them, the other constitutional issues could be addressed only after the abolition of One Unit. Following this advice, the Ordinance for the Dissolution of West Pakistan Province was issued on 30 March 1970, and West Pakistan province was divided into four provinces, the Tribal Areas, and the Capital Area.[60] In this way the aim of the anti-One Unit movement was successfully achieved.

3.2.4. THE ANTI-AYUB MOVEMENT

The anti-Ayub movement was the most successful movement of its time as it gained momentum and then a positive result very quickly. West Pakistan first showed organized resentment to the Ayub regime over the Tashkent Agreement,[61] signed by the regime with India. The opposition political parties, including the Nizam-i-Islam Party (NIP) of Choudhary Mohammad Ali, the Council Muslim League (CML) of Shaukat Hayat Khan, and Jamat-i-Islami of Maulana Maududi voiced considerable criticism as it was believed that Pakistan's position on Kashmir was weakened by the Tashkent Agreement. On the orders of the federal government, activists against the agreement, including Sardar Shaukat Hayat Khan, Inayatullah, and Sardar Mohammad Zafrullah Khan of CML, Nawabzada Nasrullah Khan, president of the All Pakistan Muslim League (APML), and Malik Ghulam Jilani and Khawaja Mohammad Rafique of the Awami League of West Pakistan were arrested. They were released almost a year later, when the government realized that the Tashkent issue was no longer alive.[62]

Ayub Khan faced the greatest trouble of his era in West as well as in East Pakistan in 1968–69. The central and provincial governments were left in no position to contain the masses. The political parties exploited the situation and a mass movement was organized against the regime of General Ayub Khan. Opposition parties in West Pakistan including CMLA, AL, NIP, JIP, and the National Democratic Front (NDF) established the Democratic Action Committee.[63] The general strife reached such an extent by October 1968, that the civil authorities had to use force to control rowdyism and lawlessness in a number of towns. Incidents of firing on mobs had taken place in Rawalpindi, Nowshera, Dhaka, and Chittagong. Prominent among the troublemakers had been political leaders from all opposition political parties, students, lawyers, ulamas, and journalists.[64]

Cabinet reached the conclusion, in its meeting held on 13 November 1968, that some of the grievances of the students and labourers, such as the non-availability of text books, debarring of third-divisioners from higher education, outdated teaching methods, and the low wages of labourers were genuine problems and the opposition parties were only trying to cash in on the situation.[65] It was because of this situation that 'Bhutto had a measure of appeal among the youth and he planned to cash in on that'.[66] The cabinet decided that the genuine problems of the students should be addressed. A committee under the chairmanship of Home Minister Chaudhry Ali Akbar Khan with representation of the provincial governments and the central education ministry and other concerned agencies should quickly consider the various problems and make their recommendations. Another committee, under the chairmanship of the Planning Commission was set up to consider the question of labour and wages and devise an effective machinery to enforce payment of reasonable wages.[67] The cabinet prioritized the early finalization of the recommendations regarding the students' problems, to be announced in the president's first of the month speech in December.[68]

The Economic Coordination Committee of the cabinet was advised by the cabinet to periodically review the availability and prices of all essential commodities. The cabinet further decided that the ruling political party must be more organized at the district and local levels. The cabinet, in its meeting on 26 November 1968, discussed the political strategy of Z. A. Bhutto, the Awami League, NAP, and finally the entrance of Asghar Khan into politics, and decided that the leaders of CML[69] must address the students, labourers, and mass gatherings on a local level, but no action was taken on this point.[70] The Governors' Conference again emphasized, in its meeting held on 12 December 1968, that PML leaders, ministers and governors must be active enough to deliver speeches to access the performance of the regime and they must support the local security agencies to control the masses and to maintain law and order.[71]

Ministers in the cabinet meeting presented different suggestions to deal with the political crisis. S. M. Zafar recommended an all parties conference. The government delegation was represented by Zafar himself, but it failed due to the boycott by Maulana Bhashani, NAP, and Asghar Khan's Tehrik-i-Istaqlal.[72] His cabinet discussed the law and order situation in East as well as in West Pakistan on several occasions and Ayub was always worried by the crippling situation. Manzur Qadir suggested on 20 March 1969 Ayub should address the nation, but he replied, 'time for addressing was gone away'.[73] Some remedial measures were taken by his cabinet, such as the removal of the State of Emergency in February 1969,[74] but to no avail. The Cabinet Committee on the Current Political Situation, comprised of Khawaja Shahabuddin, Syed Muhammad Zafar, Qazi Anwarul Haq, and Vice Admiral A. R. Khan, was assigned the duty of preparing a report on how to overcome the crisis in the country. It suggested increasing material benefits for low-paid employees.[75]

The government had to call the army into the big cities of both provinces. Agitation reached such a level that Ayub had to discuss the issue of the imposition of martial law in a cabinet meeting held on 23 February 1969. In line with cabinet's decision, a cabinet committee was formed to look into the details of the law and order situation and to report the results by the next day.[76] C-in-C of the forces Yahya Khan, who was also present in the meeting, said that martial law was essential.[77] It was finally decided on 20 March 1969, after holding many cabinet meetings, that martial law would be imposed in the country.[78]

In this way, the masses of Pakistan succeeded in ridding themselves of one military ruler, but unfortunately power was transferred to another military commander.

3.3. ISSUES OF PROVINCIAL ADMINISTRATION/ CENTRE'S INTERFERENCE IN PROVINCIAL MATTERS

This section proposes that the federal cabinet remained an important part of decision-making on issues of provincial administration. The issues which attracted the most attention of the federal cabinet were the case of Balochistan's administration, the unification of West Pakistan, the Six Points of Mujibur Rehman, the Agartala Conspiracy Case, and the NAP/JUI coalition in NWFP and Balochistan.

3.3.1. THE QUESTION OF BALOCHISTAN'S ADMINISTRATION

During the British colonial rule, Balochistan was administered by an agent of the Governor General and the chief commissioner, unlike the other provinces where representative governments were established under the governors. At the time of independence, Balochistan consisted of the British-administered territories, a vast area under the control of tribal sardars (heads), and four princely states: Kalat, Kharan, Las Bela, and Makran. The question of bringing Balochistan on a par with the other provinces was a very important one to be settled. Cabinets in the early period tried to solve this problem. Ayesha Jalal says that early prime ministers were overworked and did not have time to look into the issue relating to the upgrading of the status of Balochistan.[79] This is only partially true, as cabinets in early years spent long hours considering matters related to Balochistan.

Quaid-i-Azam Muhammad Ali Jinnah paid special attention to Balochistan. He suggested that Balochistan must be governed by an advisory committee which would be answerable to the Governor General. Such a committee would work only in the chief commissioner's part of the province, not in the tribal areas where agents to the Governor General (AGG) were responsible for carrying out duties.[80] The Quaid-i-Azam's suggestion was taken up by the cabinet of Liaquat after his death. Liaquat suggested that the mere establishment of an advisory council would not be welcomed by the people, so along with it, two advisors to the AGG should also be appointed from among the members of the advisory council to look after education, health, agriculture, roads, and veterinary services. AGG Balochistan and Sardar Abdur Rab Nishtar, Minister for Communications, said that such a step would be welcomed by the people. The PM told the cabinet that he had already instructed the AGG Balochistan to take steps for holding elections to local bodies throughout Balochistan on the widest possible franchise, besides the introduction of the advisory council.[81] Criticism was raised in cabinet about this scheme, that it was similar to the 1919 system of diarchy, which was widely criticized by the people of the subcontinent. On the basis of this criticism, the states of Balochistan were excluded from the scheme. The system of the advisory council and the appointment of two advisors to the AGG was approved in principle by the cabinet on 18 February 1948.[82]

The advisory council consisted of fifteen members, five of whom belonged to Quetta municipality, five members were to be elected at the government's discretion to represent the minorities, Balochistan States, and other interests, and five were tribal sardars. The Governor General nominated all members and a special agent who kept 'watch and word over its activities'.[83] As regards the rules, provision had been made for a minimum of four meetings a year, but it could meet more frequently. The AGG was bound to report the views of the council's meetings to the Governor General.

In practice, only urban areas like Quetta, Sibi, and the areas along the railway lines were under the direct control of the federal government. All other areas were administered by the tribal chiefs and the government exercised control over such areas through political agents.[84] Liaquat wanted the tribal region, states, and chief commissioner's territory to be merged into one, but implementation of this scheme was difficult.[85] However, the notification regarding the formation of the advisory council was issued by the Governor General after approval from a cabinet committee consisting of Liaquat Ali Khan, Mohammad Zafrullah Khan, and Sardar Abdur Rab Nishtar, Minister of Communications.[86] It started its work on 11 June 1949 for one year and its term was extended until July 1950 on the recommendation of Mohammad Zafrullah Khan.[87] In accordance with cabinet's decision, the term of the Second Advisory Council began in August 1950 and expired in August 1951. Later on, the system of two agents to the AGG was introduced on a temporary basis as reforms were under consideration for the province of Balochistan, after which an advisory council would not be required.[88]

Minister of Law, A. K. Brohi informed the cabinet on 4 November 1953 that the bill regarding Balochistan's status, defining the exact governmental and administrative set-up in Balochistan, was in progress and would be sent to the CAP sitting as the federal legislature.[89] He suggested that Balochistan should become a fully-fledged province with the governor as its head in place of the lieutenant governor. He further said that the Quaid-i-Azam and Liaquat had both promised to give provincial status to Balochistan, which had not materialized. The people of Balochistan were dissatisfied and wanted their due share of power and economic resources. Minister of Interior, Iskandar Mirza, while disagreeing, said that reforms were only promised to Balochistan. He explained that British Balochistan was only a limited area where a lieutenant governor had been appointed, and the rest of the area was administered through political agents. If full provincial status was granted, agents would be called

back and the people would be left at the mercy of despotic
feudal lords, which would be harmful for them. He proposed
'to make a start with the representative institutions without
giving Balochistan all the powers which a governor's province
had, before it was ready to assume that status'.[90]

Choudhury Muhammad Ali, Finance Minister, proposed
that a bill of amendment in the 1935 Act regarding the
enhancement of the powers and status of Balochistan must
be sent to the federal legislature. It was accepted by the
cabinet and decided that the case of Balochistan's status must
be referred to the CAP for the final decision.[91] The cabinet
further decided that CAP must amend the constitution as
soon as possible to give the status of province to Balochistan
with certain safeguards due to the special position of
Balochistan. It was an interim arrangement until the new
constitution was introduced.[92] In the next meeting of the
cabinet the draft bill regarding constitutional reforms for
Balochistan was approved and it was decided that it must
be presented in the forthcoming session of the CAP.[93] The
decision regarding the status of Balochistan read as follows:

Constitutional proposals in respect of the further Governmental
and Administrative set up of Balochistan should be finalized
early and that instead of mending the Constitution as suggested
in the summary, the above proposal should be presented to the
Constituent Assembly for incorporation to the Government of
India Act 1935, as adopted these proposals should provide for
a Governor's province in Balochistan with a certain safeguard
in view of the special position of Balochistan and it should be

made clear that these proposals were in the nature of interim arrangements till the new constitution came into existence'.[94]

The cabinet, at its meeting held on 11 November 1953, decided that the division of Balochistan into the Baloch States Union and Balochistan was unnatural and should be done away with as early as possible. It was pointed out that special position was given due to Khan of Kalat. The cabinet agreed that 'all efforts should be made to integrate the Balochistan States Union and Balochistan into One Unit'.[95]

Unfortunately, the CAP did not take the decision on this issue in time and the Cabinet of All Talents dropped the idea of granting provincial status to Balochistan in 1954 as it had started work on the One Unit Scheme. It was only in 1970, when the One Unit system was abolished, that Balochistan was given its due status. Jalal's claim that prime ministers were too overworked to discuss and decide the Balochistan issue is proved wrong after a detailed analysis of cabinet's proceedings on Balochistan.[96] The criticism must be directed towards CAP, not towards the prime ministers and their cabinets.

3.3.2. THE UNIFICATION OF WEST PAKISTAN/ISSUE OF ONE UNIT

The Cabinet of All Talents worked vigorously on the unification of all provinces and other areas in West Pakistan. Ayub Khan, Defence Minister, formally presented the One Unit Scheme in the cabinet meeting, which was approved after discussion.[97] Later, the provincial assemblies were pressurized by the federal government to pass the scheme.

Sardar Abdur Rashid's government in NWFP ratified the One Unit Scheme on the promises that his officers would be adjusted in the new province, the capital of the new province would be set up in NWFP, and that Dr Khan Sahib would not be installed as the chief minister of the new province.[98] It was approved by the Punjab Assembly on 30 November 1954 without any serious opposition.

Abdus Sattar Pirzada, CM of Sindh, was not ready to obtain approval for the One Unit scheme from the provincial assembly. He communicated to the governor his refusal to lend the desired support in favour of One Unit.[99] However, the federal government appointed Ayub Khuhro as the CM in 1954, only to get the approval of the One Unit scheme, which was successfully approved by the provincial legislature. The new CM suppressed public opinion, arrested many opposition leaders, and used coercive means to achieve this target. He changed Sindh by a military coup.[100] The One Unit Scheme was finally approved on 14 December 1954 by the Inter-Provincial Conference attended by the federal cabinet ministers, the governors of the provinces, the CMs, and the rulers of the states and their ministers. Its implementation was delayed until the new CAP was elected.[101] It was passed by the CAP on 30 September 1955 after a hot debate which lasted almost a week, with forty-three votes for and thirteen against. West Pakistan was merged into One Unit on 30 September 1955.

3.3.3. THE COALITION CABINETS

The coalition cabinets were deeply divided on issues related to the provinces including electorates, the question of the abolition of One Unit, provincial autonomy, the creation of the Republican Party, the dismissal or formation of ministries in the provinces, etc. It was on rare occasions that such conflicting issues were brought directly into cabinet meetings as they could result in further division within the cabinet or could delay decision-making. Such issues could either be settled by the PMs with the backing of their respective political parties, or by the president of Pakistan, even without consulting the PMs. The cabinets of Choudhury Muhammad Ali, Suhrawardy, and Chundrigarh had to resign because of disagreements on the above issues.[102] Because of frequent governmental changes at the centre, the governments in the provinces also kept changing. The cabinets could not introduce permanent policy to deal with the provincial political and administrative problems during the coalition cabinet's period.

3.3.4. THE SIX POINTS OF MUJIBUR REHMAN AND THE AGARTALA CONSPIRACY CASE

Ayub Khan's government had a strong grip on provincial matters at least until 1966. That is why relative calm was observed on the political scene in East Pakistan during 1966 and 1967 when the Six Points of Mujibur Rehman[103] were announced and led to a crisis. The federal cabinet had to deal with the situation as the demands included in the Six Points became popular in the province. Ayub Khan visited

East Pakistan on many occasions to deal with the issue of the Six Points. He distributed import licenses lavishly, and money was also distributed to counter the support for the Six Points, but to no avail. Ministers of the federal cabinet agreed to start a campaign against Mujib's demands, which they believed could lead to the separation of East Pakistan. Ministers from East Pakistan were asked to address large gatherings in cities to present the government's view of the Six Points.[104] It was believed that in this way they would be able to prevent the separation of East Pakistan, but cabinet's policy did not bear any fruit.

Meanwhile, a striking event took place in East Pakistan. Twenty-nine officers, men of the armed forces and civilian officers were found guilty of an attempted coup. They were arrested in December 1967 and January 1968. It later came to be known that some of them had visited Agartala[105] in India to get the Indian government's support for the establishment of an independent Bengal. It was from this time that this was referred to as the 'Agartala Conspiracy Case'.[106] Yahya Khan wanted Sheikh Mujibur Rehman's name to be included in the conspiracy without any solid evidence. Khawaja Shahabuddin, Minister of Information, was against this idea. He wrote to the president:

> So far there is no indication of any political party being involved. Therefore it would be unfortunate if Government leaders or pro-Government spokesmen were to cast reflection on them. Otherwise, the impression may gain ground that the Government is trying to take advantage of the ill-conceived

activities of a handful of disgruntled people to suppress their political rivals.[107]

Information Secretary Altaf Gauhar expressed his 'misgivings about involving Sheikh Mujibur Rahman in the conspiracy without solid evidence'.[108] Initially Ayub was ready to exclude Mujib's name, but added it later on the insistence of Yahya Khan and S. M. Zafar. Zafar claimed that he had found evidence of the involvement of Mujibur Rahman in the case; he had visited India under the name of 'Paris' to get advice and support from the Indian government.[109]

Federal ministers from East Pakistan, Khawaja Shahabuddin, Ghulam Faruque, Minister of Commerce, Altaf Hussain, Minister of Industries and Natural Resources, Qazi Anwarul Haq, Minister of Education, Health, and Labour, and Shams ud Doha, Minister of Food and Agriculture were snubbed by the president as they were not guiding their people on the right lines. He said, 'The present conspiracy was the direct outcome of the perfidy of hideous elements and their [ministers'] silence.'[110] The president gave directives to the cabinet about the Agartala Conspiracy Case which have not been declassified yet,[111] except the final point. He advised Altaf Hussain and Chaudhry Ali Akbar Khan, Minister of Home and Kashmir Affairs, to prepare a draft statement emphasizing the supreme necessity to preserve the national integrity of Pakistan and 'explaining for the benefits of the majority of the loyal elements in East Pakistan, the calamity that would befall the country if misguided activities like the Agartala conspiracy are allowed to be indulged in.'[112]

The military high command under Yahya Khan had gained power by this time and did not follow closely the decisions taken by the federal cabinet, especially in regard to issues related to East Pakistan. It wanted to establish a special tribunal to try the conspirators, but East Pakistanis, as the participants of the Governors' Conference were briefed by the director of the Intelligence Bureau, demanded an open and civil trial.[113] Ayub wanted the civilians to be tried by ordinary courts and the military personnel to be dealt with under court martial. General Yahya wanted to make it an historic public trial.[114] The trial finally started in the Dacca Cantonment on 19 June 1968, as a special tribunal which had been working since 22 April 1968 under an ordinance issued by the president. It was chaired by Justice S. A. Rahman. The Governors' Conference was informed that it seemed that 'the six chief conspirators would stand convicted and the other twenty-three, second-rankers, had even chances of conviction'.[115] Federal cabinet was hopeful that 'the political effect of the case had been an immediate shaking of the six pointers and the dampening in the activities of the opposition and Awami League in particular.'[116] Propaganda machinery was advised, in line with the decision of the Governors' Conference, that only balanced coverage should be given to the case as too much coverage could sell the cessation idea indirectly.[117]

The Agartala Conspiracy Case resulted in creating a political crisis in East Pakistan. Unfortunately, one of the accused, Flight Sergeant Zahurul Haq, died while the proceedings were in progress. With this, the proceedings came to an abrupt end in February 1969, which was a great embarrassment for Ayub's government.[118] His grip on East Pakistan was loosened. The province played an important role in his deposition from power.

3.3.5. GENERAL YAHYA KHAN AND PROVINCIAL POLITICS/ ADMINISTRATION

During General Yahya Khan's period, the major problem in West Pakistan was the unrest among industrial labour, which became very visible after the restoration of the rights to strike, lockouts, and to conduct labour agitation, on 7 November 1969. The labourers of different industries, staff of government offices, and workers of different corporations went on strike one after the other at the end of 1969 and throughout 1970. Nur Khan, governor of West Pakistan, could not normalize the situation even with the use of force. He resigned on 1 February 1970 and Lt Gen. Atiq ur Rahman was appointed as the new governor.[119] With the revival of political activity on 1 January 1970, political parties embarked on an election campaign. In the 1970 elections, the PPP emerged as the major political force in West Pakistan. The PPP mainly won seats in Punjab and Sindh. The Awami National Party and Jamiat-i-Ulema-i-Islam were successful in the two smaller provinces of NWFP and Balochistan.

Yahya Khan had inherited a difficult situation in East Pakistan, and at the same time he had no political agenda to follow. It has been recorded that, after his first broadcast to the nation on 26 March 1969, he sat in dismay and 'woefully' remarked 'what should we do now?'[120] Yahya declared on one occasion that he never tried to learn how to run the affairs of the government over the last thirty-two years.[121] Yahya visited East Pakistan after taking over the state's affairs. Yahya's government accepted many demands of the East Pakistanis which had never been addressed by past governments. These demands included: the allotment of seats in the National Assembly (NA) on the basis of population in place of parity, under which equal representation had been given to East and West Pakistan, and the promotion of Bengalis to the highest positions in the civil service. As a result, six Bengali CSP officers were promoted as secretaries in May 1969 at the federal level, and the quota for new recruitment in the civil service and military for Bengalis was enhanced, in fact doubled. One ordinance factory was also established in Dacca in April 1970.[122]

The kitchen cabinet of General Yahya discussed East Pakistan's demands in several of its meetings, but the documents are classified. The detailed study of cabinet papers has produced only some scattered files on the food situation, flooding, and the general situation in East Pakistan as well as in West Pakistan. No policy issue was discussed in the civilian cabinet meeting. The civilian cabinet was told on 2 September 1970, 'sometimes important decisions were taken at the level of the President after he had discussed the matter with a minister or some other high functionary like the Chief Election Commissioner.'[123] The civilian cabinet was not only bypassed, but also not informed about decisions in time. The Minister of Information brought to the notice of the cabinet the fact that his ministry had not been informed about the cancellation of the date of elections in certain constituencies in Balochistan and NWFP. The decision had given rise to a lot of criticism, but the Ministry of Information was not in a position to give any valid explanation because it had no prior or subsequent briefing on the reasons which led to the reversal of the previous decisions on this matter.

Minister of Communications G. W. Choudhury has also mentioned that policy issues were discussed only by the military junta. He claims himself to have been part of the kitchen cabinet and has given details of some meetings. The kitchen cabinet faced difficulties in deciding the issue of provincial autonomy while bearing in mind the six points of the AL. Some members of the kitchen cabinet, including General Hamid, General Tikka Khan, and General Omar, wanted minimum provincial autonomy, but on G. W. Choudhury's suggestion maximum provincial autonomy was granted in the Legal Framework Order.[124] The second important point was the mode of elections. Yahya clearly stated that no compromise would be made on one-man one-vote.[125] With the support of Ahsan and G. W. Choudhury, Yahya said, 'it would destroy confidence in the intentions of the military regime among the Bengalis.'[126] The inner cabinet had to accept this. Safdar Mahmood's opinion is different. He has mentioned that the issue of adult franchise was decided by 'Yahya Khan in his individual capacity'.[127] As the files of these cabinet meetings are not declassified, the exact situation cannot be ascertained, but generally Yahya used to take decisions after consultation with his close associates. The best assumption is that he declared it after it was agreed in the kitchen cabinet.

None of these attempts of Yahya Khan's government could improve the situation, and the separatist tendency in East Pakistan increased with every passing day. The situation exploded in East Pakistan after the announcement of the election results. AL, the sole successful political party in East Pakistan, began to demand broad provincial autonomy. Central government found itself in a dilemma. Yahya Khan promised to convene a session of the newly-elected National Assembly, but it was delayed without bringing the issue before a cabinet meeting.[128] Postponement of the NA session was considered by the East Pakistanis as treatment meted out to a stepchild. It triggered the demand for an independent Bangladesh.[129] In the absence of a formal civilian cabinet, which had been dissolved in February 1971, there was no recognized institution at the federal level to address East Pakistan's issues. On the suggestion of the information secretary, approval was obtained with difficulty from the president, after a long delay, to form a committee to discuss only the military action.[130]

All policy decisions, including delaying the NA session, holding talks with Mujib, and starting and ending military action were taken by Yahya and the military high command. Every step of this cabinet-less government led Pakistan towards disaster. Mujib had practically established his parallel government in East Pakistan. His directives had been followed since March 1971. General Tikka Khan, who was a hardliner, only worsened the situation further with the use of force.[131]

The military operation was over in May, but the state of affairs could not be improved. Yahya, after consulting the military high command, appointed a new civilian governor, Dr A. M. Malik of East Bengal, with full power to control the civil administration. General Niazi would look after defence only. The governor had the right to elect a council of ministers to assist him. Final approval was obtained from the president. Major General Rahim Khan was the sub-martial law administrator of Zone B under the new arrangement, and dealt with martial law cases only. The president was hopeful that these measures would expedite the process of the transfer of power to a civilian government.[132]

The government decided to hold by-elections for seventy-nine seats of the NA from 25 November to 9 December 1971.[133] This plan could not be implemented as India attacked Pakistan on the night of 20 November. Yahya was informed about this attack in the meeting of the military high command on 22 November 1971. Yahya dismissed the meeting and another was called at President House in the evening. According to Fazal Muqeem Khan, Yahya's attitude was not serious towards this very serious issue. He said, 'What can I do for East Pakistan? I can only pray'.[134] The generals decided to attack India from West Pakistan. Yahya agreed to this only under military, political, and psychological pressure.[135] Pakistani forces could not counter the attack for long and surrendered on 16 December 1971.[136] With this major defeat Yahya transferred power to the civilians.

It was an unfortunate end of Jinnah's Pakistan. East Pakistanis were brought to this fate by the injustice shown towards that province of Pakistan by governments since the creation of Pakistan. West Pakistani ministers of Ayub's cabinet thought that East Pakistanis were using pressure tactics to try to blackmail the federal government. 'It was agreed that both West Pakistan and the Centre must get tough administratively and East Pakistani disloyalty must be highlighted in the Assemblies, in the Administration and in the press.'[137] East Pakistanis could be asked to 'walk out of Pakistan if they wanted to; with this threat they could come to their senses'.[138]

This division of East and West Pakistan gained prominence under Yahya's regime. Although he tried to appoint equal number of West and East Pakistan ministers, no important portfolio was given to East Pakistani ministers.[139] Before and after the civilian cabinet (4 August 1969–22 February 1971), only the military high command existed, in which East Pakistan's representation was negligible. Yahya's kitchen cabinet, which consisted of military high command, usually discussed and decided all issues. The military junta made the situation worse, and instead of solving provincial matters, it just aggravated the situation which, in the end, resulted in the break-up of Pakistan.

3.3.6. THE NAP-JUI COALITION IN NWFP AND BALOCHISTAN

During Bhutto's period, cabinet had to deal with the changing relationship between the centre and the provinces. Now there was only one wing and there were four provinces in the remaining Pakistan: Punjab, Sindh, NWFP, and Balochistan. PPP governments were established in Punjab and Sindh, but in NWFP and Balochistan JUI and NAP formed coalition governments. Federal cabinet gradually tightened its control on NWFP and Balochistan and was directly involved in provincial matters through a new Ministry of Provincial Coordination, introduced in June 1972. Its responsibility was to establish contact and coordination between the provinces and the federal government.[140] Secondly, governors were bound, under cabinet's decision on 8 February 1973, to send monthly reports to the president on the 'State of Affairs'[141] of their provinces. Thirdly, provincial conferences which discussed and decided issues of law and order, jails, local bodies, communications, forests, and many others, were to be a regular feature. This was considered direct interference by the federal government in provincial matters as decisions in these conferences were usually taken by Bhutto and his cabinet colleagues. Sometimes, provincial governments faced difficult situations. For example, the central government announced that new universities would be opened in DI Khan, Saidu Sharif, Swat, Abbottabad, and Hazara, but the provincial governments were unable to obtain the funds.[142]

Bhutto's cabinet was given a tough time by NWFP and Balochistan's provincial governments and some other political forces. The cabinet was informed that the NAP had opposed the appointment of Sardar Ghaus Bakhsh Raisani as governor of Balochistan. The Baloch leadership was demanding that only six subjects, defence, foreign affairs, currency, interprovincial trade, communications, and the right of direct taxation, should be kept under central control.[143] They wanted provincial government control over the gas supply system.[144] NAP further criticized the appointment of late Hayat Mohammad Khan Sherpao as opposition leader in the NWFP legislature and as head of the Water and Power Development Agency (WAPDA). NAP claimed that Sherpao, in that capacity, was creating problems for the provincial government.[145] At the same time, he was serving as a federal minister.

Federal cabinet was not ready to accept these demands. The cabinet showed concern about the issue of raising armed guards by NAP and other political parties and decided that a law would be passed in the near future to ban these private armies.[146] The federal government had exercised control over Balochistan in the early years through the governor, who at times played the role of a bridge between central government and provincial political forces.

Bhutto briefed the cabinet that '... irrefutable evidence was available to show that ... some leaders of the NAP were working as foreign agents. It was necessary therefore to keep them under constant surveillance'.[147] The cabinet was also told that 'one particular leader of the NAP[148] had even discussed with Afghanistan officials the possibility of an attack by India against Pakistan and had suggested the time when it would be opportune for India to do so'.[149] It was requested by the cabinet that the head of the Intelligence Bureau and the director general of ISI should keep a watch on the activities of such political leaders.

On the other hand, a conciliatory policy was adopted towards the opposition forces. Federal cabinet was part of all the discussions that were held between the government and NAP-JUI coalition. Federal cabinet had detailed discussions on the formula for agreement presented by the PPP high command and the counter formula, presented by the NAP-JUI leadership. After considering both, cabinet approved the final terms of the agreement.[150] The Tripartite Agreement, signed with NAP and JUI on 6 March 1972 allowed NA to debate the Interim Constitution. Each political party could nominate one person to deliver a speech,[151] but discussion on the budget for the coming year, 1972–73, was not permitted. PPP supported the NAP-JUI coalition government in NWFP and they supported the PPP government at the centre. A consensus had developed between the two on how to lift martial law, and two ministries were also reserved for NAP in the federal cabinet.

The governors of the provinces were changed; Arbab Sikandar Khan and Mir Ghaus Bakhsh Bizenjo were appointed governors of NWFP and Balochistan respectively in April 1972.[152] The cabinet agreed that provincial governors should always be appointed by the president, not necessarily from the majority party, and they held office during his pleasure. Furthermore, only trustworthy people were to be appointed in both provinces due to the particular political conditions there. Although the governors of NWFP and Balochistan were appointed on 28 April 1972 from NAP-JUI circles to create good working relations between the provincial and central governments,[153] NAP-JUI did not endorse the offer of two ministries in the federal cabinet. Bhutto said, on 7 May 1972, that since 20 April he had delayed completing the cabinet at the centre, but NAP-JUI did not endorse it.[154] He completed his cabinet without the NAP-JUI.

Lack of trust on both sides hindered cooperation. Khan Abdul Wali Khan filed a complaint against the delaying tactics of the federal government regarding approval of the projects and decisions of the provincial governments and assemblies. He quoted the example of the passing of the Pashto Language Bill by the provincial assembly which remained unresolved by the federal government.[155]

This feeling of mistrust continued, and gradually Bhutto and other members of the PPP leadership started issuing statements against the NAP-JUI leadership. Their statements included humiliating terms for NAP such as 'traitors, foreign agents, puppet of capitalists, and exploiters of Pakistani workers and peasants'.[156] Anwar H. Syed's opinion is that the Bhutto government adopted a conciliatory policy towards NAP-JUI only to show Indira Gandhi that Pakistan's ethnic groups were all united. It was only within a week after Bhutto's return from India in July 1972 that federal cabinet ministers started issuing statements against NAP-JUI provincial governments and leadership.[157]

Opposition members in the National Assembly boycotted the meetings of the Constitution-making Committee chaired by Law Minister Abdul Hafiz Pirzada, so a meeting of nine major political parties was arranged to discuss constitutional issues. As a result, the Constitutional Accord was signed on 20 October 1972 in an All-Parties Conference attended by the nine major parties in the NA.[158] It stated that the parliamentary federal system of government would be the basis of the future constitution. Islamic provisions including Islam as the state religion, the condition that the President should be Muslim, and many others were agreed upon.[159] The opposition proposed amendments to the Constitution Bill moved by the government in the NA on 30 December 1972. The cabinet approved the idea that 'efforts should be made to form the Constitution with the participation of NAP if possible'.[160] It was possible for the government to agree on the Constitutional Bill on 10th April, after weeks of dialogue with the United Democratic Front, an alliance of the opposition political parties.[161] Finally, an accepted draft constitution was approved by Parliament.

In October 1972, the provincial government of Balochistan arrested the leaders of the Jamot tribe, rivals of the Mengals, in Lasbela. The tribe had revolted against the government. Governor Mir Ghaus Bakhsh Bizenjo claimed that security forces had been unable to quell the revolt so he sent his private army to deal with the Jamots. The governor of Balochistan claimed that Interior Minister Qayyum Khan and President Bhutto were responsible for developing this situation. He believed that the issue of Lasbela had not been presented to nor discussed by cabinet jointly, but it had been handled by these two people. The governor further claimed that the revolt in Lasbela was designed by Qayyum Khan himself.[162] His claim was false as federal cabinet had prepared different plans to deal with the law and order situation in NWFP and

Balochistan. Cabinet emphasized interprovincial cooperation, understanding, and planning to overcome the poor law and order situation.[163] The other plan was to raise 'separate crime police from the general police in urban areas'.[164] All provincial representatives informed the cabinet about the progress of the plan. Balochistan's report was that the separate crime police would be introduced in Quetta city only.[165] The third plan approved by the cabinet was the mounting of provincial armed resources. In response, Balochistan raised twenty-two platoons. Rules for such armed reserves were also considered by the cabinet.[166]

In its meeting held on 5 October 1972, the cabinet took the tough decision of sending army units to the Lasbela district of Balochistan to assist the provincial government in the restoration of peace. The army had authority to disarm marauding tribesmen who came from other areas. The army also had responsibility to ensure that essential supplies for the inhabitants of Lasbela district would reach there without any delay.[167] Thus, the civilian cabinet of Bhutto used the military for the first time to settle a civilian issue in Balochistan in the first year of its rule.

Bhutto appointed a secret committee on Balochistan which consisted of three members, Ghulam Mustafa Jatoi, Minister of Political Affairs and Communications, Ghulam Mustafa Khar, Governor Punjab, and Rafi Raza, later Minister of Industries and Production. Its responsibility was to find 'a satisfactory solution'[168] to the Balochistan problem. It suggested that the main areas of frequent raids by criminals and invaders were Bugti, Dukki, Nasirabad, and Lasbela, so the villagers of these areas should be provided with rifles for self-defence.[169]

On 10 February 1973, a large quantity of Russian arms was seized from the Iraqi Embassy in Islamabad. On the basis of all reports, cabinet came to the conclusion that the purpose behind collecting the arms was to start guerrilla fighting in Balochistan. The president informed the cabinet that a large number of weapons had already been distributed among tribesmen.[170] The president stated that the secessionist element was not only active in Balochistan, but also in NWFP and Sindh. Cabinet reached the conclusion, after a long discussion, that the NAP-JUI government of Balochistan was involved in the plan to secede from Pakistan with the support of Russia, and was not able to handle the alarming situation in the province; it should immediately be dismissed. In its special meeting held on 13 February, cabinet authorized the president to take a decision regarding the dismissal of the governments in the two provinces.[171] The president told the cabinet that he had met with Bizenjo and, as well as assuring him of his cooperation, he had told him that if he was to remain governor, the army must be withdrawn from Lasbela. On 15 February 1973, the governor of Balochistan and the NAP-JUI government under Sardar Ataullah Khan Mengal were dismissed and governor rule was imposed on the province in line with the decision of the cabinet.[172]

Mengal said that because everything was instigated by Khan Qayyum, the dismissal of the Balochistan government was wrong.[173] The NAP-JUI government of NWFP resigned in protest on the same day. The cabinet approved the nomination of Nawab Akbar Bugti as the new governor of Balochistan, and Mohammad Aslam Khattak as governor of NWFP.[174] Bugti had been very active in unveiling the Iraqi embassy issue.[175]

The decision to deploy the army in Balochistan was taken by the cabinet on 14 February with regret. The cabinet decided that the time for negotiation with the NAP-JUI was over as they always backed away from their promises. It was agreed that:

> The employment of force to deal with political situation is regrettable ... after the Army Action in East Pakistan in 1971. The Central Government has, however, been extremely patient and has exercised the utmost restraint in dealing with the NAP Governments in NWFP and Balochistan. The time has, unfortunately, come when political action under the constitution has become inevitable.[176]

The cabinet advised the Information Ministry to make the people aware of the distinction between the political action being taken in NWFP-Balochistan and the army action taken in East Pakistan.[177]

A special committee formed by the federal cabinet which included J. A. Rahim, Minister for Presidential Affairs, Aziz Ahmed, Minister of State for Defence and Foreign Affairs, Special Assistant Mr Rafi Raza and Special Assistant for Information Yousuf Buch, with the responsibility to note the day-to-day situation in NWFP and Balochistan and to inform the president of this together with their recommendations.[178] This committee enhanced the power and role of the centre in provincial matters. The cabinet asked the Law Ministry to frame an ordinance prescribing a severe penalty for the treasonable activities of all kinds of organizations, newspapers, magazines, and so on.[179] Under cabinet's decision, federal security police were sent to Balochistan to restore order. In addition, the cabinet decided that the army should be ready for possible action in Balochistan. It was decided in the meeting that a plan of action should be prepared based on a 'seven-to-ten day' period during which troops and equipment could be moved as close to the troubled areas as possible.[180] The president asked the interior minister to submit a list of the names of officers who were suspected of leaning towards the previous NAP government.[181]

Governor rule continued till 27 April 1973 when Jam Sahib Lasbela established a pro-PPP ministry. Maulana Shamsuddin, the deputy speaker of the Balochistan Assembly was arrested in July 1973. Khan Qayyum told the national assembly that the federal government was not involved in the arrest of the Maulana, but members of NAP/JUI did not accept this.[182] Some other tribes raised an armed revolt against the federal government over the arrest of their sardars, including Ghaus Bakhsh Bizenjo, Ataullah Mengal, and Khair Bakhsh Marri on 16 August 1973. Consequently, the military operation which had already been started in Lasbela was expanded to the whole province. Nawab Akbar Bugti resisted, but to no avail. He presented his resignation in November 1973; it was accepted in January 1974, and the Khan of Kalat, Mir Ahmad Yar Khan, was appointed as the new governor.[183]

The pro-PPP government of NWFP took its oath of office on 29 April 1973 under Inayatullah Gandapur as CM. On this development, the masses and leadership of NAP and JUI reacted violently. Wali Khan delivered some treasonable speeches. Cabinet decided that Mohammad Aslam Khattak, Governor NWFP, Major General (retd) Jamal Dar, Minister of State for Public Affairs, and others should issue strong statements condemning the treasonable speeches of Wali Khan. Cabinet planned to take action against Wali Khan, but before this, the media should expose him for his subversive utterances and fully project the government's point of view in the case of action against Wali Khan.[184] The cabinet was satisfied that the situation in the NWFP was under control.[185] The opposition members, led by Mir Ghaus Bakhsh Khan Bizenjo, claimed that the government was worsening the situation in Balochistan so was not permitted to discuss the Balochistan issue in the House.[186]

On one side the military operation was going on, and on the other side dialogue was started between the government and NAP through the US ambassador, who met Bizenjo and conveyed Bhutto's message to him, which was actually an agenda for discussion and had been approved by the cabinet. In response, Bizenjo demanded that the army must remain in the cantonments only, another security agency should be sent there, and Governor Bugti must be removed immediately. On the question of an NAP representative in the provincial cabinet, he said that if the federal government wanted a coalition government with NAP, it must be in both the provinces, and the government must be formed by the majority parties.[187] After listening to all Bizenjo's proposals, Bhutto told the ambassador that they were all counter to his own proposals, so he would discuss the issue in the cabinet and would then revert to him.[188] No compromise could be reached.

Cabinet continually discussed how to establish peace and a strong government in Balochistan. They decided that students who were incorrigibly committed to anti-state activities should be put behind bars. Secondly, the government of Balochistan should trace and arrest the gang responsible for explosions in Quetta.[189] Stanley Wolpert has stated that Bhutto announced the end of the military operation in May 1974 from Balochistan. A general amnesty was announced for those who would hand over their arms to the government by mid-October.[190] But this was not so, as the Inter-provincial Governors' Conference in its meeting held on 14 August 1974 said, 'the army must plan to finish the operation in Balochistan by the end of the year.'[191]

The Balochistan government informed the federal government that cabinet's decisions had been implemented through the commissioner and IG Police. On the cabinet's decision, interrogation teams started interrogating a large number of people, special police patrols were started, and so on. In the light of these measures, the cabinet expressed its satisfaction that the law and order situation had been brought under control.[192] The cabinet advised the Ministry of Law to take immediate action to set up a special tribunal to try the people responsible for the bomb explosions in NWFP and Balochistan. Special laws were to be enacted for this purpose, if necessary.[193] None of these measures could improve the situation to a satisfactory level in Balochistan.

The PPP, in coalition with other minor parties, established its control over the political affairs of the smaller provinces to some extent. One reason for this control was the detention of prominent leaders of NAP, including Mir Ghaus Bakhsh Bizenjo, Sardar Khair Bakhsh Marri, and Sardar Ataullah Mengal. The cabinet was informed that the detention of these leaders was essential to keep strong control on affairs in Balochistan. If they were released, they could overturn the politics of Balochistan and the temporary majority of the government party in Balochistan could be reduced to a minority, so their detention was considered to be in the best interest of Pakistan's integrity.[194] The cabinet also considered the arrest of Bugti, but avoided it due to the anticipated retaliation of his tribe.[195]

The cabinet believed that NAP was behind bombing incidents in NWFP which had increased after the return of Wali Khan.[196] The situation reached its climax on 8 February 1975 when Mohammad Hayat Khan Sherpao, Senior Minister in NWFP, was assassinated in a bomb explosion in Peshawar. Bhutto talked to Rafi Raza, Minister of Industries and Production, from New York, and ordered the arrest of the whole NAP leadership. Two days later, on 10 February 1975, NAP was banned. On the same day, PM Bhutto criticized NAP's activities while addressing the National Assembly, and said, 'We mourn the death of a great compatriot, but his death will not go in vain'.[197] Gandapur's government in NWFP and Governor Aslam Khattak were removed and governor's rule was imposed. The new governor was Maj. Gen. Syed Ghawas (retd).[198] The cabinet decided that Qayyum Khan, Minister for Interior, Mohammad Yusuf Khattak, Minister of Fuel, Power and Natural Resources, and Mir Afzal Khan, Minister for Commerce, should go through the list of NAP detainees and advise the governor of NWFP as to which of these should be released, and include additional names if necessary.[199] Secondly, it was decided that the government of NWFP should take steps to ensure that the *mullahs* did not deliver anti-government sermons. Action should be taken against those *khatibs* who were involved in such activities.[200]

Nasrullah Khattak was called back from his ambassadorial position and asked to form a coalition government of PPP and QML in NWFP, which he did, but the performance of this government was very poor.[201] Under federal cabinet's decision, a special tribunal was established at Hyderabad to try NAP leadership. Said Ahmad Khan was in charge of the case. This tribunal was highly criticized by the opposition parties, especially during the abortive talks between the PPP and the opposition.[202] Governor's rule continued in NWFP for more than a year. Governor Syed Ghawas was replaced by another military governor in March 1976.

The Jam of Lasbela's cabinet could not tackle the issue of tribal insurgency in the long run and was removed in February 1975. Federal government rule was established in Balochistan and continued till December 1976. The cabinet was satisfied that the law and order situation during this period in Balochistan had improved and was under control,[203] except in the tribal areas. Rebel tribesmen continued to wage guerrilla warfare throughout 1976. In September 1976, six army divisions were busy tackling 20,000 tribesmen. Quetta was practically under martial law. Bomb explosions were also a routine occurrence in Balochistan.[204] Civilian government was restored only on 6 December 1976 to arrange elections under Mohammad Khan Barozai including all PPP Cabinet Ministers.[205]

During Bhutto's parliamentary period, two parameters for the four provinces were followed by the cabinet at one time. On one hand, the governments of Punjab and Sindh were, to a large extent, given the freedom to solve provincial matters, as was observed in the language issue in Sindh: the provincial assembly passed a bill and decided the issue. Central government and cabinet intervened only when the situation deteriorated. As far as Punjab was concerned, it also enjoyed the trust of the federal government to a great extent. Even though the governors and CM of the province were changed time and again, they had the authority to deal with internal provincial matters to a large extent.

The governments of NWFP and Balochistan faced tough times because the opposition political parties were not submissive to the PPP government. The worst decision of the cabinet regarding Balochistan was to opt for military action in the province. If that decision had not been taken, and the issue had been settled through political dialogue, the situation could have been brought under control. It was a political government and members of the cabinet were representatives of the masses; they should have opted for the political option in resolving the Balochistan issue. The cabinet should not have approved of, or at least should have raised its voice against, the military action in Balochistan.

To sum up, it is judged that the cabinet's role in dealing with provincial political and administrative matters remained crucial during the years 1947–1977. It was during the first parliamentary period that trends were set; the cabinet started interfering in provincial matters, sometimes even transgressing democratic norms. Even the cabinets and governors of the provinces were dismissed for one reason or another. Secondly, the cabinet introduced the concept of using the army to settle provincial issues, which was not only undemocratic, but also showed mistrust of the civil authorities. Thirdly, the trend of trusting the inner cabinet to solve some provincial issues was also initiated in this period. These trends were followed during almost the whole period of this study. There were also some distinctions in the three phases. During the first parliamentary period, East Pakistanis were given importance, or at least their voices were prominent to some extent in solving the problems relevant to their province. But during Ayub Khan's military period, a discriminatory attitude was adopted towards East Pakistanis: they were not even called to attend some cabinet meetings to which only West Pakistani ministers were invited. As Ayub Khan's cabinet did not trust East Pakistani ministers, it resulted in developing mistrust towards the federal government among the East Pakistanis. By the time of Yahya Khan, this situation had reached its peak and the separation of East Pakistan took place. Bhutto inherited a truncated Pakistan and his government faced quite different problems in the provinces. It was expected that this elected government would respect the rights of the smaller provinces but in practice, the smaller provinces faced very difficult times, especially when the voice of the people was suppressed in NWFP and Balochistan, and PPP-led governments were formed in these two provinces using undemocratic means and measures. The military was used to solve political matters, elected provincial governments and governors were dismissed, and the NAP was banned. During this period, the institution of cabinet supported all these developments, and thus hindered the development of democratic values in Pakistan.

Notes and References

1. Dar, *Jinnah's Pakistan*, 211.
2. Ayesha Jalal, *The State of Martial Rule*, 85.
3. For further details on the language movement please see, Badruddin Umar, *The Emergence of Bangladesh: Class Struggle in East Pakistan, 1947–1958* (Karachi: Oxford University Press, 2004), 190–229.
4. From Governor of East Bengal Malik Firoz Khan Noon to PM Khawaja Nazimuddin, 28 February 1952, 2(1)-PMS/52, NDC, Islamabad.
5. Cabinet mtg, 12 March 1952, 73/CF/52, NDC, Islamabad.
6. Ibid.
7. Decision of the cabinet, 15 November 1953, 108/CF/53, NDC, Islamabad.
8. Decision of the cabinet, 11 April 1954, 302/CF/52, NDC, Islamabad.
9. Ziring, *Pakistan in the Twentieth Century*, 388.
10. Ibid., 389, Wolpert, *Zulfi Bhutto of Pakistan*, 197–8.
11. President's observations which he shared with his cabinet colleagues, Cabinet mtg, 24 March 1972, 128/CF/72-1, NDC, Islamabad.

12. Ibid.
13. *National Assembly of Pakistan Debates Vol. I, No. 2,* 15 April 1972, 92.
14. *National Assembly of Pakistan Debates Vol. II, No. 5,* 14 July 1972, 694.
15. Syed, *The Discourse and Politics,* 193.
16. Ibid. 193–5.
17. Surendra Nath Kaushik, *Pakistan under Bhutto's Leadership* (New Delhi: Uppal, 1985), 156; and *The Pakistan Times,* 16 July 1972.
18. Cabinet mtg, 16 May 1953, 134/CF/53, NDC, Islamabad.
19. Ibid.
20. Hamid Yousuf, *Pakistan: A Study of Political Development* (Lahore: Sang-e-Meel Publication, 1999), 53; Talbot, *Pakistan A Modern History,* 140; Ziring, *Pakistan in the Twentieth Century,* 193, and many others
21. Cabinet mtgs were held on the following dates: 21 February 1953, 25 February 1953, 26 February 1953, 27 February 1953, 10 March 1953, 20 March, and so on.
22. The prominent leaders were Ihtishamul Haq, Abdul Hamid Badayuni, Abul Hasnat, and Ataullah Shah Bokhari, Summary of the movement, presented to the cabinet by Ministry of Interior, 50/ CF/53, NDC, Islamabad.
23. Cabinet mtg, 21 February 1953, 50/CF/53, NDC, Islamabad.
24. Cabinet mtg, 25 February 1953, 50/CF/53, NDC, Islamabad.
25. Ibid.
26. Ibid.
27. Jalal, *The State of Martial Rule,* 177.
28. Cabinet mtg, 27 February 1953, 50/CF/53, NDC, Islamabad.
29. Cabinet decision, 6 March 1953, 50/CF/53, NDC, Islamabad.
30. Cabinet decision, 10 March 1953, 50/CF/53, NDC, Islamabad.
31. Ibid.
32. Ibid.
33. *Punjab Report of the Court of Inquiry Constituted under Punjab Act II of 1954 to Enquire into the Punjab Disturbances of 1953* (Lahore: Government Printing Press, 1954), 81.
34. Cabinet mtg, 20 May 1953, 50/CF/53, NDC, Islamabad.

35. From BHC Karachi to CWRO London, 30 July 1964, DO 196/318, TNA, London. This personal friend of Ayub Khan used autocratic measures and kept the grip of the central government strong till his resignation in September 1966.

36. Feldman, *From Crisis to Crisis*, 191.

37. Governors' Conference, 8 April 1961, 25/CF/60, NDC, Islamabad.

38. Ibid.

39. Cabinet mtg, 15 February 1962, 137/CF/62, NDC, Islamabad.

40. Ibid.

41. Ibid.

42. Ibid.

43. Ibid.

44. Ibid.

45. Federal cabinet decided the issue of the retirement of Lieut. Gen. Muhammad Azam Khan in April in its mtg, 25 April 1962, 280/CF/62, NDC, Islamabad.

46. Feldman, *Revolution in Pakistan*, 160.

47. Cabinet mtg, 3 March 1962, 280/CF/62, NDC, Islamabad.

48. Cabinet mtg, 6 September 1962, 280/CF/62, NDC, Islamabad.

49. Feldman, *Revolution in Pakistan*, 162.

50. Herbert Feldman, *From Crisis to Crisis: Pakistan 1962–1969* (Oxford: Oxford University Press, 1972), 174.

51. The details of the introduction of One Unit are given in the ensuing pages.

52. Selig S. Harrison, *In Afghanistan's Shadow: Baloch Nationalism and Soviet Temptation* (New York: Carngie Endowment for International Peace, 1981), 27; and Taj Mohammad Breseeg, *Baloch Nationalism: Its Origin and Development* (Karachi: Royal Book Company, 2004), 286.

53. Syed Iqbal Ahmad, *Balochistan: Its Strategic Importance* (Karachi: Royal Book Company, 1992), 167. The same incident is mentioned by Mir Ahmad Yar Khan in different words in his autobiography entitled *Inside Balochistan: Political Autobiography of Khan-i-Azam* (Karachi: Ma'aref Printers, 1975), 182–4.

54. The Nawab of Kalabagh was removed in September 1966 and General Musa was appointed as governor in his place. Altaf Gauhar,

Ayub Khan: Pakistan's First Military Ruler (Lahore: Sang-i-Meel Publications, 1993), 407.

55. Feldman, *From Crisis to Crisis,* 202.

56. From BHC Karachi to CWRO London, 2 February 1966, DO 196/316, NA, London.

57. Ibid. 9 July 1968, FCO 37/181, NA, London.

58. Feldman, *From Crisis to Crisis,* 202–4.

59. Cabinet mtg, 16 October 1968, 159/CF/68, NDC, Islamabad.

60. Feldman, *The End and the Beginning,* 58–9.

61. See the detailed terms of the treaty in Chapter 4.

62. Ziring, *The Ayub Khan Era,* 82.

63. Minutes of the Governors' Conference, 12 and 13 May 1967, 96/CF/67, NDC, Islamabad.

64. Top Secret: Summary for the Cabinet, Current Internal Situation, Causes and Remedies, 432/CF/68-1, NDC, Islamabad.

65. Cabinet mtg, 13 November 1968 and 26 November 1968, 432/CF/68, NDC, Islamabad.

66. Cabinet mtg, 26 November 1968, 432/CF/68, NDC, Islamabad.

67. Cabinet mtg, 13 November 1968, 432/CF/68, NDC, Islamabad.

68. Cabinet mtg, 26 November 1968, 432/CF/68, NDC, Islamabad.

69. Ayub's cabinet decided to form a government political party in 1962 which could be termed the King's Party. This was named the Conventional Muslim League. Its membership was given to cabinet members, members of the legislature, and other followers of the government. Ziring, *The Ayub Khan Era,* 35; and Afzal, *Pakistan, History and Politics,* 262.

70. Ibid.

71. Governors' Conference, 12 December 1968, 432/CF/68, NDC, Islamabad.

72. Interview with S. M. Zafar.

73. Cabinet mtg, 20 March 1969, cited in Baxter, *Diaries of Field Marshal Ayub Khan,* 308.

74. A state of emergency was imposed during the 1965 War which was not lifted. It was decided in September 1969 that it would be lifted, but the decision was implemented only in February 1969; stated in S. M. Zafar, *Through the Crisis* (Lahore: Book Centre, 1970), 78.

75. Governors' Conference 27 and 28 January 1969, 432/CF/68-1, NDC, Islamabad.
76. Cabinet mtg, 23 February 1969, cited in Baxter, *Diaries of Field Marshal Muhammad Ayub Khan,* 302.
77. Ibid.
78. G. W. Choudhury, *The Last Days of United Pakistan,* 39.
79. Jalal, *The State of Martial Rule,* 167.
80. Cabinet mtg, 27 January 1948, 33/CF/48, NDC, Islamabad.
81. Cabinet mtg, 18 February 1948, 33/CF/48, NDC, Islamabad.
82. Ibid.
83. Summary presented to the cabinet by the Ministry of States and Frontier Regions, 33/CF/48, NDC, Islamabad.
84. Cabinet mtg, 4 November 1953, 302/CF/53, NDC, Islamabad.
85. Cabinet mtg, 19 January 1949, 302/CF/53, NDC, Islamabad.
86. The notification was issued under Notification No. F.1 (6)-B/49 dated 26 February 1949, Cabinet mtg, 18 January 1949, 302/CF/53, NDC, Islamabad.
87. Cabinet mtg, 5 June 1950, 302/CF/53 and 33/CF/48, NDC, Islamabad.
88. Summary presented to the cabinet, 11 October 1951, 33/CF/48, NDC, Islamabad.
89. Cabinet mtg and decision, 4 November 1953, 302/CF/53, NDC, Islamabad.
90. Ibid.
91. Ibid.
92. Cabinet mtg, 9 November 1953, 302/CF/53, NDC, Islamabad.
93. Cabinet mtg, 11 November 1953, 302/CF/53, NDC, Islamabad.
94. Cabinet decision, 9 November 1953, 302/CF/53, NDC, Islamabad.
95. Cabinet mtg, 11 November 1953, 302/CF/53, NDC, Islamabad.
96. Jalal, *The State of Martial Rule, 166–7.*
97. Zarina Salamat, *Pakistan 1947–58: An Historical Review* (Islamabad: NIHCR, 1992), 86.
98. Rizwan Malik, *The Politics of One Unit, 1955–1958* (Lahore: Pakistan Study Centre, 1988), 48.
99. Ibid. 53.
100. Afzal, *Pakistan: History and Politics,* 144–5.

101. Nur Ahmad, *From Martial Law to Martial Law,* 347.

102. The details are given in the last chapter.

103. The Six Points were drawn up by a group of intellectuals who were dissatisfied with the policies of the central government towards East Pakistan. They showed the points to Nurul Amin first who delayed his reaction as he found the points to have a secessionist theme. Only then did the intellectuals take the points to Mujib who found that these matched his own ideology and took immediate action. Feldman, *From Crisis to Crisis,* 180.

104. Cabinet mtg, 24 May 1967 cited in Craig Baxter, *Diaries of Field Marshal Muhammad Ayub Khan 1966–1972* (Karachi: Oxford University Press, 2007), 100–1.

105. The Military Intelligence reported that they had conspired with P. N. Ojha, first secretary of the Indian Deputy High Commission in Dacca and visited Agartala to discuss their plan of conspiracy with Indian officers including Lt Col. Misra and Major Gauhar, *Ayub Khan,* 409.

106. Feldman, *From Crisis to Crisis,* 184–5.

107. From Khawaja Shahabuddin to President Ayub Khan, 10 January 1968 cited in Baxter, *Diaries of Field Marshal Muhammad Ayub Khan 1966–1972* (Karachi: Oxford University Press. 2007) 204.

108. Gauhar, *Ayub Khan,* 421.

109. Interview with S. M. Zafar, 104, 4th Floor, Siddique Trade Centre, Lahore, 9 December 2012.

110. Cabinet mtg, 25 January 1968 cited in Baxter, *Diaries of Field Marshal Muhammad Ayub Khan,* 206.

111. The last visit of the researcher to NDC was in August 2012.

112. Cabinet mtg, 26 January 1968, 23/CF/68, NDC, Islamabad.

113. Briefing by Director of Intelligence Bureau to Governors' Conference, 22 August 1968, 23/CF/68, NDC, Islamabad.

114. Gauhar, *Ayub Khan,* 420.

115. Briefing by Director of Intelligence Bureau to the Governors' Conference, 22 August 1968, 23/CF/68, NDC. Islamabad.

116. Ibid.

117. Ibid.

118. Feldman, *From Crisis to Crisis,* 189.

119. Ibid. 47.

120. Muqeem Khan, *Pakistan's Crisis in Leadership*, 16.

121. Hasan Zaheer, *The Separation of East Pakistan: The Rise and Realization of Bengali Muslim Nationalism* (Karachi: np, 1994), 113.

122. Rizvi, *Military, State and Society*, 124.

123. Cabinet mtg, 2 September 1970, 296/CF/70, NDC, Islamabad.

124. G. W. Choudhury, *The Last Days of United Pakistan*, 93–4. The five points included a. Pakistan must be based on Islamic ideology; b. The country would have a democratic constitution; c. Pakistan's territorial integrity must be upheld in the constitution, d. The disparity between the Wings, especially economic disparity, must be eliminated; e. Maximum autonomy would be given to the provinces.

125. Ibid. 92.

126. Ibid.

127. Mahmood, *Pakistan Divided*, 56.

128. Calling a session of the National Assembly would have given the Awami League one chance to form a government in the centre. So, the session was delayed.

129. Ziring, *Pakistan in the Twentieth Century*, 347.

130. This was presided over by the Defence Advisor and included the secretary of the cabinet, secretaries of the Departments of Information, Foreign Affairs, and Industries, an officer of cabinet division, the director general of ISI and director of Intelligence Bureau as members. Muqeem Khan, *Pakistan's Crisis*, 23–4.

131. Feldman, *The End and the Beginning*, 149.

132. Cabinet mtg, 1 September 1971, 280/CF/71, NDC, Islamabad.

133. Feldman, *The End and the Beginning*, 150–1. The government announced that there were allegations of misconduct against seventy-nine members of the NA from East Pakistan and if they were unable to answer the charges levied against them, their seats would be considered vacant. Mujib's seat was also declared vacant.

134. Muqeem, *Pakistan's Crisis in Leadership*, 160.

135. Ibid. 193 and 97.

136. As details of the war and sad demise are not directly relevant to the given topic, I have not included details of the event. For details

see various books on the war including, Saddique Salik, *Witness to Surrender* (Karachi: Oxford University Press, 1979); G. W. Choudhury, *The Last Days of United Pakistan*, and Feldman, *The End and the Beginning*.

137. Special mtg of the Cabinet (consisted of West Pakistani ministers), 28 June 1967 cited in Baxter, *Diaries of Field Marshal Muhammad Ayub Khan*, 111.

138. Ibid.

139. For details see Chapter 1.

140. William, *Pakistan Under Challenge*, 87.

141. Decision of the cabinet, 8 February 1973, 50/CF/73, NDC, Islamabad.

142. Khan Abdul Wali Khan, *Asal Haqaiq Yei Hain* (Urdu) (Karachi: Shubul Publications, 1988), 34–5.

143. Airgram from American Embassy to Department of State, Confidential A-154, 29 September 1972, Balochistan Governor's Comments on Recent Political Situation in Balochistan in Roedad Khan, *The American Papers*, 857.

144. Ibid.

145. Wolpert, *Zulfi Bhutto of Pakistan*, 199.

146. Cabinet mtg, 30 January 1972, 40/CF/72, NDC, Islamabad.

147. Cabinet mtg, 29 January 1972, 118/CF/72, NDC, Islamabad.

148. The name of that leader is not mentioned in the file of CP, but Stanley Wolpert has stated that he was the father of Wali Khan who had come back from Afghanistan after self-imposed exile of eight years.

149. Cabinet mtg, 29 January 1972, 118/CF/72, NDC, Islamabad.

150. Cabinet mtg, 6 March 1972, 97/CF/72, NDC, Islamabad.

151. Ibid. This point was added on the insistence of the opposition parties, especially of NAP and JUI.

152. Interview with Dr Abdul Hai Baluch, Superintendent House, Hostel No. 4, Punjab University, Lahore, 6 June 2012.

153. Cabinet mtg, 20 April 1972, 97/CF/72, NDC, Islamabad.

154. Statement of Zulfikar Ali Bhutto at press conference in Rawalpindi, 7 May 1972 cited in *Speeches and Statement April–June 30 1972* (E-Books) http://www.bhutto.org.com

155. Wali Khan, *Asal Haqaiq Yei Hain,* 30–1.

156. Khan, *Constitutional and Political,* 260.

157. Syed, *The Discourse and Politics,* 183.

158. A federal parliamentary system of government was agreed upon by all participants for the future constitution. Wolpert, *Zulfi Bhutto of Pakistan,* 206.

159. For details please see Hamid Khan, Constitutional and Political History of Pakistan, pages 266–8.

160. Cabinet mtg, 12 February 1973, 73/CF/73-1, NDC, Islamabad.

161. Syed, *The Discourse and Politics,* 174–5.

162. Hasan, *The Mirage of Power,* 165.

163. Cabinet mtg, 5 October 1972, 128/CF/72 II, NDC, Islamabad.

164. The progress of implementation of the G. Ahmad Report, as approved by the cabinet, 128/CF/72 II, NDC, Islamabad.

165. Ibid.

166. Ibid.

167. Cabinet mtg, 5 October 1972, 128/CF/72 II, NDC, Islamabad.

168. Wolpert, *Zulfi Bhutto of Pakistan,* 225.

169. Extracts from the recommendations made by the Cabinet Committee on Balochistan, 260/CF/72, NDC, Islamabad.

170. Cabinet mtg, 12 February 1973, 73/CF/73-1, NDC, Islamabad.

171. Cabinet mtg, 13 February 1973, 73/CF/73-1, NDC, Islamabad.

172. Ibid.

173. *Keesing's Contemporary Archives,* 21–27 May 1973, Vol. XIX 1973, Longman Pakistan.

174. Cabinet mtg, 13 February 1973, 73/CF/73-1, NDC, Islamabad.

175. Telegram from American Embassy Islamabad to Secretary of State Washington D.C. Confidential 352, February 1973, cited in Roedad Khan, *The American Papers,* 890–91; and Wolpert, *Zulfi Bhutto of Pakistan,* 211.

176. Cabinet mtg, 14 February 1973, 73/CF/73, NDC, Islamabad.

177. Ibid.

178. Cabinet mtg, 15 February 1973, 73/CF/73-1, NDC, Islamabad.

179. Ibid.

180. Cabinet mtg, 17 March 1973, 73/CF/73-1, NDC, Islamabad.

181. Ibid.

182. *National Assembly of Pakistan Debates*, 4 August 1973, Vol. 4/IV, 208.

183. 225 *Keesing's Contemporary Archives* June 24–30, 1974, Vol. XX 1974, Keesing's Publication Longman Group Limited (London); and Wolpert, *Zulfi Bhutto of Pakistan.*

184. Cabinet mtg, 22 October 1973, 73/CF/73-1, NDC, Islamabad.

185. Cabinet mtg, 10 October 1973, 73/CF/73-1, NDC, Islamabad.

186. *National Assembly of Pakistan Debates*, 11 August 1973, Vol. 4, No. 10, 568.

187. Telegram from U.S. Embassy Islamabad to Secretary of State Washington D.C, 8 June 1973, cited in Roedad, Khan, *The American Papers*, 934.

188. Ibid.

189. Cabinet mtg, 2 July 1974, 221/CF/74, NDC, Islamabad.

190. Wolpert, *Zulfi Bhutto of Pakistan*, 236 and Rafi Raza, *Zulfikar Ali Bhutto and Pakistan 1967–1977* (Karachi: Oxford University Press, 1997), 272.

191. Inter-Provincial Governors' Conference, 13 August 1974, 266/ CF/74, NDC, Islamabad.

192. Ibid.

193. Cabinet mtgs, 2–3 September 1974, 221/CF/74, NDC, Islamabad.

194. Working Paper on Present Situation in Balochistan Top Secret, 221/ CF/74, NDC, Islamabad.

195. Raza, *Zulfikar Ali Bhutto*, 272.

196. Inter-Provincial Conference, 14 August 1974, 266/CF/74, NDC, Islamabad.

197. *National Assembly of Pakistan Debates Vol. II, No. 14,* 10 February 1975, *130.*

198. Ibid. 276.

199. Cabinet mtg, 13 March 175, 223/CF/74, NDC, Islamabad.

200. Ibid.

201. Raza, *Zulfikar Ali Bhutto,* 276,

202. Ibid.

203. Inter-Provincial Governors' Conference, 15 May 1975, 140/ PROG/75-ii, NDC, Islamabad.

204. *Times*, 3 September 1976 cited in *Keesing's Contemporary Archives* 22 April 1976, Vol. XXII, 1976.
205. *Keesing's Contemporary Archives* 22 April 1977 Vol. XXIII, 1977; and Raza, *Zulfikar Ali Bhutto*, 272.

CHAPTER 4

The Formulation of Foreign Policy
and the Role of the Federal Cabinets

This chapter looks into the role of federal cabinets in the foreign policy formulation process and decision-making in matters of developing relations with the USA, Russia, China, India, and Muslim countries, particularly Afghanistan. The chapter also focuses on foreign policy issues where cabinet was not taken into confidence, or only extended formal approval of decisions. The role of the cabinet with regard to the important alliances or agreements which Pakistan signed with the other countries, and which had an impact on Pakistan's standing in world affairs is also discussed in this chapter. Such alliances or agreements include the South East Asia Treaty Organization (SEATO) 1954, the Baghdad Pact, later called the Central Treaty Organization (CENTO) 1955, the Indus Basin Treaty 1960, the Tashkent Agreement 1966, the Simla Agreement 1972, and the Delhi Agreement 1973. The cabinet, in most cases, gave prior approval to the draft agreements, but at times the agreements were signed on the initiative of the prime ministers or foreign ministers alone, and approval was sought later.

It has been generally projected by many political scientists and historians, when discussing Pakistan affairs, that the institution of the cabinet has never been effective in designing her foreign policy. It has further been stated that it was formulated by only a few civil and military bureaucrats. However, the declassified documents of cabinet proceedings have shown that the cabinets of the various regimes played an important role in decision-making. The documents consulted for this study have made it clear that the cabinet discussed and took decisions on various important issues. When representing Pakistan at an international conference or council, the Pakistani delegation followed an agenda approved by the cabinet. Furthermore, there was variation in the role of the cabinets of various regimes in dealing with foreign policy matters. It was an effective forum for decision-making under heads of state or governments such as Liaquat Ali Khan, Suhrawardy, and Ayub Khan on foreign policy issues, but ineffective under some other heads of the state like Yahya Khan and Zulfikar Ali Bhutto. Bhutto's personal knowledge and expertise were so vast in this area that he took many decisions on foreign matters on his own. He did not appoint a minister of foreign affairs in his cabinet; Aziz Ahmed was only minister of state for foreign affairs.[1] The following details will support the argument which has been presented here.

4.1. POLICY TOWARDS INDIA

Issues relating to India were most frequently discussed by the cabinets of the earlier period. Quaid-i-Azam Muhammad Ali Jinnah, while presiding over a cabinet meeting on 8 October 1947, said that India had been unduly demanding that Pakistan explain various issues. The explanations sought concerning certain points in the speech which Abdus Sattar Pirzada had delivered at the UN, was cited as an example. The cabinet decided that Pakistan's response should reach India as soon as possible. The cabinet declared, 'Our delegates are free to express their opinions and are not bound for explanations to any country.'[2] Furthermore, Pakistan never asked for an explanation on any negative remark made by India.

4.1.1. KASHMIR ISSUE

The Kashmir issue was discussed on various occasions in cabinet meetings. Minister of Foreign Affairs Zafrullah Khan shared the draft that was going to be presented in the Security Council's meeting on Kashmir.[3] The Quaid-i-Azam said, in a meeting, that the Pakistani delegation must not accept the proposal of dividing Jammu and Kashmir. Instead, the suggestion of a free and fair plebiscite would be put forward if any proposal of replacing the puppet government of Sheikh Abdullah was made. The Indian army must be driven out of Kashmir.[4] It was the cabinet, and not any single person who shaped Pakistan's policy on Kashmir. The cabinet was later informed about India's stand on Kashmir, which she adopted in the Security Council. India wanted to propose to the Security Council that independent status be given to Kashmir. The cabinet unanimously rejected the Indian proposal.[5] It also refused to give assent to the draft proposal presented in the Security Council wherein it was suggested that the armed forces of both India and Pakistan should jointly maintain order in Kashmir. Instead, the cabinet decided, in line with Quaid-i-Azam Muhammad Ali Jinnah's advice, that an independent military force should be sent to Kashmir to maintain order, and to hold a plebiscite.[6]

On the question of calling tribesmen back from Kashmir, the cabinet decided that this was not possible until Indian forces withdrew from Kashmir and arrangements for conducting an independent plebiscite had been made. The Quaid-i-Azam was not present in that meeting which is why the final decision was deferred until he was present. The Pakistani delegation had been strictly ordered to follow the line of action decided by the cabinet.[7]

In its next meeting, presided over by Quaid-i-Azam, the following passage was approved and cabled by the cabinet to the Pakistani delegation at the Security Council:

> Government still maintains that the only really practical and satisfactory solution of the Kashmir question is that Indian troops should withdraw and that there should be a neutral military force in the place of the present Abdullah regime. That is the straight course to be adopted and will immediately bring peace and the restoration and maintenance of law and order and will secure a free, fair, and impartial plebiscite. [8]

The cabinet further advised the delegation to consult the government if any changes to the final draft were under consideration.[9] In a telegram in October 1948, Nehru threatened his Pakistani counterpart with grave consequences if Pakistan did not accept Kashmir as part of India. Liaquat discussed the telegram in the cabinet and the answer to the telegram was also approved in the meeting. After explaining Pakistan's stand on the issue of Kashmir, it stated:

You have in your telegram ... threatened Pakistan with war. This is hardly the way to promote peaceful and cooperative relations between two countries. I must make it clear that the Pakistan Government cannot allow themselves to be intimated by a threat of the use of force by your government.[10]

Gurmani, Minister without Portfolio, wrote to Zafrullah Khan that he would issue guidance notes on the Kashmir policy to ensure uniformity in the official approach towards the Kashmir problem.[11]

The ceasefire agreement on the line of control was discussed on 30 July 1949 and approved by cabinet. PM Liaquat said that the ceasefire agreement was in the best interests of Pakistan as her forces in Kashmir were not strong enough to defend the area for long. The cabinet agreed that a timely decision would be effective, unlike in the case of Palestine who failed to sign in time and lost a major part of her territory.[12] From January to September 1949, the deadlock continued between India and Pakistan on the issue of Kashmir. The cabinet discussed the idea of arbitration as there was no other way to break the deadlock. The cabinet also approved the appointment of Admiral Nimitz as arbitrator.[13] On the advice of the cabinet, Liaquat wrote to inform Nehru that for the settlement of disputes between India and Pakistan, mediation was the best choice, but if disputes remained unsettled for two months after the start of mediation, then both countries should go to arbitration.[14] The cabinet met on several occasions between October 1951 and December 1953 to discuss the Kashmir issue, especially with regard to the India-Pakistan negotiations on Kashmir, through UN representative Dr Frank P. Graham and Admiral Nimitz. The line of action was always decided by the cabinet rather than any single representative, and correspondence between the Indian and Pakistani prime ministers was also the responsibility of the cabinet.[15]

4.1.2. COALITION CABINETS, 1955–58

During the period of the coalition cabinets (1955–1958), most attention was given to solving the problems between India and Pakistan. The issues which the cabinets tried to settle included the canal water dispute, pre-Partition financial matters, and post-Partition issues including trade agreements between the two countries, etc. The cabinets decided that if the World Bank's proposals did not suit Pakistan, she would reject the plan.[16] On the issue of financial matters, cabinet decided that the issue would be discussed once again in the meeting of the Pakistan-India finance ministers, and if they were unable to reach an agreement, Pakistan would ask for arbitration by three judges of the Privy Council of Great Britain. As settlement of this issue was in favour of Pakistan, which would receive a large amount of money, Pakistan was anxious to settle the issue as early as possible.[17]

The cabinet of Huseyn Shaheed Suhrawardy had approved a plan for improving Pakistan's trade relations with India. A one-year trade agreement was signed in 1956 and later cabinet authorized the Pakistani delegation to sign a three-year trade agreement if possible. Trade goods were also finalized in cabinet meetings.[18] Commerce Minister Abul Mansur Ahmad suggested improving cultural relations also. The cabinet approved the import of Hindi, Urdu, and Bengali films from India.[19] Later, in pursuance of the brief approved by the cabinet, negotiations for a new trade agreement with India were held in New Delhi from 15 to 22 January 1957. A complete summary of the negotiations and a copy of the agreement were presented to the cabinet for formal approval, which was given on 28 January 1957.[20]

Cabinet, headed by Malik Firoz Khan Noon, wanted to establish friendly relations with India. The soft spot which Noon had developed for India was not popular:[21] public opinion in Pakistan favoured developing friendly relations with India after resolving the dispute over Kashmir. The cabinets of this period played an effective role in deciding policy towards India.

4.1.3. THE INDUS WATER TREATY, 1960

With the abrogation of the Constitution in October 1958, Pakistan's external relations had been lifted out of politics. The regime had been largely able to adopt an unemotional and pragmatic approach to most of the issues. Relations with India provide an outstanding example of this, as besides the Kashmir dispute, other issues were also given importance by the cabinet and were settled.[22] The military cabinet of Ayub Khan discussed the proposed Indus Water Treaty in detail. Amendments were recommended in different areas of the agreement and the Pakistani delegation was advised by the cabinet on different aspects. It was suggested that in the proposed agreement the term 'Indian territory' should be amended to 'territory under the control of India'.[23] The cabinet decided that attempts should be made to ensure the World

Bank's role in the execution of the agreement, particularly on the issue of establishing the joint commission.[24] The cabinet finally approved the treaty on 10 September 1960. Some other relevant issues also came under discussion. Minister of Food and Agriculture, Lt Gen. K. N. Sheikh, was asked to guide WAPDA to concentrate on the replacement work and to complete related projects within a short time. He was also asked to seek an explanation from the chairman of WAPDA on disclosing the alleged effects of the treaty on irrigation without confirmation by the central government. The cabinet authorized Finance Minister Mohammad Shoaib to sign the Indus Basin Development Fund Agreement on behalf of the government of Pakistan.[25] The cabinet further decided that the president should sign the Indus Water Treaty in 1960, on behalf of the government.[26] The potentially dangerous Indus Water Dispute was settled,[27] which opened the way for the resolution of other disputes too.

4.1.4. THE PAKISTAN-INDIA WAR 1965 AND THE TASHKENT TREATY, 1966

The federal cabinet of Pakistan became involved in the issue of the 1965 War at a very late stage, i.e. after India's attack on Pakistan. But the Defence Committee of the Cabinet, as claimed by Altaf Gauhar, was involved in the different developments of the pre-1965 war era. According to him, it approved a controversial plan involving the infiltration of Pakistani guerrillas into Indian-held Kashmir. This committee was comprised of the president, the supreme commander; the C-in-C of the armed forces, the minister of finance, and the minister of economic affairs.[28] The plan was prepared by a secret committee consisting of the secretaries of the ministries of Foreign Affairs and Defence, the director of the Intelligence Bureau, the chief of general staff, and the director of military operations, under the chairmanship of Aziz Ahmed, Secretary of Foreign Affairs. The plan was presented to the Intelligence Committee of the Cabinet in February 1965. General Musa, Bhutto, and Aziz Ahmed were its members.[29] Bhutto, in the words of Altaf Gauhar, criticized the plan but later, while presiding over a cabinet meeting in the absence of Ayub, informed the cabinet that a popular revolt had broken out in occupied Kashmir, and that the situation was desperate. He suggested that Pakistan must intervene and take advantage of the situation. Operation Gibraltar started a few days later. Though the cabinet had been informed about the proposed operation in Kashmir, the details were not revealed. On 8 August, the date on which the operation was launched, four Pakistani soldiers were taken captive and their interviews were broadcast on the Indian Radio.[30] The captives revealed details of Operation Gibraltar on the Indian Radio. It was a mockery of the situation that the Pakistani people, officials, and cabinet were informed about Operation Gibraltar through the Indian Radio.[31]

The border between India and Pakistan was not demarcated at the Rann of Kutch in Sindh. Some 3,500 square miles of territory was disputed. The problem was first discussed at the diplomatic level in January 1960, but was not settled. Border clashes started between India and Pakistan at the Rann of Kutch in January 1965 and increased.[32] Pakistani forces mauled India badly after the start of intense fighting on 9 April 1965. The Indian PM's anti-Pakistan statements indicated that India was ready to attack Pakistan with full force.[33] Britain intervened and a temporary ceasefire agreement was signed between India and Pakistan.

The president told the cabinet that two agreements had been signed with India. The first agreement envisaged that the forces of both countries would go back to the positions they had held prior to 1 January 1965, within seven days. The second agreement concerned with the creation of a tribunal consisting of Pakistani and Indian delegates and one chairman. If the tribunal could not settle the Rann of Kutch dispute, the issue would be transferred to the UN Secretary General. Cabinet decided that the Foreign Office would appoint a prominent lawyer to prepare Pakistan's case for the ministerial meeting and tribunal. Manzur Qadir was considered as suitable for this position. The cabinet also decided that all evidence and supporting documents must be prepared for the case.[34] Ayub Khan told the cabinet on 12 June 1965 that nothing positive had been achieved with India on the Kutch dispute. He further informed the cabinet that he had discussed the issue with the services chiefs and all preparations had been made in case of a war with India. He briefed the cabinet about the measures taken by the armed forces. The cabinet secretary said that in case of war with India, the Defence Committee of the Cabinet (DCC) would hold daily meetings and would pass the necessary orders in the light of the situation.[35] Later the cabinet prepared a brief for the foreign minister for his meeting with the

Indian foreign minister. The composition of the delegation was also finalized, but the delegation could not go because India had, by that time, refused to take part in the talks.[36]

All the above developments indicate that India's attack on Pakistan was not sudden, as is generally believed. Selected members of the Pakistani cabinet and administration were well aware of the worsening situation on the border. The cabinet was even informed about the preparation of armed forces for war with India.

Border clashes continued between India and Pakistan throughout 1965 on the ceasefire line in Kashmir. Indian forces crossed the ceasefire line for the first time on 1 September without a formal declaration of war, and on 6 September they attacked Lahore, Sialkot, and other border areas of Pakistan. During the war, the Pakistani cabinet met on an almost daily basis as it was an emergency situation. The cabinet decided that a meeting of the Economic Coordination Committee of the cabinet should also be necessarily convened. The president briefed the ministers about the war situation on a daily basis.[37]

The Security Council passed resolutions regarding the ceasefire between India and Pakistan. The Secretary General of the UN, U Thant, visited Pakistan and India from 9–15 September 1965. The cabinet discussed U Thant's visit in detail. The president informed the cabinet that he had told the UN Secretary General that the Kashmiris were demanding liberation from India. Their brothers in Azad Kashmir naturally became infuriated and wanted to help them. The

foreign minister reported that all the major powers had
been in agreement with Pakistan about Kashmir, but all had
changed their opinion with the passage of time. President
Ayub further told the Secretary General, 'Our past conduct
shows that we want settlement of the problem peacefully'.[38]
The Secretary General mentioned in his meeting with
Bhutto that 'a new urgency had arisen because of the conflict
between these two countries'.[39] He said that Pakistan must
sign the UN Resolution for the ceasefire. The Foreign
Minister said that an unconditional ceasefire would make
the Kashmir issue a dead one once again. He requested
another resolution from the UN, which provided for the
enforcement of Security Council decisions. The Secretary
General was convinced and said that he would report back
on these ideas.[40]

The cabinet decided that maps should be prepared, indicating
the areas attacked by India, for the information of U Thant.
Detailed briefs were also prepared.[41] The cabinet assigned to
the law minister the duty of preparing Pakistan's case in full
detail for presentation to the Security Council. It was noted
by the cabinet that Pakistan was in a dilemma and agreed that
the 'great powers are not very sympathetic to our cause and
will gang up against us'.[42]

While observing the USA's unwillingness to help Pakistan,
the latter decided to take its case directly to the UNO. The
possibility of bilateral talks on the matter with the USA was
rejected by the cabinet[43] who took the US decision to suspend
arms shipments to Pakistan very seriously. Bhutto said that it
would be a fatal blow to Pakistan's defence system. Pakistan

was even ready to buy arms at commercial prices.[44] The cabinet also approved the draft of the appeal prepared by the foreign minister to be issued to all the nations of the world to come to Pakistan's help.[45]

The cabinet was told that the UN Security Council, under pressure from the USA, had passed the ceasefire-resolution. The cabinet agreed that the western powers wanted to see Pakistan subdued and wished to see the conflict resolved rather than escalating into a struggle between the great powers. The cabinet considered it unfortunate that the secretary general was not trying hard enough to seek a lasting solution to the Kashmir problem and was just trying to impose a ceasefire, which was mainly favourable to India. The cabinet decided that Pakistan must accept the peace proposals, which were relatively more favourable to Pakistan.[46] In every meeting the USA's attitude was criticized by the cabinet. On 12 September 1965, the ceasefire resolution was discussed in the cabinet meeting, where it was stated that Pakistan:

> ... demands that ceasefire should take effect on Wednesday, 22 September 1965 on 0700 hours ... and calls upon both governments to issue orders for a ceasefire at that moment and a subsequent withdrawal of all armed personnel back to the positions held by them before 5 August 1965.[47]

Some cabinet ministers were dissatisfied with the resolution. Altaf Hussain, Minister for Industries, said 'We must be firm.' Ayub snapped at him. Governor of West Pakistan, Nawab of Kalabagh, strongly favoured Ayub's idea. Bhutto discussed 'the unfavourable aspects' of the resolution. Nur Khan wanted the acceptance of the resolution immediately, without further discussion.[48] The next day, the President informed the cabinet that Pakistan had indicated to the Security Council its acceptance of the ceasefire proposals in the interests of world peace, with only one change, that it would be effective on 23 September 1965.

In a special meeting Z. A. Bhutto informed the cabinet about the details of the latest resolution of the Security Council on Kashmir. He told the cabinet that the UN had passed resolutions on 4, 5, 20, and 27 September, and a final one on 5 November 1965. The first two were about the ceasefire and withdrawal of forces; the third resolution, while referring to Kashmir in paragraph 4, had stated that the urgent need was to settle the 'underlying political problem'.[49] This key point had been emphasized again and again by Pakistan. The UN Secretary General had assured Pakistan that the UNO would act this time on the resolutions. The United Kingdom and the United States supported the same resolution inspite of bullying tactics from India.[50] France supported Pakistan's position. The president congratulated the foreign minister on the 'successful achievement of the task assigned to them especially because it was accomplished against tremendous odds'.[51]

The government of Pakistan was very active in settling the Kashmir dispute. A consensus developed among the cabinet members that the President of Pakistan, during his forthcoming visit to the USA, should try to impress upon the US leadership that the Kashmir issue needed to be settled urgently for the restoration of peace in the region.[52]

The cabinet also decided that Ayub must convey Pakistan's reservations on the attitude of the US towards Pakistan during and after the 1965 War, especially on arms aid to India, and later on the arms embargo on both countries,[53] which was actually more harmful for Pakistan and was only a 'pinprick to India'.[54] Pakistan was even prepared to buy arms rather than receiving aid from America.

The war ended, but the reason for the war, i.e. the Kashmir dispute, and the post-war issues were still unsettled. Bhutto informed the cabinet, after his visit to the USSR, that the Soviet leadership had suggested that the best option was to solve mutual problems on a bilateral level, but both the Pakistani and Indian ministers of foreign affairs suggested Soviet mediation.[55] Bhutto visited the USSR for preliminary talks before the Tashkent Summit. He briefed the cabinet that the Foreign Minister of the USSR had assured him that his PM would take a firm stand on the Kashmir issue after the Tashkent Talks.[56] Afzal's opinion is that the formal agenda for the proposed talks was not decided prior to the meeting of the Pakistani cabinet.[57]

Altaf Gauhar has mentioned the details of the cabinet meeting which was held to discuss the sole subject of the Tashkent Talks. All salient aspects of the brief[58] for the upcoming summit meeting at Tashkent were discussed. All ministers and governors attended the meeting. Discussion took place on the issues of the withdrawal of forces, settlement of the Kashmir issue, proportionate reduction of forces, and the adoption of a no-war declaration if the first three were accepted. Ayub's opinion was that India might agree on the first point, but not the second. He asked the cabinet what Pakistan should do if such a situation occurred. Shahabuddin said that India would adopt a more rigid policy on Kashmir due to its forthcoming elections: the right wing of Congress would not let Shastri, the Indian PM, agree to any concession on Kashmir. Finance Minister Mohammad Shoaib, while adopting a more realistic approach, suggested that Tashkent must be used to settle other problems like enemy property, overflights, etc. Home Minister Ali Akbar, said that the Kashmir issue was the most important problem to settle. General Musa interrupted and stated that India would never negotiate on Kashmir. Bhutto said that the Soviets would 'lean towards India', but he advised that 'Tashkent should be approached as an opportunity since it was not an exclusive Soviet initiative'.[59] Ayub informed the cabinet, 'I know people who want to risk Pakistan for the sake of Kashmir.'[60] As well as discussion, some changes were also suggested to the Pakistani draft declaration. It was suggested that the words 'defence requirements' should be substituted by the words 'other relevant considerations'.[61]

At Tashkent, sharp differences of opinion emerged between the Pakistani and Indian sides. Ayub and Bhutto insisted on the settlement of the Kashmir dispute as mentioned in the Pakistani draft of the treaty, whereas Shastri and Sardar Swaran Singh insisted on a mutual withdrawal of forces and did not refer to Kashmir. Each side rejected the other's draft. Ultimately, the Tashkent Declaration was signed on 6 January 1966 after Kosygin, the Soviet PM helped the two countries to reach an agreement.[62] On 12 January, a cabinet meeting was held to discuss the declaration. Three commanders-in-chief were also invited. Ayub stated that he went to Tashkent without any hope regarding Kashmir, but could not leave Tashkent without signing the treaty because all the major powers, the USA and Britain were with the Soviet Union on this issue. India was not ready to move an inch from its stand on Kashmir. He said that 'he had faced a stonewall during his meetings with Shastri'.[63] He admitted that, 'Militarily we have not been able to demolish the wall. We have to wait'.[64] He further explained that India wanted to sign a no-war pact and did not want Pakistan to have closer relations with China, but he clarified to the Indians that without a Kashmir settlement, this was not possible. While summing up, Ayub said that Kosygin had expressed his concern for the solution of the Kashmir dispute.[65] Bhutto remained silent during the proceedings of the cabinet meeting, creating the impression that he was unhappy with the declaration. The Pakistani delegation was not satisfied with the outcome of the talks as they considered that, overall, the Soviets favoured India.[66]

At one point Ayub asked Bhutto to provide some background on the different elements of the Tashkent Declaration, but Bhutto immediately passed this task to Aziz Ahmed. He responded very shortly on one direct question from Ayub. Although Bhutto did not oppose the declaration, his attitude was 'unconcealed'.[67] Overall, the atmosphere in the meeting was different from that of normal cabinet meetings. Ayub only gave the details of the Tashkent proceedings; ministers were not invited to ask questions so queries remained unanswered.[68] Two opinions prevailed in Ayub's cabinet regarding Tashkent.[69] The only positive development after the Tashkent declaration was the improvement of relations between Soviet Union and Pakistan.

4.1.5. YAHYA KHAN AND THE 1971 WAR

Yahya Khan's government could not perform well vis-à-vis India. Relations reached their lowest ebb when war broke out between the two countries in 1971. East Pakistan separated from the rest of Pakistan with the help of the Indian government and emerged as Bangladesh. Yahya Khan had to hand over power to Z. A. Bhutto, whose party had secured a majority of seats in the West Pakistan Assembly in the 1970 elections.

4.1.6. POST-1971 WAR ISSUES AND THE SETTLEMENT

Zulfikar Ali Bhutto successfully handled post-1971 War issues with the support of his cabinet. The Simla Agreement was the first success of Bhutto's government in the realm of foreign relations. Bhutto's ideology of bilateralism was successful at that moment. In the words of Bhutto, it was not easy to reach an agreement with Indian PM Indira Gandhi after the 1971 War. He said:

> I found myself talking in the perspective of history ... I remember asking her what the world would say if we failed, how history would judge us. I said we have been fighting for the last 25 years ... this is how the world has seen us ... I repeated that the psychological impact on our peoples and on others would be bad if we returned home in failure, she to Delhi and I to Islamabad; we must take the chance this meeting in

Simla offered. She smiled and suggested that we resume our conversation after dinner.[70]

Ministers and delegation members from both sides held talks separately. According to Bhutto, ministers were, 'building up an agreement and sending us reports on the progress they were making, that they were in agreement on this and not on that and finally that they had attained the sort of agreement I had been outlining to Mrs Gandhi'.[71]

The ice between the countries started melting with the signing of the Simla Agreement. It 'specified respect for the national unity, territorial integrity, political independence, and sovereign equality of the signatory states. Each was to refrain from the use of force against the other and to seek peaceful means to redress their differences'.[72] It was intended that the prisoners of war issue would be settled through peaceful negotiations. Pakistani Minister of State for Defence and Foreign Affairs Aziz Ahmed and his Indian counterpart Swaran Singh met in Rawalpindi in July 1973. A joint statement was issued at the end that 'all the prisoners of war would be released except the 195 charged with war crimes who would not be handed over to Bangladesh until after further discussion.'[73]

Bhutto had already prepared the ground at home for support on the Simla Agreement. Almost all political parties in the House supported him. While addressing the National Assembly, Khan Abdul Qayyum Khan, Minister of Home Affairs, said that President Bhutto was going 'with the full support of all sections of the House … and that was the only bargaining power which President Bhutto carried with him'.[74] Although the major role on the international front was played by Bhutto, he had the full support of not only the cabinet, but also of the other forces. Ministers delivered speeches in the National Assembly in support of the Simla Accord. Maulana Kausar Niazi said that in view of the prevailing circumstances and 'in view of this principle that nothing against our will and our principles should be included in the Accord, in my opinion, the Accord is the great achievement.'[75]

President Bhutto was hopeful that the issue of the return of the prisoners of war would be easier to handle than the withdrawal of troops from the borders. He said, 'Prisoners cannot be kept indefinitely. Israel has not left an inch of Arab territory but they have returned all prisoners of war ... We will certainly get back our prisoners of war'.[76] The talks between India and Pakistan were resumed in Delhi. It was to the credit of Bhutto that the Delhi Agreement was signed successfully. Bhutto signalled in New Delhi that Bangladesh would be recognized. The Indian administration was ready to sign an agreement regarding the return of 93,000 prisoners of war.[77] 195 prisoners of war were kept back by Bangladesh for trial on charges of war crimes. Later, they were also released. The Bangladesh foreign minister announced that 'the Government of Bangladesh had decided not to proceed with the trials as an act of clemency'[78] due to the appeal of Pakistan's PM to 'the people of Bangladesh to forgive and forget the mistakes of the past'.[79] The cabinet also discussed the details of the atrocities alleged to have been committed by the 195 prisoners of war later in May 1974.[80]

The next important problem related to the 1971 War for Bhutto's government was the recognition of Bangladesh. The cabinet had decided that a debate on the question of the recognition of Bangladesh should be held on TV and radio after 7 March 1973. The interviewer should be carefully selected and properly briefed by the foreign ministry, and the Peoples Party and opposition leaders should be invited to take part in the discussion.[81] The debate on the issue of the recognition of Bangladesh was opened in the National Assembly, which authorized the president to recognize Bangladesh.[82] The decision concerning the recognition of Bangladesh was taken by Bhutto's inner cabinet and the whole cabinet endorsed it later. It was just before the Islamic Summit Conference that the other ministers, including Maulana Kausar Niazi, learned about the decision.[83]

4.1.7. INDIAN NUCLEAR TEST

The Indian Nuclear Test in 1974 was highly criticized in Pakistan. The cabinet discussed the issue and adopted a formal policy on it. According to the cabinet decision, high-level action was begun by Pakistan. Pakistan recorded its reaction and concern to the UN Secretary General. The foreign secretary was sent to China, France, and Britain to explain the situation. Bhutto visited the Soviet Union. Aziz Ahmed was given the task of raising the subject at the CENTO meeting in Washington and holding discussions with US officials, and then visiting Canada, which had contributed a lot to India's nuclear capability. Bhutto himself wrote letters to many heads of state. He further said that he had not signed a 'no-war pact' with India at Simla due to the unsettled dispute over Kashmir, and that after the nuclear testing it would be impossible.[84]

In response to Pakistan's high-level action, Mrs Gandhi sent a personal letter to Bhutto through the Swiss Embassy in New Delhi on 22 May 1974.[85] Bhutto kept bilateral relations between India and Pakistan alive, but started work on creating nuclear capability for Pakistan. This programme was kept secret to a large extent and was never discussed openly in cabinet meetings during Bhutto's period. He had doubts about some of his cabinet colleagues and advisors 'regarding their contacts with USA'.[86] Minister of Production Rafi Raza had warned him of US wrath over the nuclear issue, but Bhutto did not move an inch from his decision.[87] USA exerted great pressure on Pakistan regarding the acquisition of a nuclear power plant. Aziz Ahmed told the National Assembly of Pakistan on 1 June 1977 that US Secretary of State Henry Kissinger had warned Pakistan on 8 August 1976 that if Pakistan proceeded 'with the acquisition of the nuclear plant, the US would cut off military and economic aid to it'.[88]

All governments of Pakistan during the period of this study gave utmost attention to settling Pakistan's problems with India and to improving relations with her. The role of the cabinet in this regard was mixed. The federal cabinet was highly involved in the initial years in setting the policy on Kashmir, settling financial matters, solving the water dispute, and developing trade links, etc. Ayub Khan also gave an edge to his cabinet to deal with India-related issues directly on most occasions. Unfortunately, Yahya Khan and some of his military colleagues were sole decision-makers, and under them Pakistan faced the hardest defeat on the Indian front in the shape of the loss of East Pakistan. Z. A. Bhutto did not involve the cabinet directly in dealing with issues related to India, yet he always had the confidence and support of his cabinet colleagues behind him regarding his decisions related to India.

4.2. POLICY TOWARDS MUSLIM COUNTRIES (PARTICULARLY AFGHANISTAN)

Developing brotherly relations with Muslim countries remained one of the key foreign policy principles of Pakistan throughout the period of this study. Afghanistan, out of all Muslim countries, attracted most of the attention of the cabinets of Pakistan due to its hostile attitude towards Pakistan.

4.2.1. FIRST PARLIAMENTARY REGIME, 1947–1958

Afghanistan was the only Muslim country to abstain during the vote on Pakistan's membership of the UNO and had been pressing claims to some territories of NWFP. Even then, Pakistan tried to adopt a positive policy towards Afghanistan. She provided transit and trade facilities to her. At the same time, Pakistan had imposed a check on the publicaton and broadcasting of any anti-Afghan material in the press and on radio, hoping that Afghanistan would do the same, but to no avail.[89] Relations with Afghanistan reached their lowest ebb in May 1955 when both countries closed their respective consulates. The situation was saved by the mediation of some friendly countries. The cabinet had decided that if mediation between the two countries failed, the Pakistani government would ask GHQ to take the necessary steps to safeguard Pakistan's border from an expected attack from the Afghan side.[90]

Choudhury Muhammad Ali's cabinet was successful in acquiring a 'Gentlemen's Agreement'[91] with Afghanistan through the mediation of Saudi Arabia, Egypt, and Turkey. Unfortunately, Afghanistan violated the terms of the treaty and the Foreign Minister of Afghanistan issued some anti-Pakistan statements on the issue of Khan Abdul Ghaffar Khan's arrest. Furthermore, Radio Kabul started broadcasting some anti-Pakistan programmes. To meet the crisis, the cabinet decided that the government must adopt a strict policy against Afghanistan on the violation of the 'Gentlemen's Agreement'. Moreover, the Ministry of Information and Broadcasting was asked to respond to Afghanistan's propaganda through unofficial sources. The railways and provincial governments were asked to stop the movement of consignments to Afghanistan until relations improved.[92]

Cabinet was informed on 12 October 1955 that Afghanistan had tried to interfere in the internal affairs of Pakistan by sending messages through different sources, that the implementation of One Unit should be postponed till the meeting of the Afghan PM with his Pakistani counterpart.[93] In the cabinet meeting, the PM suggested that a reply would be sent to Afghanistan through the Pakistani embassy and that there was no question of discussing One Unit or any other domestic issue with Afghanistan. If the Afghan PM wanted to visit Pakistan, he would be welcomed, but One Unit would not be discussed.[94] Suhrawardy's government signed a joint communiqué with Prince Daud of Afghanistan on 1 December 1956 with specific reference to the existence of the Pakhtunistan issue.[95]

4.2.2. AYUB KHAN'S REGIME, 1958–1969

In his first statement on foreign policy on 25 December 1958, Ayub Khan accepted the UN's charter, he rejected colonialism, and emphasized developing brotherly relations with all Muslim countries, especially with Middle Eastern countries.[96]

Because Afghanistan had adopted a hostile stance to Pakistan since its inception, that also attracted the attention of policymakers in the period of General Ayub Khan. He and his ministers criticized Suhrawardy's policy on Afghanistan. His cabinet was not ready to adopt a soft policy on this issue. Ayub refused to discuss the Pakhtunistan issue with the Afghan authorities. The Foreign Minister of Afghanistan complained that Ayub's regime was even more anti-Pakhtunistan than Iskandar Mirza, who had wanted to 'find some sort of solution'.[97] Manzur Qadir's offer on 7 March 1959 of a plebiscite in Afghanistan to determine whether the Afghan tribesmen wished to join Pakistan, resulted in more strained relations.[98] Relations reached their lowest point in September 1961 when the consulates of Pakistan in Jalalabad and Kandahar were closed. Afghanistan was also asked to close its consulate and trade agencies in Peshawar and Quetta. Relations improved a little in March 1963 when Premier

Daud and his brother, Finance Minister Nasim, whose focus of foreign policy was only 'Pakhtunistan', resigned.[99] With the efforts of the Shah of Iran, consulates were reopened in May 1963 and both sides agreed that they would do their best to create an atmosphere of good understanding, friendship, and mutual trust.[100]

During Ayub's era, the cabinet discussed issues related to Afghanistan on several occasions, and took some important decisions. The Minister for Finance was assigned the duty of coordinating a detailed scrutiny of Pak-Afghan relations with reference to the issues, including the imposition of travel restrictions, the introduction of some forms of exchange control regulations, commercial and trade relations, particularly with reference to the flow of imported goods to Afghanistan from Pakistan, and the prevention of smuggling of Afghanis into Pakistan by diplomatic missions in lieu of foreign exchange.[101] Work started on the issues but could not be completed during Ayub's reign.

Ayub took his cabinet colleagues into his confidence when recognizing new governments in Muslim countries. The cabinet approved the recognition of the new government of Syria in 1963.[102] The federal cabinet discussed the response of Muslim countries after the outbreak of war between India and Pakistan. And the offer of assistance from Saudi Arabia was warmly appreciated by the cabinet.[103] Ayub Khan told the cabinet that the PM of Iran and the Foreign Minister of Turkey had held several discussions with him. They were sincerely and extremely concerned about Indian aggression against Pakistan and the people of both these countries. Both countries had taken a firm stand in favour of Pakistan.[104]

Pakistan also responded to the causes of other Muslim countries. Pakistan displayed her solidarity with Muslim countries on the outbreak of the Arab-Israel War in 1967. The Foreign Minister of Pakistan condemned Israel for its 'naked aggression'.[105] Ayub wrote to the heads of the Arab states that Pakistan would do its utmost to render whatever 'material help' they required.[106] On the advice of the Pakistani cabinet and administration, Pakistani representatives in the UN pleaded the Arab cause effectively.

4.2.3. YAHYA KHAN'S POLICY

Yahya Khan's government dealt with Afghanistan without the involvement of the civilian cabinet. Pakistani Finance Minister Mozaffar Ali Qizilbash visited Kabul in May 1970 and signed an agreement to improve economic cooperation between the two countries. It included many fields, from the utilization of iron-ore deposits in Afghanistan to investment in Afghanistan in different fields. Pakistan agreed to provide training facilities to Afghanistan in the areas of medicine, engineering, irrigation, and fertilizers.[107]

4.2.4. SECOND PARLIAMENTARY REGIME, 1971–1977

Since the days of his foreign ministership in Ayub's cabinet, Bhutto had believed in close affinity with Muslim countries. He said:

An essential feature of the foreign policy of Pakistan is its marked emphasis on the extensive civilization of Islam as a force of emancipation and progress. The nature of this emphasis has passed through its own variations from the earlier days of Islam in this subcontinent. The quality of belief and intensity of intellectual and spiritual preoccupation with its objectives, however, have not been impaired by the passage of time.[108]

The cabinet also took an interest in expanding and consolidating Pakistan's relations with the Muslim world. Bhutto visited Muslim countries immediately after taking power, and informed the cabinet that he had explained Pakistan's stand on Bangladesh to the heads of Muslim countries, who had shown great sympathy and understanding for Pakistan's cause, for which they promised full support. He was warmly received in Iran, Turkey, Morocco, Algeria, Libya, Egypt, and Syria.[109] With the cabinet's approval, personal letters from the president were sent to the presidents of Libya and Saudi Arabia through the minister of information and the minister for food and agriculture respectively.[110] His government formed a new channel to obtain aid for Pakistan, and foreign policy took another turn. A Mirage fighter aircraft rebuilding facility was set up with the financial support of Libya. The Indus Highway, Lowari Pass Tunnel, and the nuclear power development programmes are other examples of this.[111] In particular, close relations were developed with the oil-rich West Asian Muslim countries, where a large number of Pakistani manpower was located, who became a major source of income for Pakistan in the form of foreign exchange earnings. 'Pakistan began to exploit Islamic ideology to signify and strengthen its relationship with these countries'.[112] It was to the credit of Bhutto's government that the International Islamic Conference was organized in Lahore in February 1974. Thirty-seven Muslim countries participated in it. Defence-related exchange programmes increased with the Gulf States and Saudi Arabia. Pakistan provided the best training opportunities to the officer corps of these Muslim countries.[113]

The cabinet, however, was taken into confidence on the issue of Afghanistan. Pakistan's relations with Afghanistan had been strained since the beginning. The cabinet decided to hold a detailed discussion on the subject of Pakistan-Afghanistan relations with a view to exploring the possibilities of improving the present situation.[114] The minister of state for foreign affairs was engaged in preparing a comprehensive paper dealing with all aspects of Pakistan's relations with Afghanistan. This paper was circulated in December 1972 to elicit the views of the ministries and agencies concerned. An inter-ministerial meeting was convened on 9 March 1973 after receiving the views in order to devise an agreed-upon approach. The president also gave his views on the paper before its submission to the cabinet for formal discussion.[115]

Maulana Kausar Niazi, Minister of Information and Broad-casting prepared a proposal for an all-tribes *jirga* with the help of his ministry. It was mentioned in the proposal that Kabul was organizing a *jirga* of tribal areas and had criticized the 'Pakistani government and its policies towards *Pukhtoons* and *Baluchis*'.[116] The propaganda was aimed to mislead the people and their opinions. It was suggested by Niazi that, with a view to obtaining the unanimous support of all the tribesmen of the tribal areas, an all-tribes *jirga* might be held in Peshawar in August.[117] The proposed *jirga* would include the tribal elders of the tribal areas, leading ulama and religious divines of the tribal areas, prominent tribal writers and poets, and the PM of Pakistan as chief guest. This proposal was countered by the minister of interior, and chief ministers of NWFP and Balochistan in separate letters.[118] The president accepted their opinions that paying undue attention to the tribal people and *sardars* would create further problems, so the idea of a tribal *jirga* was dropped.

Propaganda for Pukhtunistan was still alive in Afghanistan, especially after Sardar Daud's coming to power after the 1973 coup. Bhutto quickly recognized the new regime, with the approval of his cabinet. A carrot-and-stick policy was adopted to deal with Afghanistan. On one hand, goodwill messages were sent to Sardar Daud and his appointment was recognized on 22 July 1973, and on the other hand, Kabul was warned that if it revived the Pukhtunistan issue and created problems on the border 'Pakistan would take care of it'.[119] In addition, the government continued its struggle to improve relations with Afghanistan; facilities were increased for Afghan traders, and relief supplies were sent to Afghanistan during the famine of 1972–73, and in 1976 when an earthquake severely damaged the Afghan economy. Pakistan reached a limited understanding with Afghanistan on 10 June 1975, on the principles of peaceful co-existence, e.g., non-interference in each other's internal affairs and sovereignty, and respect for territorial integrity.[120] Relations between the two countries deteriorated so badly in the early months of 1976 that cabinet decided that Pakistan should be fully prepared for an Afghan attack or subversion in NWFP and Balochistan.[121] Later in 1976, Bhutto visited Afghanistan and found Mohammad Daud receptive towards the peace efforts of Pakistan. Pakistan also suspended propaganda attacks on Kabul. Daud visited Pakistan two months later. The early years of the Bhutto regime witnessed a working relationship with Afghanistan, in the words of Abdul Hafiz Pirzada,[122] which was 'transformed into promising terms in 1977'.[123]

The federal cabinet of Pakistan discussed Afghanistan-related issues on many occasions and different schemes to improve relations were brought before the cabinet for discussion, but most of the schemes could not produce positive results on a long-term basis.

4.3. POLICY TOWARDS THE USA

It is generally believed that cabinets were not usually consulted or given an important role in deciding issues related to the USA, which is not completely true. In the early days of the creation of Pakistan, the cabinet was opposed to the policy of making Pakistan an ally of the USA. During PM Liaquat's and PM Nazimuddin's periods, Pakistan's foreign policy remained independent, though a slight tilt in favour of the USA was evident. PM Liaquat Ali Khan was not completely satisfied with the West's stance on the Kashmir dispute, and was not ready to adopt a clear-cut pro-West policy, particularly on the Middle East and some other issues, althoughs some of his ministers, including Ghulam Mohammad and Gurmani, had been asking for a more pro-West stand.[124]

Pakistan was facing serious economic problems, including a shortage of wheat, rising prices, and a downward trend in the exports sector at the end of the Korean War. Ayesha Jalal says that in order to meet the challenges a secret meeting of selected members of the cabinet, i.e. Zafrullah Khan, Choudhury Muhammad Ali, Nishtar, and Ishtiaq Husain Qureshi, was held in which these members decided that a change in Pakistan's foreign policy was essential. They favoured the construction of closer ties with Washington. Nazimuddin personally had a stronger leaning towards Britain than to Washington.[125]

4.3.1. Defence Pacts: SEATO and CENTO

Federal cabinet's role was crucial in signing both the SEATO and CENTO pacts. Hamza Alavi believes that during Bogra's period, the military high command bypassed cabinet's instructions while shaping ties with the USA. In October 1954, a US Military Assistance Advisory Group was allowed to stay in the General Headquarters of Pakistan (GHQ) in Rawalpindi. A direct link was created between the Pakistan army and the Pentagon.[126] He says that most of the time cabinet was bypassed by them when taking important decisions. He believes that the cabinet was unaware of the developments which were taking place between the Pakistan Army and the Pentagon.[127] In fact, it was the cabinet of Muhammad Ali Bogra that took some important decisions regarding Pakistan-US relations. During a visit of US Secretary of State, Mr Dulles, the cabinet decided that Pakistan would follow some basic principles when discussing and deciding issues regarding Pak-US ties. The cabinet decided that it would be made clear to Mr Dulles that Pakistan would not become party to an arrangement in which Pakistan had to enter into a war if NATO countries were attacked. Pakistan would also consider how much importance would be given to the settlements of her disputes with India. The cabinet further decided that the C-in-C would be given a chance to meet with Mr Dulles, but he would not be authorized to decide any policy issues, and would only give Dulles facts and figures.[128]

Zafrullah Khan was sent to Manila with cabinet instructions to sign the SEATO Treaty only if its scope was wide enough to deal with aggression other than communist hostility. But in Manila his point of view was not accepted by the member countries, especially by the USA, and Zafarullah had to sign it against the wishes of his cabinet. His deputy argued against it, but Zafarullah told Karachi that he would resign if not permitted to act on his own.[129] While signing the SEATO treaty, he stated that it would be final only after the approval of the Pakistani cabinet. He signed the pact with the following statement:

> Signed for transmission to my government for its consideration and action in accordance with the Constitution of Pakistan.[130]

Suhrawardy's statement that the cabinet was not taken into confidence before signing the defence pact[131] is not wholly true. It went in favour of Zafrullah Khan that the cabinet had changed when he arrived back in Karachi, and included all pro-US members such as Ayub Khan, Iskandar Mirza, Choudhury Muhammad Ali, and Bogra, so Zafrullah Khan faced no difficulty in obtaining cabinet's approval for the treaty. S. M. Burke's opinion that Ayub was the main figure in foreign policy decisions from 1952 to 1958,[132] giving the impression that the cabinet was eclipsed, has also been found to be unjustifiable.

It may also be important to note here that the USA was permitted to use Pakistani air bases and was even allowed to construct new military bases without the approval of the cabinet. The federal cabinet of Pakistan was presented with a summary on 17 December 1953 concerning the rumours that Pakistan was going to provide space for the USA to open military bases in Pakistan as had been published earlier in the newspapers of other countries. China and Soviet Union both protested about it in soft and harsh words respectively.[133] Governor General Malik Ghulam Mohammad and Zafrullah Khan had indicated, in their meeting with President Eisenhower on 12 November 1953, that Pakistan could permit the USA to use the air bases of Pakistan and even to construct new ones if the US armed Pakistani forces properly.[134] The cabinet decided that telegrams would be issued to both the countries, i.e. China and Soviet Union, stating that it was only a rumour, although Pakistan reserved all rights to take decisions concerning its safety and security.[135] The cabinet might not have had formal information about the said issue.

On the other side, Pakistan signed the Mutual Defense Agreement with the USA on 19 February 1954 with the approval of the cabinet. Bogra was satisfied with this achievement and stated that 'Pakistan today enters a glorious chapter in its history and is now cast for a significant role in the world affairs.'[136] PM Bogra, along with some cabinet ministers, visited the USA in October 1954 and met President Eisenhower and the secretaries of state. The cabinet was satisfied with the close relationship between the two countries. The joint communique stated:

> Recognizing Pakistan's position in the common defence effort and following the military assistance agreement signed with the USA this spring the US will endeavor to accelerate the substantial military programs for Pakistan, which are beginning this year.[137]

Pakistan signed the Baghdad Pact, later called CENTO, which was the confirmation of the fact that Pakistan was a close ally of the USA. The cabinet of this period included two military generals (one in-service and the other retired). Other members of the cabinet also favoured a pro-US foreign policy, so it was not difficult to obtain approval for signing some more pacts with the USA. Members of the delegation chosen to attend the first meeting of the Baghdad Pact were also approved by the cabinet.[138]

The cabinet decided to give due publicity to the various agreements and pacts which Pakistan had signed with western democracies to counter the propaganda of the opposition and the leftist press.[139] PM Choudhury Muhammad Ali was successful in conveying the fact that the defence alliances would address non-communist aggression which was actually a real danger for Pakistan. On his government's initiative, the Kashmir issue was included on the agendas of the meetings of the Baghdad Pact and SEATO.[140] Suhrawardy's policy was similar. His appointment as PM was taken very well by the West, as it was believed that he would keep Pakistan 'firmly on the side of the West in foreign affairs'.[141]

4.3.2. THE SUEZ CANAL CRISIS

Suhrawardy's cabinet favoured the West on the issue of the Suez Canal, against public opinion in Pakistan which was in favour of nationalization.[142] After being briefed on the Suez Canal issue by Foreign Minister Hamidul Haq Chowdhry, the cabinet decided that Pakistan would prefer to keep the Suez Canal as an international highway as Pakistani ships passed through it, and its nationalization would have adverse effects on Pakistan's economy and trade. Suhrawardy suggested that an international conference should be called by the interested parties to deal with the issue; this was accepted by the cabinet.[143] The view that the cabinet accepted the nationalization of the canal as a legal step, and that the Foreign Minister of Pakistan, under pressure from Dulles, negated cabinet's decision[144] is incorrect. He actually followed the line of action provided by the cabinet.

Later, a conference was arranged by eighteen nations. Pakistan's Foreign Minister Noon attended the conference and put forward Pakistan's point of view. He said that the scope of negotiations must be widened and that Egypt must also be included in the discussions.[145] Suhrawardy, while addressing the CAP declared that SEATO and the Baghdad Pact were purely defensive agreements. His cabinet decided that Pakistan should not quit the Commonwealth over the Suez Canal issue as isolation would affect Pakistan negatively. However, the PM told the British High Commissioner that the attack on the Suez Canal had put Pakistan in a difficult position with regard to the Baghdad Pact and her position in the Commonwealth.[146]

> I maintain that neutrality and isolation cannot be the policy of a country that is liable to be attacked and is in danger, a country which has not got resources enough to strengthen itself against such aggression. We have, therefore, to have allies and it is fortunate for this country that we have allies who have stood by us in time of crisis.[147]

The debate in the CAP gained the support of the members of the assembly. No one raised questions about Pakistan's membership of the security alliances.[148] However, the cabinet realized later that the Baghdad Pact 'was meant to create a block against communism only'.[149]

4.3.3. THE COALITION GOVERNMENTS AND THE PRO-WEST APPROACH

All coalition cabinets not only favoured, but also publicly defended Pakistan's pro-USA and pro-West foreign policy. Foreign Minister Hamidul Huq Choudhury said, 'Pakistan was definitely opposed to communism as Pakistanis believe in democratic way of life.'[150] But at the same time, a realistic approach was adopted towards China, and problems between India and Pakistan were also addressed objectively by the cabinets. Coalition cabinets were not strong enough to change Pakistan's policy related to the system of alliances into which Pakistan had entered although some prime ministers had some reservations. Malik Firoz Khan Noon, in discussion with Dulles said: 'The Baghdad Pact was not enough to give us a sense of security and the only way of helping us was to give us an assurance that if anyone attacks us, the United States will defend Pakistan.'[151]

4.3.4. MARTIAL LAW CABINET, 1958–1962

General Ayub was one of the major advocates of the formulation of Pakistan's pro-West foreign policy before the imposition of martial law. He had been trained in the British tradition to adopt an anti-communist stand. After coming to power, Ayub announced that he saw no need to make any changes to Pakistan's foreign policy.[152] In the first cabinet meeting of Ayub's regime, an exhaustive survey of Pakistan's foreign policy was made. Most ministers agreed with Ayub's pro-West or pro-USA foreign policy. However, one dissident voice was also present: Bhutto, who said that Pakistan must look for 'basic modification in foreign policy assumptions and its conduct'.[153]

In his first statement on foreign policy, Ayub said, on 25 December 1958, that the 'structure of Pakistan's foreign policy was based on the fundamental needs of the country'.[154] Foreign Minister of Pakistan Manzur Qadir presented a summary before the cabinet that contained some directive principles of the country's foreign policy, which included a pro-USA stand on most issues. Commerce Minister Z. A. Bhutto did not agree with some of the points of that summary. He said:

> The summary created an impression that our foreign policy had been determined by our acceptance of the US aid and the course had already been set. The two vital problems for us were the problems of Kashmir and Canal waters. We had to determine how far our foreign policy had helped us to achieve the solution of these problems. It seems quite certain that in case of war with India, USA is not going to help us.[155]

He further added, 'We should not unnecessarily extend the principle of attachment to the United States.'[156] After discussions, the cabinet came to the conclusion that there was too much room for flexibility in Pakistan's foreign policy. Ayub said:

> It was a fact that we need aid and, therefore, we should not behave in a manner which would annoy those who give us aid for the development and security of our country. The aid given to us by the USA was aimed at helping us maintain our independence in an area which was threatened by communism.[157]

Ayub's martial law cabinet, which was regarded as pro-USA, had inherited an agreement concluded in August 1947 between the government of the USA and the government of Pakistan for the transit of United States military aircraft through Pakistan. The agreement had already been signed by the previous British regime on 5 July 1947 for two years. The same agreement was revived several times by both countries with some modifications. It was again revived in 1961 for three years with the approval of the cabinet.[158]

In this period, there was no forum where the question of Pakistan's foreign policy could be publicly called to account, except at the president's periodic press conferences or those of his ministers.[159] But at the same time, the cabinet was highly influential in designing policy towards other countries.

4.3.5. TRANSFORMATION IN FOREIGN POLICY; THE PRESIDENTIAL CABINET

Ayub's pro-West and pro-US foreign policy gradually transformed into a policy of bilateralism. The process of transformation began in 1962 due to both internal and external factors. With the adoption of the 1962 Constitution, broad-level changes were introduced in the composition of the cabinet. The Ministry of Foreign Affairs was taken over by Mohammad Ali Bogra. The place of the most powerful minister was taken by Zulfikar Ali Bhutto, who strongly believed in a non-aligned policy for Pakistan. However, the Finance Minister maintained his influential status among the cabinet members. Bhutto did not wish Pakistan to be part of any alliance. He has stated that he was the real policymaker in the early constitutional days, though he was finally given the portfolio of Foreign Ministry only in 1963, after the death of Mohammad Ali Bogra. Bogra had the capability to convince Ayub to accept and follow what he initiated.[160] Bogra also believed in a balanced approach towards the West and the USA. He was against extending unqualified support to the West and did not want Pakistan to be taken 'for granted'.[161]

Ayub personally gave weight to his ministers' views. Foreign policy issues were either discussed in cabinet meetings or in the inner circles of the Ayub regime.[162] He was most influenced by the views of Bogra and Bhutto.

The most important external factor to impact on the ideology of Ayub Khan was the Indo-China Border War of 1962. The USA not only extended political support to India, but also provided all the aid needed by the Indian government to improve itself economically and militarily. Pakistan protested against this and demanded that the USA should give defence aid to India only on the condition that the Kashmir dispute was solved. Pakistan failed to persuade the USA to differentiate between a neutral country and an ally. That was the time for Pakistan to search for new friends.[163] Ayub permitted Bhutto to visit the USSR and he himself visited China and signed a trade agreement with her.[164] But at the same time, Ayub also continued Pakistan's alliance with the USA. Anti-American feeling spread in Pakistan after the Indo-China Border War. Ayub told the cabinet that a top-ranking US delegate needed permission to visit Pakistan to study Pak-US relations, especially the anti-US feeling which existed in Pakistan. The President said that his government was worried not only about the emerging anti-US feelings, but also about the change in the policy of the US government towards Pakistan. The cabinet reached a consensus that Pakistan's security was in danger due to US arms aid to India, which had totally disturbed the balance of power in South Asia. The cabinet decided that the minister of foreign affairs and the minister of defence should co-operate to adopt one stand on the different issues before the arrival of the US delegation. The foreign minister must be present when the diplomat met the army chief.[165] The cabinet was very active at that time in deciding issues related to foreign policy.

The most important factor which led to change in Ayub's foreign policy was the Indo-Pakistan War of 1965. The USA remained neutral during the war, though Pakistan was her ally. Moreover, the USA imposed an arms embargo on both India and Pakistan. The cabinet criticized the US decision in its meeting held on 17 September 1965.[166]

President Ayub explained in his autobiography the circumstances which had forced Pakistan to change her position from pro-West to bilateralism. Geographically, Pakistan had three big neighbours, the USSR, China, and India. In the absence of cordial relations with India, Pakistan must have an understanding with the other two neighbours, and her relations with the USA had to be satisfactory. He was of the view that Pakistan should try to establish bilateral relations with all three big powers. Realizing the difficulties of the suggested course he said, 'It would be like walking on a triangular tightrope.'[167] It was vital to determine the 'limits of tolerance' within which the 'bilateral equation might be constructed'.[168] Pakistan should avoid taking sides on the differences that existed between the big powers. 'The basis of our foreign policy thus is that we stay within our own means.'[169]

Under the influence of circumstances, and in continuous consultation with his cabinet colleagues, Ayub's stand on foreign policy issues was modified.

4.3.6. MEDIATION BETWEEN CHINA AND USA

Yahya's only success on the diplomatic front was that of the role Pakistan played in the mediation between China and USA. Yahya delivered a letter from the US president to the president of China, of which he said that it was for the first time that a message had come from a 'Head through a Head to a Head'.[170] Later, Henry Kissinger, the American Secretary of State for Foreign Affairs, secretly left for China from Islamabad. It was due to Pakistan's support and favour in developing the relationship between China and USA that both supported Pakistan during the 1971 War.

4.3.7. THE SECOND PARLIAMENTARY REGIME

Bhutto brought the ideology of interdependence and bilateralism to Pakistan's foreign policy. During the 1971 War, he had reached the conclusion that the Super Powers' approach towards Pakistan had changed. The USA, USSR, China, and France had entered an era of détente. He believed that Pakistan must keep away from multilateral alliances and pacts. He adopted a bilateral mode of solving problems and dealing with post-1971 War issues. The ideology of Bhutto regarding foreign policy principles included the 'evolution of bilateralism, Third World mobilization through the creation of a new economic order, criticism of nuclear proliferation, and the establishment of special relations with the Muslim countries of the world on the basis of pan-Islamism'.[171] He believed that 'Pakistan must determine its foreign policy on the basis of its own enlightened national interest uninfluenced by the transient global requirements of the great powers'.[172]

Bhutto further envisioned an independent foreign policy for Pakistan. While following this ideology, Bhutto recognized North Korea, East Germany, and the governments of Vietnam and Cambodia. He also developed close ties with China, the Palestine Liberation Organization (PLO), Romania, and North Korea. Relations with the USSR and Eastern European countries were also normalized quickly.[173]

He believed that breaking the close ties with the West and USA would enhance Pakistan's esteem. Consequently, the cabinet approved the decision to withdraw Pakistan from the Commonwealth in January 1972,[174] and from SEATO in November 1972.[175]

4.4. POLICY TOWARDS CHINA

Pakistan's first cabinet adopted a pro-China policy and the People's Republic of China was recognized following a decision of the cabinet on 4 January 1950. Before this, Pakistan was not in favour of appointing an ambassador to China due to the unstable political situation.[176] During the Korean War, Pakistan did not take part in the UN vote on the resolution in which China was named as an aggressor in Korea. Pakistan established trade relations with China in 1949.[177] Though Liaquat's cabinet was generally regarded as pro-West, it was against branding China as an enemy.

His government had also refused to supply forces for the UN action against North Korea.

On the issue of China's membership of the United Nations Organization (UNO), a logical approach was adopted by the cabinet. Three opinions had emerged as a result of discussion in the cabinet meeting held on 14 September 1955. First, Pakistan should support the USA, as Pakistan was receiving aid from her; second, Pakistan should remain neutral, but in such a case no side would be happy; third, Pakistan should support China, but for that purpose Pakistan should prepare the ground and start manoeuvering. It was believed that in the case of supporting China, Pakistan would be placed in a good position as an Asian country and as a member of the Afro-Asian Group. Pakistan would be in a position to play the role of bridge between the USA and China.[178] It was decided that the government should inform USA of the move through the Pakistani embassy. The cabinet, however, decided that if 'we were really pressed hard, we should vote with the USA'.[179]

In line with the decision of the cabinet, support was extended to China. This had a positive impact and relations improved between the two countries. Pakistani PM Suhrawardy, having been invited, visited China, and ushered in a new relationship. The cabinet decided that cultural and commercial relations must be expanded. In a joint declaration, they reaffirmed their intentions to continue doing their best to facilitate the settlement of their respective problems on a just and peaceful basis.[180]

In late 1960, the cabinet began to adopt a critical approach towards the USA. Differences of opinion prevailed among the cabinet ministers on the issue of developing relations with both China and Soviet Union simultaneously, whilst maintaining relations with USA. Manzur Qadir disapproved of the idea and said that 'at the present juncture we have no alternative but to remain friendly with the West'.[181] He further said, 'We would have been faced with a very difficult choice: annoyance of China or of the USA. We had to choose between the two and the force of circumstances demanded that we backed the US.'[182]

As there was disagreement between Bhutto and Manzur Qadir, a special meeting of the cabinet was called on 18 November 1960. Ministers discussed the fact that USA was not supporting Pakistan in her disputes with India for its own reasons; therefore Pakistan must amend its policy towards the USA and should not adopt 'rigid postures towards Soviet Union and China'.[183] Bhutto pointed out that Pakistan should vote for the admission of the People's Republic of China into the UNO at its next session. Some ministers were unclear, but finally a decision was taken by the cabinet, in November 1960, in favour of Pakistan's support for China's legitimate representation at the UNO.[184] Manzur Qadir informed the cabinet that New Zealand was going to present the resolution to give a permanent seat to China in the Security Council. The cabinet decided that if this resolution was presented, Pakistan would vote in favour of China.[185]

4.4.1. The Indo-China Border War and its Aftermath

The Indo-China border war took place in October 1962, and created further complications for Pakistan. The USA pressurized Pakistan to remove its forces from the Kashmir border so that India could move its forces to the Chinese border. Kennedy wanted Ayub to assure Nehru of Pakistan's support, or at least of no opposition.[186] Ayub resisted the US pressure and decided to refuse. Ayub's cabinet was divided on the question of policy towards the Indo-China conflict. The group led by Finance Minister Mohammad Shoaib wanted to adopt a pro-America policy as had been adopted by a CENTO partner, Turkey, whose president had promised to send military hardware to India if required. The other group, led by Foreign Minister Bogra and Minister Bhutto, were asking Ayub to send forces to Kashmir for its liberation. Ayub was in a state of indecision. On one hand he did not want to lose the friendship of China, and on the other he could not afford to annoy the USA. In the end, the pro-China group was relatively more successful[187] and forces were not moved from the border.

This issue was also discussed in the National Assembly in November 1962 with full vigour. Muhammad Ali Bogra opened the discussion and stated that India and the USA had been partners in a secret arms treaty since 1951. He described this as a glowing example of 'hypocrisy and fraud'.[188] He promised to bring documents to prove this into the House in the near future. US policy to give heavy arms aid to India was also criticized. Bogra said:

... I speak in anguish and not in anger when I have to say that one of our allies had promised us that we would be consulted before any arms assistance is given to India. I regret to have to observe that this was not done.

Not only there was no declaration of war on the part of India against China or by China against India, but normal diplomatic relations continue to exist. The embassies of both countries are still functioning. All this led us to the conviction that India was not engaged in any major conflict with China but the conflict was a localized one restricted to the area under dispute.[189]

Both SEATO and CENTO were severely criticized on this occasion and it was demanded that Pakistan must withdraw from these pacts. Bhutto delivered a long speech and emphasized the pro-China policy. He said, 'I have always advocated the normalization of relations with the Soviet Union and Communist China.'[190] Bhutto, along with Minister for Industries Altaf Hussain, and Secretary for Information Altaf Gauhar, supported the pro-China policy in the Pakistani press.[191]

Zulfikar Ali Bhutto and Bogra stressed that Pakistan's foreign policy must be reassessed according to the requirements of the changing circumstances and that foreign policy must not be biased, since this could harm the national interest. Bhutto got the bit between his teeth in promoting Pakistan's relations with China.[192] Ayub was persuaded to improve Pakistan's relations with China irrespective of China's different ideological base. It was the appropriate time to take the initiative as China's relations with India and Russia were worsening.[193] Pakistan's cordial relations with China could greatly improve her bargaining position. Pakistan needed a new 'protector in place of USA'.[194] They were successful to a large extent in convincing President Ayub to change the policy.

The negotiations between China and Pakistan on the demarcation of the border between the countries were initiated by Manzur Qadir, finalized by Mohammad Ali Bogra, and signed by Bhutto. It was the first time that Pakistan had adopted an independent foreign policy.[195] Lawrence Ziring has commented: 'It was during Manzur Qadir's tenure as Foreign Minister that the first real change in Pakistan's foreign policy came about. It is interesting to note, however, that it was Bhutto who received credit for Pakistan's more independent foreign policy.'[196] Manzur Qadir claimed that 'Bhutto was the only voice in the cabinet which supported him in the policy of developing close relations with China'.[197] With this, relations with China became most cordial.[198]

Pakistan's cabinet had prepared a brief for the delegation that represented Pakistan in the UN General Assembly. The brief stated:

> The policy of Pakistan on the question of the representation of China in the UN is the same today as it was eleven years ago. The question for us is not the admission or on non-admission, as it is often described ... China had been a member of the UN since its inception and is a permanent member of the Security Council. The sole and simple question is who is entitled to represent China in the United Nations. The People's Republic of China had exercised effective authority and jurisdiction over

the whole of the mainland of China for more than twelve years. Pakistan recognized the government nearly 12 years ago ... it is clear that, in view of Pakistan, the People's Republic of China is entitled to represent China in UNO.[199]

The cabinet instructed the delegation that in the forthcoming session of the UNO, the Pakistani delegation should vote in support of the proposal to give representation to the People's Republic of China in the UNO and all its organs.[200] Foreign Minister Pirzada, succeeding Bhutto, expressed the same opinion. He said while addressing the UN General Assembly:

> The absence of the real representatives of China from the United Nations is the most important single cause of the decline of its effectiveness and the inability of the world community to deal with the problem of disarmament and to settle the many conflicts and tensions in Asia.[201]

Pakistan's pro-China policy proved to be an asset for Pakistan and the cabinet performed a very positive role in this regard.

4.5. POLICY TOWARDS THE USSR

Policy regarding Russia had been defined by the Father of the Nation Quaid-i-Azam Muhammad Ali Jinnah. He presented Pakistan as a democratic state and had said that Communism could not flourish on the soil of Islam. He further clarified that Pakistan's interests lie 'more with the two great democratic countries, namely, the United Kingdom and the USA than with Russia'.[202] PM Liaquat Ali Khan was invited to visit the Union of Soviet Socialist Republics (USSR) but he did not go. There are two points of view on this: one is that Liaquat personally wanted to visit Soviet Union. The other opinion is that some of his cabinet colleagues, including Choudhury Muhammad Ali, Ghulam Muhammad, and Zafrullah Khan,[203] who had been regarded as pro-West, changed the PM's mind. In reality he was a true follower of Jinnah, who had not been in favour of an alliance with Communism. It is assumed that while deciding the matter, the PM had borne this factor in mind.

Besides China, Bhutto wished Pakistan to develop closer ties with the Soviet Union too. He had planned a visit to the USSR, but because of some influential ministers, such as Manzur Qadir and Muhammad Shoaib, Bhutto faced great difficulties. However, due to his continuous follow-ups, the visit was sanctioned by Ayub. Bhutto was successful in signing the Oil Exploration Agreement with the USSR on 4 March 1961.[204] This marked the beginning of the working relationship with the USSR. A loan of $30 million was granted to Pakistan. Technical assistance and equipment for oil exploration were also promised. Various Pakistani officials and the foreign minister stated that the agreement did not mean a change in foreign policy,[205] but practically it had successfully broken the ice.[206] Ayub Khan had no doubt been responsible for formulating this policy, but the influence of Bhutto in many crucial matters might well have been decisive.[207]

The presidential cabinet of Ayub Khan approved the Soviet Union's offer to settle post-1965 War issues between India and Pakistan. With this, relations with Soviet Union further improved. Soviet Union's consulates general were opened in

Karachi and Dacca with the approval of the cabinet, as the embassy had moved to Islamabad.[208] The consulates general looked after trade interests and supervised the supply of Soviet machinery and equipment to Pakistan. Ayub's government continued its efforts to cultivate friendship with Soviet Russia, but Pakistan was not successful in seeking military supplies. Pakistan was gradually moving away from alignment with the West. The cabinet's point of view was represented by Foreign Minister Arshad Husain in the National Assembly. He said, regarding SEATO and CENTO, that Pakistan had lost interest in both. 'Our interest is ... confined to their cultural and economic activities with which there are some beneficial and useful projects.'[209]

General Yahya visited the USSR and the USA. He was successful in signing an agreement regarding the establishment of a steel mill, but on the political front he could not achieve much success.[210] His inexperience in handling foreign affairs was evident within a few months. During his visit to the Soviet Union in June 1969, he placed emphasis on military assistance from the Soviet president, although Kosygin had stated that Pakistan could not 'be on friendly terms at the same time with China and with the Soviet Union'.[211] Some of General Yahya's statements increased the wrath of the USSR. He annoyed the USSR by reminding her of 'its own atrocities in Czechoslovakia and the Central Asian Republics', in order to justify[212] the military operation in East Pakistan. In response Russia moved closer to India.

Bhutto's government continually tried to develop and to maximize cooperation with the USSR in economic fields.

The USSR provided support for oil exploration, provided relief to Pakistan's debt servicing position, and converted commercial loans into state loans repayable in local currency, which were utilized to pay for imports from Pakistan into the Soviet Union. Above all, the Soviet Union provided financial support for the steel mill project, which the West and the USA were not ready to entertain. The Soviet Union was impressed by the Bhutto government's initiatives of nationalization, leaving SEATO and the Commonwealth, bilateralism, and so on. Soviet Union wanted less dependence of Pakistan on the western bloc, so she helped Pakistan to achieve self-dependence in the production of heavy machinery.[213] Despite all this support from the Soviet Union, Pakistan resisted the offer to join the Asian Collective Security System, which was against including China.[214] The cabinet decided not to criticize the Soviet Union in public.[215]

In a nutshell, it is shown that there was some variation in cabinet's role and performance on issues of formulating foreign policy principles, its role in the decision-making process, and performance on issues of foreign policy. In the first phase of this study (1947–1958), trends were mostly set. Quaid-i-Azam designed basic foreign policy guidelines which were later amended and added to according to the understanding and ideology of the governments. Pakistan's foreign policy was more or less independent till 1954, and cabinet ministers' points of view and voices were given weight. It was during Muhammad Ali Bogra's premiership that civil and military bureaucracy's representatives, Malik Ghulam Mohammad, Ayub Khan, Iskandar Mirza, and

Choudhury Muhammad Ali formed the kitchen cabinet, and some foreign policy decisions were taken by them. Even then, the cabinet was not voiceless: this was clear in the brief prepared for Zafrullah Khan regarding SEATO.[216] The Cabinet of All Talents included prominent civil and military bureaucrats who, as members of the cabinet, took decisions on foreign policy issues. Coalition cabinets showed mixed performances, but almost all important foreign policy issues were discussed in cabinet meetings during Ayub Khan's regime, and different points of view were listened to carefully. Practically, Ayub, his foreign minister (whosoever that was at any time), and Bhutto, even when he was not foreign minister, were the main pillars of foreign policy formulation, but cabinet was generally not bypassed. Approval of all important issues was sought from this important institution. Even the agendas for important foreign visits by the president were approved by the cabinet.[217] However, Yahya Khan never accorded due status to his civilian cabinet and foreign policy issues were never brought there for discussion or approval. The kitchen cabinet of Yahya, which consisted of his military colleagues, was involved in formulating and decision-making regarding foreign policy issues. During Z. A. Bhutto's period, the cabinet was not very active in the formulation of foreign policy since Bhutto himself was highly interested in analysing world affairs and in deciding foreign policy matters. He believed that everyone could 'put in his weight. ... But essentially when it comes to the real decision, I am in charge of affairs'.[218] However, it is to the credit of Bhutto that the military was kept at a reasonable distance from the foreign policy formulation process. The institution of the cabinet was part and parcel of the formulation of the foreign policy of Pakistan from 1947 to 1969, but later it was generally not consulted, and only its formal approval was requested.

Notes and References

1. Surendra Nath Kaushik, Niloufer Mahdi and others have wrongly stated that Aziz Ahmed was minister of foreign affairs: he was only minister of state for foreign affairs. The portfolio of minister of foreign affairs was reserved for Bhutto.
2. Cabinet mtg, 8 October 1947, 127/CF/47, NDC, Islamabad.
3. Brief for the delegation to the Security Council presented to the cabinet, 10 January 1948, 12/CF/48, NDC, Islamabad.
4. Ibid.
5. Cabinet decision, 28 January 1948, 12/CF/48, NDC, Islamabad.
6. Cabinet mtg, 16 February 1948, 12/CF/48, NDC, Islamabad.
7. Cabinet mtg, 24 March 1948, 12/CF/48, NDC, Islamabad.
8. Cabinet mtg, 30 March 1948, 12/CF/48, NDC, Islamabad.
9. Ibid.
10. Cabinet mtg, 28 October 1948, 12/CF/48, NDC, Islamabad.
11. From M. A. Gurmani to Zafrullah Khan, 28 March 1949, 3(5)-PMS/49, GOP, PMS, NDC, Islamabad.
12. Mtg of the Defence Committee of the Cabinet, 30 July 1949, 34/CF/49, NDC, Islamabad.
13. Cabinet mtg, 2 September 1949, 34/CF/51 CP, NDC, Islamabad.
14. From Liaquat Ali Khan to Jawaharlal Nehru, 14 February 1950, 12(3)-PMS, GOP, PMS NDC, Islamabad.
15. For details of the Cabinet mtg please see Cabinet File 48/CF/51.
16. Cabinet decision, 1 June 1956, 91/CF/56, NDC, Islamabad.
17. Cabinet decision, 27 March 1957, 186/CF/56, NDC, Islamabad.
18. Cabinet mtg, 9 January 1957, 191/CF/55, NDC, Islamabad.
19. Ibid.
20. Secret Summary for the Cabinet, 'Trade Agreement with India', No 343/101/57, 28 January 1957, 191/CF/55, NDC, Islamabad.

21. From UKHC Karachi to CRO London cited in Roedad Khan, compiled, *The British Papers Secret and Confidential, India-Pakistan-Bangladesh Documents 1958–69* (Oxford: Oxford University Press, 2002), 10.

22. Brief for Parliamentary Under-Secretary of State's Visit to Pakistan, sent to CRO London, March 1960, FE 319/8 and Do 35/8926, NA, London.

23. Cabinet mtg, 25 November 1959, 674/CF/59-1, NDC, Islamabad.

24. Ibid.

25. Cabinet mtg, 16 September 1960, 674/CF/59, NDC, Islamabad.

26. Cabinet mtg, 22 July 1960, 254/CF/60, NDC, Islamabad.

27. BHC Karachi, Report Prepared for Queen's Visit to Pakistan in 1961, DO 196/128, NA, London.

28. Gauhar, *Ayub Khan*, 320–3 and M. S. Korejo, *Soldiers of Misfortune: Pakistan under Ayub, Yahya, Bhutto and Zia* (Lahore: Ferozsons, 1995), 103.

29. Gauhar, *Ayub Khan*, 320–3; Ziring, *Pakistan; At the Crosscurrent of History*, 105.

30. Ziring, *Pakistan: At the Crosscurrent of History*, 105; and Ziring, *Pakistan in the Twentieth Century*, 288.

31. Gauhar, *Ayub Khan*, 318.

32. S. M. Burk and Lawrence Ziring. *Pakistan's Foreign Policy: An Historical Analysis* (Karachi: Oxford University Press, 1990), 324.

33. From NEA Phillips Talbot to the Secretary, 30 April 1965 cited in Roedad Khan, *The American Papers*, 6–7.

34. Cabinet mtg, 30 April 1965, 130/CF/65, NDC, Islamabad.

35. Ibid. 12 June 1965.

36. Ibid. 10 July 1965.

37. Cabinet mtg, 10 September 1965, 173/CF/65, NDC, Islamabad.

38. President's Briefing to the Cabinet on his Meeting with the UN Secretary General, 450/CF/65, NDC, Islamabad.

39. Ibid.

40. Ibid.

41. Cabinet decision, 10 September 1965, 492/CF/65, NDC, Islamabad.

42. Cabinet mtg, 12 September 1965, 450/CF/65, NDC, Islamabad.

43. Ibid.
44. From BHC Rawalpindi to CRO London, 9 September 1965, cited in Roedad Khan, The British Papers, 324.
45. Ibid.
46. Cabinet mtg, 13 September 1965, Roedad Khan, The British Papers, 324.
47. Text of the Security Council Resolution on Indo-Pakistan fighting, 450/CF/65, NDC, Islamabad.
48. Gauhar, Ayub Khan, 355–6.
49. Cabinet mtg, 8 November 1965, 450/CF/65, NDC, Islamabad.
50. Ibid.
51. Ibid.
52. Cabinet mtg, 6 December 1965, NDC, Islamabad.
53. Ibid.
54. Details of the meeting of McConoughy with Bhutto, from Rawalpindi to Commonwealth Relations Office, 11 September 1965, DO 196/384 cited in Roedad Khan, The British Papers, 325
55. Special Cabinet mtg, 6 October 1965, 542/CF/65, NDC, Islamabad.
56. Cabinet mtg, 6 December 1965, 542/CF/65, NDC, Islamabad.
57. Afzal, Pakistan, 315.
58. The details of this meeting are not declassified completely. Altaf Gauhar, who attended the meeting, has given the details. Cabinet mtg, 31 December 1965, 542/CF/65, NDC, Islamabad.
59. Gauhar, Ayub Khan, 377–8.
60. Ibid.
61. Cabinet mtg, 31 December 1965, 542/CF/65, NDC, Islamabad.
62. J. N. Dixit, India-Pakistan in War and Peace (London: Routledge, 2002), 159–60.
63. Gauhar, Ayub Khan, 395.
64. Ibid.
65. Ibid. 396.
66. Incoming telegram, from American Embassy Office Rawalpindi to Secretary of State Washington, 13 June 1966 cited in Roedad Khan, The American Paper, 114.

67. Ibid., and from BHC Rawalpindi to CRO., DO196/31 in Roedad Khan, *The British Papers*, 445. Further details are given in Chater 5.

68. Ibid. 113.

69. The details of the rift are given in Chapter 5.

70. The Interview of Prime Minister Z. A. Bhutto by Mr Moti Ram, a senior Indian journalist, 23 September 1976, Rawalpindi, Naeem Qureshi Collection, National Archives, Islamabad, 7–8.

71. Ibid.

72. Burke and Ziring, *Pakistan's Foreign Policy,* 421.

73. Keesing's Contemporary Archives, 22–8 Oct. 1973, 26163.

74. National Assembly of Pakistan Debates, Vol. II, No. 1, 11 July 1972, 102.

75. National Assembly of Pakistan Debates, Vol. II, No. 3, 12 July 1972, 302.

76. National Assembly of Pakistan Debates, Vol. II, No. 5, 14 July 1972, 710.

77. Ahmed Raza Khan Kasuri, *Idhar Tum Udhar Hum: An Historical Document* (Lahore: Britannica Publishing House, n.d.), 339.

78. Ministry of Foreign Affairs Publications, *Joint Communique 1974* (Karachi: Government of Pakistan, 1977), 26.

79. Ibid.

80. Cabinet mtg, 10 April 1974, 118/CF/74, NDC, Islamabad.

81. Cabinet mtg, 3 March 1973, 128/CF/72, NDC, Islamabad.

82. Keesing's Contemporary Archives, 22–8 Oct. 1973, 26163.

83. Niazi, *Last Days of Premier Bhutto,* 10.

84. Keesing's Contemporary Archives, 24–30 June 1974, 26585; and interview of Zulfikar Ali Bhutto by Mr Khushwant Singh, editor of the *Illustrated Weekly of India,* 20 December 1976, Rawalpindi, Dr Naeem Qureshi Collection, National Archives, Islamabad.

85. She gave an assurance that India had no hegemonic designs on Pakistan, but wanted to use nuclear capability for peaceful purposes. She urged Bhutto to resume travel and telecommunication facilities between the two countries.

86. Niazi, *Last Days of Premier Bhutto,* 64.

87. Interview of Rafi Raza with Ian Talbot, *Pakistan – A Modern History*, 238.

88. National Assembly of Pakistan Debates, Vol. V, No. 3 , 10 June 1977, 203.

89. Massarrate Sohail, *Partition and Anglo-Pakistan Relations 1947–51* (Lahore: Vanguard, 1991), 339.

90. Cabinet mtg, 21 May 1955, 60/CF/55, NDC, Islamabad.

91. Cabinet mtg, 21 September 1955, 60/CF/55, CP, NDC, Islamabad.

92. Ibid.

93. Summary presented to the cabinet, 12 October 1955, 61/CF/55, NDC, Islamabad.

94. Cabinet mtg, 12 October 1955, 61/CF/55, NDC, Islamabad.

95. From BHC Karachi to CRO London, 28 April 1960, DO35/8926, NA, London.

96. Feldman, *Revolution in Pakistan,* 168.

97. *Dawn,* 29 February 1960.

98. From BHC Karachi to CRO London, 28 April 1960, DO 35/8926 and Anees Jillani, 'Pakistan-Afghan Relations, 1958–88' in *Readings in Pakistan Foreign Policy 1971–1998,* ed., Mehrunnisa Ali (Karachi: Oxford University Press, 2005), 375.

99. Burke and Ziring, *Pakistan's Foreign Policy,* 208.

100. Agreement between Pakistan and Afghanistan concluded at Tehran, 28 May 1963 in Saeeduddin Ahmad Dar, *Selected Documents on Pakistan's Relations with Afghanistan* (Islamabad: NIPS, 1986), 78.

101. Cabinet decision, 4 September 1968, 225/CF/67, NDC, Islamabad.

102. Cabinet mtg, 16 March 1963, 193/CF/63, NDC, Islamabad.

103. Cabinet mtg, 11 September 1965, 429/CF/65, NDC, Islamabad.

104. Ibid. 15 September 1965.

105. National Assembly of Pakistan Debates, Official Report, 6 June 1967.

106. Ibid.

107. *Pakistan Affairs,* 31 May 1970.

108. Speech delivered by Z. A. Bhutto, The Foreign Minister of Pakistan to the Pakistan Council for International Affairs, Karachi, 13 June 1965 in *Bhutto, Pakistan and the Muslim World,* www.bhutto.org, 3, 12 February 2012.

109. Cabinet mtg, 30 January 1972, 39/CF/72, NDC, Islamabad.

110. Ibid., 23 February 1972, 94/CF/72, NDC, Islamabad.

111. Shahid Javed Burki, *Pakistan Under Bhutto 1971–77* (London: The Macmillan Press, 1980), 154; Mahdi, *Pakistan's Foreign Policy*, 256–7 and Shafqat, *Civil-Military Relations in Pakistan*, 182–3.

112. Alavi, 'Pakistan-US Military Alliances', 1556.

113. Shafqat, *Political System of Pakistan*, 257.

114. Cabinet mtg, 7 February 1972, 53/CF/72, NDC, Islamabad.

115. Report regarding Implementation of the Decision of Cabinet, 84/CF/72, NDC, Islamabad.

116. 'Proposal for All Tribes Jirga', 256/CF/74, NDC, Islamabad.

117. Ibid.

118. Ibid.

119. *Pakistan Times*, 26 July 1973.

120. Summary presented to the Cabinet by Ministry of Foreign Affairs, 70/PROG/76, NDC, Islamabad.

121. Cabinet mtg, 13 February 1976, 70/PROG/76, NDC, Islamabad.

122. Mahdi, *Pakistan's Foreign Policy*, 125.

123. Burke and Ziring, *Pakistan's Foreign Policy*, 428.

124. Bajwa, *Pakistan and the West, The First Decade*, 37–8.

125. Jalal, *The State of Martial Rule*, 171.

126. Hamza Alavi, 'Pakistan-US Military Alliances', *Economic and Political Weekly* 33 (20–26 June 1998), 1551.

127. Ibid.

128. Cabinet mtg, 20 May 1953, 143/CF/53, NDC. Islamabad.

129. Dennis Kux, *The United States and Pakistan 1947–2000: Disenchanted Allies* (New York: Oxford University Press, 2001), 71.

130. S. M. Burke and Lawrence Ziring, *Pakistan's Foreign Policy: An Historical Analysis* (Karachi: Oxford University Press, 1990), 167.

131. Talukdar, *Memories of Huseyn Shaheed Suhrawardy*, 59.

132. S. M. Burke, 'The Management of Pakistan's Foreign Policy', in *Pakistan: The Long View*, 355.

133. Summary presented by Ministry of Foreign Affairs to the Cabinet, 17 December 1953, 314/CF/53, NDC, Islamabad.

134. Afzal, *Pakistan, History and Politics,* 131.

135. Cabinet mtg, 17 December 1953, 314/CF/53, NDC, Islamabad.

136. *Dawn*, 26 February 1954.

137. Ministry of Foreign Affairs Publications, *Joint Communique 14 August 1947–December 1957*, (Karachi: Government of Pakistan, 1977), 69. This communique was issued on the visit of PM Bogra of Pakistan to the USA, 14–21 October 1954.

138. Cabinet mtg, 16 November 1953, 95/CF/55, NDC, Islamabad.

139. Cabinet mtg, 14 December 1955, 240/CF/55, NDC, Islamabad.

140. Ahmad, *Government and Politics in Pakistan*, 54.

141. Top Secret Minute, 11 October 1957, PREM 11–2422 cited in Farooq Naseem Bajwa, *Pakistan and the West; The First Decade 1947–1957* (Karachi: Oxford University Press, 1996), 214.

142. Ibid. 63, and in Ahmed Saleem, *Tut'te Bunti Assemblian (Urdu)* (Lahore: Jang Publishers, 1990), 246.

143. Cabinet mtg, 1 August 1956, 354/CF/56, NDC, Islamabad.

144. Saeeduddin Ahmad Dar, *Pakistan's Relations with Egypt 1947–71* (Karachi: Royal Book Company, 1993), 61.

145. *Pakistan Times*, 20 September 1956.

146. Cabinet mtg, 3 November 1956, 500/CF/56, NDC, Islamabad.

147. Document No. 134, Suhrawardy's Statement during the foreign policy debate in the National Assembly of Pakistan, 22 February 1957 in K. Arif, *America – Pakistan's Relations* (Lahore: Vanguard Books, 1984), 127.

148. Keith Callard, *Pakistan's Foreign Policy: An Interpretation* (New York: Institute of Pacific Relations, 1959), 33

149. Cabinet mtg, 17 July 1958, 332/CF/58, NDC, Islamabad.

150. Top Secret, Summary presented to the Cabinet, 390/CF/56, NDC, Islamabad.

151. Noon, *From Memory*, 269.

152. Confidential From UKHC Karachi to CRO London, 28 April 1960, DO 35/8926, NA, London.

153. Z. A. Bhutto, 'A New Phase Begins', in Bhutto, Reshaping Foreign Policy, Nineteen Forty-Eight to Nineteen Sixty-Six; Statements, Articles speeches. www.bhutto.org, 103, 22 March 2012.

154. Feldman, *Revolution in Pakistan*, 168.

155. Cabinet mtg, 10 May 1960 and Dispatch by Rass Mark, *Dawn* 11 May 1960 cited in Z. A. Bhutto, *Third World New Directions*, www.bhutto.org, 61, 22 March 2012.

156. Ibid.
157. Ibid.
158. Cabinet mtg, 22 July 1960, 254/CF/60, NDC, Islamabad.
159. From BHC Karachi to CRO London, 28 April 1960, DO 35/8926, NA, London.
160. G. Noorani, 'Bhutto and Nonalignment', *Economic and Political Weekly* 11 (1976): 1957; and Feldman, *Revolution in Pakistan*, 183–4.
161. National Assembly of Pakistan Debates, Official Report, Vol. 1, No. 1, 27 June 1962.
162. Afzal, *Pakistan: History and Politics*, 246.
163. Burke and Ziring, *Pakistan's Foreign Policy*, 264.
164. Ibid. 297.
165. Cabinet mtg, 10 August 1963, 198/CF/63, NDC, Islamabad.
166. Cabinet mtg, 17 September 1965, 442/CF/65, NDC, Islamabad.
167. Ayub, *Friends Not Masters*, 115.
168. Ibid. 121.
169. Ibid. 208–9.
170. Henry Kissinger, *On China* (New York: The Penguin Press, 2011), 230; and Kux, *The United States,* 182–3.
171. Ibid. 60.
172. Z. A. Bhutto, *The Myth of Independence* (Oxford: Oxford University Press, 1969), 134.
173. Saeed Shafqat, *Political System of Pakistan and Public Policy: Essays in Interpretations* (Lahore, Progressive Publishers, 1989), 256.
174. Cabinet mtg, 30 January 1972, 38/CF/72. Bhutto informed the cabinet that the UK was going to recognize so-called Bangladesh and stated categorically that in the event of Commonwealth countries taking such a step, Pakistan would be constrained to leave the Commonwealth.
175. Talbot, *Pakistan: A Modern History*, 235 and Kaushik, *Pakistan Under Bhutto's Leadership*, 184–5.
176. Cabinet mtg, 16 March 1949, 215/CF/47, NDC, Islamabad.
177. Zarina Salamat, *Pakistan 1947–58; An Historical Review* (Islamabad; NIHCR, 1992), 210.
178. Cabinet mtg, 14 September 1955, 262/CF/55, NDC, Islamabad.

179. Ibid.
180. China-Pakistan Joint Statement, in K. Arif, *China-Pakistan Relations 1947–1980: Documents* (Lahore: Vanguard Books, 1984), 13.
181. Bhutto, *Third World New Directions,* 22 and *Dawn,* 8 November 1960.
182. Ibid.
183. Cabinet mtg, 18 November 1960, Doc. No. 197, cited in K. Arif, *America – Pakistan Relations,* 191 and 26.
184. Cabinet mtg, 18 November 1960, cited in Z. A. Bhutto, *Third World New Directions* www.bhutto.org, 22 12.06.2011; and Wolpert, *Zulfi Bhutto of Pakistani,* 66.
185. Cabinet mtg, 4 October 1961, 407/CF/61, NDC, Islamabad.
186. Gauhar, *Ayub Khan,* 201.
187. Ibid. 208–9; Feldman, *From Crisis to Crisis,* 91.
188. Ibid.
189. Statement by Mohammad Ali, Foreign Minister of Pakistan, in the National Assembly, 22 November 1962 cited in K. Arif, *China–Pakistan Relation,* 30–1.
190. National Assembly of Pakistan Debates, Official Report, 31 December 1962 and Speech of Bhutto in the National Assembly of Pakistan in Zulfiqar Ali Bhutto, *Foreign Policy of Pakistan* (Karachi: Pakistan Institute of International Affairs, 1964), 28. Bhutto advocated friendly relations with both China and Soviet Union on many other occasions also. See his speech in the National Assembly on 31 December 1962.
191. Top Secret: Note for Record: 'Pakistan: Intrigue in the High Places' From UKHC Rawalpindi to CRO London, 30 July 1965, DO 196/320, NA, London.
192. From UKHC Karachi to CRO London, 3 October 1963, DO 196/120 cited in Roedad Khan, *The British Papers,* 176.
193. Kaushik, *Pakistan under Bhutto's Leadership,* 183; and Yusuf, *Pakistan: A Study of Political Development,* 92.
194. Burke and Ziring, *Pakistan's Foreign Policy,* 292.
195. Yusuf, *Pakistan: A Study of Political Development,* 92.
196. Ziring, *The Ayub Khan Era,* 52.
197. Yusuf, *Pakistan: A Study of Political Development,* 92.

198. Werner Levi, 'Pakistan, the Soviet Union and China', *Pacific Affairs* 35 (Autumn 1962), 221.
199. Brief for the Delegation Representing Pakistan in 18th session of UNO, approved by the cabinet, 1 September 1963, 505/CF/63 and decision of the cabinet, 7 September 1963, 505/CF/63, NDC, Islamabad.
200. Cabinet decision 7 September 1963, 505/CF/63, NDC, Islamabad.
201. Document No. 9, Statement by Foreign Minister Pirzada in the UN General Assembly, 29 September 1966, cited in K. Arif ed., *China-Pakistan Relations*, 107.
202. Cabinet mtg, 9 September 1947, 67/CF/47, NDC, Islamabad.
203. She claimed that Begum Rana Liaquat invited her to accompany them on the Russia visit. Jahan Ara Shahnawaz, *Father and Daughter, A Political Autobiography* (Oxford: University Press 2002), 239, and Mushtaq Ahmad, *Jinnah and After*, 76.
204. Bhutto, *Third World New Directions*, 23.
205. From UKHC Karachi to British Foreign Office London, 3 March 1961, DO 196/128, NA, London.
206. Burke and Ziring, *Pakistan's Foreign Policy*, 212–13 and Syed, *Discourse and Politics of Z.A. Bhutto*, 32–6.
207. Yusuf, *Pakistan – A Study of Political Development*, 93.
208. Cabinet decision, 11 May 1966, 88/CF/66, NDC, Islamabad.
209. *Dawn*, 29 June 1968.
210. Ibid. 365.
211. Dennis Kux, *The United States*, 180–1.
212. Burke, 'The Management of Pakistan's Foreign Policy' in *Pakistan: The Long View*, 361.
213. Niloufer Mahdi, *Pakistan's Foreign Policy 1971–1981: The Search for Security* (Lahore: Ferozsons, 1999), 232.
214. Ibid. 231.
215. Cabinet mtg, 23 August 1974, 266/CF/74, NDC, Islamabad.
216. The details have been given in the preceding pages.
217. Cabinet concluded before Ayub's visit to the USA in 1965 that 'the President's forthcoming visit to USA would provide an opportunity to impress upon the leaders of that major World Power the need for exercising its active influence for an urgent solution of the Kashmir

problem and adopting other measures on the basis of mutual respect for each other for the restoration of peace and confidence in this region, 6 October 1965, 542/CF/65, NDC, Islamabad.

218. Zulfikar Ali Bhutto, *President of Pakistan, Speeches and Statements*, 1 October 1972–31 December 1972 (Karachi: Department of Films and Publications, Government of Pakistan, 1973), 686.

CHAPTER 5

Rifts and Changes in the Cabinets

This chapter focuses on the rifts and groupings that existed among different cabinet members because of different ideologies, regions, or at times, for personal reasons. It also highlights changes made within the cabinets through dismissals or resignations, the impact of the rifts, and changes on policymaking and the relationship between the PM or president and the cabinet as an institution. Four types of cabinet worked in Pakistan during the period of this study, i.e. single party cabinets (1947–1954, 1973–1977), coalition cabinets (1955–1958), martial law cabinets (1958–1962, 1969–1971) and presidential cabinets (1962–1969, 1971–1973). As well as these, a unique cabinet named the Cabinet of All Talents also functioned for almost a year (1954–1955). The rifts and changes in the cabinets are analysed in this chapter according to these types.

Studies of the disagreements, rifts, and ministerial changes within the cabinet of a country reveal different interest groups with varied opinions on policy issues. The working capability of a cabinet can also be affected by serious rifts. Under the British parliamentary or cabinet system, failure to abide by the doctrine of collective cabinet responsibility is the most obvious reason for a cabinet minister to either resign or be dismissed.[1] Resignation or sacking from a cabinet also takes place on issues of policy. In the case of the failure of a policy or major policy disaster, no option is left but to resign. Personal problems of either a financial or sexual nature have been another reason for sacking from the cabinet under the British system.[2] Resignation and dismissal from cabinets in Pakistan have taken place due to all these reasons in the parliamentary system, but sacking from cabinet did not need a reason every time during a military regime, as happened in the case of Mohammad Shoaib in 1966 during Ayub Khan's era.

5.1. SINGLE PARTY CABINETS

5.1.1. SINGLE PARTY CABINETS, 1947–1954

There are two defined periods when single party cabinets functioned in Pakistan. Liaquat Ali Khan's cabinet was the first one, which consisted of all Muslim League ministers. His cabinet was clearly divided between two factions: one under Fazlur Rehman, Minister of Industries, from East Bengal, and the other under Malik Ghulam Mohammad, Finance Minister, from Punjab. Fazlur Rehman led the so-called 'Bengali group' and Ghulam Mohammad led the so-called 'Punjabi group'.[3] These groups were Punjabi and Bengali in name only. The Bengali group included non-Bengalis too, like Sardar Abdur Rab Nishtar from NWFP, Minister of Communications till 1949 from NWFP, and Abdus Sattar Pirzada, Minister of Food and Agriculture from Sindh. The Punjabi group also included some non-Punjabis like Iskandar Mirza from NWFP.[4]

Malik Ghulam Mohammad and Fazlur Rehman quite often had differences of opinion. 'In temperament, they were poles apart—the one as quick and sharp as a rapier and the other as blunt and heavy as a bludgeon.'[5] It is also claimed by some historians, including Allen McGrath and Ian Talbot, that the issues were decided between these two and only then was a negotiated settlement presented in the cabinet to be approved as a matter of form.[6] No settlement could be reached on the issue of the devaluation of the currency in 1949, and conflict between these two personalities became apparent. Fazlur Rehman, in his letter to the PM, emphasized in November 1949 that the cabinet must not linger on the issue of devaluation and must make its decision as early as possible. He wrote: 'I must make it quite clear that in my opinion there is a serious danger to the success of our non-devaluation policy if uncertainty continues any longer.'[7] He further insisted that Ghulam Muhammad must be pressed for discussion and decision on a priority basis. The decision finally went in favour of Fazlur Rehman and as a result bitterness increased between the ministers on this issue specifically, and on other issues generally.[8] In some cases Ghulam Muhammad interfered in the affairs of other ministries as well. Shahabuddin, who was in Fazlur Rehman's group, was against this action of Ghulam Muhammad. Shahabuddin wrote to the PM that Ghulam Muhammad must not be permitted to interfere in the affairs of the Interior Ministry. He wrote that the administration of Karachi was the responsibility of the Interior Ministry and that the finance minister was not directly concerned with it.[9] Liaquat put his weight behind the Bengali group and the currency was not devalued.

Besides this rift in the cabinet of Liaquat Ali Khan, the dissatisfaction of Jogandar Nath Mandal, Minister of Law, Labour, and Works, was another problem. Ziring's opinion is that Mandal resigned on the question of the Objectives Resolution.[10] This opinion is not correct: if he had disagreed on the Objectives Resolution, the resignation would have taken place in 1949. He had disagreements on other points. He wanted East Bengal's cabinet to include at least two scheduled caste ministers, and if the decision was not taken soon, he 'might be forced most painfully and reluctantly to submit my resignation here in the central Cabinet'.[11] His resignation became known when he disclosed it in an interview with the correspondent of *The Civil and Military Gazette* on 3 October 1950. He mentioned that he had developed a difference of opinion with the premier of East Bengal on the issue of the treatment extended towards minorities. He also mentioned that he had problems with other cabinet ministers, but did not name them.[12] Later, Mandal migrated to India and joined the anti-Pakistan forces.

Liaquat was on a state visit to the USA in April 1950 when this incident took place. After his arrival, the cabinet decided to bring reality to the scene and to present the government's view on this issue to the world. A letter was issued by the Foreign Office in Karachi which denied the story told by Mandal. The Pakistani government had evidence that Mandal was in close contact with Dr Shyama Prosad Mukerji, an extremist Hindu leader, and with some other organizations that were trying to wreck the Delhi Agreement, popularly known as the Liaquat-Nehru Pact,[13] signed on 8 April 1950. It was also reported by the Pakistani High Commissioner in Delhi that Mandal had issued some objectionable public statements, published in a large number of Indian newspapers, to the effect that East Bengal's government was not serious in implementing the provisions of the Minority's Agreement.[14] When the PM questioned Mandal about these developments, he denied being involved and issued a statement in favour of Pakistan. He went to Calcutta after a few days to see his sick son, from where he published a letter in some Indian newspapers, in which many allegations were levelled against Pakistan. The government of Pakistan maintained that if these were correct, then he should remain in Pakistan after his resignation and fight for the rights of minorities. Some other minority leaders in Pakistan condemned his actions and said that the allegations were baseless.[15]

Punjabi-Bengali division and rifts were passed on to the next PM, Nazimuddin (1951–1953). He was a Bengali himself and led the Bengali faction of the cabinet. The Punjabi faction also included some very prominent non-Punjabi figures. They were C-in-C Ayub Khan, and Defence Secretary Iskandar Mirza. Neither of them was a part of the cabinet, but they were very close to Governor General Malik Ghulam Muhammad, and were regarded as part of the kitchen cabinet. Again, division was not on ethnic lines, but based on ideology. Nazimuddin was orthodox in his outlook and did not wish to see Pakistan become an ally of the USA or western bloc: he wanted to establish close relations with the

Muslim countries. On the other hand, the so-called Punjabi faction, including Zafrullah Khan, Choudhury Muhammad Ali, and Ghulam Mohammad, were regarded as pro-US and insisted on joining defence pacts with the West.[16]

Another rift which emerged between the members of the cabinet during the same period was over the anti-Ahmadiyya movement. It came to the surface in 1953 between Nazimuddin and Zafrullah Khan, Minister of Foreign Affairs and an Ahmadi himself. Zafrullah Khan wanted the cabinet to issue a statement condemning the attacks against the *Qadianis,* but Nazimuddin and his supporters in the cabinet were not ready to do so, despite the insistence of the Governor General.[17]

Along with some internal changes within the cabinet, Nazimuddin accepted the resignation of his brother Khawaja Shahabuddin, Minister of the Interior, Information and Broadcasting, and appointed him as governor of NWFP. His presence in the cabinet had increased tension between the two factions.[18]

Bogra's cabinet (1953–1954) also witnessed some conflicts between the Punjabi and Bengali factions. Governor General Ghulam Mohammad, a Punjabi, had selected Bogra's cabinet himself. Therefore, they were closer to the Governor General than to the PM, who was a less well-known figure in Pakistan. Bogra had been out of the country working as an ambassador in the USA. He knew little about his cabinet colleagues at the time of taking over as PM. This made the Governor General more powerful.[19] Most of the decisions were taken by the Governor General, who had the support of the Punjabi group. Throughout his premiership Bogra faced difficulties due to the Punjabi group who wanted his removal. The group included Mushtaq Ahmed Gurmani, Minister of Kashmir Affairs, States and Frontier Regions and the Interior, Sardar Bahadur Khan, Minister of Communications and brother of Ayub Khan, and Khan Abdul Qayyum Khan, Minister of Food, Agriculture, Industries and Commerce.[20] Bogra could never enjoy the support of his cabinet due to the influential Punjabi group. He did not have a complete understanding of the internal political affairs of the country at the time of his appointment as PM. Although the cabinet functioned in a normal way, there was the suspicion that the influential ministers used to reach agreement on issues in advance.[21]

This regime of a single party cabinet witnessed its end on 24 October 1954, with the dissolution of CAP.

5.1.2. The Cabinet of Zulfikar Ali Bhutto, 1973–1977

The parliamentary system was restored in Pakistan with the introduction of the 1973 constitution. This cabinet was predominantly PPP's ministers except for one Muslim League minister, Khan Abdul Qayyum Khan.[22] During this period, many forced and voluntary resignations took place. One dramatic change that occurred in this period was the shifting of the balance of power from the leftist element to the rightist in the cabinet as well as in the party. Many leftists who had helped in founding the PPP either left the cabinet or were forced to resign. J. A. Rahim, one of the founding fathers of the PPP had to leave the cabinet because of misunderstandings that developed between him and Bhutto: the first occurrence was in 1972 at the PPP convention when he showed his disagreement with Bhutto on his choice of president and speaker of the NA. After this, he started publicly criticizing Bhutto's domestic and foreign policies. Bhutto had personalized the PPP up until that time. He said 'I am the Peoples Party and they are all my creatures'.[23] Meanwhile, Aziz Ahmed[24] was appointed minister of state. Rahim, being an ex-bureaucrat, knew Aziz Ahmed personally and did not consider him good for the PPP government. In the cabinet meeting Rahim 'accused Bhutto of destroying the Party's ideology and morale'. He lashed out at Bhutto.[25] Bhutto could not tolerate this personal attack and ordered him to leave the cabinet meeting room. He was dismissed from the cabinet on 2 July 1974. Later, federal security forces (FSF) entered his home at night and beat him badly.[26] J. A. Rahim's criticism of Bhutto was harsh. Bhutto had tolerated it to the maximum, but finally took action against him.[27]

Stanley Wolpert's opinion is different from this. He states that on 2 July 1974, he, with other guests, had to wait for many hours as Bhutto was busy with some other work. Rahim left the place, saying: 'You bloody flunkies can wait as long as you like for the Maharaja of Larkana, I'm going.'[28] Late in the night he was badly beaten by the FSF at his home. This sad incident was later denied by Bhutto. He denied that the federal government was involved in the incident.[29] Mubashar Hasan summarized that the J. A. Rahim episode happened due to Rahim's criticism of Bhutto, which was intolerable for Bhutto.[30]

The next departure of an important leftist leader from the cabinet was that of Mubashar Hasan, who did not accept a cabinet portfolio in the fourth cabinet formed in October 1974. He left the cabinet for three reasons which he mentioned in a long letter to Bhutto. The reasons were Bhutto's harsh treatment of J. A. Rahim, his tilt towards the obscurantist interpretation of Islam, and the death of his mother.[31] Hasan was against the induction of rightist elements into the cabinet which were gradually gaining influence. He could not tolerate Bhutto being closer to the rightists led by Maulana Kausar Niazi. He decided to keep away from this new situation and from the cabinet.[32]

Another leftist who left the cabinet on 18 December 1974 was Khursheed Hasan Meer. According to Maleeha Lodhi, Bhutto played the politics of factionalism in the cabinet and Niazi and Meer were leading two different factions.[33] Fourteen members of the National Assembly signed a statement criticizing Khursheed Hasan Meer for trying to spread communism in the country. They accused Meer of starting a campaign against Maulana Niazi.[34] Hassan says that he resigned from the cabinet due to the direct attacks of Maulana Kausar Niazi. Bhutto did not support him well.[35] This resignation made the rightist element strong in the cabinet.

There is the other interpretation that Bhutto could not tolerate competitors in his cabinet: this is why he ousted some of his very influential ministers. J. A. Rahim, who was chief ideologue of the party and Minister of Commerce and Production, was ousted. Mubashar Hasan resigned in July

1974 which created satisfaction in Karachi's industrial sector. The most prominent exit was of Khursheed Hasan Meer who had already started sitting on the opposition benches. This left Sheikh Rashid as the only leftisit in the cabinet and he kept silent for a long time. He was comparatively submissive and did not oppose Bhutto's orders.[36] In fact, Bhutto could not tolerate any colleague being more popular than him. Maulana Kausar Niazi, who was continuously appearing publicly in his role as information minister, was dismissed from that ministry and was left with only the ministry of religious affairs.[37]

Under the 1973 Constitution, only members of parliament could be given a cabinet portfolio. Some ministers had to leave the cabinet because they were not members of either house. They were Hayat Muhammad Khan Sherpao, Minister of Fuel, Power and Natural Resources, and Ghaus Bakhsh Raisani, Minister of Food, Agriculture and Underdeveloped Areas.[38]

A reshuffle in 1974 brought in rightists as a powerful faction in the cabinet. Stalwarts of the PPP were no longer there.[39] In the absence of the staunch leftists, Bhutto faced very weak or no opposition in the cabinet. The government started giving a new direction to economic affairs.[40] A few months before the elections, a prominent change was observed in the cabinet. Two ministers of the Qayyum Muslim League, Qayyum Khan, Minister of Interior, States and Frontier Regions, and Yusuf Khattak, Minister of Fuel, Power, and Natural Resources were asked to resign. According to Rafi Raza, Bhutto's advisors, especially Hafeez Pirzada, misinformed him that he did not need the support of QML. Both the QML ministers were formally asked to resign from the cabinet. This left the PPP alone in the election contest in NWFP.[41] The presence of large number of rightists naturally influenced the policy- and decision-making of the cabinet.

The rifts in the Muslim League cabinets and PPP cabinets had one major difference: whereas Zulfikar Ali Bhutto was a powerful PM and had a strong grip on his cabinet, PMs in the early phase were divided and could not maintain a strong grip, except for Liaquat Ali Khan. Secondly, the Punjabi-Bengali divide was so prominent sometimes that it made the existence of a Bengali PM impossible. Since 1951, Punjabi Governor General Ghulam Mohammad, acting through some ministers, had made it difficult for Bengali PMs to work smoothly. The situation was quite different under Zulfikar Ali Bhutto when the president served only as a constitutional figurehead. However, the rifts and then resignations took place mostly on the basis of ideology. It can be rightly concluded that the rifts of the earlier cabinets of Pakistan were mostly region-oriented, but they erupted during Z. A. Bhutto's period mostly due to ideological differences, and sometimes due to personal clashes with the PM.

5.2. THE CABINET OF ALL TALENTS, 1954–1955

The majority of the ministers included in the so-called Cabinet of All Talents had no part in provincial or personal racketeering within the ML. They were not concerned with their own pockets or those of the province.[42] Only one prominent breach was observed in this cabinet: Suhrawardy,

Minister of Law, was unable to develop a working relationship with PM Bogra and said that he was surrounded by 'the set of crooks and Fascists'.[43] He also named Iskandar Mirza as prominent among such fascists.[44] Choudhury Muhammad Ali expressed the view in an interview with Agha Shorish Kashmiri that Suhrawardy was against Bogra's premiership.[45] Suhrawardy was a leader of national stature and did not like to work under Bogra, but had to do so in order to form the AL government in East Bengal. His public speeches and remarks in private conversation continued to be more like those one would expect from a leader of the opposition than from a member of the cabinet.[46] But this rift did not disturb the working of the cabinet and did no harm as Suhrawardy's group was not stronger than the civil-cum-military faction of the cabinet which included Ghulam Mohammad, Iskandar Mirza, Choudhury Muhammad Ali, and Ayub Khan, who together formed the real decision-making authority.

5.3. COALITION CABINETS, 1955–1958

Coalition cabinets between the years 1955–58 contained many groups and confronted several disagreements due to the presence of multiple political parties who represented their specific party programmes and policies. United Front's ministers in the cabinet of Choudhury Muhammad Ali formed a faction which developed differences of opinion on many policy issues with the ML, their coalition partner. They wanted more provincial autonomy in the 1956 Constitution. The major problem emerged after the creation of the Republican Party from within the ML. Choudhury

Muhammad Ali did not take any disciplinary action against dissident Muslim Leaguers. As president of the ML it was expected that he would take some action against such members. Pir Ali Mohammad Rashdi, Minister of Information and Broadcasting, stated on 31 August 1956, 'Prime Minister Muhammad Ali was elected to the Constituent Assembly of Pakistan on the Muslim League ticket and was bound by the advice and majority decision of the Muslim League Parliamentary Party.'[47] The ML parliamentary party decided to take disciplinary action against the Republicans, the former Muslim Leaguers.

Instead of taking action against them, Choudhury Muhammad Ali decided to convene a meeting of his coalition partners on 27 August, to which Republicans were also invited. Eleven ML members of the legislature, including two ministers, I. I. Chundrigarh and Rashdi, did not attend the meeting[48] and resigned from the cabinet on 29 August 1956.[49] This controversy led to the resignation of Choudhury Muhammad Ali from the ML as well as from the position of prime minister on 8 September 1956, despite having the support of the majority in the CAP. He informed the cabinet that, having resigned from the ML, he considered it a point of honour that he should resign also from the prime ministership.[50]

Suhrawardy's cabinet was a combination of conflicting personalities as its members belonged to different political parties. Sardar Amir Azam Khan, Minister of Information and Broadcasting, from the Republican Party, resigned from the cabinet after Gurmani's dismissal from the governorship of West Pakistan in August 1957. He was a close associate of Gurmani. His resignation was a blow to the coalition government because Amir Azam, as an *ex-officio* chief whip, was keeping the coalition together.[51]

The other area of conflict was the One Unit.[52] The Republican ministers had started a campaign to dismember the One Unit along with the left wing National Awami Party.[53] Suhrawardy publicly criticized it. In an interview he stated that it was essential to work under One Unit to avoid any delay in holding elections. Once elections had been held, the new CAP could take a decision on the issue.[54] Moreover, he was of the view that more time should be given to judging the true value of the experiment.[55] The conflict ultimately reached the point where the issue came out of cabinet meetings and entered the sphere of public discussion. The Republican Minister of the Interior Mir Ghulam Ali Talpur publicly expressed the view that no delay was possible in holding the elections if it was decided to dissolve the One Unit, and if delay occurred, even then the Republican Party would favour the dismemberment of One Unit. He overruled collective cabinet responsibility. Suhrawardy could not take disciplinary action against Talpur, and disagreement in the cabinet could not be overcome because, unfortunately, the PM did not have the right to dismiss a minister from his cabinet. Under the 1956 Constitution of Pakistan, this right was reserved for the President only.[56] By October 1957, it appeared that this coalition would not be able to work for long. But despite this, Suhrawardy announced that, as he had a majority in the Assembly on his side, he would ask for a vote of confidence on 24 October 1957.[57]

Suhrawardy called a meeting of his cabinet on 12 October 1957 at his residence in Karachi that was boycotted by the Republican ministers including Syed Amjad Ali, Minister of Finance, Muzaffar Ali Khan Qizalbash, Minister of Industries, and Commerce, and later Minister of Parliamentary Affairs, Ghulam Ali Talpur, Minister of the Interior, Mian Jaffar Shah, Minister of Food and Agriculture, and Haji Moula Bukhsh Soomro, Minister of Rehabilitation. They demanded the resignation of Suhrawardy[58] who resigned only under threat of dismissal by the president. The 'marriage of convenience'[59] between two opposing political partners proved unsuccessful.

The cabinet of I. I. Chundrigarh again included ministers from different political parties with conflicting approaches. The major coalition partners included the ML, the KSP, and the Republican Party. The main cause of friction in this cabinet was the appointment of more West Pakistani ministers to important portfolios than East Pakistanis. It caused serious misgivings in the East and remained a potential source of friction between ministers representing the two wings.[60] The ML had been a strong supporter of separate electorates since its establishment, whereas KSP was a strong supporter of joint electorates. The Republican Party supported joint electorates for East Pakistan and separate electorates for West Pakistan. ML brought up the issue for discussion in the cabinet meeting on 22 October 1957. PM Chundrigarh told the cabinet that a bill substituting separate electorates for joint electorates for the elections to the national and provincial assemblies with immediate effect would be moved in the National Assembly during its November 1957 session.[61] Republican and KSP ministers were not ready to approve the PM's idea, so the final decision was delayed.

It later appeared that Republican ministers had an agreement with the ML that they would support the ML's policy regarding separate electorates and One Unit. On the other side, KSP ministers claimed that the Republican Party had assured the KSP leadership that they would support joint electorates. The ML ministers, including Mian Mumtaz Mohammad Khan Daultana and Yousuf Haroon from West Pakistan, and Chundrigarh and Fazlur Rehman from East Pakistan, and the KSP Ministers Abdul Latif Biswas, Lutfur Rehman, and Misbahuddin from East Pakistan, continually issued public statements on the issue of electorates. Republican Party ministers including Muzzaffar Ali Qizalbash, Ghulam Ali Talpur, and Amjad Ali tried to remind the Republican Party's leaders to keep their promises.[62] But their efforts were fruitless as Malik Firoz Khan Noon and other Republican members were not ready to make any compromise. The cabinet secretariat issued a press note stating that, 'The coalition government was formed on agreement by the Republican Party to support separate electorates.'[63]

The issue of separate electorates was discussed again in the federal cabinet on 2 November 1957. The ML wanted to introduce separate electorates in place of the joint electorates under the Electorate Act and through another bill to make consequential changes in the Electorate Rolls Act.[64] Republican Party ministers stated that as they had not taken any decision on the issue yet, more time must be given to them. Later, the cabinet was informed that the Republican

Party had backed away from its position. The president informed the cabinet that the Republican Party's leadership had given their word to him and to the PM that they would support the substitution of separate electorates for joint electorates. Now the Republican Party had gone back on its promises and decided not to support the bill for separate electorates.[65] Because of this situation I. I. Chundrigarh had to tender his resignation on 11 December 1957.[66]

Malik Firoz Khan Noon was invited by the president to form the next government. Republican PM Noon's cabinet was also divided. On one level there were differences based on personal rivalry between the PM and the Republican minister Syed Amjad Ali. Noon's ally in West Pakistan was Mozaffar Ali Qizilbash, and Amjad Ali's ally was Abid Hussain.[67] On another level, problems remained between the KSP and the Republican Party. The KSP leader Hamid ul Haq Chowdhary wanted to have a seat in the cabinet which Noon was unwilling to give due to the pressure from Suhrawardy of AL, whose support was essential for Noon to remain in office.[68] The KSP and the AL had factional rivalry and the inclusion of Hamid ul Haq in the cabinet could have created problems for Noon's government.[69] However, despite this, KSP was given a cabinet portfolio in September 1958.[70]

Following KSP's inclusion in the cabinet, AL also demanded a place, which was granted to them on 2 October 1958. Three members of the AL, i.e. Sahiruddin, A. H. Dildar Ahmad, and Nurur Rahman took oath as ministers, but agreement could not be reached on the distribution of portfolios. The AL ministers wanted influential portfolios such as Interior,

Foreign Affairs, and Finance and Economic Affairs, which had already been given to Republican ministers.[71] As no agreement was reached on the issue, the AL ministers resigned from the cabinet only four days after taking oath. Suhrawardy did not want instability before the elections, which were due in February 1959. He hoped to be elected as PM after the elections. He asked his party's ministers to resign, which they did. Although both Noon and Suhrawardy cooperated to save the system, to hold elections smoothly, and to control the ambitious Mirza, their efforts were unsuccessful. President Mirza realized that his position was not safe under the parliamentary system so he paved the way for the imposition of martial law in the hope of continuing in power.

The coalition cabinets introduced a new trend in the cabinet system of Pakistan: the ministers discussed their rifts in public. If they disagreed on any issue, they issued a statement on it, which was against the accepted norms of the cabinet system. During this period, the hold of the PM on the cabinet remained weak because the constitution of Pakistan had given the right of dismissal of ministers to the president; the PM was not in a position to take any action against his ministers for disregarding cabinet discipline. During the period of coalition government ministers became more powerful while the PM became weaker due to Mirza's autocratic attitude.

5.4. CABINETS DURING THE PERIODS OF MARTIAL LAW

After the imposition of martial law by Ayub Khan in 1958, the nature of rifts and problems within the cabinets changed.

The hold of CMLA Ayub Khan on his cabinet was very strong, and the chances of rifts were meagre. If a rift emerged, the minister or ministers concerned had to leave the cabinet. Very few disagreements existed in the cabinet during the martial law period from 1958 to 1962.

5.4.1. MARTIAL LAW PERIOD, 1958–1962

During this period the ministers were mostly technocrats and worked efficiently. There was a consensus of opinion on most issues. However, the first major change in the cabinet happened in April 1960. General Azam Khan, who was a highly successful rehabilitation minister, was appointed governor of East Pakistan in April 1960 as it was a new outlet for the expression of his energies.

The first rift in the cabinet of Ayub Khan emerged over the constitution. The members of the cabinet sub-committee were divided. The committee was formed in May 1961 to examine the proposals of the Constitution Commission and to present its report. Manzur Qadir, Minister of Foreign Affairs, was its chairman, with two West Pakistani ministers, Z. A. Bhutto, Minister of Commerce, and Muhammad Shoaib, Finance Minister, and three ministers from East Pakistan, Mohammad Ibrahim, Minister of Law, Abul Kasem Khan, Minister of Industries, and Hafizur Rehman, Minister of Food and Agriculture. This committee was very important, as Ayub wanted an alternate report on the points of the Constitution Commission's Report which were unacceptable to Ayub, including a bicameral legislature, the provision of a vice president, etc.[72]

The two East Pakistani ministers, Mohammad Ibrahim and Abul Kasem Khan, disagreed with the West Pakistani ministers. Mohammad Ibrahim proposed the parliamentary form of government with adult franchise. Manzur Qadir said, 'This again will bring about chaos.'[73] Ibrahim suggested that in the case of the residential form of government, the provincial governors must be elected, and the constitution must be drawn up in consultation with the representatives of the provinces. He emphasized equal representation for both provinces in the federal cabinet and wanted a permanent seat of the central legislature in Dacca. Abul Kasem Khan was also critical of the report prepared by the Constitution Commission and emphasized equal distribution of economic resources between the two provinces. Commerce Minister Hafizur Rehman, another East Pakistani, was a silent observer on most of the issues, but said that a centralized system of government would be disastrous for the unity of the country. West Pakistani ministers wanted a strong central government under the presidential system. There was serious disagreement on the issue between the East and West Pakistani ministers. The East Pakistani ministers' point of view was not given weight. In response, Mohammad Ibrahim avoided taking part in the deliberations of the committee. Kasem Khan was disappointed and Hafizur Rehman was critical. All three were dropped from the cabinet after the introduction of the 1962 Constitution due to their disagreement over the constitution.[74] According to Mushtaq Ahmad, Mohammad Ibrahim resigned from the cabinet owing to his disagreement on the constitution, and was not dropped.[75]

Foreign policy was another area of conflict in Ayub's cabinet. Two groups emerged, one under Bhutto, and the other under Mohammad Shoaib. Bhutto prioritized an independent foreign policy and wanted to develop close relations with the communist bloc, especially China. He also wanted Pakistan to identify herself 'with the Third World causes in international politics'[76] and to seek settlement with India on a bilateral level. Mohammad Shoaib believed that foreign aid, central for economic development, was received from the USA due to the pro-west foreign policy.[77] As both were powerful ministers, it is worth mentioning that Pakistan followed the pro-west foreign policy, and at the same time started developing closer ties with China too.

The rifts in the military cabinets of Ayub's martial law period emerged in two forms: the first was the exit of the East Pakistani ministers who did not agree with Ayub Khan's constitution; the second rift was quite productive as the course of Pakistan's foreign policy underwent a positive change.

5.4.2. GENERAL YAHYA KHAN'S MILITARY REGIME, 1969–1971

Yahya Khan's military regime included military as well as civil cabinets. Both types experienced rifts. The military cabinet of General Yahya was split on different issues. The first tussle erupted between Yahya and Nur Khan, Minister of Labour, Health and Social Welfare who controlled five more departments. Nur Khan wanted to introduce some drastic reforms for labourers and students. His reforms would introduce the right to strike, lockout, and many other rights to labourers. He wanted students to have the right to 'participate in the selection and promotion of teachers including University Professors.'[78] President Yahya was against this type of reform package. The basic difference was that Yahya, General Abdul Hamid, Minister of Home and Kashmir Affairs, States and Frontier Regions, and Pirzada, PSO, wanted to take things slowly, but Nur Khan wanted to make instant changes in the system. Because Yahya was against Nur Khan's ideas, he appointed him Governor of East Pakistan.[79]

Admiral Ahsan wanted immediate elections and the early transfer of power to civilians, but other generals were not in a hurry.[80] Yahya was not tolerant of opposition, so Admiral Ahsan was appointed Governor of West Pakistan.[81] In this way, two members of the Council of Administration were ousted. All other members held opinions similar to those of Yahya.

Yahya's civilian cabinet was also divided into two distinct factions: East Pakistani and West Pakistani ministers, who clashed on almost all issues. The National Economic Council (NEC) met under Yahya's presidency on 3 February 1970. The ministers from both Wings, with the help of top bureaucrats, presented two different opinions. East Pakistani Ministers Dr Abdul Motaleb Malik, Minister of Health, Labour and Communications, Abdul Khair Muhammad Hafizuddin, Minister of Industries and Natural Resources, Muhammad Shams ul Huq, Minister of Education and Scientific Research, Ahsan ul-Huq, Minister of Commerce, and Golam Waheed

Choudhury, Minister of Communications, demanded the diversion of more developmental funds to East Pakistan, but West Pakistani ministers Sardar Abdul Rashid, Minister of Home and Kashmir Affairs, Nawab Mozaffar Ali Qizilbash, Minister of Finance, Nawabzada Mohammad Sher Ali Khan, Minister of Information and Broadcasting, Mahmood A. Haroon, Minister of Agriculture and Works, and A. R. Cornelius, Minister of Law, opposed it. They offered different reasons such as the 'lack of absorbing capacity, inadequacy of administrative machinery and the difficulty of measuring actual regional disparity and so forth'.[82]

At the end of the NEC meeting, three East Pakistani ministers, G. W. Chaudhary, Abdul Khair Muhammad Hafizuddin, and Shamsul Huq held a separate meeting and wrote a letter to Yahya. They stated that they would resign if the decision of the NEC was not revised and if more funds were not allocated to East Pakistan. They sent this letter on the assumption that Yahya would have to dismiss the cabinet if all East Pakistani ministers resigned. Yahya had to accept their demands and another special meeting of the NEC was called, at which the East Pakistani demands were accepted. Yahya said:

> My Bengali colleagues in the Cabinet have pointed out to me that the allocations to East Pakistan for 1970–71 would not narrow down the gap in regional disparity. If so I cannot be a party to it; the gap must be narrowed down.[83]

As a result, the previous decision of the cabinet was changed accordingly.

The kitchen cabinet of Yahya Khan also experienced some problems on constitutional issues. General Abdul Hamid Khan, Chief of the Army Staff, and Major General Omar, Chief of National Security, strongly opposed the principle of 'one-man-one-vote'. General Pirzada, PSO, was neutral on the issue. The conflict between General Hamid and Yahya was kept hidden from the world to a large extent.[84] This rift, at least, was settled.

5.5. PRESIDENTIAL CABINETS

5.5.1. CABINET OF PRESIDENT AYUB KHAN, 1962–1969

Pakistan's first presidential cabinet was formed with the introduction of the 1962 Constitution. This was highly controversial for the cabinet members. The two most influential ministers disagreed with the president on the provisions of the draft constitution. They were Manzur Qadir, Minister of Foreign Affairs and Commonwealth Relations, and Justice Muhammad Munir, Minister of Law and Parliamentary Affairs. Until 1962 Manzur Qadir was the most trustworthy and the main policymaker. Ayub depended on him a great deal for 'intellectualizing his ideas'.[85] but following a disagreement, he left the cabinet. There are different opinions about his departure. Lawrence Ziring says that his role as chief draftsman of the constitution made it compulsory for him to step down because his formula was not followed by the president completely. Rumours spread that they disagreed on the issue of politicizing the administration. He might have favoured the reinstatement of political parties.[86] Justice Muhammad Munir left the cabinet on 17 December 1962 over the question of indirect elections; he was in favour of direct elections.[87] The report of the Franchise Commission, headed by Justice Munir, which had suggested the direct method of elections was rejected by the special committee formed by Ayub Khan. Justice Munir resigned and started to practise law again.[88] This opinion is contradicted by Muhammad Munir. He wrote to Ayub Khan on his resignation:

> I believe that no democratic government can function in the country in which political parties are proscribed and my chief object in joining the government was to make an endeavour to convince you of the necessity of reviving collective political activity ... with the passing of the Political Parties Act individual and collective political activity commenced and now full-fledged pro-government party enjoying substantial majority in the National Assembly has come into existence, the purpose with which I joined the government has been achieved ... I therefore repeat my earlier request to you to relieve me of my present responsibilities at your convenience.[89]

This statement indicates that he resigned for personal reasons. Rifts within the cabinet were prominent when two distinct groups emerged on the scene after the Tashkent Declaration: one was the anti-Ayub faction led by Bhutto, and the other was the pro-Ayub faction led by Khawaja Shahabuddin and which included Altaf Hussain, Minister of Industries and Natural Resources, and Sabur Khan, Minister of Communications.[90] In Nurul Amin's opinion, the anti-Ayub group might stab him in the back.[91]

It is generally believed, and mentioned in the reports sent to the American Secretary of State, that after the Tashkent Declaration, Bhutto's attitude towards Ayub changed; even his facial expression was different.[92] Nor was he ready to speak in favour of the declaration in cabinet meetings. He openly announced to a private gathering after his return from Tashkent, that he had tried to convince Ayub not to accept the Soviet Union model of agreement, but he had rejected the advice.[93] Ayub understood Bhutto's stance, but wanted him to share the after-effects of the declaration. Pilo Mody has stated that Bhutto was called 'to defend government's policy but his heart was not in it'.[94] A similar opinion is given in the British High Commissioner's reports sent to the Commonwealth Relations Office. Bhutto 'played the role of loyal but an unhappy subordinate'[95] on the issue of the Tashkent Declaration. Bhutto remained pointedly silent in the enlarged cabinet meeting in which the president explained the Tashkent Declaration to ministers and officers.[96] S. M. Zafar has also mentioned that Bhutto opposed the Tashkent Declaration.[97] This interpretation is only partially true. If Bhutto was in total disagreement with Ayub Khan, he would not have defended the Tashkent Declaration in the National Assembly on 16 March 1966. He said:

> Tashkent Declaration is not a No-War pact. We cannot accept a No-War pact when the dispute of Jammu and Kashmir, Farakha Barrage, eviction of Muslims, all these problems remain to be solved … The main point in the Tashkent Declaration is that the Soviet Union has accepted for the first time that there is a dispute relating to Jammu and Kashmir.[98]

Besides explaining Tashkent, he defended Pakistan's relationship with the USA and the president's struggle to improve it. He said:

> However strains developed in the relationship between our two countries, but since the visit of our President to the United States, these difficulties and misunderstandings have been explained and at the moment our relations have improved.[99]

This indicates that Bhutto supported his government's point of view at least till March 1966. Something must have happened after that, and that something was the mood of the public which was against the Tashkent Declaration. Bhutto developed his secret sympathies with the leaderless agitation 'that was spontaneously gaining momentum'.[100] He had read the writing on the wall, that Ayub's days in government were numbered, and gradually changed his strategy. Khawaja Shahabuddin, Information Minister, explained the government's point of view and said that Bhutto should have resigned in Tashkent if his 'advice was ignored'[101] or if he 'was unhappy with the results'.[102] Ayub sent Bhutto abroad on medical leave on 6 June 1966 and later to Larkana, where he was given notice to leave the cabinet within twenty-four hours. Ayub noted in his diary that Bhutto 'started using provocative language even on international platforms and started behaving in an irresponsible and objectionable manner. Several warnings went unheeded so there was no alternative but to tell him to go.'[103]

Another reason for his dismissal from the cabinet, mentioned by many historians, is that in 1966, US Vice President

Hubert Humphrey visited South and East Asia to get the support of these countries for Vietnam and to explain the dangers of Chinese imperialist aims. Only Pakistan's response was negative. It was considered by some cabinet colleagues that Bhutto had insisted on this major change in foreign policy, so they started demanding his dismissal. As a result, Ayub dismissed two ministers in March 1966: Bhutto, who was extremely anti-America, and Mohammad Shoaib who was extremely pro-America.[104] The dismissal of Bhutto was 'a move that greatly pleased Washington, and then balanced this and upset Washington by letting his Finance Minister go'[105] because he was a channel of Pakistan-US relations in place of the foreign ministry.[106] With Shoaib's departure Americans had lost a friend at court who was capable of influencing Ayub at vital moments. Ayub respected his views and his technical competence.[107] The exit of Shoaib was a small loss to the president politically as he was not a popular figure.[108] Syed Sharifuddin Pirzada was appointed as new foreign minister and N. M. Uquailli who was a technocrat and a high-level economist, was appointed as the new finance minister.[109]

Sabur Khan, Minister of Communications, was angry and wanted to resign because his responsibilities for ports and shipping had been assigned to the newly-appointed Minister of Defence, Vice Admiral A. R. Khan. Two reasons can be identified for this: first, the admiral had convinced Ayub that it was the responsibility of the defence minister; secondly, Ayub might have been informed about the smuggling activity of Sabur Khan and wanted to curb it. Sabur Khan was among the few supporters of Ayub from East Pakistan, so he did not take any punitive action against him.[110]

Ayub Khan's commerce minister, Ghulam Faruque, was unhappy with his status as a mere minister and wanted to head the Planning Commission. Ayub told him that M. M. Ahmad was a more suitable person for the job; Farooq was not acceptable because of his temperament.[111] Later he sent a letter to Ayub in which he wrote that he wanted to be relieved of his responsibilities in the cabinet due to his ill health and old age. Ayub discussed the issue with him in a meeting and approved his resignation. He mentioned that all other allegations were only rumours;[112] Ghulam Faruque had fallen ill in December 1966 and had wanted to resign since that time.[113] Ayub appointed Ghafur Khan Hoti from NWFP in place of Ghulam Faruque. His reasons for this appointment were Hoti's intelligence, shrewdness, and quickness.[114] The resignation of Syed Mohammad Zafar, Minister of Law occurred on 21 March 1968, only four days before the imposition of the second martial law. He wrote:

> The events are turning a new corner. I don't find myself adjustable to, or in agreement with the new course of events. Therefore in fairness to you and in compliance to the oath of my office I beg to submit my resignation ... I assure you that my decision to resign is based on my own assessment of the future times.[115]

Martial law was imposed before the acceptance of his resignation. The presidential cabinet of Ayub Khan worked smoothly till 1966. The major rifts appeared after the

Tashkent Declaration and resulted in important changes in the cabinet. The situation gradually become difficult for Ayub Khan and the effectiveness of the cabinet decreased with every passing year after 1966.

5.5.2. THE PRESIDENTIAL CABINETS OF Z. A. BHUTTO, 1971–1973

Bhutto's cabinet in the pre-1973 constitutional period consisted of PPP ministers with only one exception, Khan Qayyum Khan from the ML. This presidential cabinet was ideologically divided into the leftist and the rightist factions. Even the leftist colleagues had different opinions on constitutional, political, and economic issues. The leftists, led by J. A. Rahim, Minister of Presidential Affairs, Culture Town Planning and Agrovilles, were totally against Maulana Kausar Niazi, Minister of Information and Broadcasting, Auqaf, and Hajj, and their followers. J. A. Rahim considered Maulana as an undesirable in the cabinet.[116] Khursheed Hasan Meer, Minister without Portfolio, another leftist who looked after the Establishment Division, was a factional rival of Maulana Niazi. The views of each contradicted those of the other. 'Niazi had Islamic Socialist ideology and Meer had belief in scientific Socialism'.[117] Differences of ideology was not the only cause of the rift, but both held severe personal rivalries against each other. The rift was so intense that each tried to bring about the dismissal of the other, on the grounds that both were busy conspiring against the chairman of the PPP.[118] Miraj Mohammad Khan, another prominent radical, also opposed Maulana Kausar Niazi.

In the light of this grouping within the cabinet, Bhutto appointed two landlords, Fazal Ilahi and Sahibzada Farooq Ali, as chairman of the Senate and speaker of the National Assembly respectively. Leftists in the cabinet were against this decision as they did not respect landlords' power, but Bhutto would not listen to them. The same was repeated in the Senate elections held in July 1973 when landlords were elected to 50 per cent of the seats. Leftists, especially J. A. Rahim, opposed this move publicly. This opposition widened the rift between Bhutto, the chairman of the cabinet, and his leftists colleagues, especially J. A. Rahim.[119] Aziz Ahmed's appointment as minister of state was also opposed by leftist ministers, especially J. A. Rahim. Aziz Ahmed was a former bureaucrat and had a close association with Ayub Khan. A serious rift occurred in the cabinet on his appointment as minister of state; J. A. Rahim seriously objected to it.[120]

The cabinet of Bhutto was also divided on constitutional issues. Law Minister Kasuri wanted to introduce the 'unqualified Parliamentary System'[121] in a modified form, which should give 'unchallenged status to the Chief Executive'.[122] The rift between Bhutto and Kasuri reached the point where the departure of one was necessary. Kasuri was chairman of the Constitution-Making Committee. He often argued with Bhutto on his prolonging of martial law in the country. Kasuri wanted a purely parliamentary constitution, but Bhutto wanted to continue with the presidential system or a soft parliamentary system.[123] Bhutto made a promise in his Accord of March 1972 with NAP that the rights of minorities would be safeguarded, and a constitution would be introduced 'which would ensure political participation, provincial autonomy and the economic development of their provinces'.[124] In the opinion of Kasuri, Bhutto's moves had broken the promises he had made earlier. Kasuri said that he did not want to be part of this type of underhand dealing, and resigned.[125] The other reasons for this resignation were his disagreement with Bhutto on many other constitutional issues, especially the operation of the presidential system under the interim constitution of 1972. His resignation was accepted on 4 October 1972.[126] It was an important development as he was not only the chairman of the Constitution-Making Committee, but also leader of the House in the National Assembly and vice chairman of the PPP. Laporte says that Kasuri was actually asked to resign from the cabinet or was dismissed,[127] which is incorrect.

Bhutto presented the issue to the cabinet for discussion for the first time after Kasuri's resignation in September 1972. The officials were sent out. A consensus was reached that acceptance of the resignation would mean delaying the constitution-making. Bhutto suggested that Kasuri could continue as chairman of the Constitution-Making Committee, but the cabinet, as explained by Bhutto, plainly refused to give Kasuri such a position if he resigned from the cabinet. It was decided that if Kasuri wanted to leave the cabinet, he would, on principle, have to leave the PPP and also the Constitution-Making Committee.[128] Bhutto, with the approval of the cabinet accepted the resignation of Kasuri as stated: 'Please refer to your letter of 4th October 1972; I am pleased to accept your resignation as Minister for Law and

Parliamentary Affairs with immediate effect.'[129] After Kasuri's resignation, Bhutto's close friend and lawyer Abdul Hafeez Pirzada was given both the positions formerly held by Kasuri.

A difference of opinion emerged in the cabinet on economic issues also. Leftists ministers were divided on the issue of labour reforms. One group was led by Mubashar Hassan, Minister of Finance, Planning and Development, and the other by J. A. Rahim. It was hard for the government to increase the output of nationalized industries and to fulfill all promises extended towards labourers. The finance ministry paid the managers of nationalized industries from government revenue to overcome the crisis. Labour reforms could not be fully implemented in the nationalized industries. The impact was negative for the cabinet as managers transferred their support to J. A. Rahim from Mubashar Hasan. Rahim's ministry prepared a report and leaked to the press that the PPP government was not fulfilling the promises made to the labourers. This brought to the surface the conflict between the two groups in cabinet. It was an indication that the influence of the leftists in the cabinet was getting weaker.[130]

Conflict also arose over the issue of either fast or slow socialization. Mubashar Hassan wanted it to be fast, but Abdul Hafeez Pirzada Minister of Education, Law and Parliamentary Affairs, convinced Bhutto to take time in implementing the socialist policy of the government.

The case of Minister of State for Public Affairs Miraj Mohammad Khan's resignation was also given prominence.[131] His differences with Bhutto emerged in 1970. He told Bhutto that feudalism must be abolished, whereas Bhutto's emphasis was on the abolition of capitalism 'because imperialism depended on capitalism and not on feudalism'[132] Following his appointment as minister of state for political affairs, he showed his dissatisfaction with the labour policies of the government. As a result of labour troubles in Karachi, Kausar Niazi's group adopted the opinion that communist elements were involved in the trouble and said that Miraj Khan was influenced by communism. The government adopted a policy of repressive measures towards the labourers, so Miraj decided to resign.[133]

Additional factors behind his resignation were ideological differences, changes in the manifesto of the PPP, and the most important reason was the attitude of the PPP high command towards its members and cabinet ministers.[134] Mubashar Hassan's view is different from the reasons given. He believed that Miraj Mohammad Khan enjoyed strong popularity among the workers and the portfolio given to him was useless. He was unhappy with this and resigned from the cabinet.[135] Miraj Mohammad Khan says, 'I was first warned against my habit to mix with common people. Then I was told to learn and observe the mannerism expected of a Cabinet Minister. Now I have been axed because I am trying to practise what he used to preach.'[136] He resigned from the cabinet in May 1972 and was sent to jail for the crime of publicly criticizing Bhutto's government. He called it a fascist government and said that Bhutto was a dictator.[137] This statement angered Bhutto, and Miraj was imprisoned. From this incident, the unacceptable practice of punishing opponents began in the parliamentary democracy of Pakistan.

Although both presidents had a strong grip on their cabinet, there was a strong contrast in the type of rifts that split the two presidential cabinets of the period under study. Ayub Khan's ministers were either dismissed or they resigned over matters of policy. If there was a policy clash between the president and his minister, the fate of the minister was quite evident, whereas Z. A. Bhutto's ministers were strongly divided into factions like hard leftists, soft leftists, and rightist. None of them was ready to tolerate the others. This is why the rifts of this period resulted in broad-level changes, not only during the presidential cabinet system, but also in the later period. Bhutto cleared the way for all those ministers to leave the cabinet with whom he was not comfortable; in the initial period of his rise, they were either his strong supporters or they were not.

5.6. THE RELATIONSHIP OF THE CHAIRMAN OF THE CABINET WITH HIS MINISTERS

5.6.1. THE RELATIONSHIP BETWEEN CABINET AND THE PRIME MINISTER, 1947–1958

The nature of Liaquat's relations with his cabinet was different during and after Quaid-i-Azam Muhammad Ali Jinnah's death. The Quaid-i-Azam's control over the cabinet was firm and Liaquat, too, was always eager to follow his advice, but after Jinnah's death, cabinet was divided into two distinct sections. Some of the cabinet members who considered themselves wiser than PM Liaquat would not take his orders seriously. Such ministers included Malik Ghulam Mohammad and Zafrullah Khan. However, in general his control over the cabinet was strong. At times he took decisions prior to discussing the issue in the cabinet meeting because he was confident of getting approval without any major difficulty. Such decisions included the dismissal of Mamdot's ministry during his visit to Punjab on 24 January 1949,[138] and similarly his announcement of Pakistan's support to the UNO on the Korean War issue while he was on a state visit to the USA in June 1950. It was only later that cabinet endorsed those decisions.[139] Rushbrook William's view that Liaquat took important decisions through cabinet voting seems to be partially correct. Had he been under the influence of his cabinet ministers, he would not have taken any decisions on his own. If he had opted for voting on any matter, it could be the requirement of or demand of the matter. Further, William has not mentioned the method by which voting was arranged in the cabinet meetings.[140] Generally, Liaquat's relations with his colleagues were 'in the nature of collaboration on a friendly basis, although he did not leave any doubt that he was the chief collaborator'.[141]

Nazimuddin's control over his cabinet was comparatively weak, which made decision-making difficult.[142] He mainly played the role of an umpire instead of imposing decisions in the event of a disagreement between two groups. He was the least resistant towards his cabinet colleagues.[143] Governor General Ghulam Muhammad, who had recently left the cabinet and been promoted to the seat of Governor General, had more hold on cabinet than the PM. The kitchen cabinet was also formed by the Governor General and consisted largely of outsiders like Ayub Khan and Iskandar Mirza. It also included some cabinet ministers like Choudhury Muhammad Ali and Zafrullah Khan.

Mohammad Ali Bogra could never emerge as a strong head of the cabinet like Liaquat Ali Khan. He had to depend on his cabinet colleagues who were selected by the Governor General during his first and second premierships. Generally he maintained a working relationship with his ministers. Choudhury Muhammad Ali, his finance minister, said that he had 'received the utmost consideration, courtesy and help from the honourable PM and he was dearly grateful for it'.[144] The cabinet as an institution was not a powerless body even under the weak leadership of Bogra. The cabinet decided policy regarding Punjab and other provinces while deciding that the Punjab CM must be given the opportunity to handle provincial political matters himself, and that federal cabinet should not interfere in provincial matters.[145] The kitchen cabinet of the Governor General was highly influential in foreign policy issues, yet cabinet was not voiceless. Approval was sought from the cabinet to sign the Mutual Defence Agreement with the USA on 19 February 1954.[146]

The view that Choudhury Muhammad Ali was unable to develop a close relationship with his cabinet is questionable. It is said that as a retired civil bureaucrat he always found his cabinet colleagues to be men of 'poor calibre' and thought that they were busy in 'interminable political manoeuvering'[147] due to which he was unable to concentrate on administrative matters. This study has found that he and most of his cabinet colleagues had cordial relations. He appreciated their services in the preparation of the 1956 Constitution and has recorded, 'I worked day and night and with the help of my colleagues prepared a Constitution.'[148] His ministers felt depressed at his decision to resign and thought that his departure from the political scene was a serious blow.[149] The Minister for Health, Minister of Food and Agriculture, Minister for Communications, and Minister for the Interior also expressed their sadness on the resignation of Choudhury Muhammad Ali.

Suhrawardy's relationship with his cabinet colleagues who belonged to the Republican Party had been one of conflict from the beginning. Besides the One Unit issue, Suhrawardy introduced policies such as the revision of the First Five-Year Plan and the allocation of a major share of US aid to East Pakistan, which only increased tension in the cabinet. He changed the status of the finance minister abruptly. He assumed the chairmanship of the Planning Board himself,[150] and took decisions related to finance without endorsement from Amjad Ali, the Republican finance minister who was from West Pakistan. Suhrawardy allocated local and foreign currency funds with the approval of AL ministers for East Pakistan[151] against the finance minister's will. The second major disagreement which emerged with his cabinet was on the question of supporting the US during the Suez Canal crisis when a group in his own party, under Maulana Abdul Hamid Bhashani, disagreed with him.[152] Suhrawardy successfully handled the issue and convinced his colleagues, who later endorsed his foreign policy, to support him.[153]

The hold of I. I. Chundrigarh on his cabinet was very weak and working relations between cabinet colleagues were poor. This caused the fall of his government after only fifty-eight days. Malik Firoz Khan Noon adopted a middle-way policy and avoided bringing conflicting issues into cabinet meetings, so differences of opinion could not surface. He spent eleven months of his office attempting to save the system so that elections could be held and a new government could be formed. Because of this strategy, his relations with all political parties in his cabinet were workable, though not all his efforts were fruitful, as martial law brought an abrupt end to his government on 8 October 1958.

5.6.2. THE RELATIONSHIP BETWEEN CMLA/PRESIDENT AND HIS CABINET, 1958–1971

During this period, Ayub's relationship with his cabinet was workable and at times even good. He was quite tolerant and invited his ministers to express their opinions. He always expressed his own point of view and never liked to be followed blindly. He appreciated others who put forward arguments. Ministers were able to perform their duties freely within their jurisdiction.[154] Military colleagues in the cabinet adopted this civilian culture within a few months, despite the fact that they were accustomed to military traditions.[155] General Burki remarked that he had talked frankly to the president in his days as minister and Ayub always appreciated this frank discussion.[156] Justice Muhammad Munir, Minister of Law, said that he had always received 'courtesy and consideration'[157] from Ayub Khan. S. M. Zafar claimed that Ayub Khan was flexible enough to accept the proposals which he presented, even if Ayub did not agree with him.[158] He further claimed that ministers had full freedom of expression. Ayub Khan's success lay in the fact that he supported his ministers, especially the ministers of industries, commerce, and finance, and the chairman of the Planning Commission, to experiment with new things, most of which were successful.[159]

During the meetings he usually gave details of the agenda, explaining his opinion, and only then were others invited to present their points of view, as in the meeting of 1 November 1958, when he wrote in his diary, 'I emphasized the need for exercising greater control in financial matters.'[160] Others were always invited to express themselves and to ask questions following the president's introduction.

Ayub's control over his cabinet was firm. No doubt, some of his ministers were given broad latitude, but generally they did not go against the wishes of the president. The other opinion, shared by Manzur Qadir, is that the cabinets of Ayub were not merely a rubber stamp while Qadir remained a minister. In practice, decisions were taken on the basis of a majority. Ayub gave importance to his ministers' points of view. The same view was shared by some other civilian ministers also.[161] The president praised ministers when they deserved it. He congratulated Minister for Law and Parliamentary Affairs S. M. Zafar for successfully presenting Pakistan's case to the Security Council.[162] This negates Feldman's opinion that Zafar presented Pakistan's case poorly.[163] Ayub sometimes snubbed his ministers too. He snubbed Minister for Industries, Altaf Hussain; when he tried to criticize the Cease-Fire Resolution of the 1965 War, with the words, 'We must be firm', Ayub snapped at him, saying 'I have not lectured to you and you will not lecture to me.'[164]

Yahya had two levels of relationship with his two types of cabinet. His relations with his military cabinet were good, sometime some of his military colleagues influenced his decisions, but his relations with his civilian cabinet were only distant; it was a rare occasion that he had direct meetings with them. Usually the secretaries of the ministries met Yahya once a week and were responsible for running the administration. It worked as a cabinet of sorts.[165] Bengalis were largely kept apart from the actual decision-making in both Ayub and Yahya's cabinets.

Both Ayub and Yahya were military rulers, but of different kinds. Ayub always took a keen interest in the council of ministers or cabinet affairs. He trusted his civilian colleagues more than his military colleagues. All important portfolios were given to civilian ministers, especially after 1962. His inner cabinet consisted of civilian ministers, but Yahya trusted his military colleagues more than the civilians. His kitchen cabinet always included military personnel, although they were not part of the cabinet.

5.6.3. THE RELATIONSHIP BETWEEN THE CABINET AND Z. A. BHUTTO

There are various theories about Bhutto's relations with his cabinet. One opinion is that since Bhutto had inherited power as Chief Executive and Chief Martial Law Administrator, earlier personalization of power in Pakistan's political system was maintained.[166] Bhutto adopted an arrogant attitude towards those cabinet ministers who opposed him. J. A. Rahim, Khursheed Hasan Meer, and Miraj Mohammad Khan all experienced the wrath of Bhutto.[167] Mubashar Hassan believed that ministers could not go against Bhutto and that he was the government. He did not allow freedom of expression. If anyone went against him, he would not tolerate it. That is what happened to J. A. Rahim.[168]

Bhutto gradually began to mistrust his colleagues in the cabinet. Intelligence agencies provided him with false, and sometimes true, reports about the so-called manoeuvering of his ministers.[169] Furthermore, some cabinet ministers publicly discussed secret issues which made Bhutto very angry. He said openly that ministers, when discussing secret issues openly, were doing wrong because it was unconstitutional. Their intention to let each other down was wrong.[170]

No doubt some serious differences emerged in Bhutto's cabinet, but as a politician he believed in difference of opinion. In an interview for the French daily, *Le Monde*, he stated that the government made collective decisions and collective policy but, being human, differences of opinion always exist among cabinet ministers. 'After all there is the human element also in a collective decision ... This is after all why cabinets are formed.'[171] Yahya Bakhtiar, Attorney General, who enjoyed the status of a cabinet minister, has recorded that Bhutto's attitude during cabinet meetings was tolerant. He always respected others' opinions and gave weight to them. On many occasions he changed his decision or point of view after listening to his companions.[172] A similar opinion was shared by Yusuf Khattak. He said that Bhutto's attitude towards his ministers, especially towards other parties' ministers, was polite. He suggested in a meeting that Pakistan should seek help from Saudi Arabia. In response he was sent to Saudi Arabia for the said purpose.[173] Sheikh Rashid has confirmed that the point of view of the ministers was given weight by Bhutto if it was valid.[174]

Bhutto had the habit of showing appreciation of his ministers if they performed well. On the occasion of the separation of Ministry of Information and Broadcasting from Education and Provincial Coordination, he praised the services of Abdul Hafiz Pirzada for his work at that ministry. He directed that the appreciation of the cabinet for the services rendered by him in this connection should be placed on record.[175]

In summary, differences of opinion among colleagues whether in the cabinet or anywhere else, is a natural phenomenon. It existed among cabinet ministers during all the regimes, with different causes. Regional-based conflicts emerged in ML cabinets during 1947–54, whereas ideology was the basis of rifts during the PPP regime from 1973 to 1977. Both types of rifts had positive as well as negative aspects. On one hand, ideological conflicts resulted in fruitful discussion and ideology-oriented programmes were introduced, but on the other hand, regional-based differences always resulted in a widening of the breach between the western and eastern regions of Pakistan. West Pakistani Punjabi politicians always remained more influential than East Pakistani ministers. The performance of the coalition cabinets was least productive since coalition partners always came with conflicting ideas, programmes and points of view on issues like One Unit, electorates, and others. The most negative aspect of the conflicts was that the convention of collective cabinet responsibility was strongly violated as ministers started issuing public statements against each other. However, the clash on policy issues mostly came to the surface in the presidential cabinet of Ayub Khan. This too had both positive and negative impacts. There were also minor signs of rifts between East and West Pakistani ministers. Bhutto's presidential cabinet again witnessed differences of opinion based on ideology. Leftists were more successful than the rightists, and at the same time, they were not ready to tolerate the rightists. It was a success of the period that both types of minister worked in harmony and rifts mostly remained under cover during this period at least. The military cabinets of Ayub and Yahya also had different types of rifts. In Ayub Khan's military cabinet differences of opinion were based on policy issues, which was positive most of the time, while conflicts in Yahya Khan's military cabinet always resulted in the exit of a minister. Yahya's civilian cabinet suffered some regional-based conflicts, but such conflicts had no impact on the policy and programme of the government as it was the most powerless cabinet of the period under study. The negative trend that emerged in the PPP regime was the physical abuse of some ministers who expressed a strong difference of opinion with the PM. This new tradition weakened the power and decision-making authority of the institution of the cabinet in the years to come. Overall, cabinets from 1947 to 1977 experienced differences of opinion and rifts mostly on the basis of ideology, regionalism, and policy formulation, but rarely for personal reasons.

Notes and References

1. Buckley, *The Prime Minister and Cabinet*, 44.
2. Ibid.
3. Afzal, *Pakistan: History and Politics,* 95.
4. Ibid.
5. Ali, *Emergence of Pakistan,* 375.
6. Allen McGrath, *The Destruction of Pakistan's Democracy* (Karachi: Oxford University Press, 1996), 55.
7. From Minister of Industries, Commerce and Works to Prime Minister, 12 November 1949, Confidential 3(3), PMS/49, GOP, PM'S Secretariat, NDC, Islamabad.
8. McGrath, *The Destruction of Pakistan's Democracy*, 55.
9. From Interior Minister Khawaja Shahabuddin to Prime Minister Liaquat Ali Khan, 13 February 1949, 3 (4)-PMS/49, GOP, PM'S Secretariat, NDC, Islamabad.
10. Ziring, *Pakistan in the Twentieth Century*, 107. The Objectives Resolution was presented by Liaquat Ali Khan. It established the framework for the drafting of the constitution. Criticism from minorities included the sovereignty of God, the mixture of religion and politics, and their belief that Islam's concept of democracy would keep non-Muslims as inferior. For details see G. W. Choudhury's *Constitutional Development in Pakistan.*

11. From Jogandar Nath Mandal to Chief Minister of Bengal Khawaja Nazimuddin, 3 March 1948, 3(9)—PMS/48, GOP, PM'S Secretariat, NDC, Islamabad.

12. Telegram from Pakistan High Commissioner, Calcutta to Foreign Minister Zafrullah Khan, Karachi, 10 October 1950, 3(18)-PMS/50, GOP, PM's Secretariat, NDC, Islamabad.

13. This pact sought to guarantee the rights of minorities in both India and Pakistan and avert another war between them.

14. Telegram Secret. From Foreign Office Karachi to different Foreign Offices in the World, 12 October 1950, 3(18), GOP, PM'S Secretariat, NDC, Islamabad.

15. Ibid.

16. Talbot, *Pakistan: A Modern History*, 141.

17. Jalal, *The State of Martial Rule*, 173.

18. From UKHC Karachi to CRO London, 24 October 1951, DO 35/3188, NA, London.

19. Callard, *Pakistan: A Political Study*, 139.

20. Jalal, *The State of Martial Rule*, 189.

21. Callard, *Pakistan: A Political Study*, 139.

22. The details of his inclusion are given in Chapter 1.

23. *Outlook*, 13 July 1974.

24. Former bureaucrat who also worked with Ayub.

25. Ziring, *Pakistan in the Twentieth Century*, 398.

26. Ziring 'Pakistan Political Perspective', 632.

27. Interview with Shakeela Rasheed (wife of Sheikh Rashid), History Department, University of the Punjab, Lahore, 27 September 2011.

28. Wolpert, *Zulfi Bhutto*, 240.

29. *Supreme Court Mein Bhutto Kai Bian Ka Mukamal Mattan* (Lahore: Asian Publishers) from Dr Naeem Qureshi Collection, National Archives, Islamabad.

30. Interview with Mubashar Hasan, 4-K, Gulberg-II, Lahore, 29 March 2010.

31. From Mubashar Hasan to Z.A. Bhutto cited in Hasan, *The Mirage of Power*, 256.

32. Interview with Mubashar Hasan.

33. Maleeha Lodhi, 'Bhutto, The Pakistan People's Party and Political Development in Pakistan, 1967–77' PhD dissertation, London School of Economics and Political Science, University of London, November 1980, 434.

34. Khalid Bin Sayeed, 'Political Leadership and Institution Building…', *Pakistan: The Long View,* 269.

35. Hasan, *The Mirage of Power,* 263.

36. Interview with Shakeela Rasheed, 27 September 2011.

37. W. Eric Gustafson, 'Economic Problems', 366.

38. *Pakistan Times,* 21 October 1974; Wolpert, *Zulfi Bhutto of Pakistan,* 237 and Satish, *The New Pakistan,* 88.

39. Herbert Feldman, 'Pakistan in 1974', *Asian Survey,* 15 (February 1975), 111.

40. Ibid.

41. Raza, *Zulfiqar Ali Bhutto and Pakistan,* 322.

42. From BHC Karachi to CRO London, 25 October 1954, DO 35/5405, NA, London.

43. Jalal, *The State of Martial Rule,* 201.

44. The opinion was expressed in 'The Talking Points Regarding One Unit' From BHC Karachi to CRO London, 27 December 1954, Do 35/5406, NA, London.

45. Interview of Choudhury Muhammad Ali with Agha Shorish Kashmiri, *Weekly Chatan,* Lahore, cited in Choudhury Muhammad Ali, *Task Before Us: Selected Speeches and Writings* (Lahore: Research Society of Pakistan, 1974), 300.

46. From UKHC Karachi to CRO London, 19 January 1955, DO 35/5285, NA, London.

47. *Pakistan Times,* 31 August 1956.

48. From UKHC Karachi to CRO London, 19 January 1955, DO 35/5407, NA, London.

49. *Pakistan Times,* 9 September 1956.

50. Special mtg of the cabinet, 8 September 1956, 392/CF/56, NDC, Islamabad.

51. From UKHC Karachi to CRO London, 2 April 1958, DO 35/8936, NA, London.

52. See the detailed discussion on One Unit in Chapter 3.

53. Parveen, *The Politics of Pakistan*, 201.

54. From UKHC Karachi to CRO London, 11 September 1957, DO 35/8935, NA, London.

55. Ahmad, *Government and Politics in Pakistan*, 65.

56. Ahmad, *Martial Law sei Martial Law Tuk*, 379–80.

57. *Nawa-i-Waqt*, 11 October 1957 and Talukdar, *Memoirs of Hussain*, 119.

58. Ibid. 12 October 1957.

59. Umar, *The Emergence of Bangladesh*, 325.

60. From UKHC Karachi to CRO London, 22 November 1957, DO 35/8935, NA, London.

61. Cabinet mtg, 22 October 1957, 422/CF/57, NDC, Islamabad.

62. From UKHC Karachi to CRO London, 11 December 1957, PREM 11/2027, NA, London.

63. *Pakistan Times*, 12 December 1957.

64. Ibid. 12 December 1957.

65. Special Cabinet mtg, 11 December 1957, Minutes were sent by UKHC Karachi to CRO London, DO 35/8935, NA, London.

66. From UKHC Karachi to CRO London, 11 December 1957, DO 35/8935, NA, London and *Nawa-i-Waqt*, 16 December 1957.

67. From UKHC Karachi to CRO London, 7 August 1958, DO 35/8936, NA, London.

68. At the time of formation of Noon's government Suhrawardy received a guarantee from Noon that he would not give a cabinet portfolio to KSP.

69. From UKHC Karachi to CRO London, 23 September 1958, DO 35/8943, NA, London.

70. Ministers of Federal Cabinet, Cabinet Wing, NDC, Islamabad.

71. Aziz, *Party Politics*, 46.

72. Hamid Khan, *Constitutional History of Pakistan*, 138.

73. Gauhar, *Ayub Khan, Pakistan's First Military Ruler*, 187.

74. Ibid. 188–9.

75. Ahmad, *Government and Politics in Pakistan*, 224.

76. Saeed Shafqat, *Contemporary Issues in Pakistan Studies*, 197.

77. Ibid.

78. Choudhury, *The Last Days of United Pakistan*, 51.

79. Khan, *Pakistan's Crises in Leadership*, 21.

80. Stanley A. Kochanek, *Interest Groups and Development; Business and Politics in Pakistan* (Karachi: Oxford University Press, 1983), 55.

81. Ziring, *Pakistan in the Twentieth Century*, 321.

82. Choudhry, *The Last Days of United Pakistan*, 61.

83. Ibid, 64.

84. Ziring, *Pakistan in the Twentieth Century*, 346 and Choudhury, *The Last Days of United Pakistan*, 75.

85. Ziring, *Pakistan in the Twentieth Century*, 274.

86. Ziring, *The Ayub Era*, 31.

87. Ibid.

88. Ziring, *Pakistan in the Twentieth Century*, 275.

89. From Muhammad Munir to Ayub Khan cited in Nazir Hussain Chaudhri, *Chief Justice Muhammad Munir His Life, Writings and Judgments* (Lahore: Research Society of Pakistan, 1973), iii-iv.

90. From UKHC Rawalpindi to CRO London, 22 January 1966, DO 196/316, NA, London.

91. Ziring, *Pakistan in the Twentieth Century*, 306.

92. Incoming telegram from Ambery Office Rawalpindi to Secretary of State Washington D.C., 18 January 1966 cited in Roedad Khan, *The American Papers*, 124.

93. Ibid.

94. Pilo Mody, *Zulfi; My Friend*, (Karachi, Paramount Publishing Enterprises, Reprint 2009), 109.

95. From UKHC Karachi to CRO London, 14 February 1966, DO 196/316, NA, London.

96. Ibid. 442.

97. Interview with S. M. Zafar, 104, 4th Floor, Siddique Trade Centre, Gulberg, Lahore, 9 December 2012.

98. Speech of Z. A. Bhutto in the National Assembly, 16 March 1966 cited in Zulfikar Ali Bhutto, *Reshaping Foreign Policy*, 303–4.

99. Ibid. 305.

100. Mody, *Zulfi: My Friend*, 109.

101. Bhutto's speech at Inter Collegiate Students's Body mtg, Lahore, 4 February 1967 'Pakistan's Isolation' in Bhutto, *Awakening the People*, 47.

102. Ibid.

103. Diary of Ayub Khan cited in Baxter, *Diaries of Field Marshal Muhammad Ayub Khan,* 3.

104. Gauhar, *Ayub Khan, Pakistan's First Military Ruler,* 189; Zafar, *Through the Crises,* 70 and Khalid B. Sayeed, 'Pakistan: New Challenges to the Political System', *Asian Survey,* 8 (February 1968), 97; and Burk and Ziring, *Pakistan's Foreign Policy,* 362.

105. Dennis Kux, *The United States and Pakistan 1947–2000; Disenchanted Allies* (New York: Oxford University Press, 2001), 171.

106. Shafqat, *Contemporary Issues in Pakistan Studies,* 197.

107. From BHC Rawalpindi to CRO London, 1 August 1966, DO 196/316, NA, London.

108. Ibid.

109. Ibid.

110. From BHC Rawalpindi to CRO London, 19 December 1966, DO 196/319, NA, London.

111. Baxter, *Diaries of Field Marshal Muhammad Ayub Khan,* 54.

112. Ibid. 110.

113. From BHC Rawalpindi to CRO London, 19 December 1966, DO 196/316, NA, London.

114. Baxter, *Diaries of Field Marshal Muhammad Ayub Khan,* Diary of 10 September 1967, 146.

115. S. M. Zafar, *Through the Crisis* (Lahore: Book Center, 1970), 235.

116. Hassan, *The Mirage of Power,* 180.

117. Maleeha Lodhi, 'Bhutto and the Pakistan People's Party', 434.

118. Ibid.

119. Ibid. 431.

120. Satish, *The New Pakistan,* 47.

121. Kaushik, *Politics in Pakistan,* 16.

122. Ibid.

123. Wolpert, *Zulfi,* 205 and Laporte, *Power and Privilege,* 106.

124. Hussain, *Elite Politics,* 122.

125. Ibid.

126. Satish, *The New Pakistan,* 19–22; Mody, *Zulfi: My Friend* and Ziring, *Pakistan in the Twentieth Century,* 395.

127. Laporte, *Power and Privilege,* 108.

128. Z. A. Bhutto, *Speeches and Statements Vol. 3*, 1 October–31 December 1972 Karachi: Ministry of Information and Broadcasting Department of Films and Publication Government of Pakistan, 1972–1973, 21–2.

129. From Z. A. Bhutto to Mahmud Ali Kasuri, 5 October 1972 cited in Bhutto, *Speeches and Statements*, 21.

130. Burki, *State and Society*, 122–3.

131. Miraj Mohammad Khan was Minister of State for Political Affairs. Though ministers of state are not part of this study, his resignation affected the total outlook of the government and was the first resignation in Bhutto's regime, even before Kasuri, so it has been included here.

132. Khalid Bin Sayeed, 'Political Leadership and Institution Building under Jinnah, Ayub and Bhutto' in Ziring, *Pakistan: The Long View* (Durham: Duke University Press, 1995), 262.

133. Maleeha Lodhi, 'Bhutto and the Pakistan People's Party', 314.

134. Satish, *The New Pakistan*, 22–3; and Anwar H. Syed, 'The Pakistan People's Party: Phases One and Two', *Pakistan: The Long View*, 93

135. Hasan, *The Mirage of Power*, 190.

136. Ghulam Akbar, *He was not Hanged* (1989) at www.bhutto.org, 108.

137. Ziring, *Pakistan in the Twentieth Century*, 380 and Lawrence Ziring 'Pakistan: A Political Perspective' *Asian Survey* 15 (1975), 634.

138. He informed the cabinet later in the cabinet mtg, 3 February 1949, 31/CF/49, NDC, Islamabad.

139. The decision to dismiss Mamdot's ministry was endorsed on 3 February 1949. See details in 31/CF/49, NDC, Islamabad.

140. Williams, *The State of Pakistan*, 137–38.

141. Ziauddin Ahmad, *Quaid-i-Millat*, 109.

142. From UKHC Karachi to CRO London, 17 April 1953, DO 35/5106, NA, London.

143. Ahmed, *Government and Politics in Pakistan*, 45.

144. Cabinet mtg, 11 August 1955, 236/CF/55, NDC, Islamabad.

145. Cabinet mtg, 30 December 1953, 326/CF/53, NDC.

146. *Dawn*, 26 February 1954.

147. Jalal, *The State of Martial Rule*, 233.

148. Interview of Choudhury Muhammad Ali to Agha Shorish Kashmiri, Weekly *Chatan*, in Ali, *Task Before Us*, 280.

149. Special Cabinet mtg, 8 September 1956, 392/CF/56, NDC, Islamabad.

150. For details of working and status of Planning Board please see Chapter 2.

151. Talukdar Muniruzaman, 'Group Interests in Pakistan Politics, 1947–1958', *Pacific Affairs* 39 (Spring-Summer 1966), 91.

152. Ahmad, *Martial Law sei Martial Law Tuk*, 380.

153. For more details see Chapter 4.

154. Interview with S. M. Zafar.

155. William, *The State of Pakistan*, 185.

156. Record of conversation of BHC with Gen. W. A. Burki sent to CRO London, 2 September 1967, FCO 37/179, NA, London.

157. Nazir Chaudhri, *Chief Justice Muhammad Munir*, iv.

158. Such reforms included reforms of the Bar Councils' system, enhancing the Electoral College for Basic Democrats and the status of the high courts, etc. Interview with S. M. Zafar.

159. Dobell, 'Ayub Khan', 297.

160. Muhammad Ayub Khan, *Friends Not Masters: A Political Autobiography* (Islamabad, Mr Books, 2002), 83. While giving the details of the first cabinet mtg, he says 'I gave my colleagues an assessment of the situation prevailing in the country prior to 7 Oct. 1958. I then outlined the problems that we are facing … I then explained to the Cabinet the nature of Martial Law …' At another mtg, 'I mentioned in the Cabinet that we should take up the construction of the Quaid-e-Azam mausoleum.' 81–3.

161. From BHC Karachi to CWLO London, 6 December 1958, DO 35/8946, in Roedad Khan, *The British Papers*, 99.

162. Cabinet mtg 23 September 1965, 173/CF/65, NDC, Islamabad.

163. Feldman, *From Crisis to Crisis*, 162.

164. Gauhar, *Ayub Khan*, 355.

165. Kochanek, *Interest Groups and Development*, 55.

166. Shafqat, *Civil Military Relations*, 82.

167. Sherbaz Khan Mazari, A *Journey to Disillusionment* (Karachi: Oxford University Press, 2000), 237.

168. Interview with Mubashar Hasan.
169. Hassan, *The Mirage of Power*, 264.
170. Ibid. 185–6.
171. Interview of Z.A. Bhutto for the French daily *Le Monde*, released on 26 December 1972 cited in Z.A. Bhutto, *Speeches and Statements 1 October–31 December* 1972.
172. Interview of Yahya Bakhtiar by Munir Ahmed Munir in *Siyaassi Uttar Cherhao* (Urdu) (Lahore: Atish Fishan Publications, 1985), 42.
173. Interview of Yusuf Khattak by Munir Ahmed Munir, 248.
174. Interview with Shakeela Rasheed, 27 September 2011.
175. Minutes of the Cabinet mtg, 6 March 1972, 424/CF/71, NDC, Islamabad.

Conclusion

The cabinet in Pakistan from 1947 to 1977 remained an effective decision-making institution. Its effectiveness varied during different phases and on different issues. The cabinet was highly operative and influential under Liaquat Ali Khan, Ayub Khan, and Zulfikar Ali Bhutto. It was partially influential under Khawaja Nazimuddin, Mohammad Ali Bogra, and during the period of the coalition cabinets (1955 to 1958). It was not viable during General Yahya Khan's period when the military high command was the sole decision-making authority. The cabinet's role in deciding economic and political matters remained vital during all regimes except for the Yahya Khan period. However, it was given somewhat free hand to deal with matters relating to foreign policy till 1969. Issues related to foreign policy were not brought to cabinet meetings during the periods of Yahya Khan and Z. A. Bhutto.

The selection or nomination of cabinet ministers was given due weight by all regimes. Ministers were taken from different sections of society. The present study has found no evidence to support the general perception that landlords dominated the cabinet. A study of the socio-economic profile of the ministers has established that the majority of them belonged to the group of professionals during the entire period of this study. Landlords dominated only the last cabinet (1974–1977) of Z. A. Bhutto.

The ratio of representation of one or the other group had an impact on the formulation of various policies. The urban social background of the majority of ministers led them to initiate urban-based reforms in the first decade after independence. They focused mostly on the problems of urban areas during the first parliamentary phase and neglected to initiate agricultural reforms and pro-rural policies. The situation in the later years of the first military ruler, Ayub Khan, however, was different, when a broad-based agricultural reform package in the shape of the Green Revolution was introduced. The post-1974 period of Bhutto, with a majority of the feudal ministers in the cabinet, opted for a policy of status quo, the most popular among feudal lords. This study has revealed the fact that the specific social backgrounds of the ministers had an impact on the formulation of government policies. The institution of the cabinet played a significant role in almost all of the governments regarding economic issues. In the early phase, cabinets had been successful in establishing a significant number of economic institutions, including the Planning Advisory Board, the Planning Commission, the Pakistan Industrial Development Corporation, the National Economic Committee, the Pakistan Industrial Credit and Investment Corporation, and the Pakistan Industrial Finance Corporation. The objectives and targets of all such institutions were designed by the cabinet. The cabinet kept strict control on import and export policies; import-export licences were awarded with the approval of the cabinet. The import of all such items that were produced in the country, and the export of all agricultural yields or crops which were required for the local industry were banned. This helped local industries to flourish. The cabinet determined the prices of major crops to support industry. It had direct control over all major economic activity in the country during the first parliamentary phase, which resulted in developing infrastructure and flourishing industry, but at the same time was harmful for agriculture, the backbone of Pakistan's economy. This experiment of the cabinet in the early phase enabled the future cabinets of the military regime to learn lessons from past mistakes.

General Ayub's cabinet successfully developed a strong monitoring mechanism for economic institutions and policies. The cabinet and the other economic institutions enjoyed cordial relations, worked in a harmonious way, and largely followed cabinet's advice. The cabinet used to issue a list of favoured industries for investment; investors needed the approval of the Economic Coordination Committee of the cabinet to invest in industries other than those on the list. Trade was also controlled by the cabinet or cabinet-oriented institutions such as the Economic Committee of the cabinet. The cabinet provided export incentives through direct and indirect subsidies. The import policy of the military regime's cabinet was more relaxed than in the previous era. Ministers of Commerce and Industries, Bhutto and Ghulam Faruque respectively, were highly active in initiating new trends for the promotion of exports.

Ayub's cabinet also introduced considerable changes vis-á-vis the agriculture sector. Although the cabinets consisted mostly of urban professionals and bureaucrats, Ayub's rural background and understanding of the food problem in Pakistan led his cabinets to design pro-agriculture policies.

The cabinet established institutions such as the Agricultural Policy Committees and the Agricultural Development Corporations to look after agricultural products. The export of agriculture-oriented goods was encouraged. The 'Green Revolution', which increases agricultural productivity, was a great initiative introduced by the cabinet. The perception that Ayub Khan was the sole decision-making authority in terms of the economy is unfounded. The present study has found that he listened to his ministers and advisors. Had he not listened to the expert advice of ministers like Bhutto, Mohammad Shoaib, and others in the cabinet, such outstanding economic progress would not have been achieved by his regime. It was actually the result of teamwork, whereas the role and decision-making powers of General Yahya's civilian cabinet was insignificant rather non-existent, and no prominent economic activity was initiated. His civilian cabinet was powerless and had little or no share in the decision-making process.

Two opposite views exist regarding cabinet's decision-making authority during the Bhutto era. One opinion is that Bhutto took many important economic decisions on his own and sought only formal approval from his cabinet; the second says that his cabinet decided issues relating to the economy. This study has provided evidence that the cabinet and the prime minister worked in harmony when important economic issues were decided. Neither did the prime minister try to impose decisions on the cabinet, nor did the ministers enjoy total freedom to decide issues. Ministers having a socialist ideology, like Mubashir Hassan,

J. A. Rahim, Sheikh Mohammad Rashid, Khursheed Hasan Meer, and others, were able to convince Bhutto on certain matters. But this practice was only followed until 1974, i.e. the exit of leftist ministers from his cabinet. Later, Bhutto seemed to be guiding his cabinet most of the time. The rightist element dominated the cabinet in later years. They were Rana Mohammad Hanif, Rafi Raza, Yusuf Khattak, and Feroze Qaisar. As the rightist and landlord ministers were mostly in favour of maintaining the status quo, little or no changes were introduced in the economic field in the post-1974 era. Overall, cabinet's control over the economy was stronger during this period than during previous regimes. Economic institutions including the Economic Coordination Committee of the Cabinet, the National Economic Council, the Executive Committee of the National Economic Council, and the Council of Common Interests consisted mostly of the members of the cabinet: ministers were actively involved in policymaking at all levels.

The federal cabinets, during almost all regimes, kept an eye on political matters or issues relating to the provinces. This study has provided sufficient evidence to negate some existing perceptions about the decision-making process regarding provincial political matters. Documentary evidence has been provided to negate the assertion that the anti-Ahmadiyya movement was suppressed in 1953 by the military acting on its own. The decision to impose martial law in Lahore and other cities was taken by the cabinet and not by the military high command or Iskandar Mirza. Similarly, the perception that the issue of the enhancement of Balochistan's status was neglected by the early cabinets has also been disproved. The long debates within the cabinet and the decisions on Balochistan are sufficient proof that the cabinet was seriously involved in solving the problem. Unfortunately, the introduction of One Unit did not permit the problem to be solved. However, the cabinet used delaying tactics to settle the Urdu-Bengali language crisis because it did not wish to go against the Quaid-i-Azam's decision of opting for Urdu as the national language of Pakistan. The changes of cabinets during the coalition cabinet's period (1955–1958) was so rapid that no major decisions could be taken regarding the provinces except the rapid change of ministries in the two provinces of West and East Pakistan.

The cabinet's role in deciding provincial matters was more organized and direct during Ayub's era, mostly due to the presence and successful working of the forum of the Governors' Conference. Provincial authorities were given instructions directly by the president and the federal cabinet at the Governors' Conferences, which were held regularly. The cabinet took some important decisions on political matters relating to the provinces in cabinet meetings also, without bringing them to the Governors' Conferences. Ministers were given a fair opportunity to express their opinions on those issues. The law and order situation in East Pakistan was discussed in detail on different occasions, and decisions were taken on a majority basis. At times, the president's will mattered, but Ayub usually convinced his team of ministers of his point of view instead of imposing his decision. The way of dealing with the students, the arrest of Suhrawardy, the ban on pro-AL newspapers, the Six Points of Mujibur Rehman, and the Agartala Conspiracy Case were discussed, and action was decided upon by the cabinet. Unfortunately, cabinet's grip on provincial political matters was weakened during the last year of Ayub's rule, when it moved to the control of the military high command because of the law and order situation and the separatist movement in East Pakistan.

The civilian cabinet did not perform well during Yahya Khan's period when dealing with provincial political matters. It was bypassed on most issues, as in the case of the delay and postponement of elections in some constituencies in Balochistan and NWFP. The military high command was the main decision-taking authority, but its decisions only worsened the situation, which led to the separation of East Pakistan.

The power of cabinet expanded and increased further during the Bhutto era due to the creation of the new Ministry of Provincial Coordination, after which the provincial governors were bound to send monthly reports regarding provincial matters to the president. The reports were discussed in cabinet meetings. Another element which increased cabinet's control was the provincial conferences which were held regularly. Almost all important issues relating to the provinces were discussed and decided in the cabinet meetings. The cabinet committees were also formed to deal with some specific issues such as the language controversy in Sindh. The decision to make Sindhi the provincial official language while maintaining Urdu's status as the national language was recommended by the committee of the federal cabinet.

The decision to launch a military operation in Balochistan was also taken by the cabinet. In some cases the cabinet authorized the PM to take the final decision, as in the case of the dismissal of the NAP-JUI government in Balochistan, because a strong difference of opinion had emerged among the ministers.

This study has highlighted the fact that the cabinets of various regimes played an important part in deciding foreign policy matters too. This is a direct negation of the commonly-held view that only some individuals decided matters affecting the foreign policy of Pakistan. The study has provided sufficient evidence that the institution of the cabinet played an important role in the formulation of foreign policy during the governments of Liaquat Ali, Suhrawardy, and Ayub. However, it was not an effective forum for determining foreign policy matters during the regimes of Yahya Khan and Bhutto. Neither appointed a foreign minister, and no important foreign policy matters were brought to the cabinet for discussion or decision.

Styles of decision-making in foreign policy tended to oscillate more sharply than those in the narrower confines of domestic policy. The cabinet of Pakistan was most effective in dealing with issues like the Kashmir dispute, relations with the USA and the USSR, the Suez Canal issue, and other major issues from 1947 to 1958. This study has found to be untrue the assertion that the pro-USA policy was formulated in Pakistan by a few personalities in the early 1950s. The cabinet had approved the decision to sign the SEATO with some conditions (as explained in Chapter 4) which were disregarded by Zafrullah Khan when signing the treaty. He signed it on the condition that it would be effective after it had been endorsed by the cabinet in Pakistan. The perception that Ayub Khan had been the main figure in deciding USA-related policy matters since the early 1950s is also challenged: the pro-USA policy during the Suez Canal crisis was approved by the cabinet. It believed that the nationalization of the Suez Canal would be harmful to Pakistan's trade; therefore, it should remain an independent entity. On the question of China's membership of the UN, the cabinet of Choudhury Muhammad Ali was divided into three groups. However, cabinet finally agreed to support China after convincing the USA. The military and civil bureaucrats sitting in the 'Cabinet of All Talents' were dominant enough to influence the foreign policy processes. The coalition cabinets more or less followed the pre-formulated pro-US foreign policy.

The perception of Ayub's cabinet as being powerless has also been found to be untrue as far as foreign policy is concerned. His cabinet was clearly divided into two groups, the pro-US group that was led by Mohammad Shoaib, Minister of Finance, and the pro-USSR and China faction that was led by Manzur Qadir, Minister of Foreign Affairs, and later by Z. A. Bhutto, Minister of Foreign Affairs. Bhutto's faction gradually acquired influence and convinced the president and the cabinet to develop ties with the Soviet Union, China, and the USA simultaneously. Pakistan also signed its first-ever trade agreement with the Soviet Union in 1961 due to the efforts of Manzur Qadir and Z. A. Bhutto. The cabinet also prepared a brief for China's representation in the UN.

However, cabinet was not fully involved in dealing with some of the issues related to India. The cabinet was only informed formally about the agreement on the Rann of Kutch, and not even informed on Operation Gibraltar, whereas cabinet dealt directly with issues related to the 1965 War, including the issue of the ceasefire, acquiring support from friendly countries, the problems arising from the arms embargo, etc. America's attitude was criticized frequently in cabinet meetings. The ceasefire resolution was approved in cabinet meetings and later the Pakistani government announced its acceptance. Although the cabinet prepared the terms of the Tashkent Agreement before the departure of the Pakistani delegation, some changes to the terms of the agreement were introduced on the spot. On the other hand, Yahya Khan's cabinet did not have the privilege of discussing or deciding foreign policy matters. No foreign minister was appointed throughout his rule. This important portfolio remained under the control of Yahya Khan himself, who maintained strict secrecy when dealing with matters of foreign policy.

Again, during Bhutto's rule, the cabinet did not enjoy the power of decision-making with respect to foreign policy matters, although the same cabinet was influential in deciding economic and political issues. Almost all important foreign policy issues, including agreements with India, the recognition of Bangladesh, the nuclear programme, the steel mill agreement with Soviet Union, and many other important decisions, were taken by Bhutto alone without taking the cabinet into his confidence. The cabinet discussed and decided only a few matters relating to Afghanistan.

Conflicts, rifts, and changes within the cabinets are another area of study. Evidence has been provided to show that rifts were important and had considerable impact on the working capability of various cabinets during different regimes. The rifts occurred mostly on questions of policy, and sometimes over different ideologies, or due to regional affiliations. Some such groups emerged in Liaquat's cabinet, i.e. Punjabi and Bengali, which later converted into West Pakistani and East Pakistani groups. The divide in the earlier period was on the basis of policy, as was seen in the case of the devaluation of the currency and of developing close ties with major world powers, which later converted into regional division, i.e. West Pakistani interests and East Pakistani interests.

The rifts from 1947 to 1955 were controlled and the working of the cabinet was not disturbed to any great extent, but conflicts reached a climax during the time of the coalition governments (1955–1958), when issues were taken out of the hands of the cabinet. The ministers, in some cases, did not adhere to collective responsibility and issued statements against cabinet's own decisions on certain matters, including One Unit, electorates, the creation of the Republican Party, etc. resulting in the destruction of cabinet's image, and no doubt had a negative impact on the working of the institution. Decisions on different issues were either delayed, or cabinets had to resign due to differences. I. I. Chundrigarh's government was unable to reach a consensus on the electorate issue and had to go after only fifty-eight days, and Choudhury Muhammad Ali was unable to take all his ministers along with him on the issue of the creation of, and support for, the Republican Party.

The groups and nature of the rifts within the cabinet during the period of military rule were different. Ministers enjoyed little or no political influence and were answerable to the CMLA and later, to the president of Pakistan, so rifts were easily handled. If there was no solution to the disagreement, the concerned minister would have to resign, or was dismissed. This happened to Mohammad Ibrahim, Abul Kasem Khan, and Hafiz ur Rehman, all from East Pakistan. They were dismissed from the cabinet due to a disagreement on the 1962 Constitution. The cabinet of Ayub confronted another major disagreement among its members over foreign policy issues. Bhutto being pro-China, and Mohammad Shoaib being pro-US and the West, would usually disagree on foreign policy issues. Both were influential and close to Ayub. Gradually, Bhutto's point of view prevailed and Ayub decided to develop closer ties with China also.

The rifts in Ayub's cabinet were of a controlled nature, at least before the Tashkent Declaration (1966). Later, the cabinet was divided into distinct groups: the anti-Ayub faction led by Bhutto, and the pro-Ayub faction led by Khawaja Shahabuddin, which included Altaf Hussain, and Sabur Khan, etc. This clear division of the cabinet had an impact on the policymaking process and decision-taking power of the cabinet, especially after the exit of Shoaib and Bhutto. More dismissals and resignations followed, but the situation largely remained under control and the normal working capability of the cabinet was not disturbed to any great extent. It was only during the sickness of Ayub Khan that outside elements became more influential than the cabinet and took the decision-making process into their own hands.

Yahya Khan's military cabinet was also not without conflicts, but these were not tolerated for long. Nur Khan, Minister of Labour, Health and Social Welfare, and Admiral S. M. Ahsan, Deputy Chief Martial Law Administrator, who had differences of opinion on policy matters including labour and students' reforms, and the holding of elections, were soon ejected from the Council of Administration and were assigned other duties. All the others had ideologies similar to those of Yahya Khan. The division in the civilian cabinet of Yahya Khan was on a regional basis, but as it was a powerless institution, the decision-making process was not affected by these rifts.

The single-party cabinet of Bhutto also experienced rifts on the question of ideology. His cabinet, till 1974, was divided into two clear groups, rightists and leftists. The rightists were led by Maulana Kausar Niazi, Minister of Information and Broadcasting; the leftists included prominent ministers like Mubashar Hasan, Minister of Finance, Sheikh Muhammad Rashid, Minister of Social Welfare, Health and Family Planning, J. A. Rahim, Minister of Presidential Affairs and Town Planning, and others. These leftist ministers played a significant role in increasing the decision-making capability of the institution of the cabinet. The role of the cabinet was especially enhanced in the fields of the economy, social affairs, and political matters. But on the other hand, conflicts and strong differences of opinion among leftist ministers left scars on the working of the cabinet and created divisions due to which policies could not be easily implemented. 'Soft' socialists and the members of the rightist faction both created difficulties for the smooth working of the cabinet. The situation at times resulted in dismissals and resignations.

In a nutshell, this study has found that the institution of the federal cabinet in Pakistan played an effective and significant role in the decision-making process between the years 1947 to 1977. In the field of the economy and in matters related to politics, cabinet's role was more dominant than any other institution such as the military or the bureaucracy. Under some regimes cabinet took decisions on the formulation of the foreign policy also. Differences of opinion among humans are a natural and normal phenomenon. Such differences of opinion affected the working of some cabinets, especially from 1955 to 1958. But at the same time, they also increased the working capability and decision-making authority of the cabinet during the time of Ayub Khan and in the early years of Z. A. Bhutto. Overall, some decisions of the cabinet hurt the growth of democracy in the country, such as the use of the military to solve political issues, the dismissal of provincial governments, and intolerance towards opposition forces. At the same time, the institution of cabinet remained a source of initiating democratic values in Pakistan as most of the time it shared power with the head of state and the government and played an important role in decision-making and policy formulation. This study has shown that without studying the institution of cabinet, an effective institution of the state machinery of Pakistan, huge amounts of the political history of Pakistan cannot be viewed in true perspective.

Appendix: Eras of Rule

First Parliamentary Era: 1947–1958

Single-Party Cabinets

1. Cabinet of Liaquat Ali Khan, 15 August 1947–16 October 1951

S. No	Portfolio	Period
1. Mr Liaquat Ali Khan	1. Defence 2. Foreign Affairs & Commonwealth 3. Kashmir Affairs 4. States & Frontier Regions	(15-8-47 to 16-10-51) (15-8-47 to 27-12-47) (31-10-49 to 13-4-50) (12-9-48 to 16-10-51)
2. Mr Ismail Ibrahim Chundrigarh	1. Commerce 2. Industries 3. Works	(15-8-47 to 7-5-48) do, do
3. Mr Ghulam Mohammad	1. Finance 2. Economic Affairs 3. Commerce 4. Works	(15-8-47 to 19-10-51) (1-3-48 to 19-10-51) (8-5-48 to 29-5-48) (8-5-48 to 29-5-48)
4. Sardar Abdur Rab Nishtar	Communications	(15-8-47 to 2-8-49)
5. Raja Ghazanfar Ali Khan	1. Food 2. Agriculture 3. Health Refugees & Rehabilitation	(15-8-47 to 30-12-47) (15-8-47 to 30-12-47) (27-12-47 to 30-7-48))
6. Mr Jogandar Nath Mandal	1. Law 2. Labour 3. Works	(15-8-47 to 16-9-50) (15-8-47 to 16-9-50) (31-5-49 to 10-9-49)

S. No	Portfolio	Period
7. Mr Fazlur Rehman	1. Interior 2. Information & Broadcasting 3. Education 4. Rehabilitation 5. Industries 6. Commerce 7. Works	(15-8-47 to 8-5-48) (15-8-47 to 24-10-51) (10-9-47 to 27-12-47) (8-5-48 to 10-9-49) (30-5-48 to 24-10-51) (30-5-48 to 30-5-49)
8. Sir Mohammad Zafrullah Khan	Foreign Affairs & Commonwealth Relations	(27-12-47 to 24-10-51)
9. Mr Abdus Sattar Pirzada	1. Food 2. Agriculture 3. Health 4. Law 5. Labour	(30-12-47 to 24-10-51) (30-12-47 to 24-10-51) (30-1 2-47 to 10-9-49) (16-9-50 to 24-10-51) (16-9-50 to 31-3-51)
10. Khawaja Shahabuddin	1. Interior Information & Broadcasting 2. Refugees and Rehabilitation	(8-5-48 to 24-10-51) (30-7-48 to 24-10-51)
11. Mr Mushtaq Ahmad Gurmani	1. Without portfolio 2. Kashmir Affairs	(3-1-49 to 31-10-49) (13-4-1950 to 24-10-51)
12. Sardar Bahadur Khan	1. Communications 2. Health 3. Works	(10-9-1950 to 24-10-51) (1-1-49 to 20-9-49) (15-5-50 to 31-3-51)
13. Chaudhry Nazir Ahmad	Industries	(1-1-49 to 24-10-51)
14. Dr A. M. Malik	1. Health 2. Works 3. Minority Affairs 4. Labour	(1-1-50 to 15-5-50) (31-3-51 to 24-10-51) (15-5-50 to 23-4-51) (31-3-51 to 24-10-51)

2. Khwaja Nazimuddin, 19 October 1951–17 April 1953

S. No	Portfolio	Period
1. Khawaja Nazimuddin	Defence	(24-10-51 to 17-4-53)
2. Sir Mohammad Zafrullah Khan	Foreign Affairs & Commonwealth Relations	(24-10-51 to 17-4-53)
3. Mr Fazlur Rehman	1. Commerce 2. Economic Affairs 3. Education	(24-10-51 to 17-4-53) (24-10-51 to 17-4-53) (24-10-51 to 3-2-53)
4. Choudhury Muhammad Ali	Finance	(24-10-51 to 17-4-53)
5. Abdus Sattar Pirzada	1. Food 2. Agriculture 3. Law	(24-10-51 to 17-4-53) do, do
6. Khawaja Shahabuddin	1. Interior 2. Information & Broadcasting	(24-10-51 to 26-11-51) do
7. Mushtaq Ahmad Gurmani	1. Kashmir Affairs 2. Interior 3. States & Frontier Regions	(24-10-51 to 26-11-51) (26-11-51 to 17-4-53) do
8. Sardar Bahadur Khan	Communications	(24-10-51 to 174-53)
9. Dr A. M. Malik	1. Labour 2. Health 3. Works	(24-10-51 to 17-4-53) do, do.
10. Sardar Abdur Rab Nishtar	Industries	(26-10-51 to 17-4-53)
11. Dr Mahmud Husain	1. Kashmir Affairs 2. Education	(26-11-51 to 17-4-53) (4-2-53 to 17-4-53)
12. Dr Ishtiaq Hussain Qureshi	1. Refugees & Rehabilitation 2. Information & Broadcasting	(26-11-51) to (17-4-53) (1-1-51) to 17-4-53)

3. Mr. Mohammad Ali Bogra, 17 April 1953–24 October 1954

S. No	Portfolio	Period
1. Mr Mohammad Ali	1. Commerce 2. Defence 3. Information and Broadcasting	(17-4-53 to 7-12-53) (17-4-53 to 24-10-54) (30-5-54 to 5-9-54)
2. Sir Mohammad Zafrullah Khan	Foreign Affairs and Commonwealth Relations	(17-4-53 to 24-10-54)
3. Choudhury Muhammad Ali	1. Finance 2. Economic Affairs	(17-4-53 to 24-10-54)
4. Mr Mushtaq Ahmad Gurmani	1. Interior 2. States & Frontier Regions	(17-4-53 to 24-10-54), do
5. Sardar Bahadur Khan	Communications	(17-4-53 to 24-10-54)
6. Dr A. M. Malik	1. Labour 2. Health 3. Works	(17-4-53 to 24-10-54) do, do
7. Dr Ishtiaq Hussain Qureshi	Education	(17-4-53 to 24-10-54)
8. Mr A. K. Brohi	1. Law 2. Parliamentary Affairs 3. Minority Affairs. 4. Information & Broadcasting	(17-4-53 to 24-10-54) (17-4-53 to 7-12-53) (5-9-54 to 14-10-54)
9. Mr Khan Abdul Qayyum Khan	1. Food 2. Agriculture 3. Industries 4. Commerce	(18-4-53 to 24-10-54), do, do (4-10-54 to 24-10-54)
10. Mr Shoaib Qureshi	1. Information & Broadcasting 2. Refugees & Rehabilitation 3. Kashmir Affairs	(18-4-53 to 24-10-54) do
11. Mr Tafazzal Ali	Commerce	(1-1-53 to 4-10-54)

4. Cabinet of All Talents: Second Cabinet of Mr. Mohammad Ali Bogra, 24 October 1954–11 August 1955

S. No	Portfolio	Period
1. Mr Mohammad Ali Bogra	1. Foreign Affairs and Commonwealth Relations 2. Communications 3. Health	(24-10-54 to 11-8-55) (24-10-54 to 4-11-54) do
2. Choudhury Muhammad Ali	1. Finance 2. Economic Affairs 3. Refugees & Rehabilitation. 4. Kashmir Affairs	(24-10-54 to 11-8-55) (24-10-54 to 4-11-54) (24-10-54 to 6-11-54) (24-10-54 to 6-11-54)
3. Dr A. M. Malik	1. Labour 2. Works 3. Health	(24-10-54 to 11-8-55) do 24-10-54 to 20-1-55)
4. Mr M. A. H. Ispahani	1. Industries 2. Commerce	(24-10-54 to 11-8-55) (24-10-54 to 20-12-54)
5. Maj. Gen. Iskander Mirza	1. Interior 2. States & Frontier Regions 3. Kashmir Affairs	(24-10-54 to 7-8-55) (6-11-54 to 20-1-55) do
6. General Muhammad Ayub Khan	Defence	(24-10-54 to 11-8-55)
7. Mr Ghayasuddin Pathan	1. Food 2. Agriculture. 3. Minority Affairs 4. Parliamentary Affairs. 5. Law	(24-10-54 to 15-1-55) (24-10-54 to 11-8-55) do (24-10-54 to 20-12-54) do

S. No	Portfolio	Period
8. Mir Ghulam Ali Talpur	1. Information & Broadcasting 2. Education	(24-10-54 to 12-1-55) (24-10-54 to 18-3-55)
9. Dr Khan Sahib	Communications	(4-11-54 to 11-8-55)
10. Mr Habib Ibrahim Rahimtoola	Commerce	(20-12-54 to 11-8-55)
11. Mr Huseyn Shaheed Suhrawardy	Law	(20-12-54 to 11-8-55)
12. Syed Abid Hussain	1. Food 2. Education	(15-1-55 to 11-8-55) (25-3-55 to 11-8-55)
13. Sardar Mumtaz Ali Khan	1. Information & Broadcasting 2. Kashmir Affairs	(12-1-55 to 11-8-55) (20-1-55 to 11-8-55)
14. Mr Abu Hussain Sarkar	Health	(20-1-55 to 6-6-55)

Coalition Cabinets

1. Chaudhury Mohammad Ali, 11 August 1955–12 September 1956

S. No	Portfolio	Period
1. Choudhury Muhammad Ali	1. Defence 2. Foreign affairs & Commonwealth 3. Finance 4. Economic Affairs 5. Kashmir Affairs 6. States & Frontier Regions	(11-8-55 to 12-9-56) (11-8-55 to 26-9-55 (11-8-55 to 17-10-55) (11-8-55 to 15-3-56) (17-10-55 to 12-9-56)
2. Dr Khan Sahib	1. Communications 2. States & Frontier Regions	(11-8-55 to 14-10-55)
3. Mr A. K. Fazlul Huq	1. Interior 2. Education	(11-8-55 to 9-3-56) (17-10-55 to 9-3-56)
4. Mr Habib Ibrahim Rahimtoola	1. Commerce 2. Industries	(11-8-55 to 12-9-56)
5. Syed Abid Husain	1. Kashmir affairs 2. Education	(11-8-55 to 14-10-55)
6. Mr Kamini Kumar Dutta	1. Law 2. Health	(11-8-55 to 31-8-55) (11-8-55 to 12-9-56)
7. Pir Ali Mohammad Rashdi	Information and Broadcasting	(11-8-55 to 29-8-56)
8. Mr Nurul Huq Chaudhry	1. Labour 2. Works 3. Minority Affairs	(11-8-55 to 12-9-56)

S. No	Portfolio	Period
9. Mr Abdul Latif Biswas	1. Food 2. Agriculture	(11-8-55 to 12-9-56)
10. Ibrahim Ismail Chundrigarh	Law	(31-8-55 to 29-8-56)
11. Mr Hamidul Huq Chaudhry	Foreign Affairs & Commonwealth Relations	(26-9-55 to 12-9-56)
12. Syed Amjad Ali	1. Finance 2. Economic Affairs	(17-10-55 to 12-9-56) (15-3-56 to 12-9-56)
13. Mr M. R. Kayani	Communications	(17-10-55 to 12-9-56)
14. Mr Abdus Sattar	1. Interior 2. Education	(1-1-56 o 12-9-56)

2. Huseyn Shaheed Suhrawardy, 12 September 1956–18 October 1957

S. No	Portfolio	Period
1. Mr H. S. Suhrawardy	1. Defence 2. Kashmir Affairs 3. States & Frontier 4. Economic Affairs 5. Law 6. Refugees & Rehabilitation 7. Education 8. Health	(12-9-56 to 18-10-57) (12-9-56 to 13-12-56) (12-9-56 to 18-10-57) (12-9-56 to 17-9-56)
2. Malik Firoz Khan Noon	Foreign Affairs & Commonwealth Relations	(12-9-56 to 18-10-57)
3. Mr Abul Mansur Ahmad	1. Commerce 2. Industries	(12-9-56 to 18-10-57)
4. Syed Amjad Ali	Finance	(12-9-56 to 18-10-57)
5. Mr Muhammad Abdul Khaleque	1. Labour 2. Works	(12-9-56 to 18-10-57)
6. Mir Ghulam Ali Talpur	Interior	(12-9-56 to 18-10-57)
7. Mr A. H. Dildar Ahmad	Food Agriculture	(12-9-56 to 18-10-57)
8. Sardar Amir Azam Khan	1. Information & Broadcasting 2. Parliamentary Affairs 3. Law	(12-9-56 to 5-9-57) (13-12-56 to 5-9-57)
9. Mian Jaffar Shah	Communications	(12-9-56 to 18-10-57)
10. Mr Zahiruddin	1. Education 2. Health 3. Minority Affairs	(1-1-56 to 18-10-57) do (13-12-56 to 18-10-57)

3. Mr. Ibrahim Ismail Chundrigarh, 18 October 1957–16 December 1957

S. No	Portfolio	Period
1. Mr Ismail I. Chundrigarh	1. Economic Affairs 2. Labour 3. Works 4. Rehabilitation	(18-10-57 to 16-12-57) (18-10-57 to 23-1 0-57) (18-10-57 to 24-10-57) (24-10-57 to 16-12-57)
2. Malik Firoz Khan Noon	Foreign Affairs & Commonwealth Relations	(19-10-57 to 16-12-57)
3. Mr Fazlur Rehman	1. Commerce 2. Law	(18-10-57 to 16-12-57)
4. Syed Amjad Ali	Finance	(18-10-57 to 16-12-57)
5. Mumtaz Mohammad Khan Daultana	Defence	(18-10-57 to 16-12-57)
6. Mr Mozaffar Ali Khan Qizilbash	Industries	(18-10-57 to 16-12-57)
7. Mr Abdul Latif Biswas	1. Food 2. Agriculture	(18-10-57 to 16-12-57)
8. Syed Misbahuddin Hussain	Communications	(18-10-57 to 16-12-57)
9. Mian Jaffar Shah	1. States & Frontier 2. Information & Broadcasting	(18-10-57 to 16-12-57) do
10. Mr Abdul Aleem	1. Rehabilitation 2. Works	(18-10-57 to 24-10-57) (24-10-57 to 16-12-57)
11. Mr Yusuf A. Haroon	1. Kashmir Affairs 2. Parliamentary Affairs	(18-10-57 to 16-12-57)
12. Mir Ghulam Ali Talpur	Interior	(18-10-57 to 16-12-57)
13. Mr Farid Ahmad	Labour	(1-1-57 to 16-12-57)

4. Malik Firoz Khan Noon, 16 December 1957–7 October 1958

S. No	Portfolio	Period
1. Malik Firoz Khan Noon	1. Foreign Affairs & Commonwealth Relations 2. States & Frontier Regions 3. Defence 4. Economic Affairs 5. Rehabilitation 6. Information & Broadcasting 7. Kashmir Affairs 8. Law 9. Parliamentary Affairs	(16-12-57 to 7-10-58) (16-12-57 to 7-10-58) (16-12-57 to 8-4-58) (16-12-57 to 29-3-58) (16-12-57 to 22-1-58) (16-12-57 to 22-1-58) (16-12-57 to 7-10-58) (16-12-57 to 21-1-58) (16-12-57 to 27-12-57)
2. Syed Amjad Ali	Finance	(16-12-57 to 7-10-58)
3. Mr Mozaffar Ali Khan Qizilbash	1. Industries 2. Commerce 3. Parliamentary Affairs	(16-12-57 to 18-3-58) do (27-12-57 to 18-3-58)
4. Mir Ghulam Ali Talpur	1. Interior 2. Supply	(16-12-57 to 18-3-58) (10-4-58 to 7-10-58)
5. Mian Jaffar Shah	1. Food 2. Agriculture	(16-12-57 to 7-10-58)
6. Mr Abdul Aleem	1. Works 2. Labour 3. Minority Affairs 4. Information & Broadcasting	(16-12-57 to 7-10-58) do (16-12-57 to 7-10-58) (21-1-58 to 7-10-58)
7. Mr Ramizuddin Ahmad	Communications	(16-12-57 to 7-10-58)
8. Mr Kamini Kumar Dutta	1. Health 2. Education 3. Law	(16-12-57 to 24-1-58) (16-12-57 to 7-2-58) (21-1-58 to 7-10-58)

S. No	Portfolio	Period
9. Haji Moula Bukhsh Soomro	Rehabilitation	(22-1-58 to 7-10-58)
10. Mr Mahfuzal Haq	1. Health 2. Social Welfare & Community Development	(24-1-58 to 7-10-58) (9-4-58 to 7-10-58)
11. Mr Basanta Kumar Das	1. Labour 2. Education	(7-2-58 to 7-10-58)
12. Sardar Abdur Rashid	1. Commerce 2. Industries	(29-3-58 to 7-10-58)
13. Sardar Amir Azam Khan	1. Economic Affairs 2. Parliamentary Affairs	(29-3-58 to 7-10-58)
14. Mr M. A. Khuro	Defence	(8-4-58 to 7-10-58)
15. Mr Hamidul Haq Chowdhry	Finance	(16-9-58 to 7-10-58)
16. Mr Sahiruddin	---	(2-10-58 to 7-10-58)
17. Mr A. H. Dildar Ahmad	---	(2-10-58 to 7-10-58)
18. Mr Nurur Rahman	---	(1-1-58 to 7-10-58)

Military Era: 1958–1971

1. First Cabinet of Martial Law Period, 28 October 1958–17 February 1960

S. No	Portfolio	Period
President		
General Muhammad Ayub Khan	1. Cabinet Division 2. Defence	(28-10-58 to 17-2-60) (28-10-58 to 17-2-60)
	3. Kashmir Affairs	(28-10-58 to 23-4-59)
	4. Establishment Division	
Ministers		
1. Lt Gen. Mohammad Azam Khan	1. Rehabilitation	(28-10-58 to 17-2-60)
	2. Food & Agriculture	(16-1-60 to 17-2-60) (16-1-60 to 17-2-60)
	3. Works Irrigation & Power	
2. Lt Gen. W. A. Burki	1. Rehabilitation	(28-10-58 to 17-2-60)
	2. Food & Agriculture	(16-1-60 to 17-2-60) do
	3. Works, Irrigation & Power	
2. Lt Gen. W. A. Burki	Health & Social Welfare	28-10-58 to 17-2-60
3. Mr Manzur Qadir	Foreign Affairs & Commonwealth Relations	29-10-58 to 17-2-60
4. Mr Mohammad Ibrahim	Law	28-10-58 to 17-2-60
5. Lt Gen. K. M. Sheikh	1. Interior (Home Affairs Division)	28-10-58 to 17-2-60
	2. States & Frontier Regions	(18-11-58 to 17-2-60) (23-4-59 to 17-2-60)
	3. Establishment Division	

S. No	Portfolio	Period
6. Mr Mohammad Shoaib	Finance	(15-11-58 to 17-2-60)
7. Mr Abul Kasem Khan	1. Industries 2. Works, Irrigation, & Power	(28-10-58 to 17-2-60) (28-10-58 to 16-1-60)
8. Khan F. M. Khan	Railways & Communications	(28-10-58 to 17-2-60)
9. Mr Habibur Rahman	1. Education 2. Information and Broadcasting 3. Minority Affairs	(29-10-58 to 17-2-60) (29-10-58 to 16-1-60) (11-11-58 to 16-1-60)
10. Mr Zulfikar Ali Bhutto	1. Commerce 2. Information and Broadcasting 3. Minority Affairs	(28-10-58 to 16-1-60) (16-1-60 to 17-2-60) do
11. Mr Muhammad Hafizur Rehman	1. Food & Agriculture 2. Commerce	(28-10-58 to 16-1-60) (16-1-60 to 17-2-60)

2. Presidential Cabinet (Under the Presidential election and Constitution Order, 1960), 17 February 1960–8 June 1962

S. No	Portfolio	Period
President Field Marshal Muhammad Ayub Khan	1. Defence 2. Kashmir Affairs 3. President's Secretariat 4. National Reconstruction & Information 5. Planning Division	(17-2-60 to 8-2-62) (17-2-60 to 23-4-60) (17-2-60 to 8-6-62) (20-10-60 to 25-11-60) (15-8-61 to 8-6-62)
Ministers		
1. Lt Gen. Mohammad Azam Khan	1. Rehabilitation 2. Food & Agriculture 3. Works and Water Resources	(17-2-60 to 15-4-60) do (17-2-60 to 15-4-60)
2. Mr Manzur Qadir	1. Foreign Affairs & Commonwealth Relations 2. Law	(17-2-60 to 8-6-62) (15-4-62 to 22-5-62)
3. Lt Gen. W. A. Burki	1. Health & Social Welfare 2. Minority Affairs 3. Education & Scientific Research 4. Kashmir Affairs	(17-2-60 to 8-6-62) do (2-3-62 to 8-6-62) (2-3-62 to 3-3-62)
4. Mr Mohammad Ibrahim	Law	(17-2-60 to 15-4-62)

S. No	Portfolio	Period
5. Lt Gen. K. N. Sheik Rehabilitation and Works, Housing & Water Resources abolished and Ministries of Rehabilitation. & works and Fuel Power & NR created w.e.f. 23-4-60	1. Home Affairs 2. Rehabilitation 3. Food & Agriculture 4. Works Housing & Water Resources 5. Rehabilitation & Works 6. Rehabilitation 7. States & Frontier Regions 8. Establishment Division	(17-2-60 to 14-6-60) (15-4-60 to 23-4-60) (15-4-60 to 8-6-62) (15-4-60 to 23-4-60) (23-4-60 to 7-9-61) (7-9-61 to 8-6-62) (17-2-60 to 5-8-6) (17-2-60 to 23-4-60)
6. Mr Mohammad Shoaib	1. Finance 2. Economic Coordination	(17-2-60 to 30-1-62) (30-1-62 to 6-5-62)
7. Mr Abul Kasem Khan	Industries	(17-2-60 to 8-6-62)
8. Khan F. M. Khan	Railway & Communications (Redesigned as Communications)	(17-2-60 to 8-6-62)
9. Mr Habibur Rahman	1. Education 2. Minority Affairs 3. National Reconstruction & Information	(17-2-60 to 17-4-61) do do

S. No	Portfolio	Period
10. Mr Zulfikar Ali Bhutto	1. Information & Broadcasting (Redesigned as Ministry of National Reconstruction and Information w.e.f. 10-3-60)	(17-2-60 to 1-6-60) (17-2-60 to 23-4-60) (23-4-60 to 8-6-62)
	2. Minority Affairs	(23-4-60 to 1-6-60) (3-3-62 to 8-6-62)
	3. Fuel Power & Natural Resources (Re-designated as Natural Resources Division, Ministry of Industries from 14.5.62	(25-11-60 to 10-4-61) (7-9-61 to 8-6-62)
	4. Kashmir Affairs	
	5. National Reconstruction & Information 6. Works	
11. Mr Muhammad Hafizur Rehman	Commerce	(17-2-60 to 28-5-62)
12. Mr Akhtar Husain	1. National Reconstruction and Information	(1-6-60 to 28-10-60) (10-4-61 to 17-4-61) (1-6-60 to 1-3-62) (29-6-60 to 1-3-62)
	2. Kashmir Affairs 3. Minority Affairs	(17-4-61 to 1-3-62)
	4. Education & Scientific Research	
13. Mr Zakir Husain	1. Interior	(14-6-60 to 8-6-62)
14. Mr Abdul Qadir	1. Finance 2. Commerce	(30-1-62 to 8-6-62) (28-5-62 to 8-6-62)
15. Mr Muhammad Munir	1. Law	(1-1-62 to 8-6-62)
	2. Parliamentary Affairs	

3. Presidential Cabinet After the Commencement of New Constitution (1962)
From 8-6-62 to 23-3-65

S. No	Portfolio	Period
President Field Marshal Muhammad Ayub Khan	1. President's Secretariat 2. Defence 3. Information & Broadcasting	(8-6-62 to 23-3-65) (8-6-62 to 23-3-65) (30-4-63 to 4-9-63)
Ministers		
1. Mr Muhammad Munir.	1. Law 2. Parliamentary Affairs	(8-6-62 to 17-12-62)
2. Mr Mohammad Ali	External Affairs	(13-6-62 to 23-1-63)
3. Mr Abdul Qadir	Finance	(8-6-62 to 15-12-62)
4. Mr Abdul Monem Khan	1. Health 2. Labour & Social Welfare	(13-6-62 to 7-11-62)
5. Mr Habibullah	1. Home Affairs 2. Kashmir Affairs	(13-6-62 to 23-3-6)
6. Mr Wahiduzzaman	1. Commerce 2. Health 3. Labour & Social Welfare	(13-6-62 to 20-3-65) (7-11-62 to 17-12-62) (28-10-63 to 20-1-64)
7. Mr Zulfikar Ali Bhutto	1. Industries 2. Natural Resources 3. Rehabilitation & Works 4. External Affairs	(13-6-62 to 4-9-63) (31-8-62 to 3-2-63) (24-1-63 to 23-3-65)
8. Mr Abdus Sabur Khan	Communication	(13-6-62 to 23-3-65)

S.No	Portfolio	Period
9. Mr A. K. M. Fazlul Qadir Chowdhary	1. Food & Agriculture 2. Rehabilitation & Works 3. Education 4. Information & Broadcasting 5. Labour & Social Welfare 6. Health	(13-6-62 to 4-9-83) (13-6-62 to 31-8-62) (17-8-62 to 4-9-63) (17-8-62 to 30-4-63) (3-2-63 to 28-10-63) (4-9-63 to 28-10-63)
10. Shaikh Khursheed Ahmad	1. Law 2. Parliamentary Affairs	(17-12-62 to 23-3-65)
11. Rana Abdul Hamid	1. Health 2. Labour & Social Welfare 3. Rehabilitation & Works 4. Food & Agriculture	(17-12-62 to 4-9-63) (17-12-62 to 3-2-63) (3-2-63 to 23-3-65) (4-9-63 to 23-3-65)
12. Mr Mohammed Shoaib	Finance	(15-12-62 to 23-3-65)
13. Mr A. T. M. Mustafa	1. Education 2. Information & Broadcasting	(4-9-63 to 23-3-65) (4-9-63 to 9-1-64)
14. Mr Abdullah-al-Mahmood	1. Industries 2. Natural Resources	(4-9-63 to 20-3-65)
15. Mr Abdul Waheed Khan	Information & Broadcasting	(9-1-64 to 23-3-65)
16. Al Haj Abd-Allah Zaheer-ud-Deen	1. Health 2. Labour & Social Welfare	(1-1-64 to 22-3-65)

4. President's Cabinet: 23-3-1965 to 25-3-1969

S. No	Portfolio	Period
President Field Marshal Muhammad Ayub Khan	1. Cabinet Division	(23-3-65 to 25-3-69) do
	2. Establishment Division	(23-3-65 to 25-3-69) do
	3. States & F. R. Division	(23-3-65 to 25-3-6) do
	4. Economic Affairs Division	(23-3-65 to 1-1-65) (23-3-65 to 17-8-65)
	5. Planning Division	
	6. Defence Division	
	7. Scientific Tech. Research	
	8. Home and Kashmir Affairs	
Ministers		
2. Khawaja Shahabuddin	Information & Broadcasting	(24-3-65 to 25-3-69)
3. Mr Mohammad Shoaib	Finance	(24-3-65 to 25-8-66)
4. Mr Abdus Sabur Khan	Communications	(24-3-65 to 25-3-69)
5. Mr Zulfikar Ali Bhutto	Foreign Affairs	(24-3-65 to 31-8-66)
6. Mr Ghulam Faruque	1. Commerce	(29-3-65 to 15-7-67) (1-1-66 to 15-7-67)
	2. Scientific Tech. Research	
7. Mr Altaf Hussain	1. Industries 2. Natural Resources	(29-3-65 to 15-5-68) do
8. Syed Muhammad Zafar	1. Law	(29-3-65 to 25-3-69) do
	2. Parliamentary Affairs	

S. No	Portfolio	Period
9. Kazi Anwarul Huque	1. Education 2. Health, Labour & Social Welfare	(29-3-65 to 25-3-69) do
10. Chaudhry Ali Akbar Khan	1. Home Affairs 2. Kashmir Affairs	(17-8-65 to 30-11-66) do
11. Mr A. H. M. S. Doha	1. Food & Agriculture 2. Rehabilitation & Works	(17-8-65 to 25-3-69) do
12. Syed Sharifuddin Pirzada	Foreign Affairs	(20-7-66 to 1-5-68)
13. Mr N. M. Uqualli	1. Without portfolio 2. Finance	(25-7-66 to 25-8-66) (25-8-66 to 25-3-69)
14. Vice Admiral A. R. Khan	1. Defence 2. Home Affairs Division 3. Kashmir Affairs Division	(21-10-66 to 25-3-69) (5-12-66 to 25-3-69) do
15. Nawab Abdul Ghafur Khan Hoti	1. Without portfolio 2. Commerce	(5-7-67 to 15-7-67) (15-7-67 to 25-3-69)
16. Mian Arshad Hussain	Foreign Affairs	(7-5-68 to 25-3-69)
17. Mr Ajmal Ali Choudhry	1. Without portfolio 2. Industries Division 3. Natural Resources Division	(6-7-68 to 18-7-68) (1-1-67 to 25-3-69)

5. President General Agha Muhammad Yahya Khan: President's Advisors
(26-3-1969 to 3-8-1969)

S. No	Portfolio	Period
1. Vice Admiral A. R. Khan	Defence	(26-3-1969 to 5-4-1969)
2. Mian Arshad Hussain	Foreign Affairs	(26-3-1969 to 4-4-1969)
3. Mr S. Fida Hassan	General Administration & Co-ordination	(26-3-1969 to 4-4-1969)
President		
1. General Agha Muhammad Yahya Khan, H.PIC, H.J.	1. Cabinet Division 2. Establishment Division 3. Information & Broadcasting 4. Law & Parliamentary Affairs 5. Defence 6. Foreign Affairs	(5-4-1969 to 3-8-1969)
Deputy Chief Martial Law Administraotrs:		
2. Lt Gen. Abdul Hamid Khan	1. Home & Kashmir Affairs 2. States & Frontier Regions Division	(5-4-1969 to 3-8-1969) (5-4-1969 to 3-8-1969)

S.No	Portfolio	Period
3. Vice Admiral S. M. Ahsan	1. Planning Commission including Planning & Economic Affairs	(5-4-69 to 3-8-69)
	2. Scientific & Technological Research Division	(5-4-69 to 3-8-69) (5-4-69 to 3-8-69) do
	3. Finance	(5-4-69 to 3-8-69) do
	4. Commerce	
	5. Industries & Natural Resources	
	6. Food & Agriculture Division	
4 Air Marshal M. Nur Khan	1. Communications	(5-4-69 to 3-8-69)
	2. Health, Labour & Social Welfare	(5-4-69 to 3-8-69)
	3. Rehabilitation & Works Division	(5-4-69 to 3-8-69)
	4. Family Planning Division	
	5. Scientific & Technological Research Division	
	6. Education	

6. President, General Agha Muhammad Yahya Khan's Civilian Presidential Cabinet
(4 August 1969 to 22 July 1971)

S. No	Portfolio	Period
President General Agha Muhammad Yahya Khan	1. Agriculture & Works 2. Communications 3. Cabinet Division 4. Defence 5. Economic Affairs Division 6. Establishment Division 7. Foreign Affairs 8. Information & NA 9. Law 10. Parliamentary Affairs 11. Planning Division	(4-8-69 to 14-8-69) (4-8-69 to 20-12-71) (4-8-69 to 20-12-71) (4-8-69 to 20-12-71) (15-12-70 to 20-12-71) (4-8-69 to 16-09-69) (4-8-69 to 20-12-71) do
Ministers		
1. Dr Abdul Motaleb Malik	1. Health, Labour, and Family Planning 2. Communications	(8-69 to 22-2-71) (15-8-69 to 7-10-69)
2. Sardar Abdul Rashid	Home & Kashmir Affairs and States & Frontier Regions	(4-8-69 to 22-2-71)
3. Mr Abdul Khair Muhammad Hafizuddin,	Industries and Natural Resources	(4-8-69 to 22-2-71)

S. No	Portfolio	Period
4. Nawab Mozaffar Ali Khan Qizilbash	Finance	(4-8-69 to 22-2-71)
5. Mr Muhammad Shamsul Huq	Education and Scientific Research	(4-8-69 to 22-2-71)
6. Nawabzada Mohammad Sher Ali Khan	Information and Broadcasting	(4-8-69 to 15-12-70)
7. Mr Ahsan-ul-Huq	Commerce	(4-8-69 to 22-2-71)
8. Mr Mahmood A. Haroon	Agriculture and Works	(15-8-69 to 22-2-71)
9. Mr A. R. Cornelius	Law	(17-9-69 to 22-2-71)
10. Dr Golam Waheed Choudhry	Communications	(8-10-69 to 22-2-71)

Second Parliamentary Period, 1971–1977

1. President's Council of Ministers (From 24-12-1971 to 1-5-1972)

S. No	Portfolio	Period
President CMLA Mr Zulfikar Ali Bhutto	1. Foreign Affairs 2. Defence 3. Interior 4. Provincial Coordination	(24-12-71 to 1-5-72) do, do (24-12-71 to 6-3-72)
Vice President Mr Nurul Amin	Cabinet Secretariat	(24-1 2-71 to 1-5-72)
Ministers		
1. Mr J. A. Rahim	1. Presidential Affairs 2. Culture 3. Town Planning and Agrovilles Law & Parliamentary Affairs	(24-12-71 to 1-5-72) do (24-12-71 to 1-5-72)
2. Mian Mahmud Ali Kasuri	Law & Parliamentary Affairs	(24-12-71 to 1-5-72)
3. Mr Justice Faizullah Kundi	Establishment	(24-12-71 to 1-5-72)
4. Dr Mubashir Hasan	1. Finance 2. Economic Affairs and Development	(24-12-71 to 1-5-72)
5. Shaikh Muhammad Rashid	1. Social Welfare 2. Health & Family Planning	(24-12-71 to 1-5-72)

S. No	Portfolio	Period
6. Raja Tridiv Roy	Minorities Affairs	(24-12-71 to 1-5-72)
7. Mr Ghulam Mustafa Khan Jatoi	1. Political Affairs 2. Communication and Natural Resources	(24-12-71 to 1-5-72)
8. Malik Miraj Khalid	Food and Agriculture and under Development Areas	(24-12-71 to 1-5-72)
9. Mr Abdul Hafeez Pirzada	1. Education 2. Information & National Affairs 3. Provincial Coordination	(24-12-71 to 1-5-72) (24-12-71 to 6-3-72) (6-3-72 to 1-5-72)
10. Mr Muhammad Hanif	1. Labour 2. Works & Local Bodies	(24-12-71 to 1-5-72)
11. Maulana Kausar Niazi	Information & Broadcasting, Auqaf & Hajj	(6-3-72 to 1-5-72)
12. Mr Abdul Qayyum Khan,	1. Home Affairs 2. States & Frontier Regions	(1-1-72 to 1-5-72) (18-4-72 to 1-5-72)

2. President's Ministers under the Interim Constitution (From 2-5-1972 to 14-8-1973)

S. No	Portfolio	Period
President Mr Zulfikar Ali Bhutto	1. Defence 2. Foreign Affairs 3. Pakistan Atomic Energy Commission 4. Industries	(13-5-72 to 14-8-73) (13-5-72 to 14-8-73) do
Vice President Nurul Amin	1. Cabinet Division 2. Ministry of Science & Technology	(13-5-72 to 14-8-73)
2. Mr J. A. Rahim	Production and Presidential Affairs	(13-5-72 to 14-8-73)
3. Mr Abdul Qayyum Khan	Interior, States and Frontier Regions	(13-5-72 to 14-8-73)
4. Dr Mubashir Hasan,	Finance, Planning and Development	(13-5-72 to 14-8-13)
5. Mr Ghulam Mustafa Khan Jatoi	Political Affairs & Communications	(13-5-72 to 14-8-73)
6. Hayat Mohammad Khan Sherpao	Fuel, Power and Natural Resources	(13-5-72 to 14-8-73)
7. Mr Abdul Hafeez Pirzada	1. Education and Provincial Coordination 2. Law & Parliamentary Affairs	(13-5-72 to 14-8-73) (7-10-172 to 14-8-73)
8. Maulana Kausar Niazi	Information & Broadcasting Auqaf and Hajj	(13-5-72 to 14-8-73)

S. No	Portfolio	Period
9. Mr Mahmud Ali Kasuri	Law & Parliamentary Affairs	(13-5-72 to 5-10-72)
10. Shaikh Muhammad Rashid	Health & Social Welfare	(13-5-72 to 14-8-73)
11. Mr Muhammad Hanif	Labour & Works	(13-5-72 to 14-8-73)
12. Raja Tridiv Roy	Minorities Affairs and Tourism	(13-5-72 to 14-8-73)
13. Mr Khurshid Hasan Meraj	Without portfolio	(13-05-72 to 14-08-73)
14. Sardar Ghaus Bakhsh Raisani	Food & Agriculture and Under Development Areas	(1-1-72 to 14-8-73)

3. Prime Minister's First Cabinet under new Constitution, 1973
(From 14-8-1973 to 22-10-1974)

S. No	Portfolio	Period
Prime Minister Mr Zulfikar Ali Bhutto	1. Cabinet Division 2. Defence 3. Foreign Affairs 4. Industries 5. Pakistan Atomic Energy Commission	(17-8-73 to 22-10-74) do, do (17-8-73 to 22-10-74)
1. Mr J. A. Rahim	1. Production 2. Town Planning & Agrovilles 3. Commerce	(17-8-73 to 2-7-74) do, do
2. Mr Abdul Qayyum Khan	Interior, States & Frontier Regions and Kashmir Affairs	(1-1-73 to 22-10-74)
3. Dr Mubashir Hasan	Finance, Planning & Development	(1-1-73 to 22-10-74)
4. Hayat Mohammad Khan Sherpao	Fuel, Power and Natural Resources	(17-8-73 to 13-2-74)
5. Sheikh Mohammad Rashid	1. Health & Social Welfare 2. Chairman Federal Land Commission	(17-8-73 to 22-10-74), (23-12-73 to 22-10-74)
6. Mr Khursheed Hasan Meer	1. Minister without portfolio 2. Railways 3. Communications	(17-8-73 to 22-10-74,) (30-8-74 to 22-10-74) (23-12-73 to 22-10-74)

7. Mr Ghulam Mustafa Khan Jatoi	Political Affairs & Communications	(17-8-73 to 23-12-73)
8. Mr Abdul Hafeez Pirzada	1. Education and Provincial Coordination 2. Law & Parliamentary Affairs	(17-8-73 to 22-10-74) (17-8-73 to 22-10-74)
9. Maulana Kausar Niazi	Information & Broadcasting Auqaf and Hajj	(17-8-73 to 22-10-74)
10. Sardar Ghaus Bakhsh Raisani	Food, Agriculture Rural Development	(17-8-73 to 13-2-74)
11. Mr Muhammad Hanif	1. Labour & Works 2. Fuel, Power and Natural Resources	(17-8-73 to 22-10-74), (13-2-74 to 22-10-74)
12. Raja Tridiv Roy	Minorities Affairs &Tourism	(14-8-73 to 22-10-74)
13. Mr Rafi Raza	1. Production and 2. Commerce	(1-1-74 to 22-10-74)

4. Prime Minister's Second Cabinet, Under the Constitution, 1973
(From 22-10-1974 to 28-3-1977)

S. No	Portfolio	Period
Prime Minister Mr Zulfikar Ali Bhutto	1. Ministry of Defence 2. Ministry of Foreign Affairs 3. Ministry of Interior, States and Frontier Regions	(22-10-74 to 28-3-77) (13-01-77 to 28-03-77)
1. Mr Abdul Qayyum Khan	Ministry of Interior, States & Frontier Regions	(22-10-74 to 13-1-77)
2. Shaikh Mohammad Rashid	1. Food, Agriculture and Cooperative Works, Under Developed Areas and Land Reforms 2. Food, Agriculture	(22-10-74 to 5-2-76) (5-9-76 to 28-3-77)
3. Mr Khursheed Hasan Meer	Labour, Health, Social Welfare, Population and Planning	(22-10-74 to 18-12-74)
4. Mr Abdul Hafeez Pirzada	1. Education, Science & Technology and Provincial Coordination 2. Education and Provincial Coordination	(22-10-74 to 5-2-76) (5-2-76 to 28-3-77)
5. Rana Mohammad Haneef Khan	Finance, Planning & Economic Affairs	(22-10-74 to 28-3-77)

S. No	Portfolio	Period
6. Malik Mairaj Khalid	1. Law & Parliamentary Affairs 2. Labour, Health Social Welfare and Population Planning 3. Social Welfare, Local Govt., and Rural Development	(22-10-74 to 5-2-76) (21-12-74 to 10-1-75) (5-2-76 to 27-3-77)
7. Mr Mumtaz Ali Khan Bhutto	Ministry of Communications	(22-10-74 to 28-3-77)
8. Mr Rafi Raza	Production industries and Town Planning	(22-10-74 to 28-3-77)
9. Maulana Kausar Niazi	Religious Affairs, Minority Affairs and Overseas Pakistanis	(22-10-74 to 5-2-76), (5-2-76 to 28-3-77)
10. Mr Mohammad Yusuf Khattak	Fuel, Power, and Natural Resources	(22-10-74 to 13-1-77)
11. Mir Afzal Khan	1. Commerce 2. Commerce and Tourism	(22-10-74 to 5-2-76), (5-2-76 to 28-3-77)
12. Mr Yahya Bakhtiar	Attorney General for Pakistan	(22-10-74 to 28-3-77)
13. Mr Hafizullah Cheema	1. Labour, Health, Social Welfare and Population Planning 2. Railways	(10-1-75 to 5-2-76) (5-2-76 to 28-3-77)

S. No	Portfolio	Period
14. Syed Qaim Ali Shah Jillani	1. Industries, Kashmir Affairs & Northern Affairs 2. Agrarian Management, Kashmir Affairs & NA	(5-2-76 to 17-7-76) (17-7-76 to 28-3-77)
15. Malik Mohammad Akhtar	1. Law & Parliamentary Affairs 2. Fuel Power and Natural Resources	(5-2-76 to 28-3-77) (20-1-77 to 28-3-77)
16. Mr Mohammad Haneef Khan	Information & Broadcasting	(5-2-76 to 26-3-77)
17. Mr Nasir Ali Rizvi	Housing & Works And Urban Development	(5-2-76 to 28-3-77)
18. Mir Taj Mohammad Khan Jamali	Labour, Manpower, Health, and Population Planning	(5-2-76 to 28-3-77)
19. Mian Mohammad Ataullah	Industries	(17-7-76 to 28-3-77)

Select Bibliography

A. PRIMARY SOURCES

1. UNPUBLISHED OFFICIAL RECORDS AND DOCUMENTS

(i) National Documentation Centre, Cabinet Division, Islamabad

Cabinet Files 1947, 67/CF/47, 127/CF/47, 213/CF/47, 215/CF/47.

Cabinet Files 1948, 12/CF/48, 21/CF/48, 33/CF/48, 36/CF/48, 358/CF/48.

Cabinet Files 1949, 31/CF/49, 234/CF/49.

Cabinet Files 1950, 247/CF/50.

Cabinet Files 1951, 48/CF/51.

Cabinet Files 1952, 73/CF/52, 302/CF/52.

Cabinet Files 1953, 7/CF/53-11, 50/CF/53, 108/CF/53,134/CF/53, 143/CF/53, 144/CF/53-1, 302/CF/53, 314/CF/53, 326/CF/53.

Cabinet Files 1954, 781/CF/54.

Cabinet Files 1955, 59/CF/55, 60/CF/55, 61/CF/55, 95/CF/55, 191/CF/55, 222/CF/55, 230/CF/55, 236/CF/55,240/CF/55, 262/CF/55.

Cabinet Files 1956, 91/CF/56, 186/CF/56, 203/CF/56, 354/CF/56, 390/CF/56,392/CF/56, 395/CF/56, 500/CF/56.

Cabinet Files 1957, 322/CF/57, 335/CF/57, 422/CF/57, 427/CF/57, 437/CF/57-1.

Cabinet Files 1958, 332/CF/58, 454/CF/58, 512/CF/58, 592/CF/58, 630/CF/58.

Cabinet Files 1959, 448/CF/59, 674/CF/59, 674/CF/59-1.
Cabinet Files 1960, 25/CF/60, 98/CF/60, 254/CF/60.
Cabinet Files 1961, 407/CF/61.
Cabinet Files 1962, 116/CF/62,121/CF/62-IV, 137/CF/62, 280/
    CF/62.
Cabinet Files 1963, 193/CF/63, 198/CF/63, 261/CF/63, 505/
    CF/63.
Cabinet Files 1965, 130/CF/65, 173/CF/65, 309/CF/65,422/
    CF/65, 429/CF/65,442/CF/65, 542/CF/65, 450/CF/65, 492/
    CF/65.
Cabinet Files 1966, 88/CF/66, 229/CF/66, 335/CF/66-II.
Cabinet Files 1967, 225/CF/67.
Cabinet Files 1968, 23/CF/68, 159/CF/68, 205/CF/68, 432/
    CF/68, 432/CF/68-1.
Cabinet Files 1969, 247/CF/69, 297/CF/69.
Cabinet Files 1970, 296/CF/70.
Cabinet Files 1971, 280/CF/71, 369/CF/71/II, 424/CF/71.
Cabinet Files 1972, 38/CF/72, 39/CF/72, 40/CF/72, 53/CF/72,
    84/CF/72, 94/CF/72, 97/CF/72, 118/CF/72, 128/CF/72, 128/
    CF/72-1, 128/CF/72 II, 187/CF/72, 260/CF/72.
Cabinet Files 1973, 50/CF/73, 73/CF/73-1.
Cabinet Files 1974, 113/CF/74, 118/CF/74, 221/CF/74, 223/
    CF/74, 228/CF/74, 256/CF/74, 266/CF/74, 444//CF/74.
Cabinet Files 1975, 18/PROG/75.
Cabinet Files 1976, 70/PROG/76, 73/PROG/76.

(ii) Record of the Meetings of the Cabinet Committees

Cabinet Committee on Balochistan, 260/CF/72.
Defence Committee of the Cabinet, 34/CF/49.
Defence Committee of the Cabinet, 189/CF/58.
Economic Coordination Committee of the Cabinet, 448/CF/59.
Economic Coordination Committee of the Cabinet, 130/CF/62.

Economic Coordination Committee of the Cabinet, 48/CF/66.
Economic Coordination Committee of the Cabinet, 195/CF/66.
Economic Coordination Committee of the Cabinet, 102/CF/69.
Economic Coordination Committee of the Cabinet, 102/CF/69.
Economic Coordination Committee of the Cabinet, 201/CF/69.
Economic Coordination Committee of the Cabinet, 17/CF/74.
Executive Committee of the National Economic Council, 490/CF/64.
Executive Committee of the National Economic Council, 437/CF/66.
National Economic Council, 223/CF/63.
National Economic Council, 176/CF/65.
National Economic Council, 475/CF/66.
National Economic Council, 189/CF/68.
National Economic Council, 93/CF/69.
National Economic Council 201/CF/69.

(iii) Record of the Governors' Conferences

Governors' Conference, 25/CF/60.
Governors' Conference, 359/CF/62.
Governors' Conference, 121/CF/62-IV.
Governors' Conference, 9/CF/64.
Governors' Conference, 96/CF/67.
Governors' Conference, 23/CF/68.
Governors' Conference, 432/CF/68.
Governors' Conference, 20/CF/72.
Governors' Conference, 128/CF/72-V.
Governors' Conference, 266/CF/74.
Governors' Conference, 140/PROG/75-II.

(iv) The Prime Ministers' Papers, 1947–1953

Memorandum on 'Bengali non-Bengali Question in East Bengal' attached in the letter of Ghulam Muhammad written to Liaquat Ali Khan, 22 December 1947, 3(3)-PMS/47.

Jogandar Nath Mandal to Chief Minister of Bengal Khawaja Nazimuddin, 3 March 1948, 3(9)—PMS/48.

Iftikhar Hussain Mamdot, Chief Minister of Punjab to PM Liaquat Ali, 29 March 1948, S (1)-PMS/48.

Interior Minister Khawaja Shahabuddin to Prime Minister Liaquat Ali Khan, 13 February 1949, 3 (4)-PMS/49.

M. A. Gurmani Minister without Portfolio to Mohammad Zafrullah Khan Minister of Foreign Affairs, 28 March 1949, 3(5)-PMS/49.

Fazlur Rehman, Minister of Industries, Education Commerce and Works to Prime Minister Liaquat Ali Khan 29 August 1949, 3(6)-PMS/48.

Cabinet Meeting, 18 September 1949, 53 (b), Cord/49-50-1.

Minister of Industries, Commerce and Works to Prime Minister, 12 November 1949, Confidential 3(3)-PMS/49.

Liaquat Ali Khan to Jawaharlal Nehru, 14 February 1950, 12(3)-PMS/50.

Telegram from Pakistan High Commissioner, Calcutta to Foreign Minister Zafrullah Khan, Karachi, 10 October 1950, 3(18)-PMS/50.

Telegram Secret, From Foreign Office Karachi to different Foreign Offices in the World, 12 October 1950, 3(18)-PMS/50.

Governor of East Bengal Malik Firoz Khan Noon to PM Khawaja Nazimuddin, 28 February 1952, 2(1)-PMS/52.

(v) The National Archives of Pakistan, Islamabad

Naeem Qureshi Collection

The Interview of Prime Minister Z. A. Bhutto to Mr Moti Ram, senior Indian journalist, 23 September 1976, Rawalpindi.

Interview of Zulfikar Ali Bhutto to Mr Khushwant Singh, editor of *Illustrated Weekly of India*, 20 Dec. 1976, Rawalpindi.

(vi) The National Archives, London, 1947–1977

DO 35/5043, DO 35/8945, DO 35/8950, DO 189/217, DO35/316, DO196/318, DO 196/316, DO 134/33, DO 35/8936, DO 35/8926 DO 35/3188, DO 35/5106, DO 35/5111, DO 35/5405, Do 35/5406, DO 35/5285, DO 35/5407, DO 35/8345, DO 35/8935, DO 35/8936, DO 35/8943, DO 35/8944, DO 35/5106, DO 196/128, DO 196/316, DO 196/318, DO 196/319, DO 196/320.
FCO 37/79, FCO 37/179, FCO 37/181.
PREM II-3902, PREM 11/2027, PREM 13/2851.

2. Published Sources

I. Official Publications and Printed Documents

The All-Pakistan Legal Decisions, Central Statutes, 1962, Vol. XIV, Vol. XXI, Central Statutes, 1969, Vol. XXV, Central Statutes, 1973.

Anand, C. L., *The Government of India Act 1935* (Karachi: Law Publishers, 1939).

Arif, K., ed., *China-Pakistan Relations 1947–1980: Documents* (Lahore: Vanguard Books, 1984).

America-Pakistan's Relations (Lahore: Vanguard Books, 1984).

Baxter, Craig, *Diaries of Field Marshal Muhammad Ayub Khan 1966–1972* (Karachi: Oxford University Press, 2007).

Constitution of the Islamic Republic of Pakistan 1956 (Karachi: Government of Pakistan, 1956).

The Constitution of the Republic of Pakistan 1962, All-Pakistan Legal Decisions, Central Statutes, 1962, Vol. XIV.

The Constitution of the Islamic Republic of Pakistan–1973 (Karachi: Government of Pakistan, 1973).

Dar, Saeeduddin Ahmad, *Selected Documents on Pakistan's Relations with Afghanistan* (Islamabad: NIPS, 1986).

The Gazette of Pakistan Extraordinary, Government of Pakistan, 1947–1960, Cabinet Secretariat, Karachi.

The Gazette of Pakistan Extraordinary, Government of Pakistan, 1960–1974, Cabinet Secretariat, Islamabad.

The Gazette of Pakistan, Government of Pakistan, 1969, Cabinet Secretariat, Islamabad.

The Interim Constitution of the Islamic Republic of Pakistan–1972 (Islamabad: Printing Corporation of Pakistan, 1972).

Keesing's Contemporary Archives.

Khan, Roedad, *The British Papers, Secret and Confidential India Pakistan Bangladesh Documents 1958–1969* (Karachi: Oxford University Press, 2002).

———, *The American Papers, Secret and Confidential India Pakistan Bangladesh Documents 1958–1969* (Karachi: Oxford University Press, 2000).

Ministry of Law and Parliamentary Affairs, *Constitutional Documents Vol. III* (Karachi: Government of Pakistan, 1964).

Ministry of Foreign Affairs Publications *Joint Communique 1947–1977* (Karachi: Government of Pakistan, 1977).

National Assembly of Pakistan Debates, Official Report, June 1962–1968 (Islamabad: Government of Pakistan Press).

National Assembly of Pakistan (Constitution-Making) Debates, 14 August 1972–13 April 1973 (Karachi: Printing Corporation of Pakistan Press).

National Assembly of Pakistan (Legislature) Debates, 14 April 1972–June 1977 (Karachi: Printing Corporation of Pakistan Press).

Pakistan Economic Survey (Islamabad: Government of Pakistan, 1976), 75–6.

Punjab Report of the Court of Inquiry, Constituted under Punjab Act II of 1954 to Enquire into the Punjab Disturbances of 1953 (Lahore: Government Printing Press, 1954), 81.

Supreme Court Mein Bhutto Kai Bian Ka Mukamal Mattan (Lahore: Asian Publishers).

White Paper on Balochistan (Islamabad: Government of Pakistan, 1974).

White Paper on Misuse of Media, 20 Dec. 1971–4 July 1977 (Islamabad: Government of Pakistan, 1978).

White Paper on the Conduct of March 1977 General Elections (Rawalpindi: Government of Pakistan, 1978).

White Papers on the Performance of the Bhutto Regime, 4 Volumes (Islamabad: Government of Pakistan, 1979).

II. Speeches, Statements and Memoirs

Ali, Choudhury Muhammad, *The Task Before Us* (Lahore: Research Society of Pakistan, 1974).

Ali, Syed Shafaat, *The Soldier: A Memoir* (Karachi: Royal Book Company, 2007).

Bhutto, Zulfikar Ali, *Foreign Policy of Pakistan* (Karachi: Pakistan Institute of International Relations, 1964).

The Myth of Independence (Lahore: Oxford University Press, 1969).

The Quest for Peace (Karachi: Pakistan Institute of International Relation, 1966).

Politics of the People: A Collection of Articles, Statements and Speeches, 3 Volumes, eds. Hamid Jalal and Khalid Hasan (Rawalpindi: Pakistan Publications, 1972).

Z. A. Bhutto, A New Beginning: Reforms Introduced by the People's Government in Pakistan, 20 Dec. 1971–20 Apr. 1972 (Karachi: Ministry of Information and Broadcasting Department of Films and Publication Government of Pakistan, 1972).

The Great Tragedy (Karachi: Pakistan Peoples Party Publications, 1971).

Political Situation in Pakistan (New Delhi, Vishasher Prakashan, 1968).

Speeches and Statements Vol. I, 20 Dec. 1971–31 Mar. 1972 (Karachi: Ministry of Information and Broadcasting Department of Films and Publication Government of Pakistan, 1972).

Speeches and Statements Vol. II, 1 Apr. 1972–30 June 1972 (Karachi: Ministry of Information and Broadcasting Department of Films and Publication Government of Pakistan, 1972).

Speeches and Statements Vol. III, 1 Oct. 1972–31 Dec. 1972 (Karachi: Ministry of Information and Broadcasting Department of Films and Publication, Government of Pakistan, 1972).

Speeches and Statements Vol. IV, 1 Jan. 1973–31st Dec. 1973 (Karachi: Ministry of Information and Broadcasting Department of Films and Publication Government of Pakistan, 1973).

Speeches and Statements Vol. V, 14 Aug. 1973–31 Dec. 1973 (Karachi: Ministry of Information and Broadcasting Department of Films and Publication Government of Pakistan, 1973).

Bilateralism–New Direction (Islamabad: Ministry of Information & Broadcasting, Government of Pakistan, 1976).

The Third World–New Directions (London: Quratet Books, 1977).

If I am Assassinated (New Delhi: Vikas Publishing House, 1978).

My Pakistan (New Delhi: Biswin Sadi Publication, 1979).

My Execution (London: Musawat Weekly–International, 1980).

Foreign Policy of Pakistan: A Compendium of Speeches made in the National Assembly of Pakistan 1962–64 (Karachi: Pakistan Institute of International Affairs, 1964).

'Reshaping Foreign Policy, Nineteen Forty-Eight to Nineteen Sixty-Six', Statements, Articles, Speeches, www.bhutto.org

Khan, Gul Hassan, *Memoirs* (Karachi: Oxford University Press, 1993).

Khan, Muhammad Ayub, *Speeches and Statements Vol. I, Oct. 1958–June 1959* (Islamabad: Government of Pakistan, 1959).

Speeches and Statements, July 1959–June 1960 (Islamabad: Government of Pakistan, 1960).

Speeches and Statements July 1960–June 1961, Vol. III (Islamabad: Government of Pakistan, 1961).

Friends Not Masters: A Political Autobiography (London: Oxford University Press, 1967).

Khan, Liaquat Ali, *Pakistan: the Heart of Asia* (Cambridge: Harvard University Press, 1950).

Khan, Tamizuddin, *The Test of Time; My Life and Days* (Dhaka: The University Press, 1989).

Latif, Rahat, *Bhutto's Episode: An Autobiography* (Lahore: Jang Publishers, 1993).

Mazari, Sherbaz Khan, *A Journey to Disillusionment* (Karachi: Oxford University Press, 2000).

Musa, Mohammed General (retd), *Jawan to General: Recollection of a Pakistan's Soldier* (Karachi: East and West Publishing Co., 1984).

Noon, Firoz Khan, *From Memory* (Lahore: Ferozsons, 1966).

Rashid, Sheikh Mohammad, *Jehad-i-Musalsul* (Urdu) (Lahore: Jang Publishers, 2002).

Recollections and Reflections (Lahore: PhD Publications, n.d.).

Talukdar, Mohammad H.R., *Memoirs of Huseyn Shaheed Suhrawardy: With a Brief Account of His Life and Works* (Dhaka: The University Press, 1987).

III. Interviews

Bader, Jehangir, History Department, Punjab University, Lahore, 20 June 2012.

Baluch, Abdul Hai, Superintendent House, Hostel No. 4, Punjab University, Lahore, 6 June 2012.

Habibullah, Chaudhary (Former Secretary of the Punjab Assembly), 195-G, Johar Town Lahore, 22 Oct. 2012.

Hasan, Mubashir, 4-k, Gulberg II Lahore, 29 Mar. 2010.

Ispahani, Karim (Grandson of the former Minister Mirza Abul Hassan popularly known as M. A. Ispahani), ISPI Corporation Pvt. Ltd. Building 31, West Wharf Road, Karachi.

Masood, S. M. (former Law Minister in the Punjab Cabinet, 1973–77, and later Federal Cabinet, 1977), 404 Shadman 1, Lahore, 14 Feb. 2012.

Pirzada, Abdul Hafeez, Telephonic, 8 Jan. 2013.

Rashid, Mrs Shakeela (Wife of Shaikh Mohammad Rashid who was minister in Bhutto's Cabinet), History Department, Punjab University, Lahore, 27 Sept. 2011.

Rehman I. A. (Prominent Journalist), 107 Tippu Block, New Garden Town, Lahore, 24 Dec. 2012.

Zafar, S. M., 104, 4th Flour, Siddique Trade Centre Lahore, 9 Sept. 2012.

IV. Newspapers

Dawn
Jang
Nawa-i-Waqt
The Muslim
The Nation
The News
Outlook
The Pakistan Times
Pakistan Observer

B. SECONDARY SOURCES

1. Books

A Revisionist History of Pakistan (Lahore: Vanguard, 1998).

Adams, John and Sabiha Iqbal, *Exports, Politics and Economic Development in Pakistan* (Lahore: Vanguard, 1986).

Afzal, M. Rafique, *Pakistan: History and Politics 1947–1971* (Oxford: The University Press, 2001).

Ahmad, A. S., *Pakistan Society: Islam, Ethnicity and Leadership* (New York: Oxford Publishers, 1986).

Ahmad, Masud, *Pakistan: A Study of Its Constitutional History 1857–1975* (Lahore: Research Society of Pakistan, 1978).

Ahmad, Viqar and Rashid Amjad, *The Management of Pakistan's Economy 1947–82* (Karachi: OUP, 1984).

Ahmad, Ziauddin, *Liaquat Ali Khan: Builder of Pakistan* (Karachi: Royal Book Company, 1990).

Ahmed, Ghafoor, *Phir Martial Law Agiya* (Lahore: Jung Publishers, 1988).

Ahmed, Manzooruddin, ed., *Contemporary Pakistan: Politics Economy and Society* (Karachi: Royal Book Company, 1982).

Ahmed, Mohammad, *My Chief* (Lahore: Longman Green and Co., 1960).

Ahmed, Munir, *Legislatures in Pakistan* (Lahore: Department of Political Science, 1960).

Ahmed, Mushtaq (*Jinnah and After: A Profile of Leadership* (Karachi: Royal Book Company, 1994).

Ahmed, Saleem, *Mamdot Sei Watoo Tuk: Markz-Punjab Tanaza* (Lahore: Gora Publishers, 1996).

Ahmed, Syed Sami, *The Trial of Zulfikar Ali Bhutto and the Superior Judiciary in Pakistan* (Karachi: Royal Book Company, 2008).

Ahmer, Moonis, *Pakistan and Bangladesh: From Conflict to Cooperation* (Karachi: Pakistan Study Centre, 2004).

Ajithkumar, M. P., *India-Pakistan Relations: The Story of a Fractured Fraternity* (Delhi: Kalpaz Publications, 2006).

Ali, Choudhury Muhammad, *Emergence of Pakistan* (New York: Columbia University Press, 1967).

Ali, Mehrunnisa, *Politics of Federalism in Pakistan* (Karachi: Royal Book Company, 1996).

Ali, Tariq, *Pakistan: Military Rule or People's Power* (London: Jonathon Cape, 1970).

Allen, McGrath, *The Destruction of Pakistan's Democracy* (Karachi: Oxford University Press, 1994).

Almond, Gabriel A., Powell, G. Bingham Jr, Storm, Kaare and others, *Comparative Politics Today: A World View* (Delhi: Pearson Education, 2004).

Amin, Tahir, *Ethno-National Movements of Pakistan: Domestic and International Factors* (Islamabad: Institute of Policy Studies, 1988).

Amjad, Rashid, *Private Industrial Investment in Pakistan, 1960–1970* (Cambridge: The University Press, 1982).

Anand, C. L., *The Government of India Act 1935* (Karachi: Law Publishers, 1939).

Anwar, Mehmood Rafi, *Presidential Government in Pakistan* (Lahore: Caravan Book House, 1964).

Aqeel, Abu Jaferi, *Pakistan Chronicle* (Rawalpindi: Fazli Sons, 2010).

Arif, K. M., *Working with Zia, Pakistan's Power Politics 1977–88* (Karachi: Oxford University Press, 1995).

Aslam, Mohammad, *Pakistan: Economy in Retrospect 1947–2010* (Lahore: Ferozsons Pvt Ltd., 2011).

Aziz, K. K., *Studies in the History and Politics* (Lahore: Vanguard, 2002).

Bajwa, Farooq Naseem, *Pakistan and the West: the First Decade 1947–1957* (Karachi: Oxford University Press, 1996).

Banuazizi, Ali and Myron Weiner, eds., *The State, Religion and Ethnic Politics, Pakistan, Iran and Afghanistan* (Lahore: Vanguard, 1987).

Batra, J. C., *The Trial and Execution of Bhutto* (Delhi: Kunj, 1979).

Beg, Aziz, *Before and After Revolution* (Rawalpindi: Pakistan Patriotic Publications, n.d.).

Bhatia, B. M., *Pakistan's Economic Development 1947–1990* (Lahore: Vangaurd, 1990).

Bhatti, M. H., *The Saviour of Pakistan* (Lahore: Star Books Depot, n.d.).

Bhurgri, Abdul Ghafoor, *Zulfikar Ali Bhutto: The Falcon of Pakistan* (Karachi: Szabist, 2002).

Bhutto, Benazir, *Daughter of the East: An Autobiography* (London: Hamish Hamilton, 1988).

Bindra, S. S., *Politics of Islamisation: With Special Reference to Pakistan* (New Delhi: Deep and Deep Publication, 1990).

Borrelli, Mary Anne, *The President's Cabinet: Gender, Power and Representation* (Colorado: Liynne Rienner Publishers, 2002).

Braibanti, Ralph and Howard Wrggins, eds., *Pakistan: The Long View* (Durham: Centre for Commonwealth and Comparative Studies, 1977).

Braibanti, Ralph, *Research on the Bureaucracy of Pakistan* (Durham: Duke University Press, 1969).

Britain and Pakistan: A Study of British Attitude towards the East Pakistan Crisis of 1971 (Lahore: Sang-e-Meel Publications, 2008).

Broomfield, John H., *Elite Conflict in a Plural Society* (Berkeley and Los Angeles: University of California Press, 1968).

Buckley, Stephen, *The Prime Minister and Cabinet* (Edinburgh: The University Press, 2006).

Burke, S. M., *Mainsprings of Indian and Pakistan's Foreign Policies* (Minneapolis: University of Minnesota, 1974).

Burki, Shahid Javed and Craig Baxter, *Pakistan under the Military: Eleven Years of Zia ul-Haq* (Boulder: Westview Press, 1989).

Burki, Shahid Javed, *Pakistan: Fifty Years of Nationhood* (Lahore: Vanguard, 2004).

Burney, I. H., *Outlook, Editorials, No Illusions, Some Hopes and No Fears* (Karachi: Oxford University Press, 1996).

Cabinet Government (Cambridge: The University Press, 1969).

Callard, Keith, *Pakistan's Foreign Policy: An Interpretation* (New York: Institute of Pacific Relations, 1959).

Chaudhri, Mohammad Ahsen, *Pakistan and the Regional Pacts: A Study of Pakistan's Foreign Policy 1947–54* (Karachi: Royal Book Company, 1988).

Chishti, Faiz Ali, *Bhutto, Zia Aur Main* (Lahore: Jung Publications, 1996).

Chopra, Surendra (*Pakistan's Thrust in the Muslim World: India as a Factor (A Study of RCD)* (New Delhi: Deep and Deep Publications, 1992).

Choudhury, Golam Waheed, *Transition from Military to Civilian Rule* (Essex: Scorpion Publishing Ltd., 1988).

Choudhury, Mustafa, *Pakistan: Its Politics and Bureaucracy* (New Delhi: Associated Publishing House, 1988).

Cohen, Stephen Philip, *The Pakistan Army* (Berkeley: University of California Press, 1989).

Constitutional Development in Pakistan (London: Longman, 1969).

Dar, Saeeduddin Ahmad, *Pakistan's Relations with Egypt: 1947–1971* (Karachi: Royal Book Company, 1993).

Daughter of Destiny (New York: Somon and Schuster, 1989).

Dixit, J. N., *India-Pakistan: War and Peace* (London: Routledge, 2002).

Durrani, Tehmina, *My Feudal Lord* (New Delhi: Sterling, 1991).

Federalism in Pakistan: Theory and Practice (Islamabad: National Institute of Pakistan Study Center, QAU, 1994).

Feldman Herbert, *From Crisis to Crisis, 1962–1969* (London: Oxford University Press, 1972).

Fox, R. G., *Lions of the Punjab: Culture in the Making* (Berkeley: University of California Press, 1985).

Fried, Robert C., *Comparative Political Institution* (New York: Macmillan Company, 1973).

From Jinnah to Zia (Lahore: Vanguard, 1980).

Gardezi H. N., *Understanding Pakistan: The Colonial Factor in Societal Development* (Lahore: Maktaba Fikr-i-Danish, 1991).

Gardezi, H. and J. Rashid, eds., *Pakistan: The Roots of Dictatorship* (London: Zed Press, 1983).

Gauhar, Altaf, *Ayub Khan: Pakistan's First Military Ruler* (Lahore: Sang-i-Meel Publications, 1993).

Gohar, Waseem, *Almia-i-Mushriqi Pakistan Aur Zulfiqar Ali Bhutto, 1947–1971* (Lahore: Tughliqat, 1993).

Government and Politics in Pakistan (New York: Frederick A. Praeger Publishers, 1963).

Grass Roots Government, Essays on the Genesis, Philosophy and Working of Basic Democracies in Pakistan (Rawalpindi: Pakistan Patriotic Publications, n.d.).

Grave, Frederic, *Pakistan and the Afghan Conflict, 1979–1985: With an Afterword Covering Events from 1985–2001* (Karachi: Oxford University Press, 2003).

Haq, Mahbub ul, *The Strategy of Economic Planning: A Case Study of Pakistan* (Karachi: Oxford University Press, 1963).

Hasan, Burhanuddin, *The Breaking Point: Pakistan's Turbulent 62 Years* (Karachi: Royal Book Company, 2009).

Hasan, Mubashir, *The Mirage of Power: An Inquiry into the Bhutto Years 1971–1977* (New York: The Oxford University Press, 2000).

Hasan, Syed Manzural, *Pakistan Politics in Mirror of History* (Karachi: Royal Book Company, 2009).

Hassan, K. Sarwar, *Pakistan and the United Nations* (New York: Manhattan Publishing Company, 1960).

Hassan, Pervez, *Pakistan's Economy at the Crossroads: Past Politics and Present Imperatives* (Karachi: Oxford University Press, 1998).

Hayes, Louis D., *The Struggle for Legitimacy in Pakistan* (Lahore: Vanguard, 1986).

Hennessy, Peter, *Cabinet* (New York: Basil Blackwell Ltd., 1986).

Hill, Christopher, *Cabinet Decisions on Foreign Policy: The British Experience Oct. 1938–June 1941* (Cambridge: The University Press, 1991).

Husain, Ishrat *Pakistan: The Economy of an Elitist State* (Karachi: Oxford University Press, 2002).

Hussain, Ahmed, *Strategic Issues in Pakistan's Economic Policy* (Lahore: Progressive Publishers, 1988).

Hussain, Asaf, *Elite Politics in an Ideological State* (Kent: Dawson and Sons Ltd., 1979).

Hussain, Chaudhri Nazir, *Chief Justice Muhammad Munir: His Life, Writings and Judgment* (Lahore: Research Society of Pakistan, 1973).

Hussain, Ijaz, *Issues in Pakistan's Foreign Policy: An International Law Perspective* (Lahore: Progressive Publishers, 1988).

Hussain, Syed Shabbir, *Ayub, Bhutto and Zia* (Lahore: Sang-e-Meel Publications, 2001).

Hyder, Sajjad, *Foreign Policy of Pakistan: Reflections of an Ambassador* (Lahore: Progressive Publishers, 1987).

Ikramullah, Shaista Suhrawardy, *Huseyn Shaheed Suhrawardy: A Biography* (Karachi: Oxford University Press, 1991).

Inayatullah, *Pakistan's Politics: A Personal View* (Lahore: Ferozsons, 1993).

Issues and Realities of Pakistani Politics (Lahore: Research Society of Pakistan, 2007).

Jacques, Kathryn, *Bangladesh, India and Pakistan: International Relations and Regional Tensions in South Asia* (London: Macmillan Press, Ltd., 2000).

Jaffrelot, Christopher, ed., *Pakistan: Nation, Nationalism and the State* (Lahore: Vanguard Books, 2002).

Jalal, Ayesha, *Self and Sovereignty: Individual and Community in South Asian Islam since 1850* (Lahore: Sang-e-Meel Publications, 2007).

James, Morrice, *Pakistan Chronicle* (New York: St. Martin's Press, 1993).

James, W. E. and Subroto Roy, eds., *Foundation of Pakistan's Political Economy: Towards an Agenda for the 1990s* (New Delhi 1993).

Janowitz, Moris, *The Military in the Political Developments of New Nations* (Chicago: The University Press, 1964).

Jennings, Ivor, *The British Constitution* (Cambridge: The University Press, 1962).

John, Wilson, *Pakistan: The Struggle Within* (Delhi: Pearson Education, 2009).

Johnson, Harry, *Money, Trade and Growth* (London: Allen & Unwin, 1962).

Jones, Philip E., *The Pakistan People's Party: Rise to Power* (Oxford: The University Press, 2003).

Junaid, M. M., *The Resurgence of Pakistan* (Lahore: United Ltd., n.d.).

Kak, B. L., *Z. A. Bhutto's Notes from the Death Cell* (New Delhi: Radha Krishna Prakashan, 1979).

Kasuri, Ahmed Raza, *Idhar Hum Udhar Tum* (Lahore: Britannica Publishing House, n.d.).

Kaushik, Surendra Nath, *Pakistan under Bhutto's Leadership* (New Delhi: Uppal, 1985).

Kazmi, M. R., *A Concise History of Pakistan* (Karachi: Oxford University Press, 2009).

Keith, Arthur Berriedale, *The British Cabinet System, 1830–1938* (London: Stevens and Sons, Ltd., 1939).

Kennedy, Charles H., *Bureaucracy in Pakistan* (Karachi: Oxford University Press, 1987).

Khan, Fazal Muqeem, *Pakistan's Crisis in Leadership* (Islamabad: National Book Foundation, 1973).

Khan, Hamid, *Constitutional and Political History of Pakistan* (Karachi: Oxford University Press, 2001).

Khan, Jahan Dad, *Pakistan: Leadership Challenges* (Karachi: Oxford University Press, 2001).

Khan, Khan Abdul Wali, *Aasal Haqaiq Yai Hain* (Urdu) (Karachi: Shabul Publications, 1988).

Khan, Makhdoom Ali, *The Constitution of the Islamic Republic of Pakistan 1973* (Karachi: Pakistan Publishing House, 1986).

Khan, Mohammad Asghar, *Generals in Politics: Pakistan 1958–1982* (London and Canberra: Groom Helm, 1983).

Khan, Mohammad Asghar, *Pakistan at the Cross-Roads* (Karachi: Ferozsons, 2000).

Khan, Naveed, ed., *Beyond Crisis: Re-evaluating Pakistan* (London: Routledge Taylor & Francis Group, 2012).

Khan, Rais Ahmed, *In Search of Peace and Security: Forty Years of Pakistan-United States Relations* (Karachi: Royal Book Company, 1990).

Khan, Roedad, *Pakistan—A Dream Gone Sour* (Karachi: Oxford University Press, 1997).

Khan, Shahrukh Rafi, *50 Years of Pakistan's Economy: Traditional Topics and Contemporary Concerns* (Karachi: Oxford University Press, 2006).

Kia Bhutto Nai Pakistan Tora? (Lahore: Sarang Publications, 1995).

Kissinger, Henry, *On China* (New York: The Penguin Press, 2011).

Kizlibash, H., and Khawar Mumtaz, *Pakistan's Foreign Policy and the Legislature: A Preliminary Report* (Lahore: South Asian Institute, 1976).

Kochanek, Stanley A., *Interest Groups and Development: Business and Politics in Pakistan* (Karachi: Oxford University Press, 1983).

Korejo, M. S., *Soldiers of Misfortune: Pakistan under Ayub, Yahya, Bhutto and Zia* (Lahore: Ferozsons, 1995).

Kumar, Dharma, *The Cambridge Economic History of India, Vol. II, 1757–2003* (New Delhi: Cambridge University Press, 2005).

Kumar, Satish, *The New Pakistan* (New Delhi: Vikas Publishing House Pvt. Ltd., 1978).

Kux, Dennis, *The United States and Pakistan 1947–2000: Disenchanted Allies* (New York: Oxford University Press, 2001).

Lamb, Alastir, *Kashmir: A Disputed Legacy 1846–1990* (Karachi: Oxford University Press, 1994).

Lamb, Christina, *Waiting for Allah: Pakistan's Struggle for Democracy* (New Delhi: Viking, 1991).

Laporte, Jr. Robert, *Power and Privilege: Influence and Decision-Making in Pakistan* (Berkley: University of California Press, 1975).

Laver, Michael and Kenneth A. Shepsle, *Making and Breaking Governments: Cabinets and Legislature in Parliamentary Democracies* (Cambridge: The University Press, 1996).

Law, D. A., ed., *The Political Inheritance of Pakistan* (London: Macmillan, 1991).

Lewis, Stephen R., *Economic Policy and Industrial Growth in Pakistan* (London: George Allen & Unwin Ltd., 1970).

Mahdi, Niloufer, *Pakistan's Foreign Policy 1971–1981: The Search for Security* (Lahore: Ferozesons (Pvt.) Ltd., 1999).

Malik, Iftikhar H., *State and Civil Society in Pakistan: Politics of Authority, Ideology and Ethnicity* (London: Macmillan Press Ltd., 1997).

McGrath, Allen, *The Destruction of Pakistan's Democracy* (Karachi: Oxford University Press, 1996).

Mehdi, Haider, *The Nemesis: Political Articles and Analysis* (Lahore: Heritage Publications, 2007).

Mehmood, Safdar, *Pakistan Divided* (Lahore: Jang Publishers, 1993).

Michael, Laver, *Making and Breaking Governments* (London: Cambridge Publications, 1996).

Military, State and Society in Pakistan (Lahore: Sang-e-Meel Publications, 2003).

Mody, Pilo, *Zulfi, My Friend* (Delhi: Thomason Press Ltd., 1973).

Mukerjee, Dilip, *Zulfiqar Ali Bhutto: Quest for Power* (New Delhi: Vikas, 1972).

Mumtaz, Soofia, Jean Racine, and Imran Anwar Ali, *Pakistan: The Contours of State and Society* (Karachi: Oxford University Press, 2002).

Munir, Ahmed Munir, *Siyaassi Uttar Cherhao* (Urdu) (Lahore: Atish Fishan Publications, 1985).

Munir, Muhammad, *Constitution of the Islamic Republic of Pakistan: A Commentary of the Constitution of Pakistan, 1962* (Lahore: The Punjab Educational Press, 1965).

Naseem, Ayaz, *Pak-Soviet Relations 1947–65* (Lahore: Progressive publishers, 1983).

Nayak, Pandav, *Pakistan: Political Economy of a Developing State* (New Delhi: Patriot Publishers, 1988).

Nayar, Kuldip, *Wall at Wagha: India-Pakistan Relations* (New Delhi: Gyan Publishing House, 2003).

Nayyar, K. K., *Pakistan at the Crossroads* (New Delhi: Rupa. Co., 2003).

Nazir, Muntzra, *Federalism in Pakistan: Early Years* (Lahore: Pakistan Study Centre, 2008).

Newman, Karl F., *Pakistan under Ayub, Bhutto and Zia* (Munich: Wettforum Verlag, 1986).

Niaz, Ilhan, *The Culture of Power and Governance in Pakistan 1947–2008* (Karachi: Oxford University Press, 2010).

Niazi, Kausar, *Aur Line Kat Ga'i* (Lahore: Jung, 1987).

Noman, Omar, *Pakistan: Politics and Economic History since 1947* (London: Kegan Paul International, 1988).

Outline of Economic Planning with Special Reference to Pakistan (Lahore: Bilal Books, 1992).

Pakistan at the Crossroads (Karachi: Royal Book Company, 1985).

Pakistan in Perspective 1947–1997 (Karachi: Oxford University Press, 1997).

Pakistan Muslim League Ka Dor-i-Hakumat 1947–1954 (Lahore: Sang-i-Meel Publications, 1988).

Pakistan Peoples Party: The First Phase 1967–1971 (Lahore: Progressive Publishers, 1973).

Pakistan Political Roots and Development 1947–1999 (Karachi: Oxford University Press, 2000).

Pakistan under Bhutto, 1971–1977 (London: Macmillan, 1988).

Pakistan: A Political Study (Karachi: Oxford University Press, 1958).

Pakistan: A Study of Political Developments 1947–1997 (Lahore: Sang-e-Meel Publications, 1999).

Pakistan: At the Cross Current of History (Lahore: Vanguard, 2004).

Pakistan: The Continuing Search for Nationhood (Boulder: West View Press, 1986).

Pakistan: The Enigma of Political Development (Boulder, Colo: Westview Press, 1980).

Pakistan's Lost Years (Lahore: Lion Art Press, n.d.).

Pakistan's Relations with India 1947–1966 (London: Paul Mall Press, 1968).

Papanek, Gustav F., *Pakistan's Development: Social Goals and Private Incentives* (Harvard: The University Press, 1967).

Party Politics in Pakistan, 1947–1958 (Lahore: Sang-e-Meel Publications, 1976).

Parvez Hasan, *Pakistan's External Relations* (Karachi: Pakistan Institute of International Affairs, 1958).

Politics and the State in Pakistan (Islamabad: NIHCR, 1994).

Politics in Pakistan: The Nature and Direction of Change (New York: Praeger, 1980).

Politics of Crisis (Karachi: Royal Book Company, 1987).

Quddus, Syed Abdul, *Zulfikar Ali Bhutto: Politics of Charisma* (Lahore: Progressive Publishers, 1994).

Qureshi, Hakeem Arshad, *The 1971 Indo-Pakistan War: A Soldier's Narrative* (Karachi: Oxford University Press, 2002).

Qureshi, M. Aslam, *Anglo-Pakistan Relations 1947–1976* (Lahore, Research Society of Pakistan, 1976).

Rai, Hameed A. K., *Pakistan's Foreign Policy* (Lahore: Aziz Publisher, n.d.).

Rashid, Rao, *Jo Ma Nai Dekha: Pakistani Siyasat Aur Hukmaranon Kei Androni Kahani* (Lahore: Jamhori Publishers, 2004).

Rashiduzzaman, M., *Pakistan: A Study of Government and Politics* (Dacca: The University Press, 1967).

Raza, Rafi, *Zulfiqar Ali Bhutto and Pakistan 1967–1977* (Karachi: Oxford University Press, 1997).

Readings in Pakistan's Foreign Policy 1971–1998 (Karachi: Oxford University Press, 2005).

Reconciliation, Islam, Democracy and the West (London: Simon & Schuster, 2008).

Revolution in Pakistan: A Study of Martial Law Administration (London: Oxford University Press, 1967).

Rizvi, Hasan Askari, *The Military and Politics in Pakistan 1947–1986* (Lahore: Progressive Publishers, 1986).

Rudra, A.B., *The Viceroy and Governor General* (London 1940).

Saeed, Khwaja Amjad, *The Economy of Pakistan* (Karachi: Oxford University Press, 2007).

Sahni, Naresh Chander, *Political Struggle in Pakistan* (Jullundher: New Academic Publishers, 1969).

Said, Hassan, *Pakistan: The Story Behind its Economic Development* (New York: Vantage Press, 1971).

Salamat, Zarina, *Pakistan: 1947–1958: An Historical Review* (Islamabad: NIHCR, 1992).

Saleem, Ahmed, ed., *Bhutto Ka Siasi Wirsa* (Lahore: Frontier Post Publications, 1994).

Salik, Saddique, *Witness to Surrender* (Karachi: Oxford University Press, 1979).

Sattar, Abdul, *Pakistan's Foreign Policy 1947–2009: A Concise History* (Karachi: Oxford University Press, 2006).

Sattar, Tahir, ed., *Zulfiqar Ali Bhutto Ka Supreme Court of Pakistan Main Akhri Biyan* (Lahore: Classic, 1986).

Sayeed, Khalid, B., *Pakistan: The Formative Phase* (Karachi: Oxford University Press, 1968).

Schofield, Victoria, *Bhutto: Trial and Execution* (London: Cassell, 1979).

Shabbir, Syed, *Constitutional Law of Pakistan*, Vol. I (Lahore: Vanguard Books, 2002).

Shafqat, Saeed, *Political System of Pakistan and Public Policy: Essays in Interpretations* (Lahore: Progressive Publishers, 1989).

Shah, Syed Mujawar Hussain, *Sardar Abdur Rab Nishtar: A Political Biography* (Lahore: Qadiria Books, 1985).

Shahnawaz, Jahan Ara, *Father and Daughter: A Political Biography* (Karachi: Oxford University Press, 2002).

Sham, Mahmud, *Larkana to Peking* (Karachi: National Book Foundation, 1976).

Siddique, Kalim, *Functions of International Conflict: A Socio-Economic Study of Pakistan* (Karachi: Royal Book Company, 1975).

Siyasat Dannu Ki Jabri Na Ahlian (Lahore: Jung Publishers, 1991).

Sohail, Massarrat, *Partition and Anglo-Pakistan Relations, 1947–1951* (Lahore: Vanguard, 1991).

State and Democracy in Pakistan (Lahore: Vanguard, 1997).

State and Society in Pakistan 1971–1977 (London: Macmillan, 1980).

Suleri, Z. A., *Politicians and Ayub: Being a Survey of Pakistani Politics from 1948 to 1964* (Lahore: Lion Art Press, n.d.).

Syed, Anwar H. *Pakistan: Islam, Politics and National Solidarity* (New York: Praeger Publishers, 1982).

Talbot, Ian, *Pakistan: A Modern History* (Lahore: Vanguard Books, 1999).

Talha, Naureen, *Jinnah's Role in Strengthening Pakistan's Economy 1947–48* (Islamabad: NIPS, 2008).

Taseer, Salman, *Bhutto: A Political Biography* (London: Ithaca Press, 1979).

The Ayub Era: Politics in Pakistan, 1958–1969 (Syracuse: Syracuse University Press, 1971).

The Discourse and Politics of Zulfikar Ali Bhutto (New York: St. Martin's Press, 1992).

The End of the Beginning: Pakistan 1969–1971 (London: Oxford University Press, 1975).

The Idea of Pakistan (Lahore: Vanguard Books, 2005).

The Last Days of United Pakistan (Karachi: Oxford University Press, 1998).

The Oxford Companion to Pakistan History (Karachi: Oxford University Press, 2012).

The Political Economy of Pakistan 1947–85 (London: Kegan Paul International, 1988).

The Political System of Pakistan (Karachi: Civil and Military Press, 1987).

The State of Martial Rule: The Origins of Pakistan's Political Economy of Defence (Lahore: Vanguard, 1991).

The Task Before Us: Selected Speeches and Writings (Lahore: Research Society of Pakistan, 1974).

Trivedi, Ramesh, *India's Relations with her Neighbors* (Delhi: Isha Books, 2008).

Venka Teswaran, R. J., *Cabinet Government in India* (London: George Allen & Unwin Ltd., 1967).

Wangteh Yu, *The English Cabinet System* (London: P. S. King and Son Ltd., 1939).

Warraich, Matloob Ahmad, *The Great Three* (Lahore: Book Home, 2004).

Waseem, Mohammad, *Pakistan under Martial Law 1977–1985* (Lahore: Vanguard, 1987).

We've Learnt Nothing from History: Pakistan Politics and Military Power (Karachi: Oxford University Press, 2005).

Weiss, Anita M. and Zulfiqar Gilani, *Power and Civil Society in Pakistan* (Karachi: Oxford University Press, 2003).

Wellman, Sam, *Your Government: How it Works* (Philadelphia: Chelsea House Publishers, 2001).

Wheeler, Richard S., *The Politics of Pakistan* (Ithaca: Cornell University Press, 1970).

White, Lawrence J., *Industrial Concentration and Economic Power in Pakistan* (New Jersey: Princeton University Press, 1974).

Wilcox, Wayne Ayres, *Pakistan: The Consolidation of a Nation* (New York: Columbia University Press, 1963).

Williams. L. F. Rushbrook, *The State of Pakistan* (London: Faber and Faber, 1962).

Wolpert, Stanley, *Zulfi Bhutto of Pakistan: His Life and Times* (Oxford: The University Press, 1993).

Wriggins, Howard, ed., *Pakistan in Transition* (Islamabad: Quaid-i-Azam University Press, 1975).

Yusuf, Hamid, *Pakistan in Search of Democracy, 1947–1977* (Lahore: Afro Asia, 1980).

Zafar, S. M., *Through the Crisis* (Lahore: Book Centre, 1970).

Zaheer, Hassan, *The Separation of East Pakistan: The Rise and Realization of Bengali Muslim Nationalism* (Karachi: Oxford University Press, 1995).

Zaidi, S. Akbar, *Issues in Pakistan's Economy* (Karachi: Oxford University Press, 2009).

Zaman, Fakhar and Akhtar Aman, *Z. A. Bhutto: The Political Thinker* (Lahore: People's Publishers, 1973).

Ziring, Lawrence, *Pakistan in the Twentieth Century: A Political History* (Karachi: Oxford University Press, 1997).

Ziring, Lawrence, *Pakistan's Foreign Policy: An Historical Analysis* (Karachi: Oxford University Press, 1990).

Zulfiqar Ali Bhutto of Pakistan: The Last Days (New Delhi: Vikas Publishing House, 1992).

Zulfiqar Ali Bhutto, Buchpan Sie Takhtadar Tak (Urdu) (Lahore: Iman Printing, 1988).

2. Articles in Journals

Abid, Massarrat, 'Chaudhary Mohammad Ali Ki Wizarat-i-Uzma Pur Aik Nazar', *Journal of the Research Society of Pakistan* XXV (Apr. 1988), 64–94.

Alavi, Hamza, 'Pakistan-US Military Alliances', *Economic and Political Weekly*, 33 (June 20–26 1998), 1551–7.

Ayoob, Mohammad, 'Pakistan's Political Development 1947 to 1970: Bird's Eye View', *Economic and Political Weekly*, 16 (Jan. 1971), 199–204.

Barnds, William J., 'China's Relations with Pakistan: Durability amidst Discontinuity', *The China Quarterly*, 63 (Sept. 1975), 463–89.

Burki, Shahid Javed, 'West Pakistan's Rural Works Program: A Study in Political and Administrative Responses', *Middle East Journal 23* (1969), 321–42.

'Politics of Economic Decision Making during the Bhutto Period', *Asian Survey*, 14 (Dec. 1974), 1126–40.

'Ayub's Fall: A Socio-Economic Explanation', *Asian Survey*, 12 (Mar. 1972), 201–12.

Callard, Keith, 'The Political Stability of Pakistan', *Pacific Affairs*, 29 (Mar. 1956), 5–20.

Dobel, W. M., 'Ayub Khan as President of Pakistan', *Pacific Affairs*, 42 (autumn 1969), 294–310.

Esposito, Bruce J., 'The Politics of Agrarian Reforms in Pakistan', *Asian Survey*, 14 (May 1974), 429–38.

Feldman, Herbert, 'Pakistan in 1974', *Asian Survey* 15 (Feb. 1975), 110–19.

Gauhar, Altaf, 'Pakistan: Ayub Khan's Abdication', *Third World Quarterly*, 7 (Jan. 1985), 102–31.

Gustafson W., Eric, 'Economic Problems of Pakistan under Bhutto', *Asian Survey*, 16 (Apr. 1976), 364–80.

Herring, Ronald J., 'Zulfiqar Ali Bhutto and the Eradication of Feudalism in Pakistan', *Comparative Studies in Society and History,* 21 (Oct. 1979), 519–57.

Huq Mahbub ul, 'Pakistan's Economic Development', *Pacific Affairs*, 32 (June 1959), 144–61.

Levi, Werner, 'Pakistan, the Soviet Union and China', *Pacific Affairs*, 35 (Autumn 1962), 211–22.

Maron, Stanley, 'A New Phase in Pakistan Politics', *Far Eastern Survey*, 24 (Nov. 1955), 161–5.

Muniruzaman, Talukdar, 'Group Interests in Pakistan Politics 1947–1958', *Pacific Affairs*, 39 (Spring-Summer 1966), 83–98.

Newman, K. J., 'The Diarchic Pattern of Government and Pakistan's Problems', *Political Science Quarterly*, 75 (Mar. 1960), 94–108.

Noorani, G., 'Bhutto and Nonalignment', *Economic and Political Weekly*, 11 (1976), 1957–58.

Porte, Robert La, 'Pakistan 1972: Picking up the Pieces', *Asian Survey*, 13 (Feb. 1973), 187–98.

Rose, Richard, 'The Making of Cabinet Ministers', *British Journal of Political Science*, 1 (Oct. 1971), 393–414.

Sayeed, Khalid Bin, 'Martial Law Administration in Pakistan', *Far Eastern Survey*, 28 (May 1959), 72–9.

'Pakistan: New Challenges to the Political System', *Asian Survey*, 8 (Feb. 1968), 179–90.

Suhrawardy, Hussain Shaheed, 'Political Stability and Democracy in Pakistan', *Foreign Affairs*, 35 (Apr. 1957), 422–31.

Syed, Anwar H., 'Pakistan in 1976, Business as Usual', *Asian Survey*, 17 (Feb. 1977), 181–90.

Symond, Richard. 'State-Making in Pakistan', *Far Eastern Survey*, 19 (March 1950), 45–50.

Wheeler, Richard, 'Governor General's Rule in Pakistan', *Far Eastern Survey*, 24 (Jan. 1955), 1–8.

Wilcox, Wayne Ayres, 'The Pakistan Coup D'état of 1958', *Pacific Affairs*, 38 (Summer 1965), 142–63.

Ziring, Lawrence, 'Pakistan: A Political Perspective', *Asian Survey*, 15 (1975), 629–44.

'Militarism in Pakistan: The Yahya Khan Interregnum', *Asian Affairs*, 1 (July–Aug. 1974), 402–20.

3. Theses

Hussain, Basharat, 'Nawabzada Nasrullah Khan', MPhil Thesis, History Department, University of the Punjab, Lahore, 2004.

Hussain, Ishtiaq, 'Political Institutionalization in Pakistan; A Case Study of Pakistan Peoples Party', MPhil Thesis, History Department, University of the Punjab, Lahore, 2004.

Mozaffer, Shaheen, 'Politics of Cabinet Formation in Pakistan: A Study of Recruitments to the Central Cabinet', PhD Thesis, Political Science Department, University of Ohio, Miami, 1981.

Rehman, Najeeb, 'Centre Province Relations during Bhutto Era: A Case Study of Balochistan', MPhil Thesis, History Department, University of the Punjab, Lahore, 2008.

Lodhi, Maleeha, 'Bhutto, the Pakistan Peoples Party and Political Development in Pakistan, 1967–77', PhD dissertation, London School of Economics and Political Science, University of London, November 1980, 434.

4. Research Journals

Asian Affairs

Asian Survey

British Journal of Political Science

The China Quarterly

Comparative Studies in Society and History

Economic and Political Weekly

Far Eastern Survey

Foreign Affairs

Journal of the Research Society of Pakistan

Middle East Journal

Pakistan Horizon

Pakistan Journal of History and Culture

Pakistan Vision

Pacific Affairs

Political Science Quarterly

Third World Quarterly

Index